PROGRAMMING A MULTIPLAYER FPS IN DIRECTX

PROGRAMMING A MULTIPLAYER FPS IN DIRECTX

VAUGHAN YOUNG

CHARLES RIVER MEDIA, INC.
Hingham, Massachusetts

Publisher: Jenifer Niles
Cover Design: The Printed Image
Cover Images: Vaughan Young

CHARLES RIVER MEDIA, INC.
10 Downer Avenue
Hingham, Massachusetts 02043
781-740-0400
781-740-8816 (FAX)
info@charlesriver.com
www.charlesriver.com

This book is printed on acid-free paper.

Vaughan Young. *Programming a Multiplayer FPS in DirectX.*
ISBN: 1-58450-363-7

All brand names and product names mentioned in this book are trademarks or service marks of their respective companies. Any omission or misuse (of any kind) of service marks or trademarks should not be regarded as intent to infringe on the property of others. The publisher recognizes and respects all marks used by companies, manufacturers, and developers as a means to distinguish their products.

Library of Congress Cataloging-in-Publication Data
Young, Vaughan, 1981-
    Programming a multiplayer first person shooter in DirectX / Vaughan Young.— 1st ed.
        p. cm.
    ISBN 1-58450-363-7 (pbk. with cd-rom : alk. paper)
  1. Computer games—Programming. 2. C++ (Computer program language) 3. DirectX. I. Title.
    QA76.76.C672Y68 2004
    794.8'1526—dc22
                            2004023250

Printed in the United States of America
05 7 6 5 4 3 2

CHARLES RIVER MEDIA titles are available for site license or bulk purchase by institutions, user groups, corporations, etc. For additional information, please contact the Special Sales Department at 781-740-0400.

Requests for replacement of a defective CD-ROM must be accompanied by the original disc, your mailing address, telephone number, date of purchase, and purchase price. Please state the nature of the problem, and send the information to CHARLES RIVER MEDIA, INC., 10 Downer Avenue, Hingham, Massachusetts 02043. CRM's sole obligation to the purchaser is to replace the disc, based on defective materials or faulty workmanship, but not on the operation or functionality of the product.

I would like to dedicate this book to each and every member
of my ever-growing and supportive family; with a special note to my mother—
your love and selflessness is truly amazing.

Contents

Acknowledgments

Because this is my first book, I have discovered that there is a lot more to publishing a book than simply putting words on paper. There are numerous tasks that need to be completed; I now realize why it is called a *project*, not just a book. In light of this, I want to acknowledge the dedicated and talented individuals who helped to bring this project to fruition.

First I would like to acknowledge the staff at Charles River Media for the great work they do. I want to thank Kasper Fauerby for writing the "Improved Collision Detection and Response" article and allowing me to use it in this book. Thanks to Andy Tather for his Panda DirectX Exporter, which is included on the CD-ROM, and James Boer for the great sound effects he created for the game. I also want to thank Jessica Woodward for helping me to put my knowledge and crazy ideas into legible English. Finally, I want to say "thanks" to my brother, Marcus Young, for the amazing friendship and support he provides.

Introduction

A new breed of gaming took the world by storm in 1991. A new genre—commonly referred to as the First Person Shooter (FPS)—was born in the form of *Wolfeinstein 3D*® (from id Software®). This genre revolutionized the way people played and viewed computer games; computer games were more than just a few dots moving around the screen. They became serious business and people noticed. It's games like these that put the computer game industry on the map!

Although some would argue that the FPS genre was formulated earlier than this (which it probably was), *Wolfeinstein 3D* was the first commercial title globally recognized and has therefore often been hailed as the pioneer of the genre. Several years later in 1994, a new game was released from the same company. *Doom*® was the second title to make brave new steps in the FPS genre. For the first time, players could move around and fight together (or against one another) in a 3D environment. It was truly amazing! The multiplayer experience was created. Over the following years many new FPS games were released and often referred to as *Doom* "clones," since it was this title that defined the genre at the time.

Despite all the excitement created by these titles, the most unique advancement was still to come. In 1996 *Quake*® (also from id Software), was released and this completed the final step in rounding out the genre. *Quake* was the first game to provide a true 3D experience in a FPS game. There is no doubt that id Software played a large part in shaping the genre into what it is today.

Today, the FPS genre is accelerating beyond our wildest dreams. Some of the titles contain features and enhanced visuals that are mind boggling. In fact, many of these games are so advanced—in both visuals and game play—they push the limits of even the highest-end PC.

As you progress through this book you will build your very own FPS from the ground up using Visual C++® and Microsoft® DirectX®. You will create the engine that powers it, and then build the game play on top of that. Although we won't be creating anything that will rival the next AAA blockbuster title, we will definitely create something that is both visually appealing and fun to play. More importantly, you will learn some invaluable techniques that you can take away into your own development and/or use what you create here as a foundation for your next project.

AUDIENCE

Throughout this book it is assumed that you have a working knowledge of both C++ and DirectX. Although you are not expected to have any professional level of understanding, you will be expected to know the basics. When we begin coding the game, we will jump straight into object-oriented C++ and DirectX code. We will not waste time covering the basics at the start, but many of the more involved topics will be explained as we go. However, it is strongly recommended that you learn the basics before beginning if you have not done so already.

Learning the basics is actually not that difficult. In fact, there are many resources available on the Internet; and most of them are free. If you are not already familiar with DirectX, you should take some time to read through the *DirectX Documentation for C++*, which you can locate after you have installed the DirectX Software Development Kit (SDK). The more time you spend reading this documentation, the more proficient you will become. More specifically, you should make sure that you have covered and understood the tutorials, especially the ones relating to Direct3D. These tutorials will give you an understanding of generating a basic DirectX application.

USING THIS BOOK

This book is intended to be followed in a tutorial manner—following the chapters in order from start to finish. Once you have completed the book, you may find it helpful to keep it as a reference.

Each chapter will build upon the previous, adding more functionality to the engine and the game. All of the code required for each chapter can be found on the CD-ROM, in the appropriate directory for the chapter. For each chapter, you will find a workspace that contains all of the source code built up to that point. It is recommended that you read this book at your computer so that you can actively follow along with the source code, as you will be referred to various parts of the source code as we progress. In fact, it is advisable that you develop the code yourself as you read through the book. This way you also gain the added benefit of learning through doing, and the resulting code will be in your own personal style. The book has been designed to be as practical and as "hands-on" as possible. As code is presented to you a section at a time, you should refer to the actual source code to see how that particular section relates to the surrounding code. You will also be given a full explanation of what the code is doing and why it is necessary.

When developing computer games, it is often the case that a lot of effort translates into little advancement. This is especially true when developing game engines, as you will come to realize when we start developing our engine. What this means is that sometimes we will spend quite a bit of time developing our engine and adding new features without actually seeing any visual change on screen. Therefore, it is important to remain patient during these periods; we will try to use small demos as much as possible to showcase the new features.

Since developing even a small FPS is a rather large task, it is impossible to cover every topic in depth and present every line of code. For this reason, some of the more general code or topics that are considered too trivial will not be covered. The code for these areas will still be provided, however, and you will be given appropriate instructions on how to use it. All of the code provided with this book has been prepared in a consistent format and commented thoroughly to allow you to easily read and understand it. When presented in the book, however, comments may be absent in some places for brevity.

Finally, to help speed development, we will also make use of the Direct3D Extension (D3DX) support library wherever possible. This will allow us to focus more on the development of our game rather than the low-level support infrastructure that the D3DX library already provides. For more information about the D3DX library refer to the DirectX SDK documentation.

WORKSPACE ORGANIZATION

In Part I (where we develop the engine) you will notice the presence of two projects when opening the workspace for any given chapter. These two projects are called Engine and Test. In Part II (where we develop the actual game) there is only one project in each workspace, called Game. All of the workspaces for each chapter are organized this way for the respective parts of the book.

The Engine project contains all of the source code files for what has been developed in the engine so far. We will go through the source code for the new features that have been added to the engine in the given chapter. Once you reach the second part of the book where we develop the actual game, there will be no further changes made to the engine. Therefore, it will not be necessary to add the `Engine` project to the workspace.

The `Test` project contains the source code files for the chapter specific sample application written to test the new features implemented in each chapter of Part I. The source code in these sample applications will be presented to you and discussed to ensure that you become familiar with the use of the engine.

When you move on to Part II there is no longer a need for the `Test` project since we will not be adding any new features to the engine. Instead, we will start using the `Game` project, which will contain all of the source code files for what has been developed in the game so far. We will go through this code in the same way that we discuss the engine specific code.

HOW THIS BOOK IS ORGANIZED

When developing any computer game it is often best practice to break the game into logical groups of tasks. At the highest level this generally means dividing the game into major components, then engine specific code, and the game specific code. This is exactly what we are going to do throughout this book. The book is divided into two main parts, which are subsequently divided into related chapters. The following lists the chapters in each part and an outline of what to expect in each.

> **Part I The Engine:** The first part deals specifically with the engine. We will develop all the technology that our FPS game requires.
>
> **Chapter 1 Engine Design:** Here we will roughly map out the design of our engine. This translates into what our engine needs to do and how it will do it.
>
> **Chapter 2 Framework:** This is where we develop the initial groundwork for our engine. We will set up a lot of the basic infrastructure that will support our engine's future development.
>
> **Chapter 3 Engine Control:** In this chapter, we will add two forms of engine control. The first is to control the engine's processing and the second is to accept user input.
>
> **Chapter 4 Scripting:** This chapter covers the development of an invaluable tool in game development. We will add a basic scripting feature to our engine, which will be used extensively by our game.

Chapter 5 Rendering: This lengthy chapter is the launch pad for our rendering system. Here we will implement all of the basic foundations needed to support the forms of rendering that will be implemented in later chapters.

Chapter 6 Sound: A game just wouldn't look, feel, or sound right without sound. So in this chapter we will add a sound engine that can play sound effects in a 3D environment.

Chapter 7 Networking: In order to play your games with other people you need a networking system, which is exactly what we will be adding to our engine in this chapter—allowing our FPS to be played across a Local Area Network (LAN).

Chapter 8 Materials and Meshes: In this chapter, we will implement into our engine the ability to load and render a 3D mesh (or model). In addition, we will create a system that allows us to load materials that have textures, which can be applied to the faces of our meshes in order to give them a realistic appearance.

Chapter 9 Objects: Here we will add a number of basic objects to our engine that will be used to support the games we make with it. These objects will allow us to place "entities" such as players and weapons into our game world and allow them to interact with one another.

Chapter 10 Scene Management: The final chapter for developing our engine adds the most important aspect of the engine (and probably the largest). Here we will implement a scene manager that can load, manage, and render an entire 3D scene (often referred to as a map or level). Our scene management system includes features such as frustum and occlusion culling for efficient rendering.

Part II The Game: The second part of the book deals specifically with the game. We will develop our very own FPS game using our new engine.

Chapter 11 Foundations: The first chapter of Part II involves laying down the supportive infrastructure for the game. This includes setting up the engine, developing a simple menu system, and preparing a game loop for future processing.

Chapter 12 Players: This chapter adds players to our game. Here we will develop a new type of object that can manage and control a single player in the game. Then we will create a player manager, which can watch over all of the players, ensuring they play nicely together.

Chapter 13 Weapons: The last chapter of the book focuses on adding weapons to our game. We will implement a simple system for managing the weapons in the game and the weapons each player is carrying. We will also implement a system to keep track of all the projectiles in the game for when the bullets start flying.

PREPARING VISUAL STUDIO

Before you can rush off and begin compiling the source code on the CD-ROM, you need to ensure you have your development environment correctly prepared. The source code in this book was compiled using Microsoft Visual Studio® 6, so we will quickly run through the steps you need to take to prepare Visual Studio 6. If you are using a newer version of Visual Studio (or a different compiler all together), most (if not all) of these steps will still apply; how you go about them will be a little different. In this case, you may need to refer to your compiler's documentation to determine how to carry out a particular step.

Step 1: Ensure that Visual Studio is properly installed on your computer. You should also ensure that your compiler has the latest patches and service packs applied to correct any known issues and bugs.

ON THE CD
Step 2: Install the DirectX 9.0c SDK, which you can find on the CD-ROM in the DirectX directory.

Step 3: The next step is to ensure you have the DirectX Include and Library directories set within your compiler. In Visual Studio 6, open the Options dialog from the Tools menu. From there, select the Directories tab. In the "Show directories for" drop-down list, select Include files. Ensure that your DirectX Include directory is at the top of the Directories list. If not, simply use the Up arrow on the right to push it to the top of the list. This will ensure that it is searched before the other directories. If it is not in the list at all, you will need to add it by using the New button and browsing your hard drive. Once this is done you can go to the Library files in the "Show directories for" drop-down list. You just need to repeat the process for the DirectX Library (Lib) directory, ensuring that it is located at the top of the Directories list.

Step 4: As of the DirectX 9.0c release, Visual Studio 6 is no longer supported. However, Microsoft did release a modified version of one of the core DirectX libraries, which makes it possible to compile DirectX 9.0c applications with Visual Studio 6. If you are using a later version of Visual Studio then you can ignore this step. For everyone else, you will need to copy the Visual Studio 6 compatible d3dx9.lib file from the DirectX directory on the CD-ROM to the Lib directory on your hard drive where you installed the DirectX 9.0c SDK (C:\Program Files\ Microsoft DirectX 9.0 SDK (October 2004)\Lib by default). Simply replace the existing d3dx9.lib file when prompted. If you plan on upgrading to a future version of Visual Studio, you may want to consider making a backup of the existing d3dx9.lib file before you replace it, as it is needed for future versions.

Step 5: There is one more file required to compile DirectX 9.0c applications with Visual Studio 6, called BaseTsd.h. If you have a later version of Visual Studio you may be able to skip this step. The file can only be obtained by updating your Platform SDK from the Microsoft Platform SDK Update Web site at www.microsoft.com/msdownload/platformsdk/sdkupdate/. From here you can navigate to Downloads and select Install, which will allow you to install the updated Platform SDK. Once you have the Platform SDK installed, you need to ensure the paths are set up correctly in Visual Studio. This is done in exactly the same fashion as setting the DirectX SDK paths. You need to ensure that you have both the Include and the Library paths set, which are located at <Platform SDK Installation Path>\Include\ and <Platform SDK Installation Path>\Lib\ respectively.

If you cannot download the Platform SDK for some reason, there is a quick "hack" that you can apply to the code in this book that will allow it to compile and run without the updated Platform SDK. However, it is strongly recommended that you use the Platform SDK instead. To apply this hack, simply place the following line of code at the beginning of one of the main header files, such as Engine.h.

```
typedef unsigned long DWORD_PTR;
```

That's it. Now you are ready to compile DirectX 9.0c applications (and the book's source code) in Visual Studio 6. Remember, if you are using a different compiler (or a different version of Visual Studio), you may need to double check if all of these step are necessary for you. You may also need to refer to your compiler's documentation about the specific steps involved for adding the DirectX (and Platform SDK) Include and Library directories. If you are using a newer version of Visual Studio, you can open up the workspaces on the CD-ROM and allow the conversion wizard to upgrade them for you. Once it is finished, you should be able to compile the code without any major issues.

A FINAL NOTE

You should keep an eye on my Web site (*www.coderedgames.com*) or visit *www.charlesriver.com* for updates to the book and the code as necessary. I will also have a forum set up on my Web site to allow you to raise any issues you may have with any of the material in the book, or the source code.

If you find any problems, have any comments or suggestions, or just want to say hi, please e-mail me at *vyoung@coderedgames.com*. By all means, if you find a fix for a bug, add a new feature to the engine, or make any sort of improvement that you would like to share, send it along and I will make it available for everyone.

Part I

The Engine

In this part of the book we will focus primarily on the design and development of our engine. If you are not sure what is meant by the term *engine*, just think of a car. A car has an underlying infrastructure, which includes its frame, motor, transmission, suspension, etc. This is analogous to our game's engine. You can completely change the look of a car by just replacing its chassis (or shell), while the infrastructure remains the same. The same principle applies to game development. You can take a single game engine and build two completely different games with it.

There is one inherent problem often found in game engines, however, and it is also found in the real world counterparts like the above car infrastructure example. Consider the following: if you took a car's infrastructure and decided you wanted to build a boat with it, would it be possible? Probably, but you would most likely have to "hack" away at the infrastructure to make it fit your vision. You would probably end up with a boat, but it would not have the quality or effectiveness that it could have, had you started with a boat's infrastructure. This theory is true with game development. It is very difficult to create a single game engine that can cover every genre, such as first person shooter (FPS), real-time strategy (RTS), action, adventure, etc.

For this reason, most game engines focus on a particular genre. This doesn't mean you cannot make another type of game with them, it just means that they are best suited to the type of games they were designed for. In light of this we will focus the development of our engine on a single genre—no prizes for guessing which one.

The engine that we will build over the next 10 chapters will be specifically designed for FPS development. In fact, we will even implement a few features that are very specific to FPS development. The advantage of making your game engine as specific as possible is that the resultant game is easier to create, since the engine has been designed specifically for what you are trying to achieve and therefore auto-mates a lot of the tasks for you. The disadvantage is that it increases the difficulty of creating games from other genres with the engine, at least without having to make any major changes to the engine.

Now that you have a good idea of what we are setting out to achieve in this part of the book, turn the page and let's begin with Chapter 1, "Engine Design."

1 Engine Design

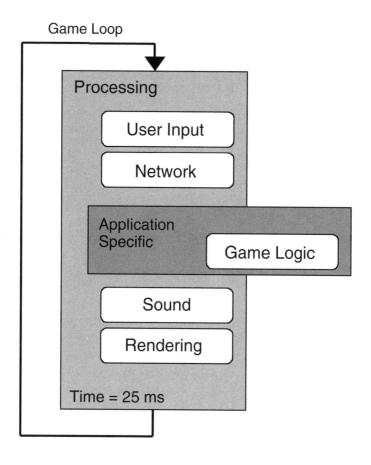

In This Chapter

■ Look at the importance of design.
■ Determine our design approach.
■ Discuss design goals and tools such as visual aids.
■ Define our engine design at a high level and run through the various components.

W elcome to the beginning of an exciting journey that we will make together. Part I is dedicated to building the engine that we will use to develop our own multiplayer FPS. To begin, we will discuss the design of our engine before we touch any code.

THE IMPORTANCE OF DESIGN

One of the most popular ways to build a computer game is to use the approach often referred to as *hacking*, which more or less entails these general steps:

1. Come up with a cool idea for a game.
2. Immediately start coding and slap together a playable demo.
3. Further develop the demo, adding more features in an attempt to lift it out of demo status.
4. Trip over poorly designed code and become bogged down with feature creep.
5. Give up on the project, either out of boredom, or claim that it was too ambitious.
6. Repeat from Step 1.

This is an example of building a computer game without the benefits of design. Many people go down this path every time they start a new project. It is very easy to do and everyone is guilty of it at one point or another, especially with small projects. You can often get away with this kind of approach on a minor weekend project, but when you attempt something serious you will quickly realize that you are going to need at least some basic design skills. So let's try to achieve a few of these skills throughout this chapter.

We will start by defining design. Some people say that design is an activity or task that needs to be completed before construction begins, and yes this is true. Take the construction of a building for example. It is no good to build the building first, and then design it. This design scenario works fine for some types of construction, such as building construction. However, it is not feasible when it comes to software development, especially computer games. It is not uncommon for software projects to run over budget and past deadline due to design difficulties. So if we cannot design our software straight out, then what do we do? We simply design it progressively—we use what is called an *evolving design*. This means that as we develop the software we also develop its design. The design is never closed, even when the project ends. Take maintenance for example. If a bug is found in the software after it is released, it may require the design to be altered in order to correct the bug. From this we can now say that for our purpose, instead of design being an activity or a task, it is actually a *process*.

Now let's go back to our example of hacking a game together and add in the process of design. Let's see how it affects the outcome of the project. Here are the new steps:

1. Come up with a cool idea for a game.
2. Put together a basic design—enough to start development.
3. Start developing a demo based on the design outline.
4. Rework the design based on the outcome and lessons learned from the demo.
5. Build a new version of the game based on the current design.
6. Rework the design based on the outcome and lessons learned from the previous version.
7. Repeat from Step 5 until the game is complete.

As you can see this is a preferable approach that actually allows for the completion of the game. Steps 3 and 4 are often large steps as you are designing and building a complete working demo, often called a *technology demo*. This demo is used to determine what is needed to build the complete game. For example, you may determine that you will need a graphical user interface (GUI) system, a sound system with 3D sound, and a rendering system that can do both 2D and 3D rendering. From here you enter a cycle of design, develop, design, develop, and so on until the game is complete. How large these design-develop iterations are, is really up to you, and will depend largely upon your confidence as a developer. If you are unsure about what you are doing, you will probably find it necessary to keep these iterations fairly tight so that development is constantly reviewed. As you become more skilled you will find that you can develop much more in between each design iteration. Just remember that it is not possible to account for everything in the design because there are far too many variable factors and unknowns. This is the main reason why we approach design using an iterative evolving process.

One thing we haven't explicitly talked about is *why* design is important, however, it is fairly obvious from our previous example. One key point to remember is that without a design process you really stack the odds against yourself. You have probably heard a lot of people say that when you first begin computer game development you should start out small; meaning, for example, that your first project should be a simple little puzzle game or a basic side scroller. This is usually said to account for the fact that beginners are generally not very competent developers; however, even someone with many years of programming experience can falter when it comes to developing a complete game. The problem doesn't lie in their ability to program, rather in their ability to implement a proper design process and the patience to maintain it. You are capable of developing anything your imagination can conceive as long as you have two key ingredients: a proper design process and a great deal of patience.

Let's just do one last thing before we move on to our engine design—dispel some common design myths. The first myth is that design is not necessary. The software development industry in general has adopted design as a common practice. In fact, there are entire standards and manuals written that are dedicated to the design of software. Unfortunately, the computer game development industry is slow to adopt these design practices so you will often find that many games are written with little design work. Lack of design is one of the main reasons why so many game projects fail—usually due to a lack of proper foresight. If you want to increase your chances of success, you should strongly consider using a design process. There are many good books written that cover every aspect of software design and even a few that are tailored specifically to computer game development. There are even a lot of free resources on the Internet that cover computer game design. As computer games become more complex, it is becoming apparent that design is very important.

The second myth is that design is more important than implementation. This also ties in with the fact that design is the largest phase. Generally speaking this is untrue. Since most games that use a design process are iterative, the design actually occurs alongside the development, so that they complement one another. Design is never more important than the implementation. Of course, without the design you have a difficult project, but without the implementation you don't have a project at all. This all leads into dispelling the final myth. You should design everything before even touching a line of code—which is more absurd than the previous two myths. When developing computer games, a lot of your time is spent researching, scouring the Internet, flipping through books, browsing help documents, etc. Why is all this research necessary? Because most of the time you are learning as you develop. You don't know everything at the beginning. You don't know what potential pitfalls you will come across. It is for these reasons that it is completely impractical to design everything before you start the implementation. The best way to approach design and minimize your risks while increasing your chances of success is to follow an iterative or evolving design process, which accommodates for the fact that you are learning as you go and allows you to make mistakes.

OUR DESIGN APPROACH

Now that you have been pumped full of propaganda about design, you can probably answer this question yourself. How are we going to design our engine? If you said we will design the entire thing at the start and then build it, you weren't paying attention and you need to go back and read the last section again. If you said we will use an iterative evolving design process, you are correct.

In this chapter, we will discuss the design of our engine at a high level. This means that we won't go into detail about specific components and their workings because we haven't built the engine yet and we are unsure how a lot of it will work. Once we have an idea of what will go into the engine, we can begin to develop the first iteration, sometimes referred to as version one, revision one, or build one. After we complete this we stop and look at how it is piecing together. We go back to the drawing board and make any necessary adjustments to the design based on what we have learned. We then begin designing the next iteration in more detail before implementing it. Finally we repeat this process for each iteration until we determine that the engine is complete for our purpose. By following this model, each chapter in Part I of the book actually makes up an individual iteration of our engine.

ON THE CD

As you read through each chapter you will find the workspace with all of the code for that chapter on the included CD-ROM. This means that the code in any given chapter is the same code from the previous chapter plus the new features and enhancements for the current chapter. Once you complete all of the chapters in Part I the engine will have enough features for us to build a game with it. This does not mean that the engine is complete. In fact its development will never be complete. After you have completed the book you can continue designing the engine, adding new features, enhancing performance, and reworking areas to keep up with changing technology. We are jumping ahead of ourselves a little here. The first step that we should concentrate on is research. That's right; your design process should always begin with research.

So what exactly do we need to research? To start with you need to know what goes into a FPS, since that is what we are making. You probably think that you already know what goes into it—flashy graphics, explosions, heaps of weapons, massive levels, and some other stuff about rendering, networking, and input too. The first few things that we listed are what we call *desirables*. These are features that we would like to have but are not essential. They are also features that are specific to the game—we are only concerned about features specific to the engine right now. More importantly we are only concerned about features that are mandatory (i.e., features that we must have). One such example is input. Our engine has to be able to support some sort of user input to allow the player to communicate with the game.

Determining all of these mandatory features can take a little time, especially if you are unfamiliar with the genre (such as if you had never played or seen a FPS before). The best way to conduct this research is to play a lot of games from your chosen genre, read reviews, research the genre on the Internet, read books about it, and talk to others who have developed games in that genre. Also, look at other engines that were written for your chosen genre. Look at how they are designed and what features they have. This will help you to gain a better understanding of them. We will run through the main features and components for our engine later in this chapter. However, before we do, let's look at a couple of more important areas of design.

USING DESIGN GOALS

Whenever you design something you will often set goals, which are what you are hoping to achieve through your design. You don't realize it, but you actually do this subconsciously with a lot of things in life. Let's look at the example of driving your car from point A to point B. As you begin the journey you have already established your first goal, which is to get to point B. You may also need to get to point B by a particular time, so subconsciously you will set another goal that dictates that you need to be at point B by that time. This goal will affect decisions that you make while driving. For example, you might decide to take the back roads knowing that the freeway is congested. Whether you realize it or not, you did this to satisfy your second goal. We can go on to say that you have a third goal which states that you would like to get to point B safely. Now disregarding the law here, if you were to encounter a stop sign you have the option to drive straight through the intersection without actually stopping. However, your third goal prevents you from doing this as you would deem ignoring the stop sign as unsafe, which would break your third goal.

As you can see, goals are used for a lot of things in life. Your current goal is to learn, which is why you are reading this book. So you can see that it is only natural to apply the theory of goals to the design of things such as software, or more specifically, computer games. Whenever you design a new piece of software you should always select a few goals that you hope to achieve, and use them to influence your design decisions. To give you an idea of what sort of goals we are talking about, take a look at Table 1.1, which lists some of the most common goals used in software design.

TABLE 1.1 Common Software Design Goals

Features	The software is to support as many features as possible.
Maintainability	The software code should be readable, neat, and well documented.
Performance	The software should operate as quickly as possible.
Portability	The software must be able to function under multiple environments.
Reliability	The software should be as accurate as possible, providing reliable data.
Reusability	The software code is easy to use again in future projects.
Stability	The software must operate under various conditions for a period of time.
Usability	The software (or code) should be clear and easy to use for the end user.

As you can see there are a few goals to choose from, and there is nothing stopping you from establishing your own. However, for the purpose of our engine design we will focus on three goals: maintainability, reusability, and usability. This doesn't mean that the rest of the goals are not important, it just means that these are the main goals that we will focus on when designing our engine. Remember this engine is entirely for learning purposes so we must keep that in mind when we choose our goals. Once you have completed this book you may want to start building your own engine. You may then choose other goals such as performance, portability, and stability.

The best way to make complete use of your chosen goals is to have them in a prominent place where they are always visible while designing your software. You may try writing them on a piece of paper and sticking it just below the screen on your monitor, this way they are right in front of you at all times. Whenever you need to make a design decision you will have your goals close at hand, which will help you to make the best decision. For example, you may be faced with the decision to choose between two font handling and rendering methods. Method A may have better performance, but less support for extended font features. While method B has greater support for these features, it is slower to render. If the performance goal was one of your top priorities and the features goal was near the bottom of your list, then the obvious choice would be method A.

Now that we have our goals chosen and prominent, how will they affect our engine design? It simply means that we will opt for methods and techniques that best satisfy our goals when we have a choice. With regard to maintainability, it means that we will endeavor to create readable, neat code that can be logically followed. Commenting the code thoroughly is also a big concern here. Browse through some of the source code on the CD-ROM to see the kind of commenting that we will use. It is much easier to maintain code that is laid out neatly and well commented rather than code that has been written with no concern about things such as formatting.

ON THE CD

Reusability means that we will try to create an engine that you can take away and reuse in another project; this is generally why we create engines. Having a reusable engine greatly cuts down the time required to develop your games. Whenever you design a new engine it is always important to identify if this engine will be used in future projects. If so, reusability should be a top priority. We will attempt to satisfy this goal by using an object-oriented design that is specific to our genre. This way it will make it much easier to build a new multiplayer FPS project with this engine.

Our final goal, usability, actually ties in closely with both maintainability and reusability. If you satisfy the first two goals, it makes it much easier to satisfy the goal of usability. For our purposes, usability indicates how easy the engine is to work with. An engine with code that is hard to maintain, poorly documented, and not reusable, tends to produce an engine that is difficult to use. We aim to create an engine that allows the user (i.e., the programmer using the engine) to invoke the functions of the engine with little effort. One way to achieve this is by creating our engine with what we call a *single point of contact* and a clean interface. A single point of contact means that the programmer uses just one class, for example, to access the main functions of the engine. We will look at this more in Chapter 2.

VISUAL DESIGN AIDS

You have probably heard the saying that a picture is worth a thousand words. Well, the picture might not actually physically say anything, but it sure does allow you to visualize something a lot easier. This is especially true when trying to visualize a complex problem. Often words cannot describe something clearly or effectively so it is necessary to depict the problem.

Let's use an example to illustrate our problem (pun intended). Pretend you had to explain to someone how the networking model works in a hypothetical game that you are working on. You may say something like the following:

Whenever a network message is received it is appended to the end of a linked list, which is processed by the network system every frame of the game loop. The network system is allowed to process messages from the list on a first-in first-out basis for a set period of time. After this time has expired, the network system must yield to allow other systems to process in that given frame.

This is the description of how a fairly typical network system receives and processes network messages. In fact, it is exactly how we are going to implement our network system. To fully understand the system, you may need to read it a little slower and visualize what the system is actually doing. The reason for this is that your brain operates best with pictures rather than words. If you try to remember back to an event that happened recently in your life, you won't receive a textual description from your brain about the event. Instead, you will receive a series of pictures—like photographs in your mind—that remind you about the event.

When you try to explain a difficult concept to someone (or even yourself), rather than trying to describe it, draw it. Let's look at our network system example again. This time we will look at Figure 1.1, which gives us a visual diagram of the system. You will probably find that this diagram is a lot easier to follow than the textual description because you didn't need to assemble a visual representation in your mind. You already had it right there in front of you.

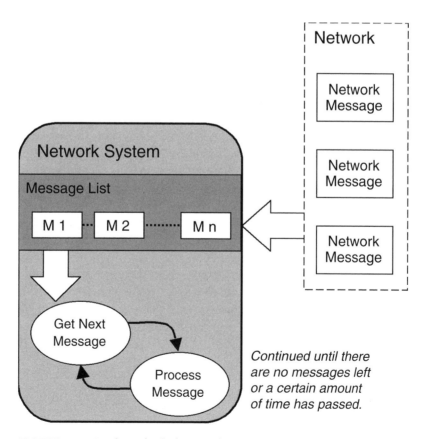

FIGURE 1.1   Our hypothetical network system receiving and processing messages.

Now you hopefully realize the benefits of drawing pictures rather than describing things verbally. However, one problem remains with drawing pictures. How do you create a picture that everyone can understand? Just like writing, it is possible for the meaning of something to be misinterpreted by the reader or viewer. In an attempt to correct this, a number of standards have been developed specifically to solve this problem and ensure that all these pictures are consistent. One of the most common standards in practice throughout the software development industry is the Unified Modeling Language (UML).

The UML defines a number of common practice forms of diagrams that have been proven within the industry. There are diagrams for mapping relationships among users, classes, and activities to name a few. You can use as much of the UML as you like and make it as complex as you like. You can even use it to map the design of entire systems without writing a single word—truly amazing! What is so important about the UML is that it can be learned and used by anyone, which means that you can draw a diagram and pass it along to your team. Everyone in the team will be able to look at it and understand exactly what is going on.

Throughout this book we are not going to use any of the UML so don't fret thinking you need to learn everything about it. Instead, you should learn at least some of the basics as it will greatly improve your ability to draw and understand diagrams that do use the UML, and will hopefully make your life a little easier when it comes to designing complex software issues.

One note to take away here is that visual design is important and a lot easier than you might think—much easier than trying to explain everything with words. If you don't want to learn a specific standard such as the UML, then come up with your own standard that you can understand. It will improve your ability to understand problems when you draw them. You will also be able to better understand your diagrams if you revisit them, for example, after a long break. Generally, however, in teams it is most effective if everyone follows the same standard or guidelines as it makes life a whole lot easier when trying to explain things to each other.

Remember that we are not building safety critical software here, so it's OK to experiment. Mistakes will enhance your design through evolution. In light of this it is not necessary to stick to a rigid design format. As long as you can create a visual design that illustrates the solution to the problem and can be understood by the required people, that's all that matters. In other words, if you can fit your design on the back of a cocktail napkin, it solves the problem, and it makes sense to everyone involved, then use it!

DEFINING THE ENGINE

At this stage we have covered a good amount of design theory. Now it is time to put some of our new skills into practice as we dive into the actual high level design of our engine. Here we will define what our engine needs to do and then define the components that make up the engine. This process is often referred to as *requirements gathering*.

To begin with, what does our engine need to do? Obviously, it needs to facilitate the creation of a FPS as easily as possible. So part of the question is in fact, what does a FPS need to do? This in turn creates a problem for us. What constitutes the engine and what constitutes the game? If we add a new feature, how do we know whether to add it to the engine or to the game code? This is a difficult question to answer as it really depends on many factors; however, through this simple design process you will better understand the differences between the engine- and the game-specific code.

In our case, we are making a simple engine specifically designed for FPSs. Therefore, we can make quite a few assumptions about the games that will run on the engine. We can assume that all of the games are in fact FPSs and they all use the same architecture as implemented in the engine. So with this in mind, let's list some tasks that we know the engine will handle:

- The engine will provide a basic framework to link all of the components together.
- All resource management (such as textures, meshes, and sounds) will be accommodated.
- The engine will provide various forms of control, both of itself and for the user.
- All rendering will be handled by the engine.
- A sound system will manage the loading and playback of sounds.
- Finally, the engine will have some sort of networking capabilities.

It's a fairly modest list, but it actually comprises a large portion of the engine—but we are not done yet. Now we enter the gray area, the area where features can seamlessly meld between engine- and game-specific code. We need to try to extract from this gray area what in fact should belong to the engine. The first topic in question (which has already been listed) is the engine control. Without going into the fine details, we know that the game needs to accept key presses and so forth in order to determine what the player wants to do. This is game specific; however we also know that the process of reading a key press is generic, so this code would be engine specific. In this particular instance, we will allow the engine to process and read input, but give the game the ability to choose what input is relevant to the game. That is one example of overcoming a gray area feature. Let's briefly look at the rest.

Scripting is another area where the game only cares for specific functionality. We will give the engine the ability to provide basic scripting, and the game can then interpret it however it pleases, just like what we will do with the user input. The game will also contain a number of objects, such as players and weapons. These objects have to be defined and processed. Normally, you would let a game define its own objects, and just provide it with the infrastructure to integrate those objects into the engine's processing. Since we know that our game is going to be a FPS, we can go one step further and actually implement the base objects into the engine, however, we will make the objects flexible enough that they can be extended or ignored completely if the situation requires it. Finally, since we know that the engine is being created for the FPS genre we are afforded the luxury of implementing the scene management directly into the engine, which can render everything from the map to all of the various objects in the scene. Let's take a more detailed look at each of the major components of our engine.

THE FRAMEWORK

The framework is a very critical area of the engine. Imagine the framework of a car. If it were designed incorrectly, you may find problems such as weakness in some areas, or insufficient room for various components, such as the engine. Like the framework of a car, the framework of a game engine is a skeleton that must eventually hold everything together and provide enough room and support for all of the components to live harmoniously. The framework also defines how the general processing flows through the engine. We have already mentioned the single point of contact for the engine, and this is exactly where it is exhibited. The framework will simply allow all of the engine components to interact with one another, while also allowing the game built on the engine to interact with each of these components, all through a single class. The framework will also handle any communication with the operating system, and provide other basic forms of functionality such as a linked list container and resource management.

The framework should also provide some degree of flexibility. We want to let the programmer have some sort of say in the way the engine will set itself up and operate. Right now it is impossible to identify every area of flexibility that will be required, however, what we can do is offer some means for this flexibility to be integrated when needed. In other words, we need to provide the programmer with a method to initialize the engine to behave in a particular way. This will all be described in more detail in Chapter 2, when we start implementing our framework.

RESOURCES

Sometimes called *assets*, resources are all of the various extras that make up a game. For example, a texture is a resource, and so is a sound effect, as is a 3D mesh. Actually, these are all primitive resources. A game may also need to use complex resources, which are combinations of primitive resources. For example, a level may consist of a number of meshes, which are covered in textures, as well as several sound effects and scripts operating around the level. This level is called a complex resource, as it is made up of two or more primitive resources. How a game handles a complex resource is really dependent on too many factors to generalize such a thing. Instead, this type of resource handling is usually left up to the game-specific code, while the engine provides the support for the primitive resources.

Fortunately, in our case, we have already made the assumption that all games built with this engine will in fact be FPSs. So for this reason we can assume that they will all use complex resources, such as maps. Based on this assumption we can give the engine all of the required functionality to support various complex resources like maps. We will cover the different complex resources that we will use as we progress through development as it is difficult to identify them all at such an early stage. We haven't even started to think about the game yet; we are still just designing the engine. So for now we will take a look at the different primitive resources that our engine will support.

We know that the engine will definitely need to support resources such as 3D meshes and sound effects, but there is another interesting resource that we want it to support: textures (i.e., images that can be rendered either on to the screen or on to the surface of a polygon in 3D space). DirectX already provides us with the basic functionality to handle textures, but we want to go a step further with them. Wouldn't it be great if we could define a texture (grass for example) so that when you walk on it, it sounds like grass, and when you shoot it, dirt flies up in the air? Well, that's exactly what we are going to do. We are going to create a resource called a *material*. A material will have a texture assigned to it as well as other properties such as how lighting affects it, and how the engine processes it. We can add anything we like to our materials, such as sound effects for when you step on them. We will cover this in more detail in Chapter 8 when we implement our material system.

Now we should note one important aspect about all of these resources. They all have similarities or several properties in common. Each one of these resources is physically located on the hard drive and therefore needs to be loaded. This means that all of these resources will have a filename, and a path pointing to where the file is located on the hard drive. When you load a resource it consumes memory. If you need to load a 3D mesh of a car, for example, and then later discover that you need another instance of that car placed somewhere else in the game world, it would be wasteful to load the 3D mesh for the car twice. It would be much better to load it once and then allow any instance of the car in the world to use the mesh, therefore only requiring memory for one copy of the 3D mesh. This is where the resource manager steps in. We will use a special class that has the ability to load any type of resource for us and always guarantee that only one copy of that resource exists in memory at any point in time, even if we tell it to load the same resource twice. We will look at the resource manager in more detail in Chapter 2.

ENGINE CONTROL

This actually consists of two separate topics. First there is the issue of controlling the engine's processing. Then there is the issue of allowing the user to provide input, which can affect how the engine processes. Without going into too much detail, engine processing is all about controlling what the engine spends its time on in each frame. For example, you may have a networking system, a sound system, a rendering system, and the game logic, which are all demanding precious processing time of which there is a limited amount in each frame. In order to allow all enough time to do their jobs without starving anyone else, you need to implement some sort of processing control. We will do this in two ways. First we will use what are called *states* and second we will use little techniques like timing to force a component to yield after a set time limit.

Every frame, the engine will run through and process everything necessary for that frame. This is called the game loop. Figure 1.2 shows an example of a simple game loop, which takes a certain amount of time to complete one iteration depending on factors such as how fast your CPU is, what video card you have, and how well the code has been optimized to run on the hardware. A typical game may consist of a number of states. For example, you may have a menu state, a cut-scene state, and an in-game state. Each frame, the engine has to decide which one of these states needs to be processed. In our example it will often be fairly obvious, however, if you were to use states at a lower level it may not be so obvious. The key point here is that not all states require all of the components to be processed. More so, each state may have different processing parameters. Rather than just processing every frame blindly, we can use the states to guide the engine as to what needs to be processed and what doesn't. For example, you may realize that in the cut-scene state, there is no network activity, so when in that state the engine may give less time to the network system (or skip it completely) and give more time to other areas like the rendering.

The second issue is user input. This is the process of accepting key presses from the keyboard or movements of the mouse, and turning them into some sort of usable information for the game. As we have previously mentioned, we will not define the exact user input for the game, but we will provide support for user input and let the game decide how to interpret it. We will achieve this through the use of a wrapper class around DirectInput. Everything about this wrapper class and the states system we already touched on will be further discussed in Chapter 3 when we add these forms of control to our engine.

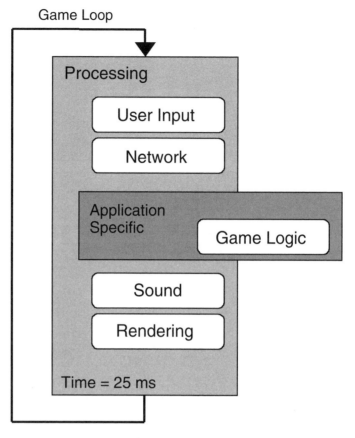

FIGURE 1.2 An example of a simple game loop.

SCRIPTING

Scripting is one of the most exciting aspects of developing computer games because it can potentially allow you to modify large portions of the game without having to recompile the code. This can be very useful in two ways: it can speed up development time when performing tasks such as balancing game mechanics because it allows you to make fine adjustments and see immediate results; and it can add value to your game in terms of allowing the end user to modify the game and potentially create his own game content, such as adding new levels, or new objects like weapons. Whenever you create any game you should always consider the impact of using some sort of scripting system, whether you create your own basic system or you use a fully featured commercial system.

For our game, we definitely want to use a basic scripting system, since we can identify a number of objects in a typical FPS that can greatly benefit from a scripting system. For example, weapons can use scripts to define properties such as how fast they can shoot, how far they can shoot, and how much damage they can do. To achieve this we will use a very basic type of script called a *property script*. A property script does not use commands like normal scripts; instead, it just lists various properties and their respective values, which can be read in by the engine. This type of system is all that we need to set the various properties of the objects in our game, like the weapons. We will go into more detail about this in Chapter 4 when we implement our scripting system.

RENDERING

One of the major areas for any game is its rendering. That is, the methods it uses to display the various images to the screen so that the game can create the environment on the screen for the player to view. This is often one of the most performance-intensive areas of a game engine, and an area that is often highly optimized. For our rendering we will use Direct3D. More specifically, we will use a Direct3D device to render vertices to the screen, which will make up polygons to form the shapes of our 3D environment. We will also use textures that will be applied to these polygons so that they look like their real life counterparts. In other words, a brick wall will look like a brick wall, when in fact it is just a few polygons with a brick texture applied to them.

One last point to keep in mind is that not all computers are the same in terms of their physical hardware configuration. Different configurations may behave differently when using the same display settings. Some computers are able to handle higher resolutions than others, so we want to accommodate this. We will build a small graphics settings interface into the engine which will allow the end user to specify how the engine will prepare the Direct3D device. We want the user to be able to adjust things such as the resolution, color depth, and the refresh rate of the display. We will cover these topics more in Chapter 5 when we add the Direct3D device to our engine.

SOUND SYSTEM

No game would ever be quite right if it didn't have sound effects—the sound of your weapon firing, the tapping of your feet as you run, or the explosion of a fuel drum being shot. It just wouldn't be the same without them, so of course we want to include them. Fortunately for us, it is very simple to implement through the use of DirectMusic. Now don't let the name fool you, it can handle a lot more than just music. Although we could develop a complete sound system through the use of DirectSound, DirectMusic is a perfect alternative as it provides a far simpler solution. In fact, it can even perform 3D sound effects through the use of DirectSound. So when your friend (or enemy) is sneaking up on your left, it will sound like he really is sneaking up on your left.

To achieve this we will use a wrapper class, which will take all of the required functionality and bind it into a tight little package that will allow you to load and play a sound with ease. If you remember back to when we were talking about resources, we identified sounds as a potential primitive resource. We also mentioned how we will use a resource manager to load our resources for use. Again, fortunately for us, DirectMusic provides interfaces that actually handle that so we don't even need a resource manager for our sound files. It just can't get any easier. Now why can't DirectX handle more resources in this fashion? In Chapter 6 we will discuss our sound system further, and then implement it.

NETWORKING

Playing a game on your own is fun, but playing a game with other people is a blast! Now if that game happens to be a board game or a card game, then you can skip this section. If, however, you are here to design a game engine that will allow two or more people to play a computer game together on different computers, then read on. Networking—in our context—is all about providing the infrastructure to allow two or more computers to communicate over a network in order to maintain the synchronized state of a game across those computers. Got it? Once again, DirectX comes to the rescue; this time in the disguise of DirectPlay, which is the component of DirectX that deals with connecting multiple computers over a network (or over the Internet, which is really just a large network) and allowing them to communicate with one another. To make it happen we will once again use another wrapper class, this time around the functionality of DirectPlay, which will give us a cleaner interface for creating our multiplayer games. DirectPlay can operate using one of two possible network architectures, peer-to-peer or client-server. In Chapter 7 (when we implement our networking system) you will see how we will actually combine these two architectures and use a hybrid model to try to gain the advantages from both architectures.

GAME OBJECTS

Objects are the building blocks of a dynamic scene. Anything that is not static is an object. For example, a weapon lying on the ground is an object that can be picked up and used. A brick in a wall is not an object because it is part of the static geometry that makes up the environment. However, if that same brick was laying on the ground it might very well be an object as the player may be able to kick it around, or pick it up and throw it. All of these objects are referred to as *game objects*. Now game objects are exactly that: they make up part of the game and are generally not implemented into the engine (although an infrastructure may be put in place for them). However, we have made assumptions about what our engine will be used for, allowing us to implement various game objects directly into the engine.

We will implement a base object into the engine that will have the ability to move around the environment, render itself, and collide with things. We will then build more objects off this base object by using the object-oriented programming concept of *inheritance*. If you have never heard of this term before, it simply means that you create a class (for example) that inherits functionality from another base class. In other words, we will create a base object with all the basic functionality used by an object. Any new objects that we later create will build off this base object and inherit (or take on) its functionality. Don't be alarmed if you have never heard about these types of object-oriented programming concepts. They will be explained to you as we progress.

These concepts allow us to define new objects with advanced functionality, such as animated objects that have the ability to animate any mesh associated with them. We can also define spawner objects that have the ability to spawn other objects such as weapons. At the same time, all of these objects will be flexible enough so that they can be derived from again to create more objects, or just ignored completely if the functionality of the specific object is not required. When it comes time to build the game you will find that a lot of the base functionality exists, due to the assumptions we made earlier, which will greatly speed the process of creating our game. In Chapter 9, we will go into a lot more detail about objects and actually implement the different types of objects into our engine.

SCENE MANAGEMENT

If you load up your favorite FPS you will notice that all of the environments that you play in are distinctive. They can be identified and separated, and have boundaries. These environments are often called levels or maps, but for us—we will refer to them as *scenes* from here on—the topic of scene management is all about managing the level or map. This doesn't just mean managing things like loading the scene, putting the players and weapons in, and so forth. It also means managing things like rendering the scene and performing collision detection between the scene and all the objects within it.

Our engine needs to be able to handle our scenes for us, which means managing all of the following tasks:

■ Loading the scene and allocating memory for everything in it.
■ Destroying the scene and freeing its memory.
■ Rendering the scene efficiently by breaking the static geometry into a hierarchy that is culled using techniques such as frustum and occlusion culling.
■ Updating and rendering all of the objects within the scene as necessary.
■ Providing collision detection between the scene and all the objects.

As you can see, our scene manager has its work cut out for it. In fact, a large portion of the engine's processing will probably be used up by this system. Therefore, this system would be the most likely candidate for any required future optimization. We will go into full detail about the scene manager in Chapter 10, the final chapter for developing our engine. After that we will be ready to develop our game.

USING THE D3DX LIBRARY

DirectX comes with a very handy library built on top of it called the D3DX library. This library is specifically designed to alleviate the programmer from many of the intricacies involved when using Direct3D. Since we are going to use Direct3D for all of our rendering, and we want to do it as easily as possible, it makes perfect sense to make use of this library.

The D3DX library provides access to a number of interfaces that expose all sorts of functionality, especially when it comes to handling, animating, and rendering meshes. It also comes with a whole lot of functions for handling mathematical calculations for everything from matrices, to quaternions, right through to vectors and planes. It truly is a very good library to wrap your head around when you first begin, as it provides a lot of the basic functionality needed to handle a 3D environment. As you become more proficient, you may find yourself wanting more out of the library. At this point you may look into developing your own similar library, which can handle all of these tasks in your own desired manner. Once you have installed the DirectX Software Development Kit (SDK), take a look at the

D3DX section of the DirectX documentation. You will find it in the Reference subsection of the DirectX Graphics section. All of the interfaces, functions, and so forth of the D3DX library are well documented so you shouldn't have too much trouble picking it up. Throughout the rest of this book you will see how we will make use of the D3DX library in our engine and in the final game, which will assist in putting some of the D3DX library's functionality into context.

SUMMARY

The first chapter is down, and we're off to a good start. We covered a lot about design in general, and then looked more specifically at the various design issues associated with our engine. We went on to briefly discuss the various components of our engine, which may have scared you off a little. Even if much of the content went straight over your head, don't worry; there is no need to go back and read it again. Everything will be explained a lot more clearly in the appropriate chapters. Chapter 1 was simply a primer to give you an idea of what we will be discussing throughout Part I of the book. In Chapter 2, we start to get our hands dirty with a bit of code as we begin to develop the framework for our engine.

2 ▪ Framework

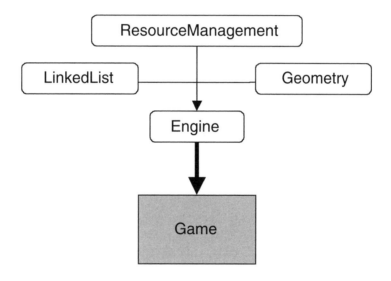

In This Chapter

- Cover a number of C++ and Windows® programming concepts.
- Begin implementation of the main `Engine` class including the supporting utilities.
- Learn about using templates to create classes such as linked lists and resource managers.
- Look at the fundamental geometry support structures and functions.

ON THE CD

W e will begin by implementing a basic framework for our engine. You can find the workspace for this chapter in the `/Source/Chapter 2/` directory on the CD-ROM.

SETTING UP DIRECTX

ON THE CD

Before we can begin it is very important that you have the DirectX SDK installed on your system and configured with your compiler. A copy of the latest version of the DirectX SDK is included on the accompanying CD-ROM.

In order to successfully compile any code using DirectX you will need to ensure that your compiler has access to the appropriate files. There are two types of files used by DirectX applications at compile time, the include files—often referred to as header files (`.h`)—and the library files (`.lib`) used by the linker. If you installed the DirectX SDK to the default path, then these files will be located in the `C:\Program Files\Microsoft DirectX 9.0 SDK (October 2004)\Include` folder and the `C:\Program Files\Microsoft DirectX 9.0 SDK (October 2004)\Lib` folder respectively. Refer to your compiler's documentation for instructions on adding these folders to the appropriate search paths. More detailed instructions are provided at the end of the Introduction, with special notes for Visual Studio 6 users, so please refer to that section if you have not read it already.

NOTE

Some of the other folders in the Include *and* Lib *directory lists may contain older versions of the same files. Therefore, it is advisable that the latest DirectX include and library folders are placed at the top of their respective directory lists to ensure that they are the first folders to be searched.*

TIP

The best way to check if you have set all the paths correctly is to open one of the workspaces included on the CD-ROM (the one for this chapter would be appropriate) and try to compile it. If you receive any error messages in the build window indicating that it cannot open a particular DirectX header file, it means you have not set the include directory path correctly. If you receive a linking error indicating that it cannot open a particular library file, it means you have not set the library directory path correctly.

USING HEADER FILES

The functionality of a particular source (.cpp) file can be represented by a header file. The header file is often referred to as the *interface*. For example, you may create a class called Animal, which represents the functionality of a generic animal within a game. This class would be defined in a header file (such as animal.h) and implemented in an associated source file. The header file therefore provides the interface to the Animal class so that the class and the functions within the class can be referenced by other files within our hypothetical game. The following example shows the class definition of our Animal class, which is placed in the header file. This then becomes the interface to the Animal class.

```
class Animal
{
public:
  Animal();
  virtual ~Animal();

private:
  bool m_alive;
};
```

Our simple class has a constructor, a destructor, and a single bool (Boolean value—true/false) member variable. For now, just ignore the virtual keyword in front of the destructor as it will be explained very shortly—it is there for correctness only. Let's move on and have a look at the actual implementation of this class, which would be placed in the source file.

```
Animal::Animal()
{
  m_alive = true;
}
```

```
Animal::~Animal()
{
  m_alive = false;
}
```

In order for the compiler to link the source of a class with the class's definition you need to include the header file at the beginning of the source file. But if you include the header file at the beginning of the source file then why bother even creating a header file? Technically, you can place your class definition at the beginning of your source file and then place the implementation below it. In fact, you can even put the implantation inside the actual class definition, as shown below.

```
class Animal
{
public:
  Animal()
  {
    m_alive = true;
  };

  virtual ~Animal()
  {
    m_alive = false;
  };

private:
  bool m_alive;
};
```

There are disadvantages to both of these approaches. First, if you place the class definition at the beginning of the source file then you lose the ability to have an independent interface to your class. This can increase the complexity of your code, which reduces the code's maintainability and subsequently, its usability. Second, if you place the implementation inside the class definition, you do not have a protected interface. The whole idea behind interfaces is to allow you to develop a class that can be used in other projects without displaying the implementation. This way anyone can view the interface to see what the class can do, but they cannot view the actual source if you wrap it up in a library.

So how does one go about including the class definition at the beginning of the source yet still maintain a separate protected interface? If you've already opened the workspace for this chapter and begun browsing the files you will notice that some of the files have one or more #include statements at the beginning. The #include statement basically tells the compiler to take the entire contents of the specified file and dump them where the `#include` statement is. Now if we go back to our previous example with the `Animal` class, we can include our class definition at the beginning of the source file by simply using an `#include` statement like the one in the following example:

```
#include "Animal.h"

Animal::Animal()
{
  m_alive = true;
}

Animal::~Animal()
{
  m_alive = false;
}
```

As far as the compiler is concerned it sees the following, which is perfect as it allows the compiler to link the source to the header, yet affords us the ease of a clean protected interface:

```
class Animal
{
public:
  Animal();
  virtual ~Animal();

private:
  bool m_alive;
};

Animal::Animal()
{
  m_alive = true;
}

Animal::~Animal()
{
  m_alive = false;
}
```

In our hypothetical game, if we wanted to create an instance of our `Animal` class (within another file) all we have to do is include the interface to the `Animal` class somewhere in the source file that will be instancing the `Animal` class. Obviously, the

`#include` statement must be placed before you attempt to use the class. Take a look at the following example:

```
#include "Animal.h"

int WINAPI WinMain( HINSTANCE instance, HINSTANCE prev, LPSTR
                    cmdLine, int cmdShow )
{
  Animal dog;

  return true;
}
```

We will employ this concept throughout the entire engine and the actual game. Virtually every class will be created with an external interface. For the engine, these interfaces will be linked (through the use of `#include` statements) to a central file called `Engine.h`, which will satisfy our requirement for a single point of contact. All the functionality of the engine will be represented by this one header file. Therefore, to use the engine, you will only have to concern yourself with including a single header file in your project, which you will see when we take a look at the first sample at the end of this chapter. We will talk more about the single point of contact a little later in this chapter.

THE VIRTUAL DESTRUCTOR

In our previous example with the `Animal` class, you will have noticed the keyword `virtual` placed in front of the class destructor. Since we are covering some basics at the moment, this seems like a good place to discuss this. Hopefully, you are already familiar with the `virtual` keyword and its use. If you not, the `virtual` keyword is used to inform the compiler that the given function can be overridden by a derived class. Let's take a look at an extended version of our `Animal` class, and a derived class called `Dog`, which obviously defines a more specific type of animal.

```
class Animal
{
public:
  Animal();
  virtual ~Animal();

  virtual void Call();
```

```
private:
  bool m_alive;
};

class Dog : public Animal
{
public:
  Dog();
  virtual ~Dog();

  virtual void Call();

private:
  bool m_alive;
};
```

Now you should already know what will happen if we create an instance of the Dog class and then call the function Call. Since this function is a virtual function, the compiler knows to call the Dog class's implementation of the Call function. However, you may not be familiar with the operation of the virtual destructor. Surprisingly, despite so few knowing about its operation, it actually operates in exactly the same way as any other virtual function. The only difference is you do not need to call the base class's implementation of the destructor to destroy the base class. The compiler does this for you.

Let's have a look at some examples. Let's say we want to invoke the Call function for our dog instance, which will play a bark sound. After the function has completed, control returns to the calling point; in other words, the function returns with no further processing. If we want to invoke the base Animal class's Call function we must manually call it from within the Dog class's Call function, as shown below.

```
void Animal::Call()
{
  // Play a generic call sound.
}

void Dog::Call()
{
  // Play a dog call sound.

  // Call the base class's Call() function.
  Animal::Call();
}
```

For the virtual destructor we do not need to make this explicit call to the base destructor as it is called automatically by the compiler after the derived destructor returns. This is actually very important, and the omission of the virtual statement is a common cause of memory leaks. Consider the following classes:

```
class Animal
{
public:
  Animal()
  {
    m_name = new char[32];
  };

  ~Animal()
  {
    delete[]( m_name );
  };

private:
  char *m_name;
};

class Dog : public Animal
{
public:
  Dog();
  ~Dog();
};
```

You may not immediately pick up on the problem here but the lack of a virtual destructor is a significant problem that will create a memory leak of 32 ? char bytes every time an instance of the Dog class is created and destroyed. The reason for this is that when you destroy your dog instance, the Dog class destructor is called but the Animal class destructor is not, unless you explicitly call it yourself from within the Dog class's destructor as we did in the previous example with the Call function. To remedy this it is just a simple matter of making the destructor virtual, which then ensures that the base class's destructor is also called when the instance is destroyed.

Whenever you create a new class you should always consider if the destructor should be virtual. Tip: the basic rule of thumb is—any class that may be derived from should have a virtual destructor. If in doubt make it virtual just to be safe. Throughout the code, in both the engine and the game, you will see many examples of the virtual destructor being put to good use. This is especially true in Chapter 9 when we start dealing with game objects that can be derived from to create new objects.

CONNECTING THE ENGINE TOGETHER

If you recall from the previous chapter where we designed our engine, we specifically stated that the engine needs to have a single point of contact. We define our single point of contact as allowing the user to incorporate the engine through one #include statement, one library file, and one main class that needs to be instanced. More specifically, the user needs to be able to access the entire engine through one global variable.

Fortunately, this is actually very easy to achieve. All that is required is that we link each source and header file in the Engine project back to one main header file, say Engine.h for example. We then create a single class called Engine that can be used to access all of the engine's functionality. The final step is to create an external global pointer such as g_engine, which can be accessed anywhere within both the Engine project and the application's project. We will allow the engine to set this pointer when the Engine class is instantiated, thus freeing the user from this task. Let's take a look at how we can use the Engine header file as this single point of contact.

The first step involves linking our Engine project with both Windows and DirectX. The first three #include statements in our Engine.h file link the project to various Windows functionality. Although we won't be using all of this functionality just yet, we will include it all now so that we don't have to come back to it later. windowsx.h is fairly obvious as to what that includes; the other two are a little more vague. stdio.h allows access to the standard file input/output functions and tchar.h allows access to the text string data type.

The second set of includes adds the functionality for the different DirectX components that we will be using. Table 2.1 shows which header file is used to access which component in DirectX. Note: there are many more header files exposed by DirectX than what we are using here. The DirectX documentation will indicate which header files need to be included when using a particular interface. As previously mentioned, we will add all the required DirectX header files now so that we do not have to return here later.

TABLE 2.1 Required DirectX Headers

d3dx9.h	D3DX Library
dinput.h	DirectInput interfaces used for both keyboard and mouse input
dplay8.h	DirectPlay interfaces used for networking
dmusici.h	DirectMusic interfaces used for all forms of sound playback

Now you have probably noticed that there is one line of code right at the beginning of the file that we have overlooked, the #define DIRECTINPUT_VERSION 0x0800. All that it is doing is defining the version that the DirectInput subsystem should emulate. It is not necessary to explicitly state this as dinput.h also defines it. If you do not include this, however, you will receive a message every time you compile your code informing you that DIRECTINPUT_VERSION is undefined. This is not a problem as DirectInput defaults to the latest version, but we will include it anyway just to prevent this message from appearing.

The next step is to link each component of the engine back to the Engine header file. You should also notice three more #include statements under the heading Engine Includes. These #include statements link the three additional header files (in the project so far) back to the Engine header file. To see how this linking works, open up the ResourceManagement header file and take a look at the ResourceManager class. You will notice that it is using a LinkedList which has been defined in the LinkedList header file. You should also notice that nowhere within the Resource-Management header file have we included the LinkedList header file. This works because everything is being linked back to one file where the compiler places the code in the order we specify the #include statements. Since we have placed the #include "LinkedList.h" before the #include "ResourceManagement.h" the compiler places the definition of the LinkedList class before the definition of the ResourceManager class. If you were to swap these #include statements around the compiler would generate an error as it would not be able to find the definition to the LinkedList class when it trys to compile the ResoureManager class.

TIP

It is very important to be aware of the order that you specify your included files. Listing them in the wrong order can cause major headaches. If it becomes too difficult to manage the ordering you can always include the headers in the specific source files that use them. The disadvantage is that you will have to do it with every source file that needs it. This can become confusing in its own right.

Finally, there is one last #include statement you need to be aware of. This is the one located at the beginning of every source file. Open up the file Engine.cpp for an example. You will see the line #include "Engine.h" at the beginning of the file. When we discussed using header files previously we saw how a source file must include its header file in order for the code to compile. If the code is using one or more other interfaces it must also include the header files of those interfaces as well. To prevent you from having to include multiple header files in every source file we will simply include all of the header files in the Engine header file and then just include the Engine header file at the beginning of each source file, as shown in the source files for this chapter's workspace. We will do this virtually every time we add a new source file to the project from chapter to chapter.

MEMORY MANAGEMENT

Gone are the days of concerning yourself over limited memory. These days the average computer system has enough memory for you to do almost anything you like as long as you do not fall victim to one of a programmer's worst enemies, the memory leak. Despite having so much memory to play with, it is still finite and can still run out if you abuse it. Abusing memory generally happens through sloppy programming and a lack of housekeeping, so it's important to clean up properly and release memory you are no longer using. If your system does run out of memory you can expect it to become unstable and potentially crash the operating system, which is no fun for anyone. Thankfully, the latest operating systems are becoming much better at cleaning up unused memory for you, especially if your application crashes unexpectedly. Nevertheless, you should not rely on your operating system. Instead you should have your own method for managing memory and releasing it properly.

You can get very elaborate memory management systems these days that will create, track, and free all memory for you. These systems are often foolproof and can almost guarantee to never let a memory leak slip through the cracks (pun intended). We won't be using anything half as elaborate as this, as it can be very detailed. However, we encourage you to delve deeper into this area (via the Internet, for example) and come up with your own reusable method to manage memory that you can use in your future projects. It will save you many headaches in the long run.

As previously alluded to, we will be using a very simple method to manage our memory. To begin with we will use the standard new operator to create everything from class instances to storage containers such as arrays and linked lists. You will see many examples of the new operator as we progress.

In order to free our memory, we will use three simple macros as shown in the Engine header file: SAFE_DELETE, SAFE_DELETE_ARRAY, and SAFE_RELEASE. Each macro takes as input a pointer to an address in memory, and is used to free a particular type of memory. The SAFE_DELETE macro frees any memory created with the new operator except for arrays, in which case the SAFE_DELETE_ARRAY macro should be used. The SAFE_RELEASE macro is a special one that will only free memory that was allocated through the creation of a DirectX COM (Component Object Model) object, which uses the IUnknown interface.

NOTE

COM is a very detailed topic and its explanation is beyond the scope of what we need to do. In fact, for our purposes COM is virtually transparent. If you would like to learn more about COM you should refer to the DirectX documentation as it provides a very detailed and clear explanation.

Whenever you create one of these DirectX objects, you are indirectly allocating all the required memory for the object. The only way to release this memory is to call the Release function exposed by the object's IUnknown interface, which is exactly what the SAFE_RELEASE macro does. Now you might be wondering why we are bothering with these macros when the DirectX objects already have a Release function and when an equivalent delete operator exists to free memory created with the new operator. The answer is safety. The macros ensure that we do not try to destroy memory that was never allocated. For example, if you try to call Release on a NULL pointer you will receive an access violation error. The SAFE_RELEASE macro prevents this mistake from occurring.

The last point to make about our memory management method is to make good use of your own memory. You will need to remember to free any memory that you previously allocated. This is why you should take time to develop your own memory management method that works for you. Sometimes just keeping a note of what has been allocated is sufficient. For larger projects this may not be good enough.

ENGINE SETUP STRUCTURE

As you will remember from our design in Chapter 1, we decided that we wanted to have a method to allow the programmer to initialize the engine to behave in a particular way. To put it in more simple terms, we want to have an engine setup structure. The engine setup structure is nothing more than a struct definition which can be instanced and then filled out. Think of it like a form that you fill in and then pass to the engine. The engine takes this form and then sets itself up according to what you specified. An important point we should keep in mind is that the programmer should be able to fill in as much or as little of this so-called form as possible. In other words, the engine should have a set of default parameters for each entry in the form, just in case the programmer does not specify a value for a particular entry. Here is the beginning of our engine setup structure.

```
struct EngineSetup
{
  HINSTANCE instance;
  char *name;

  EngineSetup()
  {
    instance = NULL;
```

```
    name = "Application";
  }
};
```

Our engine setup structure is pretty plain at the moment. This is okay because our engine is also pretty plain at the moment. As the engine expands we will add more entries to the engine setup structure, which will give the programmer more options to customize the engine's behavior. You will notice the constructor, which will establish the default value for each parameter. Now let's take a quick look at the two parameters currently in the structure.

First you have the `instance`, which is the handle of the application. This is passed to you by Windows when you specify the `WinMain` function, which you will see when we create our first sample application to test the engine. All you need to do is pass this handle over to the engine so that it knows which application it is working with. The second parameter is the `name`, which is nothing more than the name of the application. This text will appear in the title bar of a windowed application.

COMMUNICATING WITH WINDOWS

Any application that runs on your computer has to answer to the operating system. In other words, an application cannot just greedily hog the system, ignoring all requests from the operating system. For that reason, an application should contain what is called a *window procedure* (or `WindowProc`) call-back function. The prototype for this function generally looks like the following:

```
LRESULT CALLBACK WindowProc( HWND wnd, UINT msg, WPARAM wparam,
                             LPARAM lparam )
```

Just because we have to define this function in our application doesn't mean we actually get to call it. In fact, we never call it. Instead, the function is called whenever our application receives a message from Windows, even if the message was originally generated by our application. You are expected to implement the function so that when it is called it can handle any message sent to it by Windows. To assist you, Windows passes four parameters to you through the function call. First there is the `HWND wnd`, which is a handle to the window that received the message, which is usually your application window. Then there is the `UINT msg`, which is an identifier to identify the incoming message. Finally you have the `WPARAM wparam` and the `LPARAM lparam`, which are just parameters that can be used by any of the incoming messages. The best way to handle a call to this function is to check the `msg` to see what message has arrived, and then use the data in the `wparam` and/or `lparam` to process the message.

There are many different messages that you need to support, but fortunately for us Windows offers a default message handler that can handle any of the messages with a default response. This means that we can choose which messages we want to support and then let the default message handler take care of the rest. There are far too many messages to list them all, but Table 2.2 shows some of the most commonly used messages.

TABLE 2.2   Common Messages

WM_ACTIVATEAPP	Focus is about to change to or from the current application.
WM_COMMAND	User activated messages from menu items and child controls.
WM_CREATE	The application has created a new window.
WM_DESTROY	The application is destroying a window.
WM_PAINT	A request has been made to paint a portion of the application's window.
WM_SIZE	Indicates that the size of the application's window has changed.

For the purpose of our engine, we are only interested in supporting two of the common messages: WM_ACTIVATEAPP and WM_DESTROY. Shown below is the complete implementation of our WindowProc call-back function, supporting both of these messages and using the default message handler for the rest.

```
LRESULT CALLBACK WindowProc( HWND wnd, UINT msg, WPARAM wparam,
                             LPARAM lparam )
{
  switch( msg )
  {
    case WM_ACTIVATEAPP:
      g_engine->SetDeactiveFlag( !wparam );
      return 0;

    case WM_DESTROY:
      PostQuitMessage( 0 );
      return 0;
```

```
        default:
          return DefWindowProc( wnd, msg, wparam, lparam );
    }
}
```

You can see here that we are using a `switch` statement to determine which message is to be processed. When we receive a `WM_ACTIVATEAPP` message we flip the flag used by the engine to indicate if our application is active or not. Flipping means that if the value was true, it now becomes false and vice versa. When the `WM_DESTROY` message is received we make a call to `PostQuitMessage`, which tells Windows that the thread that our application is running on has requested to be terminated. In other words it shuts our application and engine down. When we implement the `Engine` class you will see how this all fits in.

THE ENGINE CLASS

Now let's move on to something a little more rewarding. The `Engine` class is the main workhorse of the entire engine. It is the entry point and will also be our single point of contact. To use the entire engine, the programmer should only have to create a single instance of this one class. Let's have a look at Figure 2.1, which shows the `Engine` class being used as a single point of contact.

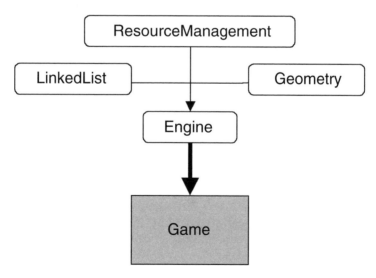

FIGURE 2.1   The `Engine` class as a single point of contact.

Now let's take a look at the definition for the Engine class.

```
class Engine
{
public:
  Engine( EngineSetup *setup = NULL );
  virtual ~Engine();

  void Run();

  HWND GetWindow();
  void SetDeactiveFlag( bool deactive );

private:
  bool m_loaded;
  HWND m_window;
  bool m_deactive;

  EngineSetup *m_setup;
};
```

As you can see, the Engine class is very basic at the moment as it really just defines the skeleton of our engine. As we progress through the rest of the chapters we gradually build our engine, therefore, this class constantly changes. So it is a good idea to take a look at the Engine class in each chapter to see the new changes. For now we will discuss the Engine class in its current state.

You can see that it has four member variables, the first of which is m_loaded. This variable is used internally by the engine to indicate whether or not the engine is actually loaded. The m_window variable is a handle to the application window used by the engine, and can be retrieved by calling the GetWindow function (this is the same handle that is passed to you by the WindowProc function when the application receives a message from Windows). The next variable is m_deactive, which is the flag that gets flipped by the WindowProc whenever the application's window loses or gains the focus. Finally we have m_setup, which is an internal copy of the setup structure used to create the engine.

The first three functions are of greater interest to us so we are going to look at them one by one, starting with the constructor. The constructor accepts, as optional input, a pointer to an engine setup structure that is filled with the options of how the engine should set itself up to operate.

```
Engine::Engine( EngineSetup *setup )
{
  m_loaded = false;

  m_setup = new EngineSetup;
  if( setup != NULL )
    memcpy( m_setup, setup, sizeof( EngineSetup ) );


  g_engine = this;
```

First the `m_loaded` flag is set to false to indicate that the engine has not yet been loaded. Then a default engine setup structure is created. If an engine setup structure was passed to the constructor, its details are copied to replace the default engine setup structure. The `g_engine = this` statement is used to make our engine global. We won't discuss this now, as it will be covered in great detail later in this chapter.

```
WNDCLASSEX wcex;
wcex.cbSize        = sizeof( WNDCLASSEX );
wcex.style         = CS_CLASSDC;
wcex.lpfnWndProc   = WindowProc;
wcex.cbClsExtra    = 0;
wcex.cbWndExtra    = 0;
wcex.hInstance     = m_setup->instance;
wcex.hIcon         = LoadIcon( NULL, IDI_APPLICATION );
wcex.hCursor       = LoadCursor( NULL, IDC_ARROW );
wcex.hbrBackground = NULL;
wcex.lpszMenuName  = NULL;
wcex.lpszClassName = "WindowClass";
wcex.hIconSm       = LoadIcon( NULL, IDI_APPLICATION );
RegisterClassEx( &wcex );
```

The next step is to fill in a WNDCLASSEX structure, which is used to define how we want the application window to be set up. You will notice that the third entry in this structure is where we set our WindowProc that we discussed earlier in the chapter. This links the WindowProc up to this application window so that messages can be received by it. We also set the instance from our engine setup structure so that the window knows which application it belongs to. The only other important property is the lpszClassName, which we set to WindowClass. This is used to reference the window class. Once we are satisfied with our window class we can register it with RegisterClassEx so that we can later create the window.

```
CoInitializeEx( NULL, COINIT_MULTITHREADED );

m_window = CreateWindow( "WindowClass", m_setup->name,
                         WS_OVERLAPPED, 0, 0, 800, 600, NULL,
                         NULL, m_setup->instance, NULL );

srand( timeGetTime() );

m_loaded = true;
}
```

We use the CoInitializeEx function to initialize the COM library with multi-threaded concurrency so that it can be used later by our application—remember that we briefly mentioned that DirectX heavily relies on COM. The next step is to create the actual application window that we registered a couple of steps back. We use the CreateWindow function, which accepts a whole lot of parameters and returns a handle to the new window, which we store in m_window. Below is the prototype for the CreateWindow function.

```
HWND CreateWindow
(
  LPCTSTR lpClassName,   // Registered window class name.
  LPCTSTR lpWindowName,  // Name to appear in title bar.
  DWORD dwStyle,         // Style of the window.
  int x,                 // Horizontal position of window.
  int y,                 // Vertical position of window.
  int nWidth,            // Width of the window.
  int nHeight,           // Height of the window.
  HWND hWndParent,       // Handle to a parent window.
  HMENU hMenu,           // Handle to a menu.
  HINSTANCE hInstance,   // Handle to an application instance.
  LPVOID lpParam         // Additional window creation data.
);
```

The second to the last step is to seed the random number generator with the current time using srand and timeGetTime, which will be used later when we want to generate random numbers. The last step is to set the m_loaded flag to true to indicate that the engine is now loaded. Once the engine has been created and has finished loading you should call the Run function, which will enter the engine into a continuous processing loop (the game loop).

```
void Engine::Run()
{
  if( m_loaded == true )
  {
    ShowWindow( m_window, SW_NORMAL );

    MSG msg;
    ZeroMemory( &msg, sizeof( MSG ) );
    while( msg.message != WM_QUIT )
    {
      if( PeekMessage( &msg, NULL, 0, 0, PM_REMOVE ) )
      {
        TranslateMessage( &msg );
        DispatchMessage( &msg );
      }
      else if( !m_deactive )
      {
        unsigned long currentTime = timeGetTime();
        static unsigned long lastTime = currentTime;
        float elapsed = ( currentTime - lastTime ) / 1000.0f;
        lastTime = currentTime;
      }
    }
  }

  SAFE_DELETE( g_engine );
}
```

First, the function checks if the engine is in fact loaded; if so, it proceeds to show the application's window. It then prepares a MSG structure, which is used to store details about messages that have been sent to the application's window. We then enter into a while loop, which is terminated when we receive a WM_QUIT message. This is a game loop where we process window messages and the frames of our application. We use the PeekMessage function, which checks if a message is waiting for our application's window to process. If so, we process the message using TranslateMessage and DispatchMessage, which will dispatch the message to our WindowProc. Otherwise, if there are no messages waiting to be processed we check whether or not our application is active. If it is active, we can process a single frame for our application. At the moment our engine does nothing more than calculate the elapsed time between frames, which is stored in a float variable called elapsed. This means that the elapsed variable will hold the number of seconds that passed since the last frame was processed. You will find that when the engine is running it will process frames so quickly that this value will actually be less than one. For example, if the engine were to process 40 frames per second you would find that the elapsed variable would hold a value around 0.025. The last step that occurs in the Run function is the call to SAFE_DELETE(g_engine), which basically destroys the engine for us. This line is only reached once the while loop has terminated, which only occurs when the engine is instructed to quit or shut down. So at that point it is safe to destroy the engine.

When the engine is destroyed the destructor is called. The implementation of the destructor is shown below.

```
Engine::~Engine()
{
  if( m_loaded == true )
  {
    // Engine specific stuff will be destroyed here.
  }

  CoUninitialize();

  UnregisterClass( "WindowClass", m_setup->instance );

  SAFE_DELETE( m_setup );
}
```

The destructor checks to see if the engine was previously loaded successfully. If so it will proceed to destroy all of the components that are specific to the engine. At the moment we do not have any components that need to be destroyed. Later on when we start to add things like sound and network support—these components will be destroyed here. The next step is to close the COM library with a call to CoUninitialize. We then remove our window class using UnregisterClass, and finally we destroy our engine setup structure.

NOTE

Remember that our Engine *class is very basic at the moment. As previously mentioned it will constantly expand throughout the rest of the chapters in Part I while we build the engine. So you should always keep an eye on this class in each chapter to see what is new. Don't worry though, all the significant changes will be pointed out and discussed so you won't miss anything important.*

MAKING THE ENGINE GLOBAL

One of the most crucial aspects of an engine is usability. The whole reason anyone ever uses an engine is because it is supposed to be easier and faster to learn and use than it is to implement your own equivalent. We have already established that one of our goals for the engine is usability, so we must take active steps to support this decision. One of the key aspects of usability is accessibility, which in our case is loosely defined as the ease of accessing the features of the engine. We want to make our engine as accessible as possible in order to maintain our goal of usability. Fortunately, we already have a very easy to implement solution available to us due to previous design decisions we have made.

We have already decided that our engine must have a single point of contact, and we have taken the steps to implement this. Due to this design we now have a class that will completely encapsulate the engine's functionality: the Engine class. The problem we now face is that virtually every component of our engine and the future games we plan to build with this engine must have access to all of these features. One way to achieve this is to simply pass a pointer to an instance of our Engine class around to all the various components that will require it. There are three problems with this solution:

1. We already know that almost every component will need access to some or all of the engine's functionality.
2. It is easy to forget which component is using which feature. This makes it difficult to implement changes later, which lowers the maintainability of the code.
3. The code can become messy and unorganized, which can lead to problems such as NULL pointers.

There is a much better solution: make the pointer to the Engine class instance global.

There are some people who will argue that using global variables is not a good idea, and their reasoning is valid. Most people who argue this point generally stand by the fact that global variables are dangerous for a number of reasons, including:

- It is easy to lose track of the variable and its scope.
- They can become unintentionally corrupted due to logical errors.
- When used in excess they defeat the principle of object-orientated coding practices.

All of the above points are valid, however, they all have a single flaw—they are dangerous due to human error. They all revolve around the fact that *you,* the programmer, will make a mistake while using them. So, in conclusion, the ability to create a global variable is for your benefit, however, you must be aware of the pitfalls. This way you are less likely to stumble into them. If you use global variables sparingly and correctly you should not have any problems.

With this in mind, we will use a global variable as a pointer to an instance of our Engine class. This way every component of our engine and the future games will be able to access this pointer and therefore access the engine's functionality. You will notice the following line of code at the beginning of the Engine source file:

```
Engine *g_engine = NULL;
```

This single line of code defines our global pointer instance of the Engine class. This variable is created immediately upon execution and is set to NULL, which indicates that the engine has not yet been created. We now have our empty pointer, but it is not actually global yet. We need to add another line of code to the end of the Engine header file.

```
extern Engine *g_engine;
```

By using the extern keyword we define our variable as an external, in other words a global variable. The variable is now truly global and can be accessed from any source or header file that includes the Engine header file.

We have two tasks left—setting the global variable and destroying it. We could leave this job up to the programmer using the engine, but that doesn't lend itself toward better usability. We want the engine to be able to handle these tasks on its own. Fortunately, implementing this is even easier than making the variable global. To set the pointer we just add the following line to the beginning of the Engine class constructor:

```
g_engine = this;
```

The this keyword is actually a pointer to the instance of the class that the this keyword was used in. So, in our example, the this keyword acts as a pointer to the instance of the Engine class that is being created when the constructor is called. By setting our global pointer to the this pointer, we tell our global pointer to point to the address in memory where the actual instance of our new Engine class exists. The final step is to free the memory that this pointer points to when we are finished using this instance of the Engine class. We do this using the last line of code in the Run function of the Engine class.

```
SAFE_DELETE( g_engine );
```

This uses the first of the memory management macros that frees the memory pointed to by the given pointer, which in our case is the pointer to the instance of the Engine class. With that we have finished making our engine global. This may have been a little complicated, but it is an important part of our engine that you will need to be aware of. If you didn't quite grasp how this works you should go back and reread this section and ensure that you have the code for this chapter open as it will help to put everything in context.

TEMPLATES

Let's now take a quick look at the concept of *templates* and what they are used for. You know that all variables are of a particular type, called a *data type*. For example, you could have a variable of type int, or float, or bool (these are primitive data types). A variable can also be a class or structure type, or a pointer to a class or structure instance. There are many possibilities, and with that comes many conflicting data type problems. The question is what happens if you want to perform an operation on variable A (of type int) and then perform that same operation on variable B (of type bool). This is where templates come into play. In essence, templates are used to perform the same operations on multiple data types. Let's take a look at the following oversimplified example.

Imagine you had to write a function that can add two int values and give the result. You would easily solve this problem by writing a single function that would take as input two int values, add them together, and then return the result. Now what if you need to perform the same operation with float values, yet still maintain their precision. Obviously, you wouldn't be able to use the same function you used for the int values—but that's not a problem is it—instead we can simply create a new function that handles the float values. However, the problem can become worse. What if later you also need to perform the operation for double values? As you can see, we are starting to grow a collection of functions that do the same thing. Their definitions would look something like this.

```
int AddInts( int value1, int value2 );
float AddFloats( float value1, float value2 );
double AddDoubles( double value1, double value2 );
```

What if it was possible to compress all of these functions into one, capable of handling any data type? Well it is. This is the purpose of templates. When using templates, your new function would look something like the following:

```
template< class Type > Type Add( Type value1, Type value2 );
```

This is a template function that accepts any data type, attempts to add them using the + logical operator, and then returns the result in the same data type. In other words, you can "plus" two int values together, or two float values together using the same function. That is the purpose of the class Type parameter, which allows you, the programmer, to specify which data type you want the function to use. It will then accept two values in the specified data type and return the result in the same data type. You would use this single function to achieve the same result as the three previously stated functions.

```
int myInt = Add< int >( 5, 45 );
float myFloat = Add< float >( 3.2, 17.47 );
double myDouble = Add< double >( 29.4967, 12.01568 );
```

There is a lot more to templates than just functions. You can even create whole classes that are templates. Take a look at the following example:

```
template< class Type > class Maths
{
public:
  Type Add( Type value1, Type value2 );
  Type Multiply( Type value1, Type value2 );
  Type Divide( Type value1, Type value2 );
};
```

This shows a template class that is used for some basic mathematic operations. We can create an instance of this class and specify which data type it will work with, and then perform any of the operations in that type as shown below.

```
Maths< float > *floatMaths = new Maths< float >;
float addTest = floatMaths->Add( 2.45f, 15.9f );
float multiplyTest = floatMaths->Multiply( 10.0f, 5.5f );
float divideTest = floatMaths->Divide( 16.4f, 4.0f );
```

The first line of code creates the instance of the Maths class of type float. The next three lines of code each perform an operation from our new class using floating-point variables. The three functions all return values of type float, since that is what we used to create the class.

Classes are probably the most common area where you will use templates; it is best to think of a template class as a blueprint. In other words, it is not a class definition, but a blueprint for a class definition. The actual class definition is created when you instance the template class with a set of parameters. You should also note that in our previous examples we only used one parameter; however, you can use more than one, as in the following example:

```
template< class Type, int size > class MyData
{
public:
  void SetData( Type data );
  Type GetData();

private:
  char buffer[size];
};
```

We could continue discussing templates for quite some time, however, you don't need to know a great deal about templates in order to use them; you just need to be aware of them. If you had any trouble understanding how templates are used, don't worry about it too much as you will see them put to use throughout the rest of this book. Seeing a concept in use in real code (rather than some abstract example) is far more beneficial than pages of explanation. However, if you would like to learn more about templates, there is a huge amount of free resources available on the Internet. For now though, let's move on to a couple of foundational `Engine` classes that make use of templates.

LINKED LISTS

There are many different ways to store data that is used by an application. You can store all of your data in individual variables, however, this becomes unmanageable very quickly and is difficult to extend. Alternatively, you can store all of your data in arrays, which are nothing more than fixed lists of predetermined data types. This option is much easier to manage than single variables, but it still suffers from the problem of extendibility. If you create an array to hold five items and later you decide that you need eight items, you need to modify the size of the array and recompile the code, unless you are using a specialized array class that can handle resizing.

One of the best ways to store your game data is in a particular type of storage container called a linked list. A linked list is similar to an array except that it is much better at resizing itself dynamically at runtime. A very good real life example that mimics a linked list is a train with carriages. Each carriage is connected to two other carriages at most—one at either end. When multiple carriages are linked they form a continuous chain. You have a head, which is the locomotive, and a tail, which is the caboose. The carriages can be rearranged, new ones can be added, and old ones can be removed. At all times the train maintains a continuous link from head to tail.

As far as computer programming is concerned there are two main types of linked lists that can be employed, the singly linked list, and the doubly linked list. The singly linked list uses elements that only maintain a link with the next element in the list, while the doubly linked list uses elements that maintain links with both the next and previous elements. Figure 2.2 shows the difference between a singly linked list and a doubly linked list.

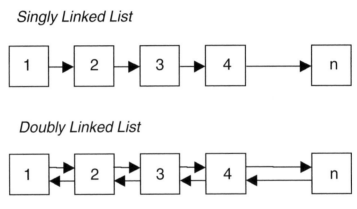

FIGURE 2.2   Difference between a singly linked list and a doubly linked list.

Singly linked lists use less memory as each element only stores one pointer to the next element in the list. However, the disadvantage with singly linked lists is that it is harder to insert items into the list because you need to traverse the list to locate the previous item in order to maintain the links. This is one of the main reasons why doubly linked lists are often used instead. Since each element maintains a link with both the next and previous elements it makes it much easier to insert items into the list. Additionally, tasks such as sorting the list are much easier with doubly linked lists.

CAUTION

There is one major drawback to linked lists that other storage containers such as arrays do not suffer from. It is harder to locate individual items in a linked list because you need to traverse the list and check each item. This is not such a problem for small lists, but if you have a list that contains thousands of items and you need to find one of them, it can take some time, especially if the item you are looking for is near the end of the list. The computation effect can compound very quickly if you are searching large lists multiple times per frame. If you are working with a fixed data set or you know the maximum number of elements at design time then it may be a good idea just to use an array, which will afford you the luxury of locating items quickly based on their index in the array.

Open up the `LinkedList.h` file, which shows the definition and implementation of the `LinkedList` template class. It is important to remember that this class is a template, which means it is not actually a class definition. It is rather a template (or a blueprint) for a class definition. The actual definition of the class is not created until you create an instance of the class specifying a particular data type, as previously discussed. You don't need to concern yourself with this as it is all handled for you by the compiler. Just remember to specify a type when you create a new instance of the `LinkedList` class.

The `LinkedList` class uses a small structure called `Element`, which stores the data for a single element in the list. Here is the definition for the `Element` structure, including its basic implementation.

```
struct Element
{
  Type *data;
  Element *next;
  Element *prev;

  Element( Type *element )
  {
    data = element;
    next = prev = NULL;
  }

  ~Element()
  {
    SAFE_DELETE( data );
```

```
    if( next )
      next->prev = prev;
    if( prev )
      prev->next = next;
  }
};
```

The Element structure is internal to the LinkedList template class, which allows it to use the Type parameter specified in the LinkedList template class definition. The data variable stores the actual data for this element using the type specified by the linked list. The next two variables store pointers to the next and previous elements in the linked list, allowing the element to maintain itself as a link in the list. The constructor sets the element's data and clears the linking pointers. The LinkedList class is responsible for actually linking the new element into the list correctly. Finally, the destructor is designed so that it automatically destroys the data the element holds (freeing its memory), and it gracefully removes the element from the list without breaking the linked list. Notice how it rejoins its previous element with the next element in the list and vice versa. Figure 2.3 shows how this works.

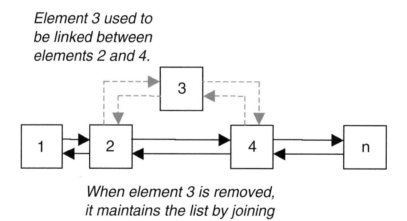

FIGURE 2.3 An element gracefully removing itself from a linked list.

The LinkedList class is a rather large class and would take up too much space to show it all here. Instead, you are encouraged to look through the source code to the LinkedList class and read the comments. They will inform you what each function performs in the linked list. There is a constructor that prepares the list, and an equivalent destructor, which will empty the list when it is destroyed. By emptying the list, all of the elements in the list are destroyed, which in turn destroys all the data being held by the elements. There are functions to add elements, insert elements, and remove elements from the linked list, as well as manually empty the list. Additionally, there are a whole host of functions that allow you to access any of the elements in the list. You can iterate through the list one element at a time, access the first or last element, and even return a random element from the list. Finally, you should be aware of two more functions exposed by the LinkedList class: ClearPointers and ClearPointer. These functions are designed to destroy all of the elements in the list or a single given element in the list, respectively. What makes these functions special is that they do not destroy the data that is being held by the elements. This is useful for when you have a linked list of pointers to data that is being stored elsewhere. These functions will allow you to destroy the linked list without affecting the data.

Be careful though as this can cause memory leaks if you accidentally call these functions on linked lists that do in fact store data and not just pointers.

Despite the host of features the LinkedList class comes with, using it is surprisingly easy. The reason for this is that all of its underlying works are completely transparent. To use the LinkedList class all you need to do is create it, add and remove elements, and then finally destroy it. The following is a basic example of using a linked list with float values.

```
LinkedList< float > *list = new LinkedList< float >;

list->Add( new float( 5.0f ) );
list->Add( new float( 3.7f ) );

SAFE_DELETE( list );
```

Remember that the LinkedList class is not limited to primitive data types such as int and float. It can handle any data type or class that you create. For example, you can create a linked list of players in your game. You will see many examples of the LinkedList class as we progress. In fact, the next component of our engine—the resource manager—coincidentally uses a linked list.

RESOURCE MANAGEMENT

Resources are often referred to as assets and they represent all the tangible components of your game that allow it to operate. A resource can be anything from a
texture or mesh to a sound or script. All engines have to be able to handle resources
to varying degrees, since without them you cannot present an entertaining experience to a player. Imagine trying to play a game without sound, scripts, meshes, or
textures—a very plain game indeed. Our engine is no exception, and we need a
method to handle these resources.

Obviously, the methods you use to load and process a sound file are different
from the methods you use to load and process a mesh file, and so on for any type
of resource. However, one thing they all have in common (at least in our case) is
that they are all file based, and must be loaded into memory and later freed from
that memory. We can take advantage of these commonalities and implement a
Resource class that stores a few details about a generic resource. Open up the
ResourceManagement.h file and take a look at the Resource class, which encapsulates
the basic details of any resource. These are the name of the resource, the path to the
resource, and the complete filename (i.e., the path with the name appended to it).
The resource also uses a reference count, which you will see in use very shortly. As
previously mentioned, this is the base class for any resource. To create a new resource, such as a sound file, you would create a new class that derives from this one
as shown in the following example:

```
class Sound : public Resource
{
public:
  Sound( char *name, char *path = "./" );
  virtual ~Sound();
};
```

All you need to do in the Sound class constructor is pass the name and path over
to the Resource class constructor so that it can set itself up correctly, as shown:

```
Sound::Sound( char *name, char *path )
      : Resource< Sound >( name, path )
{
  // Load the sound resource.
}
```

You can now use your new resource and access all of its basic details provided by the Resource class, such as its name, path, and complete filename (i.e., name appended to the path). Of course, it is up to you how you go about loading and destroying the resource as well as what to do with it once it is loaded. One more point is that the true potential of the Resource class is not realized until you combine it with the ResourceManager class.

The ResourceManager class is actually what really makes the whole resource system so effective. If you look further down the ResourceManagement.h file you will see the definition and implementation of the ResourceManager class combined. Here is the class definition of the ResourceManager (without the implementation).

```
template< class Type > class ResourceManager
{
public:
   ResourceManager( void (*CreateResourceFunction)
       ( Type **resource, char *name, char *path ) = NULL )
   ~ResourceManager()

   Type *Add( char *name, char *path = "./" )
   void Remove( Type **resource )

   void EmptyList()

   LinkedList< Type > *GetList()
   Type *GetElement( char *name, char *path = "./" )

private:
   LinkedList< Type > *m_list;

   void (*CreateResource)( Type **resource, char *name,
                           char *path );
};
```

The ResourceManager class is another template class that requires a type to be set when the class is instanced. What this means is that you need a resource manager for each type of resource you plan to use. For example, if you wanted to support sound effects, textures, and meshes, then you would need three separate resource managers. When a new instance of the ResourceManager class is created, the constructor is called, which simply prepares the resource manager, creating a linked list using the specified type. The constructor also accepts a pointer to a function called

`CreateResourceFunction`. This is actually a call-back function that is called every time the resource manager is told to add (i.e., create) a new resource. When you call the `Add` function, the resource manager creates a new resource from the given name and path. However, if the `CreateResourceFunction` call-back has been set, then it will be called by the `Add` function instead. This allows you to set a function in the application specific code that is used to create that type of resource. This way you can create resources that are specific to your game. If you do not require any specific loading of a resource, you can leave the call-back function set to `NULL` and the resource manager will use the default loading code for the resource provided by the engine. You will see how we will make use of the call-back function later when we implement our game, but for now take a look at Figure 2.4, which shows the relationship between resources, resource managers, the engine, and the application—in terms of who requests information from whom.

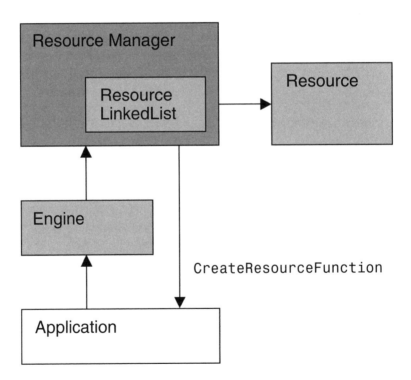

FIGURE 2.4 The relationship among resources, resource managers, the engine, and the application.

The Remove function allows you to remove any resource from the resource manager. This is where the reference count for the resources comes into play. When you add a new resource, the reference count for that particular resource is incremented to one. If you try to add the same resource again, instead of loading the resource all over again, the resource manger just returns a pointer to the already existing copy of the resource and then increments its reference count to two. So every time you ask the resource manager for a copy of this particular resource, the resource manager just gives you a pointer to it (as it is already in memory) and increments its reference count. This way the resource manager can keep track of how many instances of this particular resource are being used. Whenever something finishes using the resource it tells the resource manager to remove the resource. The resource manager decrements the reference count on the resource and then checks if it has reached zero. If so, then there is nothing using the resource and it is safe to destroy it. Note: the EmptyList function will destroy all of the resources stored in the resource manager without regard to their reference counts.

The last two functions, GetList and GetElement, will return a pointer to the resource manager's internal linked list, and a pointer to the resource with the given name and path, respectively. The GetList function is useful for when you want to manually iterate through the resource manager's resources or alter the resources. However, when playing around with the resources in the list, be careful that you do not change their names, paths, or reference counts as this will hinder the resource manager's effectiveness and may cause memory leaks.

At the moment we have no real use for the resource management system as we have not implemented any resources yet. When we get to Chapter 4, however, we will implement the first of our resources: scripts. Then you will see our resource system at work.

GEOMETRY

You may or may not have noticed it yet, but there is one more file we have yet to discuss—the Geometry.h file. If you open up the file and have a quick scroll through it, you will probably agree that it is the most complicated looking file so far. Fortunately, you will probably never have to directly use anything in this file as it is all support code. This means that it is code that is used by other classes and functions throughout the engine. Nevertheless, we will take a quick look at it so that you are at least familiar with it. If you want to learn more about it, read through the code, as it is well commented.

First you have three structures called Vertex, LVertex, and TLVertex. These three structures are used to define a point in 3D space called a *vertex*. Meshes and other 3D geometry are made up of these vertices, which are connected to form the 3D shape. Figure 2.5 shows the role that a single vertex plays in 3D geometry.

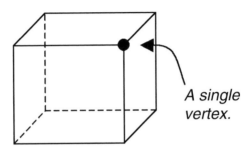

A single vertex.

FIGURE 2.5   A vertex in 3D space.

The Vertex structure is used for vertices that are transformed (had their position calculated in 3D space), lit, and textured by DirectX. The LVertex structure is used for vertices that are transformed and textured by DirectX, but lit by the engine. The final structure, TLVertex, is used for vertices that are only textured by DirectX. Their position and lighting are calculated by the engine. The Vertex structure is the most commonly used structure as everything is handled by DirectX for us. If you want to use the other structures, some of the components need to be calculated manually.

The next four structures, Edge, IndexedEdge, Face, and IndexedFace are used for storing information about edges and faces in 3D geometry such as meshes. An edge is the line between two vertices, so the Edge structure stores a pointer to each of these two vertices. The IndexEdge, however, stores an index value for its two vertices. These indices are usually used when the vertices are stored in something like an array or an index buffer, which is a special type of buffer used by DirectX to store vertices in an optimized fashion. A face is made up of three vertices, and covers the area between those vertices. The Face structure stores pointers to these vertices while the IndexedFace structure stores the vertices' indices.

NOTE

Faces are one-sided, which means that only one side of the face can been seen. This is called the face's front side and is determined by the face's normal. The normal is a vector (like a line) perpendicular to the face, pointing away from the front side. The normal is determined by the order in which the vertices in the face are specified, which is usually in a clockwise order.

Figure 2.6 shows the relationship between vertices, edges, and faces, including the face normal.

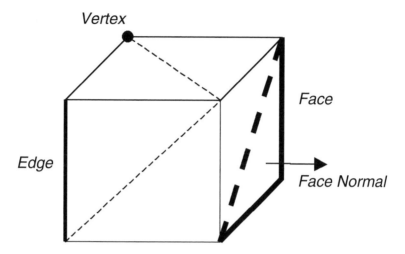

FIGURE 2.6 Relationship between vertices, edges, and faces.

Finally, we have a set of inline functions used for testing contact between various geometrical shapes. If you are unfamiliar with the `inline` keyword, all it does is instructs the compiler to replace calls to the function with the actual code from the function at compile time. By making a function inline, you remove the overhead of the function call. The disadvantage is that it increases the size of the compiled code, which means you end up with a larger executable file.

The first of these inline functions is the `IsBoxInBox` function, which tests if a 3D box has made contact with another 3D box. You pass the function the extents of the two boxes and it returns true if they are in contact, otherwise it returns false. The function prototype is shown as:

```
inline bool IsBoxInBox( D3DXVECTOR3 box1Min, D3DXVECTOR3 box1Max,
    D3DXVECTOR3 box2Min, D3DXVECTOR3 box2Max )
```

The next function is the `IsFaceInBox` function, which tests if a 3D face has made contact with a 3D box. You pass the function the vertices of the face and the extents of the box and it returns true if they are in contact, otherwise it returns false. The function prototype is shown as:

```
inline bool IsFaceInBox( Vertex *vertex0, Vertex *vertex1,
  Vertex *vertex2, D3DXVECTOR3 boxMin, D3DXVECTOR3 boxMax )
```

Next, there is the `IsBoxEnclosedByVolume` function, which tests if a 3D box is completely enclosed by the given volume. A volume can be any 3D convex shape defined by a set of planes. You pass the function a linked list containing the set of planes for the volume as well as the extents of the box and it returns true if the box is completely inside the volume, otherwise it returns false. The function prototype is shown as:

```
inline bool IsBoxEnclosedByVolume(
  LinkedList< D3DXPLANE > *planes, D3DXVECTOR3 min,
  D3DXVECTOR3 max )
```

Then we have the `IsSphereOverlappingVolume` function, which tests if a 3D sphere is in contact with the given volume. You pass the function a linked list containing the set of planes for the volume as well as the translation (position in 3D space) and radius of the sphere and it returns true if the sphere is in contact with the volume, otherwise it returns false. The function prototype is shown as:

```
inline bool IsSphereOverlappingVolume(
  LinkedList< D3DXPLANE > *planes, D3DXVECTOR3 translation,
  float radius )
```

Finally, there is the `IsSphereCollidingWithSphere` function, which can test if a moving 3D sphere makes contact with another moving 3D sphere. You pass the function a pointer to a `float` variable, the translation of both spheres, along with the sum of the velocity vectors of both spheres, and the sum of the radii of both spheres. The function returns true if the spheres make contact with one another, otherwise it returns false. If the spheres do collide, the floating-point variable `collisionDistance` that you passed in will be filled with the actual distance to the point of collision. The function prototype is shown as:

```
inline bool IsSphereCollidingWithSphere( float *collisionDistance,
  D3DXVECTOR3 translation1, D3DXVECTOR3 translation2,
  D3DXVECTOR3 velocitySum, float radiiSum )
```

As you can see there is quite a bit going on in this file. Some of it may seem a bit complicated, but as previously mentioned you will probably never need to directly play with any of this stuff, so you can breathe a sigh of relief. When you become a little more confident you may want to look deeper into some of these functions and even add some of your own functionality. Consider this to be the beginning of your growing 3D geometry library, if you haven't already got one. Throughout the rest of our engine development you will see these various structures and functions put to good use, which will assist you in better understanding them when you see them in a useful context.

TESTING THE FRAMEWORK

ON THE CD

Now that we have everything in place, let's create a simple little application that will test our framework. You can find the test application in the Test project in the workspace for this chapter. There is only one file in the project called Main.cpp, which has all the code in it for our test application. If you open the file you will see that we have two #include statements. The first one—#include <windows.h>—is for the basic Windows functionality that our application will use. The second one—#include "..\Engine\Engine.h"—is the interface of our engine. Since our engine has a single point of contact, we only need to include one header file. The engine includes the rest for us. The next step is to implement the WinMain function, which is the main function that all Windows applications have to implement. It is the entry point to your application. Below is the implementation of our WinMain function.

```
int WINAPI WinMain( HINSTANCE instance, HINSTANCE prev,
                    LPSTR cmdLine, int cmdShow )
{
EngineSetup setup;
setup.instance = instance;
setup.name = "Framework Test";

new Engine( &setup );
g_engine->Run();

return true;
}
```

The WinMain function has a number of parameters that are passed to it by Windows. The only one that we need to concern ourself with is the HINSTANCE instance, which is a handle to our application instance. Although this is not mandatory, it is a good idea to pass this handle to the engine through the Engine- Setup structure. That way the engine has some method of referencing our application. In the EngineSetup structure, we can also set the name of our application. This name is what will appear in the title bar when the application is run in windowed mode (i.e., not full screen). The next step is to create an instance of our `Engine` class and pass the `EngineSetup` structure to it. This will call the `Engine` class constructor, which will point the global `g_engine` pointer to the address in memory of our `Engine` class instance. The last step is to call the engine's `Run` function, which will put the engine into a continuous loop until we exit. At the moment, we do not have any method of exiting from our test application, so if you run it you will need to shut it down by pressing Alt + F4. In Chapter 3, we will implement a method to shut our engine down, when we add user input to the engine.

SUMMARY

This has been a very diverse chapter indeed. We have covered a lot of topics so don't be afraid to reread anything that you have forgotten. We first covered preparing visual studio, and then we moved on to some C++ topics that were going to come in handy. We implemented the main `Engine` class and the supporting engine setup and memory management utilities. We talked about templates, linked lists, and resources, and implemented a resource management system. Finally, we looked at all the supporting geometry structures and functions that we will later need.

In Chapter 3, we are going to start adding some real functionality to the engine. We will implement two important forms of engine control. The first will allow us to control the processing of the engine and the second will allow the user to interact with applications built using the engine.

3 Engine Control

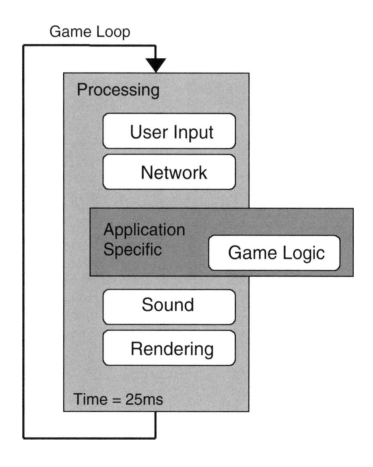

In This Chapter

- Discuss engine control and Finite State Machines.
- Discuss the viewer structure used for defining the virtual 3D view point.
- Cover states for managing what the engine processes and when it processes it.
- Look at user input through the use of a DirectInput wrapper class.

ON THE CD

Now that our engine has a basic framework we will proceed to add various forms of control to the engine. You can find the workspace for this chapter in the /Source/Chapter 3/ directory on the CD-ROM.

WHAT IS ENGINE CONTROL?

When you ask someone what a game engine is, usually they first think of 3D rendering. Although they are correct in respect to the fact that most game engines are used to handle 3D rendering, they are missing the much broader picture. That is, a game engine has to be able to facilitate the creation of an entire game, not just its 3D rendering requirements. Throughout the development of our engine we must keep this in mind, and plan for an engine that will encompass virtually all our needs for a FPS game engine.

One mistake that a lot of amateur developers make is to forgo appropriate engine control early in the development process. Instead, they opt to hammer out the 3D rendering capabilities of the engine before they even attempt to control the engine, so to speak. However, before we go any further let's define engine control. More specifically, let's take a look at what constitutes appropriate engine control. For our purposes we will define engine control as two separate (but related) aspects.

- Engine Processing
- User Input

Engine processing is defined by the methods and procedures put in place to control what the engine processes at any point in time. For example, most engines run using what is referred to as a *game loop*. The game loop is simply a continuous loop, which executes over and over again until it is aborted (usually by the user exiting the game or application). Often these loops will execute 30+ times per second, which is defined as your *frame rate* or *frames per second* (fps—note the lowercase).

If your game loop is running at 40 fps then each frame theoretically consumes 2.5% of one whole second, which equates to 25 ms (milliseconds) per frame. In other words, your game loop completes one full execution every 25 ms. Now a typical engine will do quite a lot in a single frame, which is where engine processing control comes into play. Since you have such a limited amount of time each frame, you have to spend it wisely. Take a look at Figure 3.1 to help visualize our example.

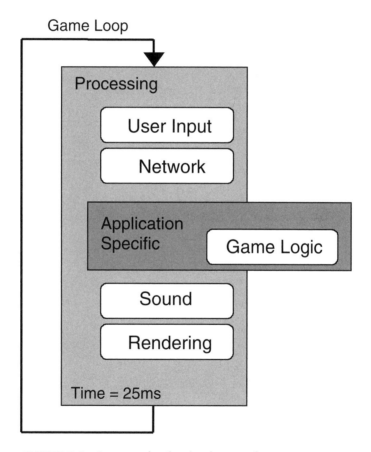

FIGURE 3.1   An example of a simple game loop.

This is a very simple example and there are a number of things that are not shown, but it has the major components. Controlling our engine processing is really all about managing that 25 ms and determining what slice of time is given to each component. Let's say that combined, our user input, network, sound, and rendering consumed 18 ms. This would leave us with a mere 7 ms for application-specific processing such as game logic, which may include time-consuming operations such as artificial intelligence. Now we've actually gone a lot deeper here than is necessary, however, it is important for you to be aware of this so that you can understand some of the design decisions we will make later on such as:

- Limiting the amount of collision detection iterations
- Yielding network message processing after a set time period
- Restricting the size of our scene hierarchy

For now we can focus on the broader picture as far as engine processing is concerned. At this level we will create a system that can manage how the components from Figure 3.1 work together to process a single aspect of the simulation, otherwise referred to as a *state*. This system is often called a *finite state machine* (FSM), which can be used in many contexts in programming. We will discuss this a little later and look at how we will use it to solve our engine processing issue at a high level.

Before we move on we will quickly touch on our second form of engine control: user input. Although not the same as managing the engine's states and its processing, it is still a form of control as it allows the user to control the engine to a degree, but more importantly control the game built on the engine. It is the engine's responsibility to provide this control. Therefore we will implement user input into our engine natively through the use of a DirectInput wrapper, which we will take a look at later.

FINITE STATE MACHINES

We will be using a simple form of an FSM for managing the various states that our engine may need to process at any point in time. Before we relate this to our situation, let's briefly discuss the FSM. This is actually a very simple concept if you just break down the words and look at them individually.

First we have the word *finite*, which basically means limited. In terms of an FSM it refers to the number of states. Although theoretically not impossible, it is humanly impossible and completely infeasible to have an infinite number of states. We can infer that all state machines are finite and therefore have a limited number of states based on how many you define for it. We will look at a visual example shortly.

The second word is *state*. A state is the disposition and behavior of a given entity at a given point in time. For example, you might call the state you are in right now, the reading state. When you go for a walk, you may call this the walking state. Later on you will sit down to a meal, which you could call the eating state. A more simplified example would be a light switch that has only two states, the on state and the off state. The switch can only be in one of these states at a time.

The final word is *machine*, which can simply be defined as a system. If you think about it, a machine is really nothing more than a system. It receives an input, processes it, and gives an output. Take the engine in a car for example. Although it is a machine, you can call it a system since it receives an input (fuel), processes it (internal combustion), and gives an output (energy). To be more concise though, our FSM is really a dynamic machine since it can change the way it processes, which means that it can accept and deliver different inputs and outputs respectively. The reason why it can change is because it can change states. When a car engine is running it only has one state, therefore it can only accept input for that state, process it, and give that same form of output every time—whereas our FSM is more akin to a slide projector. Although the slide projector doesn't change, its input, the processing (to a degree), and the output can. You can change the slide (input), which will cause the light to behave differently as it passes through the slide (processing), which gives a different projected image (output).

So we can now conclude that an FSM is a system that can dynamically change its input, processing, and output based on a finite set of defined states. Figure 3.2 shows a basic FSM for a hypothetical animal. The animal has an internal FSM which can change to any of the shown states; however, it can only be in one state at a time. While in a particular state the animal will behave differently to represent that state. Now the real questions are, how does the FSM change states, and how can we use it in our engine?

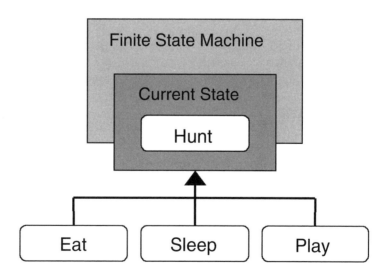

FIGURE 3.2 A basic FSM for a hypothetical animal.

The answers are fairly simple. Any FSM can change states in two ways: automatically and manually. An FSM can change to a different state automatically through the direction of the current state. For example, the hunt state for our animal in Figure 3.2 may have an instruction in it that informs the FSM to change to the eat state automatically when the animal catches its prey. The second method is to change manually, which means that the user of the FSM intervenes causing the FSM to change to the desired state. If we go back to our animal example again we could say that after chasing its prey for some time the animal grows too weary to continue the hunt so it forces its FSM to change to the sleep state.

The final question still remains: how can we use this in our engine? Well, we are going to create a system that will allow the user of the engine to define one or more states for the game. The system will then ensure that the engine processes the correct state at the correct time, while providing the user with the power to transition between these states as necessary. This will ensure that our engine is not wasting valuable processing time on features that are not being used at that time. We will discuss the system in more detail when we implement it later in this chapter.

VIEWER SETUP STRUCTURE

Before we can implement our state system we need to look at a little obscure structure called the *viewer setup structure*. This structure will be used by the state system so it is necessary to cover it now. You can find the structure's definition at the start of the State.h file, and you will probably notice that it is empty at the moment—you will soon see why.

The viewer setup structure is used to define the parameters used by the engine when deciding what to display on the screen in a given frame. For example, the engine will need to know where the player is standing in the game world and what direction the player is facing so that the engine can compute what needs to be rendered on the screen for each frame. It is the game programmer's job to inform the engine of these details through the use of the viewer setup structure. At the moment, however, our engine is not really capable of rendering anything, so we don't have to worry about this just yet. It is an example of what the viewer setup structure will be used for in the future.

Right now our viewer setup structure is not needed for anything, but much like the engine setup structure, it will expand over time as we add entries to it. If you take a look in the Run function of the Engine class from Engine.cpp you will notice that we are creating an instance of the viewer setup structure. Strictly speaking we do not need to do this just yet since the structure has no use at the moment, but it is there so that we don't forget about it later. When we implement the state system later in this chapter you will see what it is actually used for.

STATE SYSTEM

We have already covered a lot of the theory surrounding the state system earlier in this chapter, so we will just jump straight into its very simple implementation. Here is the definition for the State class, which can be found in State.h.

```
class State
{
public:
  State( unsigned long id = 0 );

  virtual void Load();
  virtual void Close();

  virtual void RequestViewer( ViewerSetup *viewer );
  virtual void Update( float elapsed );
  virtual void Render();

  unsigned long GetID();

private:
  unsigned long m_id;
};
```

The first thing you will probably notice is all the virtual functions. If you have a look at the implementation for all the functions in this class (which can be found in State.cpp) you will soon realize that this class doesn't really do anything. Now you're probably thinking that we are going to add implementation to the class as we go, but in actual fact this class is pretty much complete. That's all there is to this class. So what is the point of a class with a bunch of functions that do nothing? Well, the best way to look at it is to consider this class as a pseudo template class, since it isn't a real template class like we discussed in Chapter 2. What this means is that although you could create an instance of this class, you never would, since it cannot do anything. Instead, this class is designed to be overridden with your own state classes with your own custom implementation behind each of the virtual functions. We have to provide this base class with all of the empty virtual functions so that the state system has a consistent interface to work with. If we didn't do this then the state system may try to call a function on one of your states that you have forgotten to implement. At least in this case you have the base State class to fall back on so that the system does not break.

Let's quickly run through each of the functions. First we have the constructor, which you use to perform any one-time initialization of the state's members such as setting them to NULL. The constructor is also used for setting the identification number of the state. Each state that you create should have a unique identification number, which you pass to the state through the constructor. This identification number is then stored in m_id and can be retrieved with a call to GetID. You can use whatever number you like for a state, just as long as you keep a note of the number as it is used to reference the state. When you tell the engine that you want to switch to a new state, the engine will ask you for the unique identification number of the state that you want to switch to. You can assign a state's identification number to a constant using the #define keyword. This will allow you to reference the state using a more tangible name rather than some abstract number.

You have probably also noticed that there is no destructor. The reason for this is that everything for a state should be loaded and shut down using the Load and Close functions, respectively. You don't ever need to call the Load or Close functions. They are called for you by the engine. All you need to do is implement your loading and shut down code within them on your derived class. In fact, you don't need to ever call any of the virtual functions in your derived class. They are all called by the engine. All you need to do is implement the functions that you are interested in handling. For example, the RequestViewer function is called so that you can fill a viewer structure that has been passed to you by the engine. This is so that the engine has the information it needs to render the current frame, as we discussed earlier in the chapter. If you create a state that doesn't need any rendering capabilities, then you do not need to bother implementing this function in your derived class. Instead, you can just let it fall back on to the empty function from the base State class.

The Update and Render functions will be called by the engine to allow you to update your state and perform any additional rendering for your state. When the Update function is called, the engine will pass the elapsed time since the last update to you. This value is stored in the floating-point elapsed variable and you can use this value for anything from timing through to interpolation across time. We will design our engine to handle a lot of the rendering automatically, however, the Render function is provided so that you can perform your own specialized rendering that is not covered by the engine. It is important to note that the Render function will be called after the engine has performed its own rendering. Usually this won't make any difference, but if you try to do special effects that use alpha blending, for example, you will need to bear in mind that they will blend with what has already been rendered.

INTEGRATING THE STATE SYSTEM

So the state system is virtually complete, except for the viewer structure, which we will complete in a later chapter. For now though, let's integrate what we have into our engine. Obviously, the first step is to link our new `State.cpp` and `State.h` files into the engine. You will probably remember that this is achieved by adding an `#include "State.h"` statement to the `Engine.h` file and an `#include "Engine.h"` to the beginning of the `State.cpp` file. That's the easy part. The next step is to add three new member variables to the `Engine` class.

```
LinkedList< State > *m_states;
State *m_currentState;
bool m_stateChanged;
```

As you can see, `m_states` is a linked list that stores all of our states. Every time we add a new state to the engine it is stored in this list, which is why we need to keep unique identification numbers for each state so that we can later tell them apart. `m_currentState` is just a pointer to the state that currently has control. This is the state that the engine is currently processing each frame. The final member variable is `m_stateChanged`, which is an internal flag used by the engine to indicate if the state has been changed during the current frame. Along with these variables we are also going to add a few functions to the `Engine` class.

```
void AddState( State *state, bool change = true );
void RemoveState( State *state );
void ChangeState( unsigned long id );
State *GetCurrentState();
```

The most interesting functions are the `AddState` and `ChangeState` functions, which can be found in the `Engine.cpp` file. The `RemoveState` function is pretty straightforward as it just removes the state from the engine that matches the supplied `state` pointer. The `GetCurrentState` function just returns the state that is currently being processed, which is the state that is pointed to by the `m_currentState` pointer.

`AddState` simply adds to the engine the new state that is passed in through the `state` pointer. The `change` flag is used to indicate whether or not you want the engine to immediately switch to the new state as soon as it is added. The implementation of `AddState` is shown here:

```
void Engine::AddState( State *state, bool change )
{
  m_states->Add( state );

  if( change == false )
    return;
```

```
    if( m_currentState != NULL )
      m_currentState->Close();

  m_currentState = m_states->GetLast();
  m_currentState->Load();
}
```

ChangeState is used to manually switch the engine's processing to a new state. When you call ChangeState you must pass in the unique identification number of the state to which you want to change. ChangeState will iterate through the list of states until it finds the state that you want to change to. It will then shut down the current state and proceed to load the new state. Once this is done it sets the m_stateChanged to true so that the engine knows that the state has changed. This is used by the engine in the Run function so that it does not accidentally try to process a state that is no longer in control. The implementation of the ChangeState function is shown here:

```
void Engine::ChangeState( unsigned long id )
{
  m_states->Iterate( true );
  while( m_states->Iterate() != NULL )
  {
    if( m_states->GetCurrent()->GetID() == id )
    {
      if( m_currentState != NULL )
        m_currentState->Close();

      m_currentState = m_states->GetCurrent();
      m_currentState->Load();

      m_stateChanged = true;

      break;
    }
  }
}
```

If you have a look at the EngineSetup structure (also found in Engine.h) you will notice that we have added a new member, void (*StateSetup)(), which is set to NULL by default. It may look a little strange at first, but it is actually a call-back function like the one used by the ResourceManager template class that we looked at in the last chapter. How it works is you create a void returning function with no parameters in your application specific code. Then you set the StateSetup pointer to point to your new function. When the engine is created it will call this function so that you can set all the states you are going to need for your application. This allows your state setup to be integrated into the loading of the engine. Note: this is not entirely necessary, but it helps to create more robust code. Setting your states this way will help to prevent you from trying to set states when the engine has not yet been loaded.

Now if you switch over to Engine.cpp and take a look at the Engine class constructor you will see that we prepare the linked list that will store all of the states the engine will use. We also set the m_currentState pointer to NULL to indicate that the engine does not yet have a state to process, as shown here:

```
m_states = new LinkedList< State >;
m_currentState = NULL;
```

Near the end of the constructor we check if a state set up function is being used. If so, then we call the function to allow the programmer to set all the states that are going to be used by the application.

```
if( m_setup->StateSetup != NULL )
m_setup->StateSetup();
```

Now moving down to the destructor you can see that we are starting to make use of that little area we left open for destroying all our engine components that were loaded in the constructor. We start with the linked list that stores all the states. First we check if there is a current state; if so, then we allow it to close itself down. Then we use the SAFE_DELETE macro to destroy the m_states linked list, as shown here:

```
if( m_currentState != NULL )
  m_currentState->Close();
SAFE_DELETE( m_states );
```

The Run function is the last place where we need to make changes in order to bring the state system to life. First we check if there is a current state; if so, then we need to call the RequestViewer function so that the programmer can fill the Viewer-Setup with the details needed to render the current frame. Since we are not doing any rendering yet, the ViewerStructure is empty and does not need to be filled in. We put this here anyway so that as soon as we start adding entries to the Viewer-Setup it will be all ready to go, as shown here:

```
if( m_currentState != NULL )
  m_currentState->RequestViewer( &viewer );
```

The last step is to set the `m_stateChanged` flag to false, then call the `Update` function on the current state, assuming there is one. The reason we need to set `m_stateChanged` to false is because it is during the `Update` function that you have the opportunity to call the `ChangeState` function and cause the engine to switch to a new state. When this happens, `m_stateChanged` will be set to true, which is checked in the next line of code shown below. If it is true, then the `continue` keyword is called. The `continue` keyword is used to stop any further processing inside the current `do`, `for`, or `while` loop and jump straight back to the beginning of the next iteration of the loop. Since this code is inside a `while` loop, this means that anything below the `continue` keyword that is inside the `while` loop will be skipped (when it is actually called), and a new iteration of the `while` loop will begin. We do this to prevent any further processing on the current state, since the current state has changed and is no longer the same state that began this iteration of the `while` loop.

```
m_stateChanged = false;
if( m_currentState != NULL )
  m_currentState->Update( elapsed );
if( m_stateChanged == true )
  continue;
```

So there you have it. The state system has been fully integrated into our engine. Of course, we will need to return to some of these areas later to add new things, especially the `ViewerSetup` structure.

USING THE STATE SYSTEM

Now that we have our state system working, let's take a little crash course in the use of it. It really is quite simple. All you need to do is to derive a new class from the `State` class, and override any of the virtual functions that you want to support. The following is an example:

```
#define TEST_STATE 1

class TestState : public State
{
public:
  TestState ( unsigned long id );

  virtual void Load();
  virtual void Close();
```

```
    virtual void RequestViewer( ViewerSetup *viewer )
    virtual void Update( float elapsed )
    virtual void Render();
};
```

Then you just need to create a state setup function that the engine can call so that you can add your new state, like in the following example:

```
void StateSetup()
{
  g_engine->AddState( new TestState( TEST_STATE ), true );
}
```

If you had more than one state and you wanted to switch to this state for example, you would call the ChangeState function from within the current state's Update function. You just need to pass the unique identification number of the state you want to change to, which we have defined using the #define TEST_STATE 1 statement. Here is an example:

```
g_engine->ChangeState( TEST_STATE );
```

Now you should have enough knowledge to use the new state system to your heart's content. It's really quite simple. With that out of the way we can now move on to the second form of engine control—user input.

USER INPUT

We want our engine to be able to support user input through two devices, the mouse and the keyboard. We could support other devices like joysticks, but they are not so common among FPS, so it is not really necessary. Now we won't actually implement the keys and so forth that are used by the game as that is very much a game-specific area. Instead we will implement a class that wraps around Direct-Input (called a wrapper class) to provide all of the basic input functionality that we need, at a higher level. This means that many of the underlying DirectX operations will be transparent and you will be able to harness the power of user input with greater ease. So let's take a look at the Input class definition, which can be found in the Input.h file and is reproduced here:

```
class Input
{
public:
```

```
    Input( HWND window );
    virtual ~Input();

    void Update();

    bool GetKeyPress( char key, bool ignorePressStamp = false );

    bool GetButtonPress( char button,
                          bool ignorePressStamp = false );
    long GetPosX();
    long GetPosY();
    long GetDeltaX();
    long GetDeltaY();
    long GetDeltaWheel();

private:
    HWND m_window;
    IDirectInput8 *m_di;
    unsigned long m_pressStamp;

    IDirectInputDevice8 *m_keyboard;
    char m_keyState[256];
    unsigned long m_keyPressStamp[256];

    IDirectInputDevice8 *m_mouse;
    DIMOUSESTATE m_mouseState;
    unsigned long m_buttonPressStamp[3];
    POINT m_position;
};
```

This is a very busy little class, and there are a number of things we need to cover. Fortunately, many of the functions are pretty straightforward, just returning a single value of some sort. We will cover all of the various member variables as we look at the implementation of the functions starting with the constructor, which accepts as input a handle to a parent window. This should be the main window that you will be running the application on. Our engine creates a window for you to use and the handle can be retrieved by call GetWindow from the Engine class. You can use the handle returned from this function to supply the Input class constructor. The constructor then stores a copy of this handle in its own internal variable (as it will need it later in other functions), which is shown here:

```
    Input::Input( HWND window )
    {
      m_window = window;
```

```
DirectInput8Create( GetModuleHandle( NULL ),
                    DIRECTINPUT_VERSION, IID_IDirectInput8,
                    (void**)&m_di, NULL );
```

;The first major task is to create the DirectInput object, which is achieved by calling the `DirectInput8Create` function. You will notice that it has an 8 in it, which signifies Version 8 of DirectInput. Even though we are using DirectX 9, DirectInput did not undergo any major changes so it still uses the same interface that was developed for DirectX 8. The definition for the `DirectInput8Create` function is shown here:

```
HRESULT WINAPI DirectInput8Create
(
  HINSTANCE hinst, // Instance handle of the application module.
  DWORD dwVersion, // Version of DirectInput the application uses.
  REFIID riidltf, // Unique identifier of the desired interface.
  LPVOID *ppvOut, // Pointer to receive the interface.
  LPUNKNOWN punkOuter // Used for aggregation, leave it as NULL.
);
```

The `m_di` pointer will store the address to our new DirectInput object after the function returns. Once we have our DirectInput object we can go about preparing our devices, which are the physical input devices such as the keyboard and the mouse. Preparing each device is surprisingly similar. You create the device, set the data format that it will use, then set the device's cooperation level, and finally acquire the device. Let's go through the process for the keyboard.

The first call is to the `CreateDevice` function that is exposed by our new DirectInput object that we just created. The prototype for this function is shown here:

```
HRESULT CreateDevice
(
  REFGUID rguid, // GUID of the device to create.
  LPDIRECTINPUTDEVICE *lplpDirectInputDevice, // Pointer to
                                              // receive the
                                              // device.
  LPUNKNOWN pUnkOuter // Used for aggregation, leave it as NULL.
);
```

All you really need to be worried about is passing in the correct globally unique identifier (GUID) for the device you want to create, and a pointer to point to the address of the new device. We use the `GUID_SysKeyboard` to specify a keyboard device, which will be pointed to by `m_keyboard` after the function returns, as shown here:

```
m_di->CreateDevice( GUID_SysKeyboard, &m_keyboard, NULL );
```

Once the device is created we can use its pointer to access it. The first thing we need to do with it is set its data format with a call to `SetDataFormat`. The data format is what describes how the data will be arranged for this device. There are a number of predefined data formats, which we can make use of. For our keyboard we will use the `c_dfDIKeyboard` data format, which is shown here:

```
m_keyboard->SetDataFormat( &c_dfDIKeyboard );
```

The second step in preparing our device is to set the cooperation level, which indicates how this device will share input with other applications. You can operate a device in either the foreground or the background, and in exclusive mode or nonexclusive mode. Table 3.1 shows the details of each flag.

TABLE 3.1   Input Device Cooperation Flags

`DISCL_NONEXCLUSIVE`	Your application shares access to the device.
`DISCL_EXCLUSIVE`	Your application has exclusive access to the device.
`DISCL_FOREGROUND`	Input only received when the application has the focus.
`DISCL_BACKGROUND`	Input can be received all the time, regardless of the focus.

These flags can be combined, however, `DISCL_NONEXCLUSIVE` and `DISCL_EXCLU-SIVE` are mutually exclusive and so are `DISCL_FOREGROUND` and `DISCL_BACKGROUND`. We will operate our keyboard device with foreground, nonexclusive cooperation, which means that our application can only receive input from the keyboard while the application has the focus. Additionally, other applications can also receive input from the keyboard at the same time if they need to. This is shown as:

```
m_keyboard->SetCooperativeLevel( m_window, DISCL_FOREGROUND |
                                 DISCL_NONEXCLUSIVE );
```

The last step in preparing our keyboard device is to acquire it, which allows us to retrieve input from the device. You can only retrieve input from a device while you have it acquired. A device can be unaquired either manually (by calling `Unac-quire` on the device) or when certain events happen like your application loses the focus, or another application tries to acquire the device with exclusive access. Acquiring the device is very simple, as shown:

```
m_keyboard->Acquire();
```

Now we have to repeat the process with our mouse device. It is pretty much exactly the same steps; we just change a few of the parameters in the various calls. If you take a look at the next four lines of code you will see how we change the device and the data format to represent a mouse device rather than a keyboard device.

```
m_di->CreateDevice( GUID_SysMouse, &m_mouse, NULL );
m_mouse->SetDataFormat( &c_dfDIMouse );
m_mouse->SetCooperativeLevel( m_window, DISCL_FOREGROUND |
                              DISCL_NONEXCLUSIVE );
m_mouse->Acquire();
```

Once created and prepared, a pointer to our new mouse device is stored in the m_mouse member variable. Finally, our Input class constructor is coming to a close with one last line of code, which clears a stamp that we will use later. Stamps are just numerical values (usually of type long) that are incremented every frame. So in the first frame m_pressStamp would be 0, in the second frame it would be 1, then 2 in the third frame, and so on. We use stamps to track when something last occurred, or in what frame a particular event last occurred. In the Input class we will use this stamp to track when keyboard keys and mouse buttons were last pressed.

```
    m_pressStamp = 0;
}
```

Our Input class also has a destructor, which uses the SAFE_RELEASE macro to destroy our DirectInput object and both of the input devices when the class is destroyed, as shown here:

```
Input::~Input()
{
  SAFE_RELEASE( m_di );
  SAFE_RELEASE( m_keyboard );
  SAFE_RELEASE( m_mouse );
}
```

UPDATING USER INPUT

We have seen how the Input class creates and destroys itself; now we need to look at how it keeps the user input updated. In other words, every frame the Input class needs to be able to query the devices to check if the user is trying to provide any input. This is achieved through the use of the Update function exposed by the Input class. This function needs to be called once per frame, every frame in order for it to do its job. Let's take a look at the Update function to see how it works.

When you glance at it (found in Input.cpp), you can easily pick out the two main while loops. The first is used to check for keyboard input and the second is used to check for mouse input. Checking for input on either the keyboard or the mouse is almost an identical process, with the only difference being the pointer to the device that we use, and the way we store the input data.

```
void Input::Update()
{
  static HRESULT result;

  while( true )
  {
    m_keyboard->Poll();
```

When we enter the first while loop, we begin by polling the device in question, which is the keyboard device in this instance. Polling means that you instruct the device to update its input data and is achieved by calling Poll, which is exposed by the input device interface. A call to this function should be made at least once every frame in order to keep the input data fresh and up-to-date.

```
    if( SUCCEEDED( result = m_keyboard->GetDeviceState( 256,
                (LPVOID)&m_keyState ) ) )
      break;
```

Once the device has been polled, the second step is to get the device state with a call to GetDeviceState. This function allows you to retrieve the input data from the device and store it for later use. Since this is a keyboard device, we pass our array our m_keyState char values to the function. After the function returns, our array will contain a char value for each key on the keyboard to represent whether or not the key is pressed. We use one of the DirectX macros—SUCCEEDED—to check if the function was successful. If so we can break out of the while loop as we have the input data for this frame.

```
      if( result != DIERR_INPUTLOST && result != DIERR_NOTACQUIRED )
        return;

      if( FAILED( m_keyboard->Acquire() ) )
        return;
  }
```

If the function failed we go on to check why it failed. There are two particular reasons that we are interested in, which are the most common reasons why a device might fail. The first is because the device is lost and the function will return DIERR_INPUTLOST to indicate this. The other reason is that the device has not been acquired, which means the function will return DIERR_NOTACQUIRED. In either case the solution is to reacquire the device, which is achieved with a call to Acquire on the device.

```
  while( true )
  {
    m_mouse->Poll();
    if( SUCCEEDED( result = m_mouse->GetDeviceState(
                    sizeof( DIMOUSESTATE ), &m_mouseState ) ) )
      break;
    if( result != DIERR_INPUTLOST && result != DIERR_NOTACQUIRED )
      return;

    if( FAILED( m_mouse->Acquire() ) )
      return;
  }
```

After the keyboard device has been queried, we then go on to check the mouse device. As previously mentioned, the process is almost identical. The main difference is the way in which we store the input data when we call GetDeviceState. Instead of using a char array we need to use a MOUSESTATE structure. This structure allows us to retrieve information about the mouse's movement, its scroll wheel (if it has one), and up to four buttons on the mouse. If for some reason you want to support a mouse with more than four buttons you can use the MOUSESTATE2 structure, which lets you support a whopping eight buttons on a mouse.

```
    GetCursorPos( &m_position );
    ScreenToClient( m_window, &m_position );

    m_pressStamp++;
  }
```

The final steps involve collecting the position of the mouse cursor on the screen and incrementing the press stamp. The GetCursorPos retrieves the coordinates of the mouse cursor on the screen and stores them in a POINT structure called m_position. ScreenToClient then makes the coordinates relative to the application's window. That way, a coordinate of 0, 0 refers to the upper left-hand corner of the application's window rather than the screen.

The POINT structure has an x and a y component, which measures how far out the cursor is along the x and y axes of the screen, respectively. The top left-hand corner of the screen is coordinate 0, 0 with x increasing to the right of the screen and y increasing down the screen. Figure 3.3 shows how the coordinate system works.

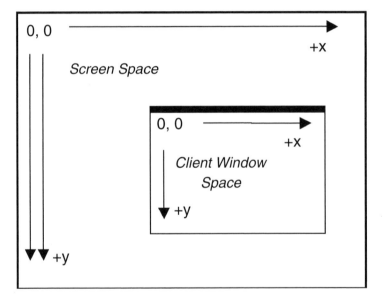

FIGURE 3.3   The mouse cursor coordinate system.

RETRIEVING INPUT

Once the Input class has been updated, you can then retrieve the current input from it using a number of functions. There is a function for checking keyboard keys and one for checking mouse buttons. There are also a number of functions for retrieving the mouse's position and movement, including its scroll wheel.

The first function is `GetKeyPress`, which returns true if the requested keyboard key is pressed. You can check any of the keys on the keyboard, and DirectX has a special `char` key code for each key, which you need to pass to `GetKeyPress` so that it knows which key to check. Table 3.2 shows some of the common keys you might want to check for a game. Their names give away which key they are used for.

TABLE 3.2   Common DirectX Key Codes

DIK_W	DIK_UP
DIK_A	DIK_LEFT
DIK_S	DIK_DOWN
DIK_D	DIK_RIGHT
DIK_SPACE	DIK_LCONTROL

`GetKeyPress` also accepts a second parameter, `ignorePressStamp`, which is false by default. If you remember, our `Input` class has a press stamp that is incremented each frame. This press stamp is used to keep track of when each key was last pressed. The reason why we do this is because it allows us to prevent a key press from registering multiple times if we do not want it to. Imagine if you wanted to check if the user pressed the spacebar, and then toggle a flag (i.e., flip it between true or false) every time the spacebar was pressed. If the user presses and holds the spacebar down, then it would register as being pressed every frame and your flag would constantly switch between true and false every frame. If you do not want it to do this then you need to use the press stamp. When a key is pressed and you check it for the first time, its press stamp is set and it returns true. Then if you check the same key again, either in the same frame or subsequent frames, it will return false as the press stamp will indicate that the key is already pressed and checked, therefore it is no longer a valid press. Despite the fact that using a press stamp is very simplistic, it is just fine for our purposes. The following is the implementation of `GetKeyPress`, showing the press stamp in action.

```
bool Input::GetKeyPress( char key, bool ignorePressStamp )
{
  if( ( m_keyState[key] & 0x80 ) == false )
    return false;

  bool pressed = true;
```

```
    if( ignorePressStamp == false )
      if( m_keyPressStamp[key] == m_pressStamp - 1 ||
          m_keyPressStamp[key] == m_pressStamp )
        pressed = false;

  m_keyPressStamp[key] = m_pressStamp;

  return pressed;
}
```

To retrieve the state of a mouse button we use a very similar function. The only
difference is that we are testing against the four mouse buttons so we need to pass
in the number of the button we want to check, which is between 0 and 3. 0 is for the
first button, 1 for the second, 2 for the third, and 3 for the fourth. Then we use the
rgbButtons component of the MOUSESTATE structure to check the button in question.
The press stamp works in exactly the same way for mouse buttons as it does for keyboard keys.

```
bool Input::GetButtonPress( char button, bool ignorePressStamp )
{
  if( ( m_mouseState.rgbButtons[button] & 0x80 ) == false )
    return false;

  bool pressed = true;

  if( ignorePressStamp == false )
    if( m_buttonPressStamp[button] == m_pressStamp - 1 ||
        m_buttonPressStamp[button] == m_pressStamp )
      pressed = false;

  m_buttonPressStamp[button] = m_pressStamp;

  return pressed;
}
```

The next two functions—GetPosX and GetPosY—allow us to retrieve the x
and y coordinates of the mouse cursor on the application's window. GetDeltaX and
GetDeltaY allow us to retrieve the change in the mouse's x and y movement since
the last frame. The final function—GetDeltaWheel—gives us the change in the
mouse's scroll wheel since the last frame. The implementation of these functions is
very basic and can be found in Input.cpp.

INTEGRATING THE INPUT SYSTEM

Integrating the new input system is done in a very similar way to the state system we did earlier. The first step is to always ensure you get the right #include statements in the right spots. The Engine.h file will need #include "Input.h" and the Input.cpp file will need #include "Engine.h".

Next we need to create a variable within our Engine class that will store a pointer to an instance of the Input class—like Input *m_input. We will also add the GetInput function, which will allow us to gain access to this pointer. The Engine class constructor will need to create an instance of our Input class and assign it to the m_input pointer, as shown here:

```
m_input = new Input( m_window );
```

In the Engine class destructor we also need to destroy the input object by using the SAFE_DELETE macro, in the same way that we destroyed the states linked list earlier. Finally, we move on to the Run function where we need to add a few lines of code, as shown:

```
m_input->Update();

if( m_input->GetKeyPress( DIK_F1 ) )
  PostQuitMessage( 0 );
```

We call the Update function on the Input class every frame to allow the input devices to update. We will then also check if the user has pressed the F1 key on the keyboard. If so, we will instruct the engine to shut down with a call to PostQuitMessage. This will send a WM_QUIT message to our application's window, which will allow our continuous while loop to break as that is the message it breaks on.

TESTING THE STATE AND INPUT SYSTEM

Now that our new state system and input system have been integrated, it is only fitting that we end with another little test application to see them in action. You can find the test application in the Test project in the workspace for this chapter. There is only one file in the project called Main.cpp, which has all the code in it for our test application. When you open the file you will see that we have defined a new class called TestState, which is a new state that we have derived from the base State

ON THE CD

class. We have overridden the Update function so that we can test if the user presses the Q key. If so, we exit from the test application, which tests our input system. Additionally, you can press the F1 key to exit the application as it is built into the engine.

You will also notice that we have defined a state setup function that we pass to the engine through the use of the EngineSetup structure. This allows us to add our new state to the system when the engine is created. When we add the new state we also instruct the engine to switch to it immediately so that as soon as the engine begins processing, it will process this state. Then we do not need to switch to it later to get it running.

SUMMARY

In this chapter, we covered two interesting topics: engine processing and user input. We implemented a state system, which will allow us to control what our engine processes. We also implemented an input system that is capable of handling both keyboard and mouse devices. We went through the steps of integrating our new systems, which is what we will need to do every time we add something new to the engine. Finally, we looked at a little test application that showed off all our hard work, which wasn't very exciting since we still have no way of stimulating our senses with fancy graphics and blasting sounds. This will all come in time—but not now. Chapter 4 covers scripting, where we will implement a basic scripting system tailored for our purposes.

4 Scripting

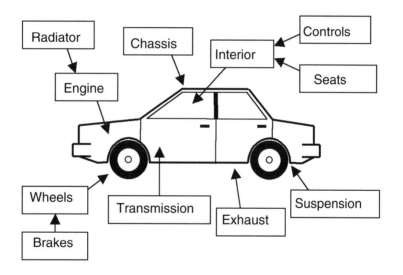

In This Chapter

- Learn about the benefits of scripts.
- Discuss the importance of encapsulation and automation in object-orientated programming.
- Look at the design and implementation of our scripting system.

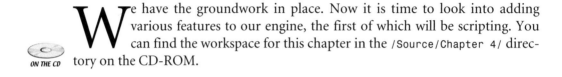

W̲e have the groundwork in place. Now it is time to look into adding various features to our engine, the first of which will be scripting. You can find the workspace for this chapter in the /Source/Chapter 4/ directory on the CD-ROM.

BENEFITS OF SCRIPTS

We will start by defining what a script actually is. By now you should be familiar with standard C++ code, and if you look at any of the code you have written you will notice that among other things, it consists of two fundamental aspects: variables and commands. What this means is that your code is using commands to invoke various events from the compiler in order to make the computer behave in a particular way. To facilitate this, you also use a number of variables throughout your code so that values can be passed around and used in calculations in order to determine which commands should be called by the compiler. Take a look at the following pseudo code:

```
myVariable = 5
if myVariable > 5 then
  Call CommandA
else (i.e. myVariable is equal to or less than 5)
  Call CommandB
```

Now without going into all the details of how a compiler works, we can just simply pretend here that this pseudo code is like a script for your compiler. The compiler reads it and uses it to invoke functions on the operating system and whatever other systems you are working with. myVariable is nothing more than a variable, which you use for your own calculations. All that really matters in the script is what CommandA and CommandB equate to. Based on this model you can create your own scripting system that allows you to use variables and commands. In fact, the variables can even be system generated. This means that you access variables from within the actual game code, or even the engine code, and either use their values or alter them in real-time!

As for the commands, they would link up to various functions within the code of the game and even the engine. For example, you could have a command that tells the game to invoke an explosion effect. The command may look something like the following:

```
CreateEffect_Explosion( location )
```

When the scripting engine reads this command, it will inform the game to invoke the necessary functions to create an explosion effect at the given location, which could be a 3D coordinate. All this sounds really cool, doesn't it? Unfortunately, the downside is that scripts can be awfully slow, especially when done incorrectly. This is often caused by the fact that scripts are processed in real-time, which means that the system has to slow down to the speed at which the script can be read. This is similar to what happens when you try to read a book out loud. If you read a paragraph in your head (without mouthing the words), you will find that you can read a lot faster than when you actually verbalize the words. The reason for this is that your brain can process text much faster than what you can speak. The scripting engine is the same. Although the commands and the internal engine can operate very quickly, it is often bottlenecked by the slow file input/output (IO) speed. Fortunately for us, we do not need such a fully featured solution. Therefore, we do not need to be as concerned with such problems.

As mentioned in Chapter 1, we are going to use a basic script system that we will implement ourselves. We briefly looked at how we are going to use property scripts, but let's look at them in more detail here. If you remember back to how we defined a normal script, and remove the part about commands, you've basically defined a property script. In other words, a property script contains nothing more than a list of variables with values that can be accessed by the game for whatever reason. Often these property scripts are used to define various objects in your game world. For example, you may have a weapon object that has properties such as rate of fire, range, and damage. You could easily set up a property script (for each of your weapons) that has three variables in it containing the values that the system would use, as shown here:

```
rof = 120
range = 200
damage = 50
```

What the actual value represents really depends on your game, but you see the principle. For example, the rof could be in rounds per minute, and range could be in meters, feet, yards, or whatever is appropriate to the scale used in your game. We also need to consider the type of data that the variable stores. In this example, we have three values that are obviously going to be represented by a numerical data type such as an `int` or a `long`, or even an `unsigned char` (assuming the values never went out of scope). But what happens if we want to store a letter, a word, or a whole sentence? In fact, come to think of it, what if we wanted to store a floating-point value or a Boolean (true or false) value? What about complex data types such as color information or 3D coordinates? Well, not to worry as we will take all of this into account when we implement our system.

Finally, the reason why we do not really need to concern ourselves with the performance issues found with real-time scripting systems is because our system will rarely be used in real-time. Think about the most common places that a property script would be used, such as defining game object properties. All of these details usually only need to be loaded once at startup. After that the system has the data in memory and no longer needs to read from the script. Therefore, although the script is being read at runtime, we will rarely need to read a script in real time during performance critical code.

THE SCRIPT SYSTEM

We have an understanding of what a script is and we've defined what type of script we will be using. However, up to this point we have omitted a very large detail. That is, how do we handle these scripts? We can't just open up a text editor, hack out some values, save it, and expect our game to miraculously know how to read the script. Well, actually we can, with a little help from us, of course. We just need to implement a reusable (remember our goals), automated system that we can call to read any script and pass us the values we need at crunch time. Take a look at Figure 4.1, which diagrams how our scripting system will work.

From Figure 4.1 you can see that our scripting system will actually sit on top of the resource management system. This is because our scripts are essentially resources. If you recall from Chapter 1, we defined a resource as something that is stored on your hard drive for example, which has a filename and a path to the file. The resource can be loaded and stored in volatile memory for the duration of the application's execution. You will also see that our scripting system is made up of two core components: scripts and variables. Actually, the system only directly manipulates the scripts. The scripts then manipulate their internal variables. The important point here is that we have identified two components, or objects, of our scripting system. Therefore, using an object-orientated approach we can immediately assume that they will be our two classes that we need to implement. Remember that our resource management system is already in place and implemented. So as long as we provide the code to load and handle the scripts, they will work fine as generic resources without having to create any special script management class. We will cover this in greater detail a little later in this chapter when we take a little

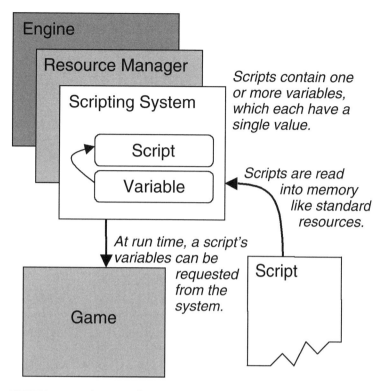

FIGURE 4.1 Diagram of our scripting system.

detour and look at two important topics of object-orientated programming: *encapsulation* and *automation*.

If you look at the flow of operation you can see that a script is first loaded by the script system, which is really just an instance of the resource manager in disguise using templates. The script class will be invoked to load the script and all of its internal variables, which are instances of the variable class. Once loaded, the game can then request the value of any of these variables from the script. Since the script has been loaded, the values are accessed directly from memory rather than reading from the physical resource, which will eliminate our file I/O bottleneck even if we were to request a value during performance critical code.

We also previously touched on the idea of storing different types of values in our variables—different data types and even complex data types. To achieve this we will give all of our variables a type identifier, which will allow us to identify what sort of data is being held by the variable so that we know how to read and manipulate it. Obviously though, we will have to provide the implementation for each of our data types, but this is fairly trivial.

Since we are going to run the scripts through the resource management system we don't need to worry about what is going on with the memory. Even if you load a hundred scripts, with many of them being repeat loads (i.e., the same script loaded more than once), and then you mess it up by forgetting to close half of them, you can still relax. The resource manager is extremely forgiving and will efficiently clean up. However, in order for it to work you must load your scripts through the resource manager. If you load them independently, you will need to independently destroy them. We are getting a little ahead of ourselves here. We haven't even implemented the scripting system yet; but first let's have a look at how our scripts will be composed.

SCRIPT COMPOSITION

Let's just briefly look at the composition of a basic script that our system will be able to read. Scripts are entered into a text file and read in by the system. Essentially the system reads in variables with user-defined values in them. The programmer can then access these variables in the code at runtime, and query them for the data. Additionally, we want to be able to put comments in our scripts so that we can provide descriptive details if necessary. To achieve this we will use *variable blocks*. A variable block is simply a group of variables that are bound by something so that anything outside of the block is ignored. We will define the bounds around our variable blocks with two statements, #begin and #end, as shown in the following example:

```
This is outside the block, therefore it will be ignored.
#begin
This is inside the block, therefore it will be read by the system.
#end
```

This will also allow us to have multiple blocks, which will help to make longer scripts more readable as variables can be logically grouped and comments can be placed part way through the script. The only restrictions are that blocks cannot be placed inside one another (nested) and every #begin statement must be closed with a matching #end statement. Here is another example:

```
The first block.
#begin
Some data inside this block.
#end

The second block.
#begin
Some more data inside this block.
#end
```

The next important aspect is the variables, which must be placed inside the blocks. Every variable is described in the following format, which is the name of the variable followed by the variables type followed by the value for the variable:

```
name type value
```

This should be enough information for us to start work. Later when we look at how to use the system we will cover more intricate details, but for now let's begin implementation.

VARIABLE CLASS

Now that we know what we are creating, we're on to the tricky part (just kidding). The implementation is actually the easy part. In fact, if you are confident with your C++ and file I/O skills you can probably just open up the header and source files (`Scripting.h` and `Scripting.cpp`) and read through the code yourself; otherwise, keep reading and we will step through the important parts together.

The first class to implement is the `Variable` class. The reason we need to implement it first is because the next class (the `Script` class) will use it. It would be silly to implement the `Script` class if it doesn't even have an implementation for its variables ready to go. Now if you go ahead and open the `Scripting.h` file you will see an enumeration at the beginning of the file. It should look similar to this:

```
enum{ VARIABLE_BOOL, VARIABLE_COLOUR, VARIABLE_FLOAT,
      VARIABLE_NUMBER, VARIABLE_STRING, VARIABLE_VECTOR,
      VARIABLE_UNKNOWN };
```

An `enum` statement is just a simple way of listing a sequential set of constants. The idea is to set a value for the first constant and then each one after is incremented by one. So, if you were to define an enumeration like this:

```
enum{ CAT = 47, DOG, BIRD, FISH };
```

obviously, the first constant would be equal to 47 while DOG would equal 48 and FISH would equal 50. However, if you do not specify a value for the first constant like we did in our first enumeration, then it defaults to zero. This means that the constant VARIABLE_UNKNOWN would be equal to 6.

So, let's begin by looking at the class definition for the `Variable` class.

```
class Variable
{
public:
```

```
    Variable( char *name, FILE *file );
    Variable( char *name, char type, void *value );
    virtual ~Variable( );

    char GetType( );
    char *GetName( );
    void *GetData( );

private:
    char m_type;
    char *m_name;
    void *m_data;
};
```

Now there is nothing too out of the ordinary here, except for the fact that there are two class constructors and also that strange looking FILE *file variable in the first class constructor. This is actually a pointer to an instance of a structure that contains a data stream for the open file on the hard drive. The file should be a text file (*.txt) that contains the script's variables and their values. This constructor is obviously called when you are creating a script variable from a script text file. The char *name is just the name of the variable that is being created. The second constructor is used when a script variable is created from scratch. In other words, a script does not exist yet. In fact, the script in which the variable belongs is most likely being created and this new variable will belong to it. The extra two parameters used in this constructor indicate the type for the variable and the actual value to go into the variable. It is important that the value matches the type. This means that if the variable is set to a string type, for example, you should pass in a string value. You will see plenty of examples of how this is used later on.

After the destructor you can see three more functions plus three matching class member variables, which store the type, name, and the data within the variable, respectively. The three functions are used to access any of this data as necessary. For example, you may need to know the type of a particular variable, so you would call the GetType() function, which would then return one of the types from the type enumeration that we looked at earlier. The most common function you are likely to use is the GetData() function, which will return a void pointer containing the address of the data stored in this variable. The pointer will need to be cast into a usable pointer, which is done based on the type of the variable. Once again you will see examples of this when we implement the actual Script class later in this chapter, so don't stress if this sounds a little daunting. It really is very simple. Actually, once we have implemented the Script class you will probably never have to touch this class again because the script class handles all the loading and interpreting of the scripts for you.

At this point we could go through and look at the inner workings of the Variable class. However, this is really unnecessary as it is not a crucial component. The most interesting class to look at here is the Script class as it is the class you will use the most, so we will just get on with dissecting it instead. If you are really interested in the workings of the Variable class, open up the Scripting.cpp file and check out the first half of the file, with the most interesting function being the first class constructor. By following the comments you should be able to see how the variable loads its data based on its type. This is very useful to learn in case you ever want to add your own types to the class. You would first need to add the type to the type enumeration, then add the loading code in both of the constructors and finally add the return code used by the GetData() function for your new type.

ENCAPSULATION AND AUTOMATION

What's going on? Where is the Script class? By the heading you have probably guessed that we are not moving on to the Script class yet. Instead, we are going to take a little detour through object-oriented programming land. So the question is, why are we discussing this now; it seems a little out of place doesn't it? We are suppose to be talking about scripting here not object-oriented programming. The problem is that if we were to look at all of this back at the start it would be harder to understand as we would not have any real code to use as examples. It is just convenient that the Script class we are about to look at employs these theories, so it makes sense to cover it now when we have some physical code to look at. Throughout the book we will sometimes make little detours from the topic at hand to discuss some other aspect or theory of programming that is relevant to what we are doing at the time. Anyway, let's get on with the theory again.

Encapsulation and automation are two very important aspects of programming that will make your life a whole lot simpler. They go hand-in-hand with other great buzzwords like abstraction and polymorphism. All of these terms are names for various forms of programming techniques that are specifically designed to reduce the complexity of your code, therefore making it easier to maintain and easier to use in future projects. Remember those other buzzwords we talked about in Chapter 1, maintainability, reusability, and usability. Now these words are beginning to mean something.

Let's have a look at some simple definitions that are tailored to our situation. Encapsulation means that you combine functionality to create a higher level (this is called *abstraction*) component that performs the same task independently. In other words, the component is self-sufficient; it does not rely on outside assistance to perform its duties. This includes the data it uses as it is very important that the classes are created based on the data they manipulate. This is one of the major reasons why classes in object-oriented programming work the way they do. The idea is that you combine all of the functionality for a particular object into a class, which can operate completely independently receiving input and giving the output it was designed to give. This then leads straight into the topic of automation, where you create objects that when combined can produce a high level result through a series of low level input/outputs and processes. So you really see the benefits of automation when you stack multiple objects on top of one another, each with its own particular role. Combined, they work together for a greater cause. In fact, this is another example of encapsulation at an even higher level. Figure 4.2 gives a visual illustration of all this jargon.

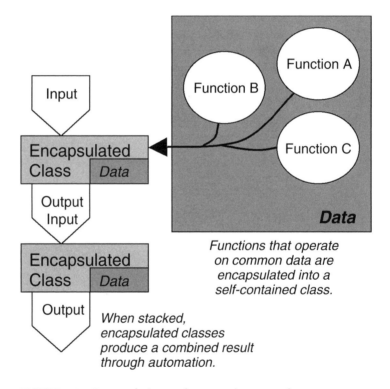

FIGURE 4.2   Encapsulation and automation at work.

Let's use an example to better understand how these two concepts work. We will use a car as our example and imagine that we have to model it in terms of objects. The most obvious breakdown would be to separate the engine from the rest of the car and define them as two separate objects that work together. Furthermore, we could separate other aspects of the car such as the seats and the wheels, and define them as objects, too. In fact, we could go as low in the hierarchy as we like, separating everything down to the last nut and bolt, but this would be completely unnecessary. So how do you know when to stop? Well, the simple answer is to look at the data that is being processed, and then break things up into logical groups that manipulate common data.

If we look at the engine we can see that it uses data such as fuel and air intake, oil, water, and acceleration and torque as well as potential and kinetic energy in order to produce an output—power to the drive shaft. Some may argue that some of this data is actually input (such as acceleration), but that is beside the point. The important note here is that no other part of the car needs to manipulate this type of data in order to operate, so we can deduce that the engine is a separate component that can be encapsulated. This means that all of the engine's data is encapsulated with it, too. If you want, you can further break down the engine into more components by identifying which parts manipulate unique data. Before subdividing an object, always ensure that the proposed data is not being used by any other object. Additionally, if a component does not use similar data to another component, then do not combine them. This theory is what will prevent you from making silly errors such as combining the suspension with the engine, or the brakes with the transmission, for example. So the moral of the story is, always encapsulate based on data rather than functionality. If we did group components based on functionality we would end up with objects that combined parts like the engine with the transmission as they are both used to move the car. However, they are different components that act on completely different data. In fact, the transmission provides an input for the engine. Figure 4.3 shows a simple breakdown of our car based on data.

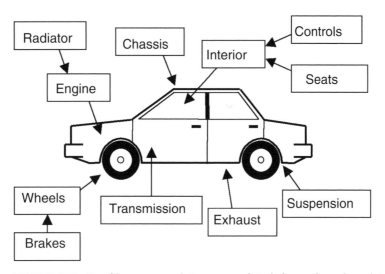

FIGURE 4.3 Breaking a car up into encapsulated classes based on data.

Automation is a fundamental key of software design, especially for logic intensive applications such as computer games. Let's continue with our car example and see how automation can greatly simplify the process of moving the car. The first step is to apply acceleration using the car's controls, which then provides input to the engine informing it to increase its revolutions, which creates the output of energy. This energy passes through the transmission and down the driveshaft, which is finally translated into power at the wheels. Therefore, the output of the engine becomes an input for the transmission, which gives another output that finally becomes an input for the wheels. Now if we were to look at the car as a complete system (i.e., we encapsulate the car's components into a higher level class) we can provide a single input to the car to inform it to move, and the car will in fact move due to automation, which states that each component will fulfill its role in order to produce a greater output. So, which component of the car actually produced the output; which one moved the car? They all did; combined they produced the final result. We have a set of objects that are fully self-sufficient and will receive input, act upon it, and give the appropriate output, which becomes the input of another object. This whole process continues without interruption and more importantly without interference. We do not need to provide any of the components with any outside assistance, hence the reason why the whole process is automated, as shown in Figure 4.4.

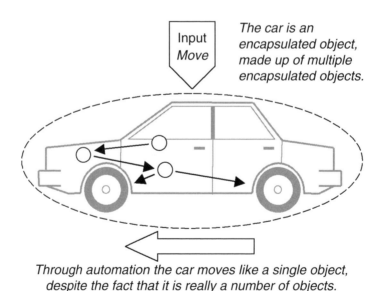

Through automation the car moves like a single object, despite the fact that it is really a number of objects.

FIGURE 4.4 Our car represented as an encapsulated object, moving through automation.

What makes this so amazing is that since each subobject of the car is encap-sulated, it means that they can be modified or replaced without affecting other components. For example, you could change the wheels and expect the engine to operate exactly the same. You could also make modifications to the engine and expect the transmission to operate correctly (however, this may change the input to the transmission, which could result in an unexpected output). The only limitation you have is the interfaces between the components. For example, you could not change the controls to apply acceleration using radio waves as the engine has no facility to accept that type of input. In the same way, you cannot replace the engine if the connection it uses to the transmission is different. The golden rule is that as long as you satisfy the inputs and provide the correct outputs you can really do whatever you like in between.

In extreme situations you can change the interface if necessary, however, this is not recommended. It may not be such a problem in a car, but it can become a real problem when it comes to software. The reason for this is that if you were to create a new version of a particular component and you changed the interface, then you can potentially break every other component of an older version that attempts to use the new interface. It is often a good idea to continue to support the old inter-faces, which is called *backwards compatibility*. In fact, DirectX does this extensively. With every new iteration of DirectX, many of the interfaces are changed, however, it does not affect the operation of applications that rely on the old interface. For ex-ample, you can run an application that was built using DirectX 8 and still expect it to run without any problems on a system that uses DirectX 9. So, if you do need to change an interface it is always a good idea to leave in support for the old interface as well.

SCRIPT CLASS

That's probably enough beating on the theory drum. Now it is time to get back on topic, and hopefully you will see how all that theory about encapsulation and au-tomation fits into place. We have taken a quick tour of the Variable class, which should give you enough understanding to move on to the real meat of this topic: the Script class. You already know the Script class uses the Variable class within it, which is the reason why we had to cover it first. So, let's take a look at the class definition for the famous Script class we have being talking so much about.

```
class Script : public Resource< Script >
{
public:
  Script( char *name, char *path = "./" );
  virtual ~Script();
```

```
    void AddVariable( char *name, char type, void *value );
    void SetVariable( char *name, void *value );

    void SaveScript( char *filename = NULL );

    bool *GetBoolData( char *variable );
    D3DCOLORVALUE *GetColourData( char *variable );
    float *GetFloatData( char *variable );
    long *GetNumberData( char *variable );
    char *GetStringData( char *variable );
    D3DXVECTOR3 *GetVectorData( char *variable );
    void *GetUnknownData( char *variable );

private:
  LinkedList< Variable > *m_variables;
};
```

As you can see the Script class inherits from the Resource class as a script shares all the properties of a tangible resource, so there is no reason why we shouldn't link it into our resource management system. We have to remember that our Resource class is actually a template, meaning that it is a blueprint for a class, not a class definition as we discussed in Chapter 2. This means we have to provide the Resource class with a type so that the compiler knows how to build the class for us. In this case, we provide it with the type Script as shown by the Resource< Script >.

The Script class uses a whole host of functions to manipulate the variables within it, which are stored in a linked list called m_variables. We also know that our linked list implementation is a template class, so we have to specify a type for it, too. In this case, we are using our Variable class that we have already implemented. This will create a linked list class of type Variable for us to store all of our variables for each script in an orderly fashion. If you haven't picked up on it already, we are actually using encapsulation and automation here. Let's have a look at how it is being used in this real example, not some abstract car.

Automation is a real fundamental key of software design when you are talking about logic intensive applications such as computer games. Imagine trying to implement our Script class if it were to internally manage all of the script variables, which are stored in a manual linked list, also managed by the Script class. The class would soon become very messy, unmanageable, and prone to errors, which would defeat the purpose of our first design goal of maintainability. So instead we create a series of encapsulated classes each with a specific job that they can handle without any support. This way we can safely build classes such as our Script class on top of our resource management and linked list storage technology without any hassle, knowing that everything will work the way it is supposed to. If anything does go wrong, it makes the process of debugging and repairing the fault a whole lot easier.

Instead of just saying that we have a problem within our Script class somewhere, we can narrow the problem down by identifying which of the subclasses may be causing the problem. This ultimately means that we deal with simpler code, despite that fact that combining the classes produce a greater, more complex output.

We mentioned this before, but here it is again: it is very important that you separate your components or classes based on data rather than functionality. That is, each class is encapsulated around the data that it processes rather than the functionality it provides. If we look at our Script class you can immediately see that it uses the Variable encapsulated class to manage each of the variables within the script, rather than trying to manage all of the variables itself internally. Now why did we break the scripts up and encapsulate them in two separate classes? The Variable class deals specifically with variable data, while the Script class cares little for that data. The Script class doesn't care what is in a particular variable, or what type it is, or even what its name is. If the Script class needs any of this information it will just ask for it from the appropriate instance of the Variable class. Additionally, we have the Resource class and the LinkedList class that only care about storage data such as the script's file information and the number of variables in the script, respectively. Once again, if the script needs any details from a particular variable, it can just request the variable from the linked list, and then ask the variable for the information. Figure 4.5 shows how the Scripting System is designed using encapsulation and automation.

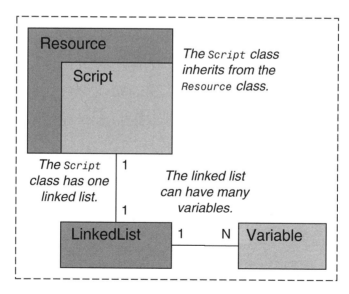

The entire design is encapsulated into a single component called the Scripting System.

FIGURE 4.5 Scripting system design utilizing encapsulation and automation.

This whole design is called the *Scripting System* and allows us to use it like an encapsulated component in much the same way that we used the car from the example earlier in the chapter. We can issue commands to the Script class or request information back from it and expect it to behave in a particular way and give a particular output despite the fact that it does not do all of the work. All of the other components that it utilizes work together through automation to create a greater output. Let's look at one more figure to help solidify this. Figure 4.6 shows how the system works together to provide a single output.

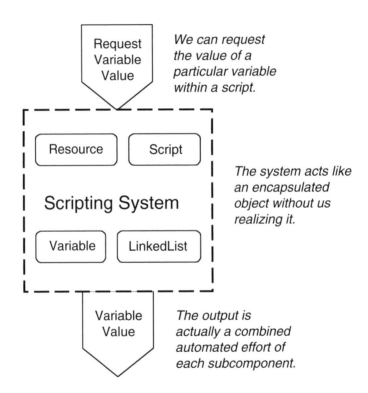

FIGURE 4.6 The Scripting System producing its output.

Developing code this way will ultimately assist in satisfying all three of our design goals. First, the code will be easier to maintain as it is separated into data specific classes. This makes it easier to identify problematic areas and code that requires attention. Second, the goal of reusability is far easier to satisfy. Instead of having components that rely on one another (as they process the same data), you have encapsulated data independent classes that can be altered or replaced at will.

For example, we could completely replace the implementation of our `Variable` class, `Resource` class, or `LinkedList` class without changing a single line of code from the `Script` class (as long as the interfaces do not change). This is because they are grouped around the data they process, rather than the functionality they provide combined. If we were to integrate all of this functionality together it would make it hard to isolate, replace, or repair problems with any one component such as our linked list. Third, you should also note here that usability is greatly increased as many of the intricate details of the systems operation can be hidden, allowing the programmer to use the system as a complete package. The programmer only needs to be concerned with the input to the system and the output from it, ignoring all of the steps in between.

Now—back on topic—let's continue dissecting our `Script` class. We will look at some of the functions within the Script class in more detail, starting with the constructor.

```
Script::Script( char *name, char *path )
        : Resource< Script >( name, path )
{
```

The constructor starts by accepting a name and path for the script to load. This is standard practice for any particular physical resource, as the resource management system requires these two parameters. As you can see they are immediately passed to the `Resource` class constructor since the `Script` class inherits from the `Resource` class. Remember that this inheritance is what will allow our scripts to be managed by the resource management system later on, which is a key aspect of our memory management because it will prevent multiple instances of the same script from being loaded into memory. It will also ensure that all scripts are freed from memory at shutdown, preventing memory leaks.

```
m_variables = new LinkedList< Variable >;
```

Next, we create an instance of our `LinkedList` class, which will store the variables in this script. Since the `LinkedList` class is a template class, we must specify the type for it to use, which in this case is our `Variable` class. The next step is to attempt to open a file handle to the physical text file that has been specified in the parameters of the constructor.

```
FILE *file = NULL;
if( ( file = fopen( GetFilename(), "r" ) ) == NULL )
  return;
```

The `FILE *file` is a structure that will store the details of the stream for the open file and the `fopen` function is a standard input/output function (specified in `stdio.h`) that opens a file. Here is the prototype for `fopen`.

```
FILE *fopen( const char *filename, const char *mode );
```

The first parameter is the complete filename of the file to be opened. This includes the path to the file and the file extension. The second parameter is the mode in which to open the file. Table 4.1 shows the different modes that can be used to open a file.

TABLE 4.1   `fopen` File Opening Modes

r	Opens the file for reading. The file must exist.
w	Opens the file for writing. The contents of the file are destroyed if it exists.
a	Opens the file for appending. The file is created if it does not exist.
r+	Opens the file for both reading and writing. The file must exist.
w+	Opens the file for both reading and writing. The contents of the file are destroyed if it exists.
a+	Opens the file for reading and appending. The file is created if it does not exist.

We will use the `Getfilename` function specified in the `Resource` class, which will return the complete filename (including the path and extension) for the script resource. We will open the file using mode r, which will allow us to read data from the file but not to modify it. If the script file does not exist or an error occurs, `fopen` will fail and return `NULL`. We check this to prevent any further operation on an invalid script resource. Now we are going to step the complexity up slightly as we look at the method of reading in the variables from the script.

```
bool read = false;
char buffer[MAX_PATH];
fscanf( file, "%s", buffer );
while( feof( file ) == 0 )
{
```

First we have `read`, which is used to determine whether we are reading from the script or not. The reason for this is that our scripts can contain things like comments, which we obviously do not need to read in. Next we have `buffer`, which is a character array that we will use to read words (referred to as strings) from the script, one at a time. The next step is to use `fscanf`, which allows us to read formatted data from the stream. Here is the prototype of `fscanf`.

```
int fscanf( FILE *stream, const char *format [, argument ]... );
```

The first parameter is just the stream for the open file and the second parameter is the format of the data you are looking for in the stream. There are many formats that you can look for and Table 4.2 gives a brief list of some common formats.

TABLE 4.2 Common Stream Formats

%c	Single byte character
%d	Decimal integer value
%f	Floating-point value
%s	String of up to the first whitespace character

We are interested in reading one string at a time, so we will use the `%s` format. In the last option parameter we will pass in our `buffer`, which will come back containing the next string found in the stream. Then we enter into a `while` loop that will constantly check the `file` stream using `feof`, which returns a nonzero value when the end of file (eof) is reached. At that point, we can break from the loop as we are at the end of the script and there is nothing left to read.

```
if( read == true )
{
  if( strcmp( buffer, "#end" ) == 0 )
    read = false;
  else
    m_variables->Add( new Variable( buffer, file ) );
}
```

What we do here is check if we are supposed to be reading a variable from the script. If so, we then check our buffer to see if we have reached the end of a variable block. This is achieved by using strcmp to check if our buffer contains the #end statement. strcmp basically compares the two strings and returns 0 if they are identical, which is what we are looking for. If we have reached the end of a variable block then we need to indicate that we are no longer looking for variables, at least until the next #begin statement is found. Otherwise, if an #end statement was not found, then we have obviously found a new variable.

We then use the Add function from our linked list to add the new variable to the end of the list. We pass the buffer and the file to the constructor of the new variable so that it can load itself. When this returns, the file stream will have its position indicator moved to the end of the value for this variable, ready to start reading the next variable. This is because the Variable class constructor reads the appropriate characters from the file stream in order to extract the new variable's type and value.

```
else if( strcmp( buffer, "#begin" ) == 0 )
   read = true;
```

If we are not supposed to be reading variables then we are not in a variable block, so we need to check if we are about to enter one. We do this by using strcmp again, however, this time looking for the #begin statement. If it is found then we indicate that we have entered a new variable block and we can start reading variables.

```
    fscanf( file, "%s", buffer );
  }

  fclose( file );
}
```

The final step in the while loop is to read the next string from the file stream. The loop will then flip back to the start and the process will repeat. This will continue until the eof marker is encountered and the loop is terminated. Once the loop ends the script is fully loaded and we can finally close the file stream using fclose.

The next three functions in the Script class are AddVariable, SetVariable, and SaveScript. These functions are used for creating scripts at runtime, which we will do very rarely. AddVariable will allow you to add a new variable to a script, specifying its value, while SetVariable will allow you to change the value of a variable in a script. SaveScript will write the script to the text file that you specify. These functions are luxury items, and you can peruse the source code for them in your own time. As usual, they are commented so you can follow them fairly easily.

The rest of the functions are used to access the value of any particular variable within a script. We will just look at one of them as they are all very similar, differing only by what they return. We will look at `GetNumberData`, which will be a fairly commonly used function.

```
long *Script::GetNumberData( char *variable )
{
  m_variables->Iterate( true );
  while( m_variables->Iterate() != NULL )
    if( strcmp( m_variables->GetCurrent()->GetName(), variable ) \
        == 0 )
      return (long*)m_variables->GetCurrent()->GetData();

  return NULL;
}
```

The function takes one parameter, which is the name of the variable that you want the value of. The function then iterates through the linked list of variables in the script using `strcmp` to find the variable with the matching name. If the variable is found, it requests the data from the variable and returns a pointer to the data, which is cast into a `long` value. If the variable is not found, `NULL` is returned.

There you have it. That concludes the implementation of our scripting system. Spend some time looking through the actual source code if something is not quite clear as there are more comments there. It is not really necessary to understand exactly how this all works right now, so don't stress if something seems complicated. For now all you need to understand is how to use the system, which we will discuss next. You only need to know its inner workings if you plan to alter it later or add your own variable types.

THE RESOURCE MANAGER

Unless you plan on loading, reading, and destroying scripts yourself, you should always load them using the resource management system. For this reason we will add a new resource manager called `m_scriptManager` to the `Engine` class. If you open the `Engine.h` file you will be able to see the new manager as well as the function `GetScriptManager`, which allows you to access the script manager from other parts of your projects external to the `Engine` class. Note that the `ResourceManager` class is a template class so we must specify a type for it. In this case, we use the `Script` class as the type.

In the constructor of the `Engine` class (found in `Engine.cpp`) you will see where we create the script resource manager.

```
m_scriptManager = new ResourceManager< Script >;
```

We then destroy it in the destructor as shown here:

```
SAFE_DELETE( m_scriptManager );
```

This is the first of several resource managers that we will be adding to our engine over time. Each one will be added in the same fashion, only differing in name and the type of resource it handles.

USING THE SCRIPT SYSTEM

If you thought implementing the scripting system was easy, then you are going to laugh at how easy it is to use. First, we will look at the different types that you can use for your variables. Table 4.3 lists all the currently supported types and gives a description of each.

TABLE 4.3 Supported Script Variable Types

bool	A true/false Boolean value. This is a case-sensitive value. Any value that does not match the string "true" will evaluate to false.
colour	A RGBA (red, green, blue, alpha) color value. Each component is a float value (ranging from 0.0–1.0). Each component must be separated by at least one space.
float	A float value.
number	A numeric long value.
string	A character string consisting of alphanumeric characters. If the string consists of multiple words (i.e., words separated by spaces) then the entire string must be enclosed in a set of inverted commas (i.e., "string goes here").
unknown	The special unknown type. If a variable has an undefined type, then it is given this type. This type of variable is stored by the system as a character array. The programmer can access the variable at runtime and return its character array; however, it will be up to the programmer to interpret the data into a usable format. Therefore, the unknown type can effectively be used to store variables with a custom (or user-defined) type.
vector	A 3D (x, y, z) vector, each component is a float value, and must be separated by at least one space.

The following is an example of a basic script using each of the supported data types:

```
This is a comment as it is outside the variable block.
#begin
ballColour colour  1.0 0.0 0.65 1.0
my_var     float   27.3978
text       string  Testing?
someData   number  1243
MyStory    string  "Once upon a time..."
myStory    string  "...there was a very tall tree."
made_up    code    jdf93mf093j
userVar    unknown OOOJHM-935TKY-473HUR
position   vector  20.5 79.938 -4.0
WORKING    bool    true
#end
```

There are a couple of interesting points to note here. First, the variables MyStory and myStory are unique since their case differs. Variable naming is case-sensitive, and you should always give your variables unique names (i.e., no two variables in the same script with the same name). Second, the variable made_up will default to an unknown type since the type cannot be recognized by the system.

The next step is to load the script. There are two ways you can achieve this, either through the resource management system (recommended) or on your own. If you load it yourself, you are responsible for destroying it and making sure you do not load multiple copies of it; otherwise, you waste memory. The script resource manager will handle all of that for you if you choose to load the script through it. The following is an example of loading a script through the resource manager:

```
Script *myScript = m_scriptManager->Add( "script.txt" );
```

This will attempt to load the script called script.txt, which is located in the same directory as the executable file. If the script loads successfully, myScript will contain a pointer to the loaded script. If you later decide to remove the script from the script resource manager you can do the following:

```
m_scriptManager->Remove( *myScript );
```

Alternatively you can load and destroy the script yourself as in the following example:

```
Script *myScript = new Script( "script.txt" );

SAFE_DELETE( myScript );
```

Either way, once you have your script loaded you can access the value of any of the script's variables as shown in the following examples:

```
myScript->GetFloatData( "my_var" );
myScript->GetStringData( "MyStory" );
myScript->GetVectorData( "position" );
```

As you can see, it really is a breeze to use the scripting system. The most important point to remember is that if you load a script yourself, you must destroy it. Otherwise, use the script resource manager and it will do it for you.

SUMMARY

Our scripting system is now fully operational and you should be able to create scripts to your heart's content. We even took some time out to look at some important object-oriented programming topics: encapsulation and automation. Finally, you saw exactly how easy it is to create, load, read, and destroy your own scripts.

Unfortunately, we didn't have an example of the system at work in this chapter. However, you will be sure to see it in operation in Chapter 5 when we look at rendering. One of the first topics that we will cover will be the Direct3D device enumeration. You will see how we will use the scripting system to save and load the device settings that the user selects so that the next time he loads the application he won't have to adjust all the settings again. We've even found a non-game specific use for the system.

5 Rendering

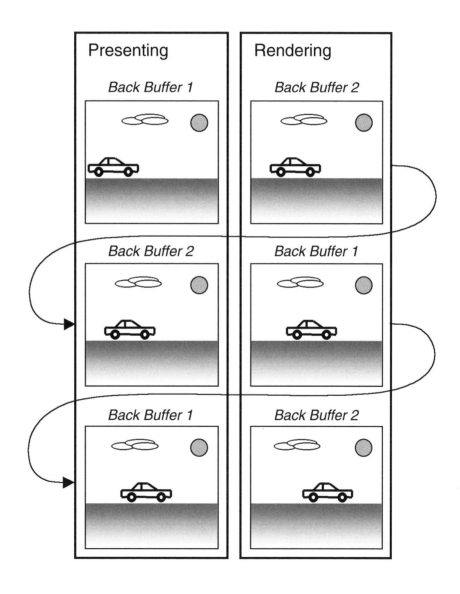

In This Chapter

- Talk about Direct3D and how it handles rendering.
- Implement the Direct3D device and an enumeration dialog for setting up the device.
- Add a basic font rendering system for displaying text.

Finally, we are getting to the exciting parts. By the end of this chapter you will be able to actually see something on the screen. Admittedly, it will only be some text, but we have to start somewhere. You can find the workspace for this chapter in the /Source/Chapter 5/ directory on the CD-ROM.

DIRECT3D RENDERING

Direct3D is one of the major components of DirectX. Before DirectX 8, there were two separate components for handling all rendering. There was Direct3D, which obviously did all 3D rendering, and DirectDraw, which handled everything in 2D. Now these two components have been combined into one, flying the banner of DirectGraphics. However, most people still refer to it as Direct3D, which is what we will call it. Besides, many of the Direct3D interfaces still maintain this name, so it makes it a lot easier when talking about it. A complete discussion of Direct3D could span multiple chapters. We will briefly look at a few of the common topics that will affect us. If you want to read more about Direct3D, how it works, and what it can do, take a look the *DirectX Graphics* section of the DirectX SDK documentation. The *Getting Started* section of the *Programming Guide* should be of particular interest.

Direct3D is an application programming interface (API) that is used primarily for displaying graphics on the screen. This is usually achieved by rendering 3D geometry through the use of the computer's video card (called the *display adapter*). What makes Direct3D so good at doing this is that it uses what is called a *hardware abstraction layer* (HAL). The HAL is a device-specific interface provided by the manufacturer of the video card. A different HAL is designed specifically for each display adapter and provides access to the functionality that the display adapter can support. Direct3D communicates directly with the HAL, and by developing applications that make use of this relationship, you open yourself up to a world of lightning fast rendering possibilities. Figure 5.1 shows the relationship between your application, Direct3D, and the display adapter.

As suggested by the name, Direct3D renders in 3D. Everything in 3D is represented by a physical position in 3D space. To define the position of anything, you

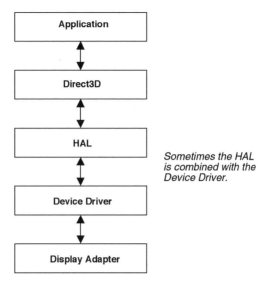

FIGURE 5.1 The relationship between your application, Direct3D, and the display adapter.

use a set of coordinates—x,y,z. This is called a Cartesian coordinate system, of which there are two types—a left-handed and a right-handed system. Direct3D uses a left-handed Cartesian coordinate system to represent 3D space. Under both systems the x and y coordinates operate in the same way as in a 2D system, with the positive x-axis pointing to your right, and the positive y-axis pointing straight up. When you move to 3D you add the third dimension, which is the z-axis. In a left-handed system the positive z-axis points away from you, while in a right-handed system the positive z-axis points toward you. Figure 5.2 shows the difference between the two Cartesian coordinate systems.

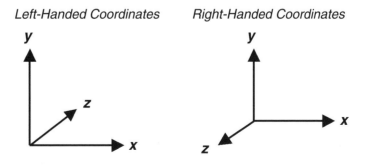

FIGURE 5.2 The difference between the two types of Cartesian coordinate systems.

Direct3D uses *primitives* to render things in this 3D space. In Chapter 2, we looked at 3D geometry and the role that vertices, edges, and faces play. Primitives are really nothing more than 3D geometrical shapes made up of vertices, which can be connected by edges to form faces. The simplest primitive is a single vertex located in 3D space. The most common type of primitive that we will work with is a triangle, or polygon (called a face). A face is made up of three vertices that are connected to form a triangle-shaped face. Complex meshes can be created when you combine multiple faces. Everything from a cube to a car or a human character are all made from simple triangular faces. When you apply textures to the triangles Direct3D can render them so that they look like the intended object.

As you should already be aware (from Chapter 2), a face has what is called a face normal. The face normal indicates which side of the face is the front side, calculated by the order in which the vertices that make the face are specified. Since Direct3D uses a left-handed coordinate system, you must specify a face's vertices in a clockwise order to achieve the correct face normal. The face normal is a perpendicular vector that points away from the front of the face. It is used by Direct3D to determine if a face is visible or not. If a face's normal is pointing away from the view point (i.e., the virtual eye that views the 3D world), then Direct3D determines that the face is not visible, so it is not rendered—this is called *back face culling*. Figure 5.3 shows how Direct3D culls back faces.

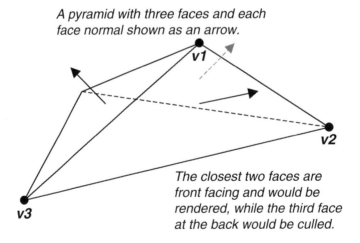

A pyramid with three faces and each face normal shown as an arrow.

v1

v2

The closest two faces are front facing and would be rendered, while the third face at the back would be culled.

v3

FIGURE 5.3   The face normal used by Direct3D for back face culling.

Not only does every face have a normal, but every vertex also has a normal. This is called the *vertex normal* and it is used for calculating effects such as lighting. Basically, Direct3D calculates the amount of light that hits a surface based on the angle between the light source and the vertex normal. Figure 5.4 shows how Direct3D uses the vertex normal to calculate lighting across a set of faces.

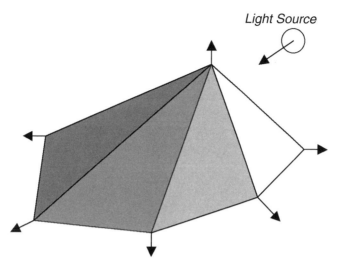

Light Source

*The extreme difference in lighting between the two
faces at either end is due to the angles between
each vertex norma and the light source.*

FIGURE 5.4   The vertex normal used for lighting.

Direct3D can also apply different types of shading to the faces. Figure 5.4 shows faces that are lit with flat shading, which means that each face is shaded with a single color and intensity. Direct3D also offers Gouraud shading, where the color and intensity on each vertex is calculated and then interpolated across the surface of the face, which gives far superior image quality. Figure 5.5 is an example of how Gouraud shading works. We will use this type of shading by default for all of our rendering.

Another interesting aspect of Direct3D is its ability to texture primitives. This is another area where the face normal comes into play as Direct3D only applies textures to the front side of a face. In order to correctly place a texture across a face—and even across multiple faces—Direct3D uses texture coordinates. Every vertex that is used by a face to be textured should have texture coordinates. Textures are divided into what are called *texels*, which are the individual color values in a texture. The texels are stored like a grid across the texture with the columns being referred to as a texel's *u* value and the rows being referred to as a texel's *v* value. So each u,v coordinate references one texel from the texture. A texture coordinate specifies where the texture should be applied to the vertex. In other words, you specify a u, v coordinate and Direct3D maps the texture onto the vertex starting at that u,v coordinate. Figure 5.6 shows how a texture is mapped to a face using u,v texture coordinates.

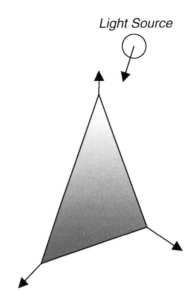

Light Source

FIGURE 5.5 An example of Gouraud shading.

Despite the u,v coordinates ranging from 0 to 1, the texture can be any pixel size you like (such as 512, 512).

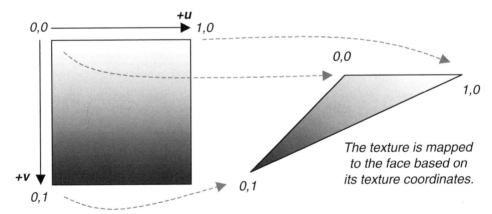

The texture is mapped to the face based on its texture coordinates.

FIGURE 5.6 Mapping a texture to a face using u,v texture coordinates.

As you can see, Direct3D can do quite a bit, but the amazing part is that we have barely scratched the surface. Direct3D is capable of far more than what we have briefly covered. Unfortunately, we don't have enough pages to cover every exciting aspect of Direct3D. So, it's time to move on to something a little more specific: the Direct3D device (referred to as the *device*).

THE DEVICE

The device is the heart of Direct3D. Other than the Direct3D object itself, the device is one of the first objects you will create and the last one you will destroy. Every device is created specifically to run on the display adapter within the computer it is created on. The reason for this is that each display adapter, its driver, and the HAL created for it, is different in terms of capabilities. Not only that, but also there are a host of parameters that you can adjust when creating the device. This means that any given device is extremely specific to the given instance of the application. When the device is destroyed and re-created, it can very well be different again.

Direct3D can create two types of devices. The HAL device (which is the one you always want to use) and the reference device. The HAL device—as we previously mentioned—is specific to the current display adapter and supports only the capabilities of that piece of hardware. The advantage is that Direct3D can run all supported functions through the hardware, which is extremely fast. The reference device, however, is pretty much the opposite. It supports every feature of Direct3D as it is implemented entirely in software; the disadvantage is that it is very slow.

Under almost all circumstances you should use the HAL device. The only time you should use the reference device is when you want to test a feature of Direct3D that your HAL device does not support.

When you create a new device, there are a number of parameters that you can set to control how the device behaves. Some of the most common include the color depth, resolution, and the refresh rate. However, the device also supports many advanced settings for everything from stencil buffers to anti-aliasing. Just as the HAL has different capabilities, so does the display adapter which can only support particular parameters. Valid combinations of these parameters are referred to as *display modes*. A device is made up of the display adapter on which it runs and the display mode—and settings—selected for it to operate under. Since there are countless combinations of devices that can be created on your display adapter, it is often necessary to enumerate the display adapter. This means that we query the display adapter for all the valid combinations of parameters with which to create a device.

Rather than talking about enumerating the display adapter, let's move on to the next section where we will present a class that can enumerate our display adapter and then display the options to the user using a dialog. The various parameters can be selected and a valid device will be created from the selection.

DISPLAY MODE STRUCTURE

There is one last thing we need to do before we see the `DeviceEnumeration` class. We must look at a little structure called the `DisplayMode` structure (found in `DeviceEnumeration.h`). The `DisplayMode` structure will store the details of a single valid display mode with which we can create a device. Here is the definition of the structure:

```
struct DisplayMode
{
  D3DDISPLAYMODE mode;
  char bpp[6];
};
```

If you haven't picked up on it yet, we have just created this structure to be a wrapper around the `D3DDISPLAYMODE` structure that is already provided for us by Direct3D. The reason that we have done this is because Direct3D does not work with individual color depths. Instead, it works with display formats, which define how the color data of each pixel on the screen is stored. Table 5.1 shows some common display formats used by Direct3D.

TABLE 5.1 Common Display Formats

D3DFMT_X1R5G5B5	16-bit color—5 bits for each color and 1 reserved bit.
D3DFMT_A1R5G5B5	16-bit color—5 bits for each color and a 1 bit alpha channel.
D3DFMT_R5G6B5	16-bit color—5 bits each for red and blue and 6 bits for green.
D3DFMT_X8R8G8B8	32-bit color—8 bits for each color and 8 reserved bits.
D3DFMT_A8R8G8B8	32-bit color—8 bits for each color and an 8 bit alpha channel.
D3DFMT_A2R10G10B10	32-bit color—10 bits for each color and a 2 bit alpha channel.

From a programmer's point of view it is perfectly fine to work directly with these display formats. However, from a user's point of view it can be a little confusing. When was the last time you went into the options of a computer game to change the color depth, and you were presented with a list of display formats? So to make life a little easier for our end user we will store a little string that will be a textual description of the display format, in a recognizable format. So D3DFMT_A1R5G5B5 would be represented by "16 bpp" and D3DFMT_A8R8G8B8 would be represented by "32 bpp" for example—where bpp stands for *bits per pixel*, which is just another way of referring to color depth.

Finally, let's have a quick look at the definition of the D3DDISPLAYMODE structure provided by Direct3D.

```
typedef struct _D3DDISPLAYMODE {
  UINT Width;        // Width of the display area.
  UINT Height;       // Height of the display area.
  UINT RefreshRate;  // Refresh rate of the display.
  D3DFORMAT Format;  // Display format (colour depth).
} D3DDISPLAYMODE;
```

Both the Width and Height are specified in pixels, and should generally match the size of the application's window. The RefreshRate is a measure of how often the display updates, and is usually specified between 60 Hz and 85 Hz. Finally, the Format is what stores one of the display formats that we have already talked about.

Direct3D offers a lot more display formats than what you saw in Table 5.1, however, these are some of the most common formats and therefore the formats that we will be working with. If you would like to see a complete list of display formats offered by Direct3D, refer to the D3DFORMAT *enumerated type under the Direct3D reference section of the DirectX SDK documentation.*

Now that we have a place to store our display formats that will be enumerated from the display adapter, we can look at the DeviceEnumeration class.

DISPLAY ADAPTER ENUMERATION

Let's quickly recap some of the important points that have brought us this far. By now you are aware of the Direct3D device. It is used by Direct3D to handle all of our rendering. There are two types of devices that Direct3D can create: the HAL device and the reference device. We are only interested in the HAL device as the reference device (despite being 100% accurate in terms of capabilities) is far too slow for an interactive 3D application. The HAL device is specific to the video card (which we call the display adapter) in your computer. In other words, it is designed to support the capabilities of that particular display adapter. For this reason, we need to create a device that specifically addresses that HAL, which means the device used for one display adapter will be different from the device used for another display adapter. In addition to this, the display adapter probably won't support every combination of display modes. For example, some display adapters won't support resolutions of 1600×1200, and some may not support refresh rates greater that 100 Hz. Since the device can be created with so many different parameters it makes it difficult to specify the creation of one device combination and expect it to work across multiple computers, each with a different display adapter. This is especially true when creating multiplayer games as you can guarantee that the game will be played on more computers than just your own.

As you can see, it makes perfect sense to provide the end user with a means to customize the setup of the device to operate correctly on his particular computer. At the simplest form it could be a matter of allowing the user to select a resolution; however, you don't have to stop there. You can make it as elaborate as you like, allowing the user to adjust every aspect of the device's creation. To see a good example, just run any of the sample applications that ship with the DirectX SDK (they can be found in the DirectX Sample Browser) and press the F2 key once it is running. The Direct3D Settings dialog will open. If you have a quick look at this dialog you will see how many different options you can adjust when creating the device. In our engine, we will use a dialog similar to this, but not half as elaborate. We will simply support the most commonly adjusted parameters, such as whether or not the user wants to run in a windowed mode. If the user opts for a full screen mode, we will allow parameters such as the v-sync, color depth, resolution, and refresh rate to be adjusted.

To handle this entire enumeration process we will use the `DeviceEnumeration` class. The implementation of this class is a bit lengthy, and may seem somewhat daunting at first. But as with anything, if you start playing with it—changing things around to see their effects—you will eventually learn how it works. This is one of the best ways to learn any form of programming. When you find code you don't understand, start tinkering with it. Rewrite it in your own style and adjust things you don't like. By doing these simple exercises you will soon master the topic at hand. Before you rush off to start playing, let's at least have a look at the `DeviceEnumeration` class so you have an idea of how it all works. We will start with the class definition, as shown below (found in `DeviceEnumeration.h`).

```
class DeviceEnumeration
{
public:
  INT_PTR Enumerate( IDirect3D9 *d3d, HWND window );

  INT_PTR SettingsDialogProc( HWND dialog, UINT uiMsg,
                              WPARAM wParam, LPARAM lParam );
```

```
    D3DDISPLAYMODE *GetSelectedDisplayMode();
    bool IsWindowed();
    bool IsVSynced();

private:
    void ComboBoxAdd( HWND dialog, int id, void *data, char *desc );
    void ComboBoxSelect( HWND dialog, int id, int index );
    void ComboBoxSelect( HWND dialog, int id, void *data );
    void *ComboBoxSelected( HWND dialog, int id );
    bool ComboBoxSomethingSelected( HWND dialog, int id );
    int ComboBoxCount( HWND dialog, int id );
    bool ComboBoxContainsText( HWND dialog, int id, char *text );

private:
    Script *m_settingsScript

    D3DADAPTER_IDENTIFIER9 m_adapter;
    LinkedList< DisplayMode > *m_displayModes;
    D3DDISPLAYMODE m_selectedDisplayMode;
    bool m_windowed;
    bool m_vsync;
};
```

You probably agree that it is starting to look a bit ugly, but don't be concerned—we'll break it down. The first interesting point to note about this class is that it has no constructor or destructor. This is simply because the class is a utility class that does not need to allocate any permanent memory. What this means is that the class is a one-off use class that is invoked when the engine is loaded to create the device. Once the device is created, this class is never touched again. All of the class's functionality can be wrapped up inside a few public functions that create and destroy any memory that it needs within these function calls. The first two functions—Enumerate and SettingsDialogProc—are of particular interest to us, so we will explore them after we have covered the rest of the class definition.

After you have used the class to enumerate the display adapter and the user has selected his desired options, the first step is to determine if the user wants to run in windowed mode. This is achieved with a call to the IsWindowed function, which will return true if the user wants to run in a window. Running in a window is fairly straightforward as the entire required device setup information is already available to you—we will discuss this later. If, however, the function returns false, then the user wants to run in full screen. Once you have determined the window mode you can use the GetSelectedDisplayMode function, which will return to you a pointer to the D3DDISPLAYMODE containing the details of the display mode configuration that the user selected. This will give you the resolution (i.e., width and height of the screen), the refresh rate, and the display format with which to create the device. Additionally, you can use the IsVSynced function, which will return true if the user wants the display to sync to the refresh rate. This means that the video card will wait until the monitor is ready to refresh the display before rendering the next frame. This allows for smoother animation and reduces visual artifacts such as tearing (when the image appears to tear across the screen due to fast movement). However, it means that rendering updates will be capped to the refresh rate of the monitor. This is generally not a problem because a monitor's refresh rate is usually at least 60 Hz.

TIP

Direct3D refers to the v-sync as the presentation interval. The default is a presentation interval of one, which means that the video card updates every time the monitor refreshes. This is synonymous to the v-sync being enabled. You can tell when v-sync is enabled, because the frame rate runs at the same speed as the refresh rate.

Within the DeviceEnumeration class there are a number of private functions used for manipulating combo boxes. A combo box is just a common Windows control that looks like a text box with a little arrow on the right—you have probably used one a number of times. When you click on the arrow, a list of options appears below. We will be using combo boxes on the dialog to allow the user to select from the valid options for the device creation on his display adapter. These functions are used for various forms of combo box manipulation. We won't cover their implementation because they are only used by the dialog window. You will never need to use them directly; hence the reason why they are declared as private, which means that they cannot be accessed outside of this class. If you are interested in how they work, take a look in DeviceEnumeration.cpp, at the end of the file.

Finally, the DeviceEnumeration class has a number of member variables, which we will run through now. First, we have m_settingsScript, which is a script. We are actually making use of our new scripting system. Since we didn't have a sample application to test the scripting, you will get to see it at work here when we have finished implementing our display adapter enumeration system. m_settingsScript will store the user's selected display settings. After enumeration is completed, the engine will write the settings to the script so that it can be loaded next time. This will prevent the user from having to reenter the settings every time the engine is started. The engine can read from the script and set itself up from the stored selection.

Next, we have `m_adapter`, which is a `D3DADAPTER_IDENTIFIER9` structure. This structure contains all of the information about the display adapter in the user's computer. Here is the definition of the structure:

```
typedef struct _D3DADAPTER_IDENTIFIER9 {
  // Name and description of the driver (for presentation only).
  char Driver[MAX_DEVICE_IDENTIFIER_STRING];
  char Description[MAX_DEVICE_IDENTIFIER_STRING];

  char DeviceName[32]; // Name of the display adapter.

  // Identifies the version of the 32 bit driver components.
  // Use this for Win32 applications.
  LARGE_INTEGER DriverVersion;

  // Identifies the version of the 16 bit driver components.
  // These are not available for Win32 applications.
  DWORD DriverVersionLowPart;
  DWORD DriverVersionHighPart;

  DWORD VendorId; // Identifies the manufacturer of the chip set.
  DWORD DeviceId; // Identifies the type of chip set.
  DWORD SubSysId; // Identifies the board.
  DWORD Revision; // Identifies the chip set's revision level.
  GUID DeviceIdentifier; // Unique identifier for the adapter.
  DWORD WHQLLevel; // The adapter's WHQL validation level.
} D3DADAPTER_IDENTIFIER9;
```

This structure is extremely extensive and we don't need this much information. We will use the structure for one purpose: to display the name and driver version of the display adapter in the user's computer. This information is not really necessary, but we will present it anyway since it is simple to do.

The last four member variables are used for storing information about how to create the device. `m_displayModes` is a linked list of display modes, which will store all of the valid display mode combinations after the display adapter has been enumerated. Once the user selects a display mode it will be stored in `m_selectedDisplayMode` so that you can access it to create the device based on the user's selected settings. The last two—`m_windowed` and `m_vsync`—indicate if the user has selected windowed mode and v-sync, respectively. As previously mentioned, these settings are accessed using `IsWindowed` and `IsVSynced`, respectively.

ENUMERATING DISPLAY MODES

When we looked at the `DeviceEnumeration` class, there were two functions that we were particularly interested in: `Enumerate` and `SettingsDialogProc`. Let's look at the implementation of the first of these two functions—`Enumerate`. This function is used to begin the whole display adapter enumeration process. It accepts a pointer to a Direct3D object as input, which is used to gain access to the display adapter information and for enumeration purposes.

```
INT_PTR DeviceEnumeration::Enumerate( IDirect3D9 *d3d )
{
  m_displayModes = new LinkedList< DisplayMode >;

  m_settingsScript = new Script( "DisplaySettings.txt" );

  d3d->GetAdapterIdentifier( D3DADAPTER_DEFAULT, 0, &m_adapter );
```

The first step is to prepare some of the member variables for enumeration. First, the display modes linked list is created, and then we create a new script called `DisplaySettings.txt` and assign a pointer to it, which is stored in `m_settingsScript`. Finally, we gain access to our display adapter's information with a call to `GetAdapterIdentifier`, which is exposed by the Direct3D object. For the first parameter we pass in `D3DADAPTER_DEFAULT`, to indicate that we want the details of the primary adapter. The only other important parameter is the last one, which is a pointer to the `D3DADAPTER_IDENTIFIER9` structure that you want filled with the adapter's information.

```
D3DFORMAT allowedFormats[6];
allowedFormats[0] = D3DFMT_X1R5G5B5;
allowedFormats[1] = D3DFMT_A1R5G5B5;
allowedFormats[2] = D3DFMT_R5G6B5;
allowedFormats[3] = D3DFMT_X8R8G8B8;
allowedFormats[4] = D3DFMT_A8R8G8B8;
allowedFormats[5] = D3DFMT_A2R10G10B10;
```

What we are doing here is creating a list of display formats that we are interested in finding display modes for. We are only interested in 16-bit and 32-bit display formats, and we only really care for the most commonly found of these formats. When we enumerate the adapter it can potentially return many different display formats that it supports. The problem is that we don't want to use all of the available formats because they are not all appropriate. For example, there are a number of 8-bit formats that your display adapter may support, but we don't want an 8-bit format because it is restricted to 256 colors. That is far too few colors to produce acceptable image quality. To combat this, we decide which formats we want to support and then enumerate the adapter looking for display modes that use these formats. This brings us to the next step, which is to enter into a `for` loop to enumerate the adapter using each of the formats that we are interested in.

```
for( char af = 0; af < 6; af++ )
{
  unsigned long totalAdapterModes = d3d->GetAdapterModeCount(
                    D3DADAPTER_DEFAULT, allowedFormats[af] );
```

As soon as we enter a new iteration of the `for` loop we immediately request (from Direct3D) the total number of display modes that the adapter supports for the display format that we are checking against. We retrieve this information from the `GetAdapterModeCount` function exposed by the Direct3D object. We always use `D3DADAPTER_DEFAULT` to indicate that we are only interested in the primary display adapter. We also pass to the function the display format for which we want to know how many display modes are available. Once we have the total number of display modes that this adapter supports using the specified display format, we enter into a second `for` loop. This time we are looping through each of these particular display modes that the adapter supports.

```
for( unsigned long m = 0; m < totalAdapterModes; m++ )
{
  D3DDISPLAYMODE mode;
  d3d->EnumAdapterModes( D3DADAPTER_DEFAULT,
                    allowedFormats[af], m, &mode );
```

Once in this loop, we first ask Direct3D for the display mode in question and store it in the temporary `D3DDISPLAYMODE` structure called `mode`. We then use the `EnumAdapterModes` to gain access to the details of a particular display mode. As usual, we use `D3DADAPTER_DEFAULT` to indicate that we are working with the primary adapter. We also pass in the display format that we are currently looking at, as well as the index of the display mode that we want the details of. Next, we do a quick little check to see if the display mode is too small. Any display modes that have a height less than 480 pixels is too small for our purposes. The minimum resolution that we want to support is 640×480 pixels. If the display format is too small we skip it with the `continue` keyword. Remember that the `continue` keyword makes control return back to the next iteration of the immediately enclosing loop in which the keyword was encountered.

```
if( mode.Height < 480 )
  continue;

DisplayMode *displayMode = new DisplayMode;
memcpy( &displayMode->mode, &mode,
        sizeof( D3DDISPLAYMODE ) );
if( af < 3 )
  strcpy( displayMode->bpp, "16 bpp" );
else
  strcpy( displayMode->bpp, "32 bpp" );

m_displayModes->Add( displayMode );
  }
}
```

If the display mode passes our size test, it is considered to be a valid display mode. We then create a new DisplayMode structure and copy the details of the display mode into it using memcpy. The next step is to create a little textual description to represent the display format, which we will later use to display the color depth to the user. Since we know that our first three display formats use 16-bit color, we can check this and then create an appropriate description. This textual description is stored in the bpp char array found within the DisplayMode structure. Finally, we add the new display mode to our linked list of display modes. We then return to the start of the loop to check the next display mode. Once we have checked all of the display modes for the current display format, we go back to the beginning of the first loop to start the process again with the next display format that we are interested in.

```
return DialogBox( NULL,
                  MAKEINTRESOURCE( IDD_GRAPHICS_SETTINGS ),
                  NULL, SettingsDialogProcDirector );
}
```

By the time the function reaches this point it will have completed enumerating the display adapter. The linked list m_displayModes will be filled with all of the valid display modes that the adapter supports for the display formats that we were interested in. We are now ready to present it to the user so that he can decide which of the valid display modes he wants the device to operate with. This is the purpose of our last line of code in the function. The `DialogBox` function will create the dialog that you specify and display it to the user. Here is the prototype for the `DialogBox` function:

```
INT_PTR DialogBox
(
  HINSTANCE hInstance, // Handle of the executable's module.
  LPCTSTR lpTemplate,  // Template of the dialog box to load.
  HWND hWndParent,     // Handle of the application's window.
  DLGPROC lpDialogFunc // Dialog procedure call-back function.
);
```

The first parameter of the function can be safely ignored and left as NULL. The second parameter is an identifier that instructs the function as to which dialog needs to be loaded. We use the MAKEINTRESOURCE macro to convert the name of the dialog (which is an `integer` value) into a resource type that is compatible with the function. Don't worry about where the dialog came from, or how you create it, as we are going to cover all of that next. You can safely ignore the handle to the parent (application's) window, by setting it to NULL. The last parameter is the function that is to be used as the dialog's procedure call-back, just like the main application window. We will further discuss this later in this chapter.

DIALOG RESOURCES

Whenever you use a Windows application you will more often than not encounter various windows with controls on them. These controls can range from buttons to text boxes (or edit boxes) to combo boxes and tree controls, just to name a few. All of these controls are placed on a window that you can usually resize, minimize, close, and so forth. A dialog (sometimes called a dialog box) is really just a window that is used to query the user for input—and is therefore a temporary window created by the main application window. The dialog can contain any controls necessary in order to receive the appropriate input from the user.

Visual C++ allows you to add dialogs to your project, which may be activated at runtime as you saw previously when we called the `DialogBox` function. When you create the dialog you must give it a name that you will use to reference the dialog at runtime. If you take another look at the `DialogBox` call we made in the Enumerate function, you will see that we told it to load the dialog called IDD_GRAPHICS_SETTINGS, which is the name of the dialog we are going to use to solicit the graphics settings from the user. When you create new dialogs, you can customize them as you like and add any controls that you need. Every time you add a new control to a dialog, you must also give the control a unique name, which is used at runtime to manipulate the control and access any information from it that the user may have entered.

Dialogs are stored in a special script file that Visual C++ uses called a resource template (.rc files). If you were to look inside one of these files with a text editor you would see that it has much information in it about the various resources that are stored. If there are any dialogs in there, you would notice that it specifies all the details about each control on the dialog, such as its name, position, and any details specific to that control. The Test project in the workspace for this chapter has a resource template file in it called Resource.rc (it is actually located in the Engine directory, but included in the Test project), which includes all the details about our graphics settings dialog. When in Visual C++, you can view the resources that are stored in the file and open them. If you open our graphics settings dialog you will see all of the controls on it.

If you decide to experiment with the graphics settings dialog, just remember that the code relies on those controls and their unique names. So you may find that the application might crash unexpectedly if it attempts to access a control that you have changed or deleted.

When you add and save a new resource in a project for the first time, Visual C++ will ask you to specify the name of the new resource template file that will store your resources. When you save it, Visual C++ will create a second file called resource.h. The Engine project in the workspace for this chapter has one of these header files in it. If you open it you will see a list of #define statements. This header file defines the names of each dialog and each control so that you can access them at runtime.

In order to use our new dialog resource we need to link these two files into the appropriate projects. It is important to note that the resource template file must be accessible by the application executable. In other words, you must include it in the project that builds the actual executable. We have two projects: the Engine project and the Test project. The Engine project does not build an executable (it creates a library file), so it does not need the resource template file. The Test project on the other hand does build an executable and will need the resource template file. The Resource.h file needs to be accessed by any project that needs to use the resources. Since our engine will be accessing the graphics settings dialog and its controls at runtime, the Resource.h file needs to be included into the Engine project.

So, simply put, we need to add the resource template file to the Test project (or whichever project is building the executable), and the Resource.h file to the Engine project. To add the `Resource.h` file to the engine, it is just a matter of adding another `#include` statement within the `Engine.h` file along with the other already existing engine includes. Adding the resource template file to the `Test` project is even easier. You don't need to add any code; the file just needs to be present in the project. You can see how this is all set up by opening the workspace for this chapter and looking at how the two files are positioned.

Although the two files are separated across the two projects, they must be physically located together on the hard drive (in the same directory) because the resource template file relies on the `Resource.h` file. This can be altered by opening up the resource template file in the text editor and adjusting the path to the `Resource.h` file if necessary.

USING DIALOGS AT RUNTIME

We now have our graphics settings dialog linked with our engine, and we have our display adapter enumeration up and running—well, almost. There are two more steps we need to take before we can use the whole enumeration system. At the end of the `Enumerate` function we made a call to `DialogBox` in order to display our graphics settings dialog to the user. The next step is to retrieve the information from the dialog so that we know how the user wants the device to be created. The final step is then to integrate the whole display adapter enumeration process into our engine. Before we do that, let's have a quick look at how we will use the dialog resource to get the required information from the user.

We have already learned that a dialog is just another type of window, and if you remember in Chapter 2 (when we created the main application window), you know that windows receive messages. Therefore, we can conclude that dialogs also receive messages, which is exactly how they are used. Whenever the user interacts with the dialog, a message is sent to the dialog informing it of the event that occurred. Some examples include the user's clicking on a control on the dialog or entering some data into one of the dialog's controls. Some events are specifically for the dialog itself, such as when the user activates, closes, moves, or resizes the dialog (assuming those actions are possible with the dialog in question). In order to handle these events when they occur at runtime, you need to assign a dialog procedure call-back function (called a `DialogProc`) to the dialog, in the same way that we used a window procedure call-back function for the main application window in Chapter 2. In fact, the dialog procedure call-back function works in exactly the same way as the window procedure call-back function. So we won't bother going through the details of how the function works; instead, we will just take a look at some of the important events that we will support within the function.

The function that we are using for our dialog procedure call-back is the SettingsDialogProc. It is assigned to the actual dialog when you call the DialogBox function—it is specified as a parameter of the function. Now you may notice that we are not passing the actual name of the dialog procedure call-back function; instead, we are passing another function called SettingsDialogProcDirector. This function is just a director, which calls the SettingsDialogProc function in our DeviceEnumeration class using the global g_deviceEnumeration pointer. We cannot use the SettingsDialogProc function directly as it belongs to a class that needs to be instantiated.

Once we are inside the SettingsDialogProc, we use a switch statement to determine the message that has been received. The first message that we are interested in handling is the WM_INITDIALOG message, which is received when the dialog is loaded. The following code is used to prepare the dialog and load in the initial settings for all the controls, as shown here:

```
// Display the adapter details and its driver version.
char version[16];
sprintf( version, "%d",
         LOWORD( m_adapter.DriverVersion.LowPart ) );
Edit_SetText( GetDlgItem( dialog, IDC_DISPLAY_ADAPTER ),
              m_adapter.Description );
Edit_SetText( GetDlgItem( dialog, IDC_DRIVER_VERSION ), version );

// Check if the settings script has anything in it.
if( m_settingsScript->GetBoolData( "windowed" ) == NULL )
{
  // The settings script is empty, so default to windowed mode.
  CheckDlgButton( dialog, IDC_WINDOWED, m_windowed = true );
}
else
{
  // Load the window mode state.
  CheckDlgButton( dialog, IDC_WINDOWED, m_windowed =
                  *m_settingsScript->GetBoolData( "windowed" ) );
  CheckDlgButton( dialog, IDC_FULLSCREEN, !m_windowed );

  // Check if running in fullscreen mode.
  if( m_windowed == false )
  {
    // Enable all the fullscreen controls.
    EnableWindow( GetDlgItem( dialog, IDC_VSYNC ), true );
    EnableWindow( GetDlgItem( dialog, IDC_DISPLAY_FORMAT ),
                  true );
```

```
EnableWindow( GetDlgItem( dialog, IDC_RESOLUTION ), true );
EnableWindow( GetDlgItem( dialog, IDC_REFRESH_RATE ), true );

// Load the vsync state.
CheckDlgButton( dialog, IDC_VSYNC, m_vsync =
                *m_settingsScript->GetBoolData( "vsync" ) );

// Fill in the display formats combo box.
ComboBox_ResetContent( GetDlgItem( dialog,
                       IDC_DISPLAY_FORMAT ) );
m_displayModes->Iterate( true );
while( m_displayModes->Iterate() )
  if( !ComboBoxContainsText( dialog, IDC_DISPLAY_FORMAT,
      m_displayModes->GetCurrent()->bpp ) )
    ComboBoxAdd( dialog, IDC_DISPLAY_FORMAT,
            (void*)m_displayModes->GetCurrent()->mode.Format,
             m_displayModes->GetCurrent()->bpp );
ComboBoxSelect( dialog, IDC_DISPLAY_FORMAT,
                *m_settingsScript->GetNumberData( "bpp" ) );


char text[16];

// Fill in the resolutions combo box.
ComboBox_ResetContent( GetDlgItem( dialog, IDC_RESOLUTION ) );
m_displayModes->Iterate( true );
while( m_displayModes->Iterate() )
{
  if( m_displayModes->GetCurrent()->mode.Format ==
      (D3DFORMAT)PtrToUlong( ComboBoxSelected( dialog,
       IDC_COLOUR_DEPTH ) ) )
  {
    sprintf( text, "%d x %d",
            m_displayModes->GetCurrent()->mode.Width,
            m_displayModes->GetCurrent()->mode.Height );
    if( !ComboBoxContainsText( dialog, IDC_RESOLUTION,
                               text ) )
      ComboBoxAdd( dialog, IDC_RESOLUTION,
                   (*void)MAKELONG(
                   m_displayModes->GetCurrent()->mode.Width,
                   m_displayModes->GetCurrent()->mode.Height
                   ), text );
  }
}
ComboBoxSelect( dialog, IDC_RESOLUTION,
          *m_settingsScript->GetNumberData( "resolution" ) );
```

```
// Fill in the refresh rates combo box.
ComboBox_ResetContent( GetDlgItem( dialog,
                        IDC_REFRESH_RATE ) );
m_displayModes->Iterate( true );
while( m_displayModes->Iterate() )
{
  if( (DWORD)MAKELONG(
        m_displayModes->GetCurrent()->mode.Width,
        m_displayModes->GetCurrent()->mode.Height ) ==
        (DWORD)PtrToUlong( ComboBoxSelected( dialog,
        IDC_RESOLUTION ) ) )
  {
    sprintf( text, "%d Hz",
              m_displayModes->GetCurrent()->mode.RefreshRate );
      if( !ComboBoxContainsText( dialog, IDC_REFRESH_RATE,
                                 text ) )
        ComboBoxAdd( dialog, IDC_REFRESH_RATE,
              (*void)m_displayModes->GetCurrent()
                                  ->mode.RefreshRate ), text );
  }
  }
  ComboBoxSelect( dialog, IDC_REFRESH_RATE,
                *m_settingsScript->GetNumberData( "refresh" ) );
  }
}
```

That is one scary looking piece of code! We will simply run through what is actually happening here; we won't dissect it line by line because it is very specific to this dialog and these controls. A lot of the code is just manipulating the dialog and its controls, which we are not interested in. We just want to focus on how this affects our whole process of display adapter enumeration. The comments have been left in to make it a little easier for you to follow the code.

First, we display the name of the display adapter and its driver version to the user. To do this we use the m_adapter D3DADAPTER_IDENTIFIER9 structure that we filled back in the Enumerate function. The second step is to check if the settings script is present. The first time the application runs, the settings script will not exist, so by default we set up the dialog so that windowed mode is selected. If there is a valid settings script, then we read the settings from it and set up all the controls on the dialog so that they match the settings in the script. If the settings script indicates that it should run in windowed mode, then it is easy to set up as we can ignore all the controls for selecting a display mode combination. Otherwise, we have to go through each of the display mode controls and set them based on the settings in the script.

The first step (when running in full screen mode) is to enable all of the controls for selecting a display mode. These controls are disabled by default, as the default setting is to run in windowed mode. We then need to set the checkbox based on the flag for the v-sync. It if is true, then we check the checkbox; otherwise, it is cleared. The final step is to fill in the combo boxes for each of the three display mode settings—the display formats, the resolutions, and the refresh rates. When we fill in each of these, we also select the appropriate setting from the list based on the setting in the script. Once the dialog is set up correctly, we are ready for the user to start adjusting the settings, which of course will send more messages to the dialog.

The next type of message that we want to support is the WM_COMMAND message. This message is sent to the dialog procedure call-back function whenever the user interacts with one of the controls on the dialog, such as clicking on it. Table 5.2 shows the controls on the dialog that we are interested in receiving messages about. It also gives a description of what we will do with that control.

TABLE 5.2 Supported Dialog Messages

IDOK	When the user clicks the OK button we want to save the selected settings and write them to the script. We then close the dialog so that the engine can carry on with creating the device.
IDCANCEL	If the user clicks the Cancel button, then we will close the dialog and return failure code so that the engine knows that the user has exited.
IDC_COLOUR_DEPTH	This combo box allows the user to select his desired color depth for full screen mode only. Once selected, the resolution combo box is updated so that only resolutions that support this color depth are displayed.
IDC_RESOLUTION	This combo box allows the user to select his desired resolution for full screen mode only. Once selected, the refresh rate combo box is updated so that only refresh rates that support this resolution are displayed.
IDC_WINDOWED IDC_FULLSCREEN	These two controls are option controls, which allow the user to select one or the other. When windowed mode is selected, all the controls for adjusting the display mode are disabled. When full screen mode is selected, all display mode controls are enabled. Additionally, the color depth combo box is filled in with the supported display formats.

Let's have a look at the code for what happens when the user clicks the OK button. Once again, the comments have been left to help you follow the code.

```
// Store the details of the selected display mode.
m_selectedDisplayMode.Width = LOWORD( PtrToUlong(
                ComboBoxSelected( dialog, IDC_RESOLUTION ) ) );
m_selectedDisplayMode.Height = HIWORD( PtrToUlong(
                ComboBoxSelected( dialog, IDC_RESOLUTION ) ) );
m_selectedDisplayMode.RefreshRate = PtrToUlong(
                ComboBoxSelected( dialog, IDC_REFRESH_RATE ) ) );
m_selectedDisplayMode.Format = (D3DFORMAT)PtrToUlong(
                ComboBoxSelected( dialog, IDC_DISPLAY_FORMAT ) ) );
m_windowed = IsDlgButtonChecked( dialog, IDC_WINDOWED ) ?
                                      true : false;
m_vsync = IsDlgButtonChecked( dialog, IDC_VSYNC ) ? true : false;

// Destroy the display modes list.
SAFE_DELETE( m_displayModes );

// Get the selected index from each combo box.
long bpp = ComboBox_GetCurSel( GetDlgItem( dialog,
                                IDC_DISPLAY_FORMAT ) );
long resolution = ComboBox_GetCurSel( GetDlgItem( dialog,
                                      IDC_RESOLUTION ) );
long refresh = ComboBox_GetCurSel( GetDlgItem( dialog,
                                    IDC_REFRESH_RATE ) );

// Check if the settings script has anything in it.
if( m_settingsScript->GetBoolData( "windowed" ) == NULL )
{
  // Add all the settings to the script.
  m_settingsScript->AddVariable( "windowed", VARIABLE_BOOL,
                                 &m_windowed );
  m_settingsScript->AddVariable( "vsync", VARIABLE_BOOL,
                                 &m_vsync );
  m_settingsScript->AddVariable( "bpp", VARIABLE_NUMBER, &bpp );
  m_settingsScript->AddVariable( "resolution", VARIABLE_NUMBER,
                                 &resolution );
  m_settingsScript->AddVariable( "refresh", VARIABLE_NUMBER,
                                 &refresh );
```

```
  }
  else
  {
    // Set all the settings.
    m_settingsScript->SetVariable( "windowed", &m_windowed );
    m_settingsScript->SetVariable( "vsync", &m_vsync );
    m_settingsScript->SetVariable( "bpp", &bpp );
    m_settingsScript->SetVariable( "resolution", &resolution );
    m_settingsScript->SetVariable( "refresh", &refresh );
  }

  // Save all the settings out to the settings script.
  m_settingsScript->SaveScript();

  // Destroy the settings script.
  SAFE_DELETE( m_settingsScript );

  // Close the dialog.
  EndDialog( dialog, IDOK );
```

First, the selected display mode details are stored in the m_selectedDisplayMode DisplayMode structure. We then destroy the linked list of display modes as it is no longer needed. Then we store the index of the selected item from each of the combo boxes. We do this because the next step is to write all the selected details to the settings script so that the next time the application is loaded, the combo boxes can have the selections restored. If the settings script is empty (which it would be the first time the application is run), we add the settings to the script; otherwise, we just change the values of the existing settings. Finally, we tell the script to save itself to file, and then we delete it since we are finished with it. The last line of code is a call to EndDialog, which allows us to close the dialog window and return a value that we can later use to determine if the user clicked the OK button or the Cancel button. Since this code is processing the OK button, we pass the ID of the OK button as the return value, which is IDOK.

There you have it. Now you can see how the dialog is used to display the different device setup options to the user and how to retrieve the user's desired settings. We didn't cover the rest of the code for the other controls on the dialog as they are fairly straightforward. If you open up DeviceEnumeration.cpp you will be able to peruse them yourself. Table 5.2—which you saw earlier—shows you an outline of what happens when the user activates the code for each control.

Now that we have our whole display adapter enumeration process implemented, we need to integrate it into the engine so that the graphics settings dialog is displayed to the user every time the engine is started. When the user selects his desired settings and clicks the OK button, we want the engine to take those settings and create a compatible Direct3D device. So let's get on with that.

INTEGRATING THE DEVICE ENUMERATION

Before we can create the device, we need to add the DeviceEnumeration class to our engine so that it can be used to gather the information needed to create the device. The first step, as usual, is to link the DeviceEnumeration.h and the DeviceEnumeration.cpp files into the Engine project. You can probably remember how this is done as we have already done it a few times in previous chapters. It is just a matter of adding the #include "DeviceEnumeration.h" statement to the Engine.h file and the #include "Engine.h" statement to the beginning of the DeviceEnumeration.cpp file. Now the class is integrated and ready to use.

You will probably notice that there are a whole lot of new additions to the Engine class; we will cover them all in due course. For now let's jump over to the Engine class constructor (found in Engine.cpp) and put our new DeviceEnumeration class to work. Before the main application window is created, you will notice a few new lines of code, similar to what is shown here:

```
IDirect3D9 *d3d = Direct3DCreate9( D3D_SDK_VERSION );

g_deviceEnumeration = new DeviceEnumeration;
if( g_deviceEnumeration->Enumerate( d3d, NULL ) != IDOK )
{
  SAFE_RELEASE( d3d );
  return;
}
```

The first line creates our Direct3D object (which is required to enumerate the display adapter) using the Direct3DCreate9 function. The function only takes one parameter, which should always be set to D3D_SDK_VERSION. It is just an identifier that DirectX uses to ensure that the application is built using the correct header files, as they can change with newer versions. The next step is to create an instance of our DeviceEnumeration class. The class comes with its own global variable called g_deviceEnumeration, which we must use for the instance of our class. The reason for this is that the dialog procedure call-back function requires access to the same instance of this class. If you remember back to when we set the dialog's procedure call-back function, you will remember that we could not use the call-back function from within the class; therefore we needed some way to access this class. To solve the problem, we use the same theory that we applied to the Engine class, which was to create an external variable that can be accessed anywhere.

Once our DeviceEnumeration class has been instantiated, we can proceed to call the Enumerate function, passing the pointer to our new Direct3D object. The call to Enumerate is wrapped inside an if statement, which checks the return value from the function. If the function returns anything but IDOK, then we know that the user did not click on the OK button on the dialog (if the user clicks the Cancel button, the function will return IDCANCEL). If this is the case then we don't want to continue creating a device, and therefore we don't want the engine to load. So, we destroy our Direct3D object and return from the Engine class constructor. This means that the m_loaded flag will not be set to true since it is the last line of code in the constructor. So when the application calls the Run function, the m_loaded flag will indicate that the engine has not been loaded and it will drop out (calling the Engine class destructor on its way). Therefore, the application will terminate.

Otherwise, if the return value is IDOK, then we can continue on to create the device. If you look at the next line of code you will see that we have made a change to how the main application window is created:

```
m_window = CreateWindow( "WindowClass", m_setup->name,
    g_deviceEnumeration->IsWindowed() ? WS_OVERLAPPED : WS_POPUP,
    0, 0, 800, 600, NULL, NULL, m_setup->instance, NULL );
```

In the past, we set the third parameter of the CreateWindow function call to WS_OVERLAPPED, which means that we created an overlapped window (i.e., a standard window with a title bar and a border). However, when you run in full screen mode, you should really use WS_POPUP, which is for a pop-up window. A pop-up window does not have any of the extras that the overlapped window has, such as the title bar and the border. They are not necessary for full screen mode as they are never seen nor used.

We know that one of the options on the graphics settings dialog is the option of running in either window or full screen mode. Since we have already asked the user for their preferences, we can now query the DeviceEnumeration class for the windowed mode so that we can decide which window style we need to use. We do this by calling the IsWindowed function and then using the ?: conditional operator on the function's return value. It is easiest to think of this operator as an if...else statement. It tests the expression (which is the value on the left of the ?) for a true/false value. If the expression evaluates to true, control is passed to the left of the : ; otherwise, control is passed to the right. So if you look back to our code you can see that if IsWindowed returns true, then WS_OVERLAPPED is used; otherwise, WS_POPUP is used.

NEW ENGINE SETUP PROPERTIES

You are probably eager to create the device so that we can start rendering things. However, before we do that we will quickly jump back and take a look at all the new entries in the EngineSetup structure. There are two new entries—float scale, and unsigned char totalBackBuffers, which are set to 1.0 and 1, respectively, by default in the structure's constructor.

When you work with 3D graphics, everything is represented in *units*. A unit is an arbitrary measurement that can be scaled to real-world measurements. For example, you may have a line in 3D space that is four units long. In the real world, this means nothing as we have no idea how long one unit is. It is like asking someone how long a piece of string is. 3D modeling packages are designed like this on purpose to allow you to decide how long a unit is—this is called the *scale*. You might decide that one unit equals one foot, or one meter, or even one kilometer or one mile. When you create the engine, you need to indicate what scale you want to operate in. This is because there are a number of components, including some aspects of DirectX, that need to know how long one unit is. DirectSound is one such component that uses a scale, as it can work with 3D sounds.

A 3D sound can be placed anywhere in 3D space and can then be heard based on its distance from an imaginary microphone that you also place somewhere in 3D space. In order for DirectSound to calculate how loud the sound is, it needs to work out the distance between the sound and the microphone. DirectSound works on the principle of how many meters can fit into one unit. Since this is the way in which DirectSound works by default (and it is one of the major components that relies on scale), we will adapt, and therefore operate using the same principle. What this means is that the scale property in the EngineSetup structure is in meters per unit. By default it is set to 1.0 (which is the same default that DirectSound uses), meaning that one meter fits into one unit. Written differently, it means that one unit equals one meter. You can change this value so that your 3D environment operates in any scale you like. For example, you may want one unit to equal two meters (effectively halving the size of everything). In this case, you would set the scale property to 0.5. You could go the other way and double the size of your 3D environment by making one unit equal to half a meter. In this case, you would set the `scale` property to 2.0. Finally, you can change the scale to operate in a measurement other than meters, such as feet, for example. To do this you just need to work out what percentage of one meter is consumed by one foot. This value then becomes your new scale. In this case, we know that one meter equals 100 centimeters and one foot equals about 30.48 centimeters. All we have to do is divide 30.48 by 100 (the number of centimeters in one meter) and we will have the scale, which is 0.3048. If you set the `scale` property to this value, your 3D environment will be scaled to operate in feet.

The last new entry in the `EngineSetup` structure is the `totalBackBuffers`. Direct3D uses what are called *back buffers* to present rendered scenes to the screen. Generally speaking, an application uses two back buffers (unless you operate in windowed mode, where you can only use one). While Direct3D is rendering the current frame onto one of the back buffers, the other one (which has the last frame drawn on it) is presented on the screen. Once Direct3D has finished rendering, it then swaps the back buffers around so that it now renders on the one that was just presented, while the one it just finished rendering to is presented to the screen. This process continues for the lifetime of the application (as long as Direct3D is rendering). If the application is running at 40 fps, it means that Direct3D is rendering, displaying, and switching the back buffers 40 times per second, which is how an animated scene is smoothly presented to the user. Figure 5.7 shows how the process works.

There are a number of different ways in which Direct3D can use the back buffers to present the scene on the screen, but we won't go into that right now. All you need to worry about at the moment is that you can adjust how many of these back buffers Direct3D will use. When you create a windowed application, Direct3D will ignore whatever value you specify here as it can only use one back buffer in windowed mode. However, in full screen mode you can use as many as you like. The most common number of back buffers is either two (called *doubled buffering*) or three (called *triple buffering*). The more buffers you use, the smoother the transition between frames, which creates smoother animation. Admittedly, it is difficult to pick up any differences with the human eye. The disadvantage to using more back buffers though, is that it consumes more memory. Let's look at an example. If you run at a resolution of 1280 × 1024 with 32-bit color depth, then one back buffer will consume 1280 × 1024 × 32 = 41,943,040 bits of memory. Since there are eight bits in one byte, this equates to 5,242,880 bytes of memory. In other words, one back buffer would use 5.2 MB of memory. If you were to use three of them, then it would consume almost 16 MB of memory on the video card. You will also want to load textures, meshes, vertex data, and so forth into video memory. So as you can see, if memory is a big issue for you then it may not be feasible to use a lot of back buffers. Alternatively, you can reduce the resolution and/or the color depth, which will lower the amount of required memory.

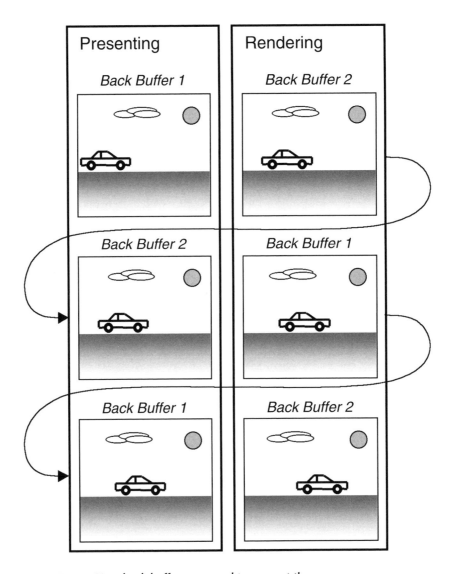

FIGURE 5.7 How back buffers are used to present the scene.

If you set the back buffer count too high, the device creation may fail. The number of back buffers that can be supported depends on the capabilities of the display adapter and the available memory. For the best compatibility you should not attempt to create a device with more than three back buffers. In fact, you may even consider making it an option for the end user. This will increase compatibility with older hardware that cannot support as many back buffers.

ENGINE CHANGES

The last thing we need to look at before we create our device is the changes that have occurred to the Engine class since the last chapter. Remember that this class will change frequently as new features are added to the engine. So let's run through what's new in this chapter.

First we have four new public functions, as shown:

```
float GetScale();
IDirect3DDevice9 *GetDevice();
D3DDISPLAYMODE *GetDisplayMode();
ID3DXSprite *GetSprite();
```

The first one is pretty obvious; it simply returns the scale that the engine is operating in. This is the same value that you set in the EngineSetup structure. The second function returns a pointer to our Direct3D device, which we will be creating shortly. The third function returns a pointer to the D3DDISPLAYMODE structure containing the current display mode details. These are the same details that the user selected when the display adapter was enumerated. The last new function returns a pointer to the ID3DXSprite interface that we will create after we have created the device. A sprite is simply a 2D image that can be drawn on the screen like a picture. Since Direct3D works entirely in 3D, the ID3DXSprite interface (which comes from the D3DX library) is intended to simplify the whole process of drawing sprites on the screen.

In addition to these new functions, there are also four new member variables, some of which are used by the above-mentioned functions. These new variables are shown here:

```
IDirect3DDevice9 *m_device;
D3DDISPLAYMODE m_displayMode;
ID3DXSprite *m_sprite;
unsigned char m_currentBackBuffer;
```

Just by looking at them, it is fairly obvious what each one stores. The first one, m_device, stores the pointer to our device that we will be creating shortly. m_displayMode is the structure that stores the current display mode that is being used by the device, and m_sprite is our ID3DXSprite interface, which is created after you create the device. The last one m_currentBackBuffer needs a little explanation. The back buffers that Direct3D uses—combined—are called a *swap chain* because the buffers are presented in a circular sequence. In other words, they are swapped around like they are connected in line by a chain. When you instruct Direct3D to present a new frame, the whole chain is pulled around one place (called a *flip*, or *flipping*), effectively rotating the buffers so that the first buffer becomes the last and the second buffer becomes the first. Figure 5.8 gives a visual illustration.

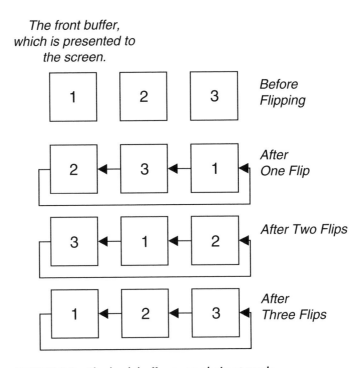

FIGURE 5.8   The back buffer swap chain at work.

m_currentBackBuffer is used to keep track of which buffer is at the front of the swap chain at any time. In other words, every time the swap chain is flipped, m_currentBackBuffer is incremented by one until it exceeds the total number of back buffers, at which point it is reset to one (the start of the swap chain). We will touch on the reasoning behind this briefly, but it will become more apparent when we develop the actual game in Part II. The game that we will create will use a dialog for its menu system (just like the graphics settings dialog). These dialogs are not rendered by Direct3D; instead, they are drawn by the Graphical Device Interface (GDI), which is part of Windows. The problem is that the GDI can only be drawn on to the first buffer in the swap chain, which means that if the swap chain is flipped around to any buffer other than the first one, the dialog will not be visible on the screen. We need to keep track of which buffer is at the front of the swap chain so that when we try to display a dialog, we can flip the swap chain around the appropriate number of times to bring the first buffer to the front of the swap chain.

DIRECT3D DEVICE CREATION

We have covered pretty much everything we need in preparation for creating our device. The device is created in the Engine class constructor (found in Engine.cpp), right after we finish enumerating the display adapter and creating the main application window.

There is quite a bit of new code that has been added here. Not all of it is specifically for creating the device, but it is all related. We will look at the creation of the device first. In the next section, we will cover the rest of the supporting code.

```
D3DPRESENT_PARAMETERS d3dpp;
ZeroMemory( &d3dpp, sizeof( D3DPRESENT_PARAMETERS ) );
d3dpp.BackBufferWidth =
      g_deviceEnumeration->GetSelectedDisplayMode()->Width;
d3dpp.BackBufferHeight =
      g_deviceEnumeration->GetSelectedDisplayMode()->Height;
d3dpp.BackBufferFormat =
      g_deviceEnumeration->GetSelectedDisplayMode()->Format;
d3dpp.BackBufferCount = m_setup->totalBackBuffers;
d3dpp.SwapEffect = D3DSWAPEFFECT_DISCARD;
d3dpp.hDeviceWindow = m_window;
d3dpp.Windowed = g_deviceEnumeration->IsWindowed();
d3dpp.EnableAutoDepthStencil = true;
d3dpp.AutoDepthStencilFormat = D3DFMT_D16;
d3dpp.FullScreen_RefreshRateInHz =
      g_deviceEnumeration->GetSelectedDisplayMode()->RefreshRate;
if( g_deviceEnumeration->IsVSynced() == true )
  d3dpp.PresentationInterval = D3DPRESENT_INTERVAL_DEFAULT;
else
  d3dpp.PresentationInterval = D3DPRESENT_INTERVAL_IMMEDIATE;
```

We start by filling in a D3DPRESENT_PARAMETERS structure. This structure is used by Direct3D to create the device; it contains virtually all of the parameters needed for setting up the device to behave in a particular way. The definition of the structure is shown here:

```
typedef struct _D3DPRESENT_PARAMETERS_ {
    // The width and height of the back buffer.
    UINT BackBufferWidth, BackBufferHeight;

    // The display format for the back buffer surface, and the
    // total number of back buffers to use.
    D3DFORMAT BackBufferFormat;
    UINT BackBufferCount;

    // Anti-aliasing support, and its quality.
    D3DMULTISAMPLE_TYPE MultiSampleType;
    DWORD MultiSampleQuality;

    // Indicates how the swap chain will be handled.
    D3DSWAPEFFECT SwapEffect;

    // Handle of the main application window.
    HWND hDeviceWindow;

    // Indicates if the device should operate in a window or not.
    BOOL Windowed;

    // Depth-stencil buffer support and the format of the buffer.
    BOOL EnableAutoDepthStencil;
    D3DFORMAT AutoDepthStencilFormat;

    // Additional creation flags from D3DPRESENTFLAG.
    DWORD Flags;

    // The refresh rate and the presentation interval (v-sync).
    UINT FullScreen_RefreshRateInHz;
    UINT PresentationInterval;
} D3DPRESENT_PARAMETERS;
```

We do not need to concern ourselves with all of the parameters, so to ensure that the ones we don't use have a default value in them, we clear the memory of the structure using ZeroMemory. After that we can start filling in the parameters of the structure that we are interested in. First, we set the back buffer width, height, and format from the settings that the user selected on the graphics settings dialog. These are accessed by calling the GetSelectedDisplayMode function from the DeviceEnumeration class. Then we reference the appropriate member of the D3DDIS-PLAYMODE structure that it returns. We also need to set the total number of back buffers that we want the swap chain to have, which we get from the `EngineSetup` structure that was passed into the constructor. The next parameter tells the device how it should handle the back buffer swap chain. Table 5.3 lists each of the three options that you can choose from.

TABLE 5.3 Swap Chain Effects

D3DSWAPEFFECT_FLIP	Uses multiple back buffers in a circular list, rotating the list every time a new frame is presented. This effect is best used on full screen applications.
D3DSWAPEFFECT_COPY	Utilizes a single back buffer (regardless of how many are set) to copy the contents of the buffer to the screen. This ensures that the back buffer contents are not changed and is best suited for windowed applications.
D3DSWAPEFFECT_DISCARD	Allows the display driver to switch between the first two effects. This is the best effect to choose in almost all circumstance as it will ensure that the most efficient swap effect is used at all times.

We will use `D3DSWAPEFFECT_DISCARD` to allow the most efficient swap effect to be chosen by the display driver. We set `hDeviceWindow` to the handle to our main application window, and indicate whether it is running in windowed or full screen mode with the `IsWindowed` function from our `DeviceEnumeration` class. Next, we indicate that we want the device to use a depth-stencil buffer, and we also set the format for the buffer. Table 5.4 shows some of the most common formats that can be set for the depth-stencil buffer.

TABLE 5.4 Common Depth-Stencil Buffer Formats

D3DFMT_D16	16-bit depth buffer.
D3DFMT_D15S1	16-bit depth buffer, 1-bit stencil buffer.
D3DFMT_D24X8	24-bit depth buffer.
D3DFMT_D24S8	24-bit depth buffer, 8-bit stencil buffer.
D3DFMT_D32	32-bit depth buffer.

The depth buffer (sometimes called the *z-buffer*) is used by Direct3D for rendering geometry in 3D space. If you have two faces in 3D space and one of them overlaps the other, the depth buffer is used to determine which face is rendered at any given pixel. Every time you render something, the pixels that are affected on the screen are tested against the depth buffer to ensure that only the face closest to the viewer actually affects the color of the pixels (unless of course you are using special effects such as transparency and alpha blending). Without the depth buffer, Direct3D has no real way to tell which face is in front of which when they are mapped to pixels on the screen. Therefore, faces can be rendered in the wrong order, causing hidden faces to become visible.

TIP

When we start rendering a real scene with plenty of faces (such as in Chapter 10), try disabling the depth buffer by setting EnableAutoDepthStencil *to false and see what happens. For our depth-stencil buffer, we will use the* D3DFMT_D16 *format, which means that we will not be using the stencil buffer. The stencil buffer is used for techniques such as stencil shadowing, silhouettes, decals, and other special effects. We won't be implementing anything like that so we don't need the stencil buffer.*

Finally, we just need to set the refresh rate and the presentation interval (which is the v-sync. We set the refresh rate based on the user's choice from the graphics settings dialog, which we get from the RefreshRate property of the D3DDISPLAYMODE structure returned by GetSelectedDisplayMode (in the DeviceEnumeration class). As for the presentation interval, we just call IsVSynced, also from the DeviceEnumeration class. If the function returns true, we set PresentationInterval to D3DPRESENT_INTERVAL_DEFAULT, which is the equivalent of switching v-sync on. If the function returns false, we set PresentationInterval to D3DPRESENT_INTERVAL_IMMEDIATE, which means that v-sync is switched off.

Once we have filled in the D3DPRESENT_PARAMETERS structure, we no longer need the DeviceEnumeration class, so we can destroy our instance of it. We then move on to creating the device as shown here:

```
SAFE_DELETE( g_deviceEnumeration );

if( FAILED( d3d->CreateDevice( D3DADAPTER_DEFAULT, D3DDEVTYPE_HAL,
            m_window, D3DCREATE_MIXED_VERTEXPROCESSING, &d3dpp,
            &m_device ) ) )
    return;

SAFE_RELEASE( d3d );
```

Creating the device is just a matter of calling the `CreateDevice` function that is exposed by the Direct3D interface. The prototype for the function is shown here:

```
HRESULT CreateDevice
(
   // Display adapter. Use D3DADAPTER_DEFAULT to indicate the
   // primary display adapter.
   UINT Adapter,

   // The device type. Use D3DDEVTYPE_HAL for a HAL device.
   D3DDEVTYPE DeviceType,

   // Handle to the application's window.
   HWND hFocusWindow,

   // Options for controlling the device creation and behavior.
   DWORD BehaviorFlags,

   // Pointer to a filled D3DPRESENT_PARAMETERS structure.
   D3DPRESENT_PARAMETERS *pPresentationParameters,

   // Address of a pointer to store the new device.
   IDirect3DDevice9** ppReturnedDeviceInterface
);
```

It is pretty much self explanatory as to what we pass in to each parameter. For the first parameter we just pass `D3DADAPTER_DEFAULT` to indicate that we want to create a device on the primary display adapter. The second parameter is set to `D3DDEVTYPE_HAL` for a HAL device. Alternatively, you could set it to `D3DDEVTYPE_REF` if you need to use the reference device to test a feature that your display adapter does not support. We then set `hFocusWindow` to `m_window`, which is the handle to our application's window. The next parameter—`BehaviorFlags`—is of interest because you can use it to set a number of flags. Most importantly, you use it to instruct the device on how it should process vertices. There are three flags that control how the device processes vertices, which are shown in Table 5.5.

For our device we will use `D3DCREATE_MIXED_VERTEXPROCESSING` so that the device can use both hardware and software vertex processing. The next parameter of the `CreateDevice` function is where we pass in a pointer to the `D3DPRESENT_PARAMETERS` structure that we filled out earlier. This allows the device to create itself based on all of the additional parameters, some of which were set by the user—using the graphics settings dialog. Finally, the last parameter is just the address of the pointer that we want to use for the new device. We will pass in the `m_device` member variable for this parameter.

TABLE 5.5 Vertex Processing Flags

D3DCREATE_HARDWARE_VERTEXPROCESSING	Vertex data is processed by the display adapter. This generally provides the best performance, however, capabilities are limited to whatever the display adapter supports.
D3DCREATE_SOFTWARE_VERTEXPROCESSING	Vertex data is processed in software by DirectX. Although not always the best for performance, it does provide a fixed set of capabilities, which are guaranteed to be the same on different computers.
D3DCREATE_MIXED_VERTEXPROCESSING	This mode allows the device to perform both hardware and software vertex processing.

When we make the call to CreateDevice, we wrap it up in an if statement to check if the function call fails, by using DirectX's FAILED macro. The function can fail for a number of reasons, such as an invalid parameter that may have been set by the user.

NOTE

Remember that (as previously mentioned) a common cause of device creation failure is the back buffer count being set too high. To minimize the chance of failure, you should also ensure that you have a compliant video card and the correct version of DirectX installed on the system. If the device creation fails, the Engine *class constructor will return without setting the* m_loaded *flag to true. This ensures that the* Run *function does not try to process. If the device is successfully created, then we no longer need the Direct3D interface, so we can safely release it.*

INTEGRATING THE DEVICE

Now we have the device created and ready to use; however, there are a number of additions to the Engine class that we must go through to allow the device to work with our engine. We will start with the Engine class constructor and pick up from where we left off. Right after we finish creating the device, we need to prepare it for use by setting some default parameters on it.

```
m_device->SetRenderState( D3DRS_LIGHTING, false );

m_device->SetSamplerState ( 0, D3DSAMP_MAGFILTER,
                               D3DTEXF_ANISOTROPIC );
m_device->SetSamplerState ( 0, D3DSAMP_MINFILTER,
                               D3DTEXF_ANISOTROPIC );
m_device->SetSamplerState( 0, D3DSAMP_MIPFILTER,
                               D3DTEXF_LINEAR );
```

There are four parameters that we want to change the default setting for on our new device. The first is the lighting, which is set to true by default. This means that Direct3D will calculate lighting on all the vertices in a scene by default. We don't want it to do that as we don't always want Direct3D to process lighting unnecessarily. For example, we may create a state for our menu system that does not need any lighting. It would be a waste for Direct3D to calculate lighting on our scene unnecessarily. To switch lighting off we make a call to SetRenderState, which is exposed by our new device. For the first parameter we pass in D3DRS_LIGHTING to indicate that we want to adjust the lighting. The second parameter we set to false to tell Direct3D to stop calculating lighting. If we need to switch lighting on for something, we can just call this function again with the same parameters, except we set the last one to true instead of false.

The SetRenderState function is a very useful function that allows you to adjust many properties that affect the device's processing. Everything from rendering quality and alpha transparency to fog and stencil buffer properties can be adjusted with this one function. It is just a matter of setting the first parameter to the property that you want to adjust and the last parameter to the value that you want to adjust the property to. There are far too many properties to list here, so instead you should take a look at the D3DRENDERSTATETYPE enumerated type in the *Reference* section of the *DirectX Graphics* section, found in the DirectX SDK documentation.

After changing the default lighting, we need to adjust the default texture filtering. There are three parameters that make up the texture filtering: the magnification filter, the minification filter, and the mipmap filter. When a texture is applied to a face it is often enlarged or shrunken to fit on the face correctly, which is called magnification and minification, respectively. The problem is that when a texture is stretched or compressed in this fashion it can lose quality. Magnification of a texture can cause it to become blocky as many screen pixels are mapped to one texture texel. Minification of a texture can cause it to become blurry as many texture texels are mapped to one screen pixel.

When a texture goes through minification it can use a number of mipmaps to improve the visual quality of the image. Mipmaps are smaller versions of the original texture, which are pre-generated either using a separate software package or during runtime when the game is loading. If a texture has a set of mipmaps, Direct3D decides which mipmap to use when the texture is rendered based on a number of factors. The problem is that when two different mipmaps of the same texture are rendered side-by-side, a hard line between them is often apparent. To remove this visual artifact and improve the transition between mipmaps, Direct3D uses the mipmap filter. The whole purpose of texture filtering is to reduce these types of visual artifacts and increase the quality of the rendered image. There are a number of different texture filtering modes that can be used. Table 5.6 shows the three most common modes of texture filtering.

TABLE 5.6 Common Texture Filtering Modes

D3DTEXF_POINT	Uses the closest texel to the desired pixel value. This is the poorest form of texture filtering; however, it is the most computationally inexpensive. This is the default texture filtering.
D3DTEXF_LINEAR	Bilinear interpolation whereby the average of a 2×2 box of texels around the desired pixel is used.
D3DTEXF_ANISOTROPIC	The best form of texture filtering that takes into account the angle between the textured face and the plane of the screen. This is also the most computationally expensive.

For the first two texture filters, we will use D3DTEXF_ANISOTROPIC, and for the mipmap filter, we will use D3DTEXF_LINEAR by default, which is set with three separate calls to SetSamplerState—also exposed by our new device. The first call sets the magnification filter by passing D3DSAMP_MAGFILTER, the second call sets the minification filter by passing D3DSAMP_MINFILTER, and the third call sets the mipmap filter by passing D3DSAMP_MIPFILTER.

The next step is to set up what is called the *projection matrix*. We will set a default projection matrix; however, it can always be changed later on if necessary. The best way to visualize the projection matrix is like thinking about the workings of a camera, as the DirectX SDK puts it. When you use a camera, you can adjust the lenses, which allow you to increase or decrease the field of view (FOV), and zoom in and out. The projection matrix is used for virtually exactly the same purpose. If you imagine the viewpoint in 3D space, which is used to view our scene—it is just like a camera. The projection matrix is used to define an imaginary pyramid that extends in the direction the camera is viewing, with the apex of the pyramid positioned where the camera exists in 3D space. Figure 5.9 gives an illustration.

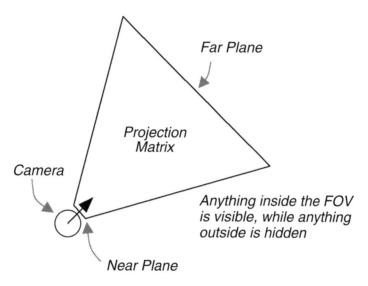

FIGURE 5.9   The projection matrix, like a pyramid, extends away from the camera in 3D space.

From Figure 5.9 you can also see that the projection matrix defines what is called a *near* and *far clipping plane*. The near clipping plane indicates that any geometry that comes closer to the camera than this clipping plane is ignored and therefore not rendered. The far clipping plane does the opposite. It indicates that any geometry that is beyond this imaginary plane is considered to be too far away from the camera, so it is ignored and therefore not rendered. This is an excellent way to help reduce the amount of faces that the engine has to render (especially when combined with some sort of fog), which is a common technique employed in many FPS games. You will often notice that when you look into the distance, the fog becomes thicker and thicker up until the point that you cannot see anything anymore. The engine is set up so that the far clipping plane sits just behind the point where the fog becomes so thick that you can no longer see anything. This way, the engine does not have to render all the faces in the distance and because of the fog, you do not realize that nothing is being rendered in the distance. Now let's look at the code for setting up our projection matrix.

```
D3DXMATRIX projMatrix;
D3DXMatrixPerspectiveFovLH( &projMatrix, D3DX_PI / 4,
    (float)d3dpp.BackBufferWidth / (float)d3dpp.BackBufferHeight,
    0.1f / m_setup->scale, 1000.0f / m_setup->scale );
m_device->SetTransform( D3DTS_PROJECTION, &projMatrix );
```

Our projection matrix is stored in a D3DXMATRIX structure, which is a generic 4 × 4 matrix used by DirectX. To calculate our projection matrix, we use the D3DXMatrixPerspectiveFovLH, which is another utility function supplied by the D3DX library.

Notice the LH on the end of the function name. This indicates that it sets up a projection matrix for a left-handed coordinate system. If we were using a right-handed coordinate system then we would need to use the D3DXMatrixPerspectiveFovRH function instead. The prototype for the left-handed version of the function is shown below (the right-handed version is exactly the same).

```
D3DXMATRIX *WINAPI D3DXMatrixPerspectiveFovLH
(
  D3DXMATRIX *pOut, // A matrix to store the result.
  FLOAT fovy,       // The field of view.
  FLOAT Aspect,     // View space width divided by the height.
  FLOAT zn,         // The near plane.
  FLOAT zf          // The far plane.
);
```

For the first parameter we pass in projMatrix, which is the matrix structure that will store our new projection matrix. For the second parameter we use D3DX_PI / 4, which indicates that we want a 90-degree FOV. The third parameter is very simple as it is just the width of the screen divided by the height of the screen. We can get this information from the back buffer that our device uses. By dividing the width by the height, it will give us our aspect ratio. So, if you were to use a resolution of 800 × 600, then the aspect ratio would be 1.33, which is the standard ratio for most resolutions. Finally, we just need to set the near and far clipping planes. That is the distance these planes are from the camera. This is the first time that we are making use of the new scale parameter in our EngineSetup structure. By default, we want to set the near plane to 0.1 and the far plane to 1000.0; however, this may not always be appropriate. So, to ensure that our clipping planes are at a reasonable distance, we need to divide them by the scale.

Now, we have created the projection matrix, but it is not over. The problem is that our device doesn't know anything about our new projection matrix, so we need to set it in the device. To do this we call the SetTransform function on our device. This function is used for setting a number of other types of matrices as well, but we don't need to worry about that, at least not for now. We will cover them as they arise. For now, all we need to concern ourselves with is setting the projection matrix, which is achieved by setting the first parameter of the function to D3DTS_PROJECTION to indicate that we want to set the projection matrix. For the second parameter, we pass a pointer to the D3DXMATRIX structure that contains our new projection matrix; and that's all there is to it. The device is now set with the correct project matrix. As long as you do not change the projection matrix, you won't have to set it on the device again for the life of the device. Now we only have a few more steps to address and then we have covered all the new code in our Engine class constructor.

```
m_displayMode.Width = d3dpp.BackBufferWidth;
m_displayMode.Height = d3dpp.BackBufferHeight;
m_displayMode.RefreshRate = d3dpp.FullScreen_RefreshRateInHz;
m_displayMode.Format = d3dpp.BackBufferFormat;

m_currentBackBuffer = 0;

D3DXCreateSprite( m_device, &m_sprite );
```

As you can see in the above code, we need to keep a copy of the display mode that the device is using so that it can be accessed later if necessary. To do this, we just copy the required details across to our m_displayMode member variable, which is a D3DDISPLAYMODE structure. We then set the m_currentBackBuffer to 0 so that it starts with the first back buffer, and finally we create our ID3DXSprite interface, with a call to D3DXCreateSprite. This function is provided by the D3DX library and it accepts two parameters. The first is the device that the interface is to work with and the second is the address of the pointer to store our new ID3DXSprite interface.

Now that we have created everything, we must remember to destroy everything when we are finished. There are two new additions to our Engine class destructor, which are shown below. All we are doing is releasing our two new interfaces. First the `ID3DXSprite` interface, then the `IDirect3DDevice9` interface.

```
SAFE_RELEASE( m_sprite );

SAFE_RELEASE( m_device );
```

In the `Run` function (of the `Engine` class), we can now add our rendering support, which also allows us to support the `Render` function from the `State` class. The code is shown here:

```
m_device->Clear( 0, NULL, viewer.viewClearFlags, 0, 1.0f, 0 );
if( SUCCEEDED( m_device->BeginScene() ) )
{
  if( m_currentState != NULL )
    m_currentState->Render();

  m_device->EndScene();
  m_device->Present( NULL, NULL, NULL, NULL );

  if( ++m_currentBackBuffer == m_setup->totalBackBuffers + 1 )
    m_currentBackBuffer = 0;
}
```

First, we call the `Clear` function on our device, which allows us to clear the view port. The view port is like a window into 3D space. It contains what is seen by the virtual camera. The `Clear` function can clear the view port so that it does not contain data from previously rendered frames. This `Clear` function takes a number of parameters, but we only really need to worry about one of them. The prototype for the function is shown here:

```
HRESULT Clear
(
  // Used for clearing specified portions of the view port.
  DWORD Count,
  const D3DRECT *pRects,

  // Flags to indicate which surfaces are to be cleared.
  DWORD Flags,

  // A 32-bit color value to clear the render target to.
  D3DCOLOR Color,
```

```
    // The value to clear the depth buffer to.
    Float Z,

    // The value to clear the stencil buffer to.
    DWORD Stencil
);
```

When we clear the view port, we will always clear the entire thing, so we can ignore the properties for clearing just certain portions of it. The last three parameters are used to specify what each respective buffer should be cleared to. We will just use the default values for each of these, which is 0 (black) for Color, 1.0 for Z, and 0 for Stencil. We only need to worry about setting the appropriate flags in the Flags parameter. The Flags parameter can be set to one or more of the flags shown in Table 5.7.

TABLE 5.7 Clear Flags

D3DCLEAR_STENCIL	Clears the stencil buffer to the value specified by Stencil.
D3DCLEAR_TARGET	Clears the render target to the color specified by Color.
D3DCLEAR_ZBUFFER	Clears the depth buffer to the value specified by Z.

We won't be specifying any of these flags in the function call, as we cannot assume what needs to be cleared. Instead, we will pass in the viewClearFlags from the ViewerSetup structure that we receive from the RequestViewer function, which is called on the current state. This will allow each state to determine what needs to be cleared. For example, if one state is using a depth buffer, but another one is not, then only the state that is actually using the depth buffer needs to worry about clearing it.

Remember that clearing these surfaces is somewhat computationally expensive and should be done as little as possible. For standard 3D rendering to the entire view port (which is what we will be doing in the game that we build later), you really only need to worry about clearing the depth buffer.

After we have performed any view port clearing, the next step is to allow the device to prepare itself before rendering the current frame. This is achieved by calling

BeginScene with our device. We wrap the call inside an if statement so that we can check if it is successful, using the SUCCEEDED macro provided by DirectX. If the function succeeds, then it is safe to render the current frame. First, we check if there is a current state, and if so, we call its Render function to allow the state to perform any of its own rendering. This is for specialized rendering that is not handled by the engine. As you will see later, the engine will actually handle a lot of the scene and object rendering for you. Once we have completed rendering for this frame, we then call the EndScene, and the Present functions on the device, in that order. Every time the BeginScene function is called, there must be an equivalent EndScene call to inform the device that rendering is complete. The Present function then performs a flip on the swap chain to present the back buffer (with the currently rendered scene on it) to the screen. The Present function has a number of parameters that allow it to perform special functions, such as only presenting part of the back buffer rather than the whole thing. We do not need any of these features so we will leave all of the parameters set to NULL, to perform a standard presentation operation.

Now that we have flipped the swap chain, we need to keep track of which back buffer is at the front. So we need to increment the member variable m_currentBackBuffer. At the same time, we check to see if by incrementing the variable we will exceed the number of back buffers. If so, we know that the swap chain has done a complete revolution and we are back at the start of the chain (i.e., the first back buffer is at the front of the swap chain). To indicate this we need to set m_currentBackBuffer back to 0.

Since we are talking about the back buffers, we might as well look at the last change to the Engine class, which is found in the ChangeState function. The new code is shown here:

```
while( m_currentBackBuffer != 0 )
{
  m_device->Present( NULL, NULL, NULL, NULL );

  if( ++m_currentBackBuffer == m_setup->totalBackBuffers + 1 )
    m_currentBackBuffer = 0;
}
```

What is happening here is that every time we change to a new state (by calling the ChangeState function), we want to bring the first back buffer to the front of the swap chain. This ensures that any states which use the GDI (such as for drawing dialogs) will have the front buffer immediately available so that whatever the GDI draws will be visible. To do this we enter into a while loop that breaks when the first back buffer is at the front of the swap chain. In every iteration of the loop we call Present (on the device) to flip the swap chain. We then increment m_currentBack-Buffer, and reset it back to 0 when it exceeds the total number of back buffers. The while loop will detect this reset and drop out so that it stops flipping the swap chain, at which point we are guaranteed that the first back buffer is at the front of the swap chain.

Phew! Our device is created and set up, all ready to use for some serious rendering. Unfortunately, we don't have anything exciting to render just yet. In fact, we won't even be adding mesh support until Chapter 8. So, how are we going to test our shiny new device? We will add a simple little Font class that can render text to the screen—so read on.

FONTS

We are going to add a very basic font rendering class to our engine. We will have a quick look at the interface for the Font class so that you know how to use it, but we won't spend any time going through the actual implementation because the class can be considered just a basic cutdown version of CD3DFont that comes with the DirectX samples, with some adjustments so that it fits nicely into our engine. At a later stage you may find a use for a fully featured font rendering system, at which point you may want to implement your own, or integrate the CD3DFont class—as it has many more features. For now we will begin by looking at the Font class definition, which is shown below and can be found in Font.h.

```
class Font
{
public:
  Font( char *name = "Arial", short size = 10,
        unsigned long bold = FW_NORMAL, bool italic = false );
  virtual ~Font();

  void Render( char *text, float x, float y,
               D3DCOLOR colour = D3DCOLOR_COLORVALUE( 1.0f, 1.0f,
               1.0f, 1.0f ) );

private:
  bool PrepareFont( HDC hDC, bool measure = false );
```

```
private:
  IDirect3DStateBlock9 *m_states;
  IDirect3DVertexBuffer9 *m_vb;
  IDirect3DTexture9 *m_texture;
  unsigned long m_textureWidth;
  unsigned long m_textureHeight;
  float m_textureCoords[96][4];
  short m_spacing;
};
```

It is a fairly small class, but it has a number of member variables, which we will run through now. The first one—m_states—is used for storing the current state of the device before rendering any text. This is because the Font class modifies the device state (such as the various render states that can be adjusted with SetRenderState) so that it can perform its rendering correctly. Once it has finished rendering, it needs to restore the device state back to what it was before the Font class started rendering.

The next member variable is m_vb, which is a vertex buffer. We haven't discussed vertex buffers because we have not needed them yet. You will see vertex buffers in use quite a bit in the later chapters when we start rendering the scene and the meshes within it. To quickly touch on it now—a vertex buffer is like a big pool that contains all of the vertices necessary to render a particular piece of 3D geometry. For example, if you were to create a vertex buffer that held the vertices for a single face, then it would have three vertices in it. You can then pass the vertex buffer to Direct3D and tell it to render it. Direct3D will render the face that is made up by the three vertices. This is the general principle behind vertex buffers; however, there is a lot more to them than this simple example—but we won't go into it right now. All you need to know is that m_vb stores the vertices of the faces that the text is rendered with. Each character is made up of two faces with a texture applied to them. The texture has a picture of the character on it in the selected font.

The next three member variables are used for the actual texture that has all of the characters printed on it. This texture is stored in an IDirect3DTexture9 interface called m_texture. You will learn more about this interface in Chapter 8 when we implement materials and meshes. m_textureWidth and m_textureHeight store the width and height of this texture. The last two variables are used for identifying the individual characters on the large texture. m_textureCoords has the u, v coordinates of each character, and m_spacing indicates the amount of pixel spacing on either side of each character.

To use the Font class it is just a matter of creating an instance of the class, which will set up the class ready to begin rendering. The constructor accepts as input the name of the font to use (which must be a font that is registered on the system), the size of the font, and two flags to indicate if the font is bold and/or italic. Each of these parameters has a default value, so you do not need to specify all of them. Once the Font class has been instantiated, you can render text with it by calling Render. The first parameter of the function accepts a pointer to the text to render and the next two parameters indicate the position of the screen to render the text. The position is specified in pixels along the x-axis and the y-axis—a value of 0, 0 would indicate the upper left corner of the screen. The last parameter is an RGBA color value to specify the color of the text.

The last step before the Font class can be used by the engine is to include it into the engine. This is done in the same way as everything else. We just need to place the appropriate #include statements in the appropriate files. You can see this by opening Engine.h and Font.cpp to see the #include statements. If you are interested in learning how the Font class works, just have a look through Font.cpp. The code has been presented as clearly as possible and comments have been placed to assist you to understand it. Now that the new Font class has been integrated, all we have to do is have a look at an example of how to use it, which is shown here.

```
// Create a default font.
Font *font = new Font;

// Render some text with the default settings.
font->Render( "here is some text" );

// Render some yellow text, part way down the screen.
font->Render( "some yellow text", 0, 100,
              D3DCOLOR_COLORVALUE( 1.0f, 1.0f, 0.0f, 1.0f ) );

// Destroy the font.
SAFE_DELETE( font );
```

The only problem with the code is that the calls to Render *must be made in between the calls to* BeginScene *and* EndScene *on the device. Since the* Font *class uses our engine's device, we can only expect the* Font *class to be able to render anything when the device is ready. For this reason, it is always best to call the* Render *function on the* Font *class from within the* Render *function of the* State *class, as this is called by the engine from within the calls to* BeginScene *and* EndScene. *You will see this when we test the engine in the next section.*

TESTING THE DEVICE

ON THE CD

We have now finished adding all of the new features for this chapter, which concludes another iteration of our engine. All we have to do now is have a look at the little test application for this chapter, which tests the new features. You can find the test application in the Test project of the workspace for this chapter. We are using the same test application that we wrote in previous chapters; we are simply modifying it so that it tests what we are interested in. For example, one new change is in the WinMain function where you can see that we are now specifying a value for totalBackBuffers.

If you have a look at the TestState, you can see a number of new additions. Most notably we are using the new Font class to test the device's rendering. Notice how we create and destroy the instance of the Font class in the Load and Close functions (of the TestState class), respectively. We then perform any text rendering using the Font class from within the Render function of the TestState class. You can also see in the RequestViewer function, we specify D3DCLEAR_TARGET in the viewClearFlags, to indicate that we want the render target cleared in between frames. The best way to see how this works is to try running the application with this line of code commented out. You will see that the fps display is completely unreadable; this is because the previous frames are not being cleared and the new ones are being rendered over the top.

Speaking of fps, if you take a look in the Update function of the TestState, you will see that we are using the elapsed variable to calculate the current frame rate. This is stored in a character array, which is then passed to the Render function of our Font class. This shows how the Font class can accept text either directly or from a character array.

SUMMARY

Although we have only covered a couple of topics in this very long chapter, we covered them in detail. After a little theory about Direct3D, we went on to implement a complete display adapter enumeration system that allows the user to specify how he wants his device to be set up. We then looked at the process of creating the device and went through all of the new additions to our Engine class that relate to the device. Finally, we added a basic font rendering class so that we can test the device to ensure that everything is working correctly.

We have our rendering support up and running, but that only satisfies one of our senses—sight. There is another sense that must be tended to if we are to create a completely immersive environment: hearing. In Chapter 6 we will implement a sound system into our engine with the capability to play all of our sound effects and music. It will even be capable of playing 3D sounds so that sounds appear to originate from a source.

6 Sound

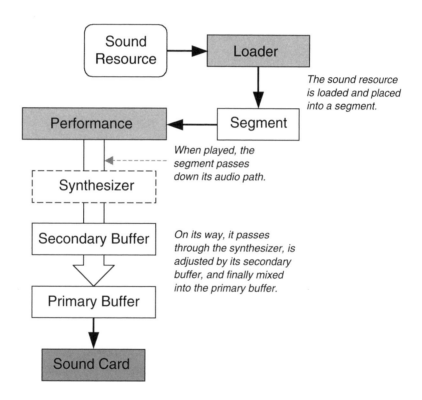

The sound resource is loaded and placed into a segment.

When played, the segment passes down its audio path.

On its way, it passes through the synthesizer, is adjusted by its secondary buffer, and finally mixed into the primary buffer.

In This Chapter

■ Discuss the components of DirectX that make sound possible.

■ Cover 3D sound and learn about 3D vectors for managing objects in 3D space.

■ Implement our sound system complete with 3D sound capabilities.

In the last chapter, we added our Direct3D device so that we can start rendering things, but as great as that is, it's no fun if we can't hear anything. We want to be able to hear our weapon when we shoot and hear our footsteps when we walk. In this chapter, we will implement a sound system to handle all of this. You can find the workspace for this chapter in the /Source/Chapter 6/ directory on the CD-ROM.

ON THE CD

DIRECTMUSIC

There are two components in DirectX that have the ability to play sound: Direct-Sound and DirectMusic. Despite what the names may suggest, DirectMusic is not just for playing music, it can do almost everything that DirectSound can do. Yes, it is true that DirectMusic is specially designed for playing back music, but the point is that it is not limited to just music. In fact, DirectMusic is considered to be a more full-featured interface, especially in terms of its dynamic music playback capabilities. There have not been many changes to either of these components in this revision of DirectX; they have just been fine-tuned and enhanced here and there to increase performance.

So the question is, what is the difference between the two components? Put simply, it is usability versus low level control. If we ignore the extra features supported by DirectMusic (for its music capabilities) just for a moment, the real difference between the two components is that DirectMusic provides a user friendly environment, while DirectSound provides greater control. DirectSound is best suited to those who want absolute control over every aspect of sound playback at a low level, such as managing hardware resources. Some examples include sound synthesizing software developers, or someone who is developing an advanced sound engine. The trade-off is that DirectSound is a little more involved and harder to work with—it has a steeper learning curve. If you are not doing anything out of the ordinary and you just want some sound and music in your game, DirectMusic is the way to go. By sacrificing a bit of low level control you benefit from an extremely easy-to-use interface that will have you playing sounds in just a few minutes, literally—and when it comes to music playback, you will be blown away by the host of features supported by DirectMusic.

You should keep in mind that even though they are two separate components, they are still very much interrelated, and you will find that we will often use various interfaces from both components, especially when we look at 3D sound. In light of this, we will discuss the specific DirectSound interfaces as we use them. For now, let's have a more detailed look at DirectMusic, and how we can use it for our sound playback.

DirectMusic opens up a whole world of sound and provides a lot of features; including some of these common features:

- Load and play sounds in MIDI or WAV format.
- Use dynamic music playback through the use of DirectMusic producer.
- Control the volume, pitch, and pan of sound through the use of DirectSound.
- Locate sound in 3D space through the use of DirectSound.
- Apply effects to sounds, use styles for music playback, and other advanced features.

As you can see from this brief list, there are a couple of aspects of DirectMusic that rely on DirectSound, such as the ability to use 3D sounds. Now that we know what DirectMusic can do, let's have a look at how it works.

DirectMusic uses a number of interfaces to achieve its sound playback. The first one is the *loader*. Sounds—like scripts, textures, and meshes—are resources, which exist on the hard drive, for example, and need to be loaded before they can be used. We have already developed a resource management system, but as far as sounds go, we don't need it. DirectMusic uses the loader to load and mange sound resources. In other words, it does everything our simple resource management system can do, plus a whole lot more. Unfortunately, it is specific to sound resources, so we cannot take advantage of it for other types of resources.

Once a sound has been loaded, DirectMusic uses what is called a *performance*, to manage the flow of sound data to the synthesizer. The performance interface is the most important unique interface that DirectMusic uses—it is unique because you generally only ever create one of them. It controls everything to do with sound playback, including all of the housekeeping and resource management that is inherently involved with sound playback. The performance can manage the playback of multiple sounds at the same time so that they can be ultimately blended together to give a perfect output through your speakers. Despite the performance interface being your best friend, surprisingly, you very rarely need to touch it. Once it is created, it just does its job and you never really need to tend to it. This is another reason why DirectMusic is so easy to use, as you will see when we implement our sound system.

The last two major interfaces that we will use are for *segments* and *audio paths*. These two interfaces go hand in hand with one another, as the former stores the sounds, and the latter is used to play the sounds. Once a sound is loaded, it is stored in a segment, which in essence is just like a block of sound data that can be passed to the DirectMusic for playback at will. An audio path is like a footpath for the sound segment to travel down. This imaginary foot path starts at the performance and goes all the way down to what is called the *primary buffer*. On the way it passes by a couple of interesting tourist destinations where sound segments love to visit, such as the synthesizer and the DirectSound buffers. DirectSound uses buffers to manage the playback of particular sounds. For example, you may have a buffer for your gunshot sound, and another buffer for your footstep sound. Each of these buffers has parameters that can be adjusted, which affect the playback of that individual sound, such as the sound's volume, or its frequency. Additionally, you can acquire a 3D sound buffer for a given sound, which will allow you to adjust parameters such as the sound's position, velocity, and direction in 3D space. The primary sound buffer is a unique sound buffer used by DirectSound to mix all of the sounds on the secondary sound buffers into one combined sound that is then pushed through your sound card. The primary sound buffer is also used for controlling global 3D sound parameters.

As you can see, the process it fairly involved. Thankfully, it is all very easy to implement and a lot of these underlying processes are completely transparent, meaning you will never see them nor concern yourself with them. You have probably noticed that near the end of the whole process we started talking quite a bit about DirectSound. The reason for this is that ultimately it is DirectSound that manages the sound playback at a low level with the sound buffers. DirectMusic sits on top of the whole process and just passes the required information to the sound buffers. Before we move on to implementing our sound system, take a look at Figure 6.1, which will hopefully give you a better understanding of how the process of sound playback works.

This has given you a quick introduction to DirectMusic with a touch of DirectSound. There is quite a bit more to this whole topic than what we have looked at here—much of it centered on advanced music playback and sound control, which we do not need. As with anything, the best way to learn is through doing. So let's spend less time discussing, and let's start implementing our sound system.

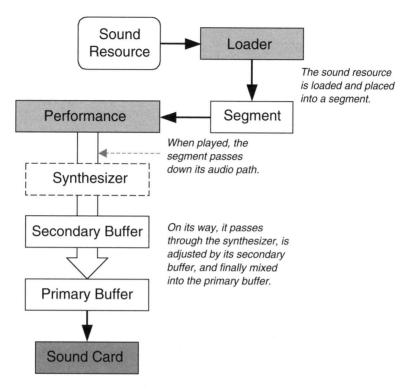

FIGURE 6.1   The process of sound playback through DirectMusic and DirectSound.

THE SOUND SYSTEM

To bring our sound system to life; there are three classes that we need to create. The first of these three classes is the main SoundSystem class. This class is used for the overall management of the sound system, and will create and maintain our loader and performance, among other things. The class definition for the SoundSystem class is shown below (and can be found in SoundSystem.h).

```
class SoundSystem
{
public:
  SoundSystem( float scale = 1.0f );
  virtual ~SoundSystem();

  void UpdateListener( D3DXVECTOR3 forward, D3DXVECTOR3 position,
                       D3DXVECTOR3 velocity );
```

```
    void GarbageCollection();

    void SetVolume( long volume );

    IDirectMusicLoader8 *GetLoader();
    IDirectMusicPerformance8 *GetPerformance();

private:
  float m_scale;
  IDirectMusicLoader8 *m_loader;
  IDirectMusicPerformance8 *m_performance;
  IDirectSound3DListener8 *m_listener;
};
```

Based on our previous discussion of DirectMusic, you should have no trouble understanding what is in the class just by looking at the definition. The only thing you have not seen yet is the IDirectSound3DListener8 interface. This is the interface used by DirectSound to determine whether or not a 3D sound can be heard. If it can, it has to determine (based on its position) what volume the sound should be played at through each speaker to simulate the 3D environment. Rather than discussing everything here, let's just move straight to the implementation and we can talk about each topic as it comes up. So to begin with we will look at the destructor, which is shown below. The SoundSystem class implementation can be found in SoundSystem.cpp.

```
SoundSystem::SoundSystem( float scale )
{
  CoCreateInstance( CLSID_DirectMusicLoader, NULL, CLSCTX_INPROC,
                    IID_IDirectMusicLoader8, (void**)&m_loader );

  CoCreateInstance( CLSID_DirectMusicPerformance, NULL,
                    CLSCTX_INPROC, IID_IDirectMusicPerformance8,
                    (void**)&m_performance );
```

The class constructor accepts as input the scale that the system is to work in. This is the same scale that is passed to the engine through the EngineSetup structure, and is specified in meters per unit. Once in the constructor, the first step is to create the DirectMusic loader, which is a COM object, so we use CoCreateInstance to create it. In the first parameter, we must pass in the class identifier of the object that we want to create, which is CLSID_DirectMusicLoader in this case. The fourth parameter is also of interest as here we specify which interface the object is to use by passing in a reference to the required interface, which is IID_IDirectMusicLoader8. The last parameter is the only other one that concerns us as here we pass the address of the pointer that will store the requested interface pointer. Since we are creating the loader object, we pass in `m_loader` for this parameter.

Once we have created the loader object, we need to do the same to create the performance object. Once again, we use the `CoCreateInstance` function to create the object interface, only this time we must change the parameters to reference a performance object rather than a loader object. For the class identifier, we use `CLSID_DirectMusicPerformance` and for the interface reference we use `IID_IDirect-MusicLoader8`. For the last parameter, we pass in `m_performance` to store the interface pointer for our new performance object. Now that we have our two main objects created we are ready to begin the painless process of initialization.

```
m_performance->InitAudio( NULL, NULL, NULL,
                          DMUS_APATH_SHARED_STEREOPLUSREVERB, 8,
                          DMUS_AUDIOF_ALL, NULL );
```

The main task that needs to be done is initializing the performance so that it is ready to start playing sounds. This is done with one quick and easy call to `InitAudio`, which is exposed by our performance object. The prototype for this function is shown here:

```
HRESULT InitAudio
(
  // The address of two pointers, one for the DirectMusic object
  // and the other for the DirectSound object.
  IDirectMusic** ppDirectMusic,
  IDirectSound** ppDirectSound,

  // Window handle used by DirectSound.
  HWND hWnd,

  // The default audio path type.
  DWORD dwDefaultPathType,

  // The number of performance channels to allocate.
  DWORD dwPChannelCount,

  // Flags for requesting special features.
  DWORD dwFlags,

  // Address of a DMUS_AUDIOPARAMS structure for specifying the
  // synthesizer parameters.
  DMUS_AUDIOPARAMS *pParams
);
```

It may look like a rather large function, but don't let it scare you—it's just a mouse disguised as a tiger. Most of the parameters we don't even need to bother with and can just set them to NULL, which will give us the default behavior; that just so happens to be exactly what we want. The first two parameters allow you to specify the DirectMusic and DirectSound objects that you want the performance to use. We will set them both to NULL, which means that the performance will create both of these objects internally for its own private use. This doesn't bother us because we don't need access to either of these objects. We can also leave the third parameter set to NULL, which means that the performance will use the handle of the foreground window (i.e., the window with the focus) to attach to the DirectSound object. We are happy with this too, as we only have one application window and it will always be the foreground window when the performance is created.

The performance can also have a default audio path inside of it that allows you to quickly play a sound without having to bother creating an audio path for it first. We will make use of this default audio path by passing in the type of audio path we want the performance to use in the fourth parameter. If you set this parameter to NULL, the performance will not use a default audio path. Table 6.1 shows the different audio paths you can create—we will use the last one for stereo sound playback with reverb, which is the best for ordinary sound, including music. Remember this is just the default audio path, so it doesn't need 3D playback. We will create separate audio paths for the sounds that need that support.

TABLE 6.1   Audio Path Types

DMUS_APATH_DYNAMIC_3D	Uses a 3D sound buffer for 3D sound playback.
DMUS_APATH_DYNAMIC_MONO	Single channel playback for mono sound.
DMUS_APATH_DYNAMIC_STEREO	Dual channel playback for stereo sound.
DMUS_APATH_SHARED_STEREOPLUSREVERB	Stereo sound with reverb.

The next parameter indicates the number of performance channels that we want to allocate. Each audio path uses one of these channels when it plays a sound. In other words, the more channels you allocate, the more sounds you can play back simultaneously. The downside is that more channels equals more overhead, which can hit on performance and memory. It is often a good idea to allow the end user to adjust this based on his computer's configuration. We will set the parameter to 8 by default, which will be plenty of performance channels for our purposes.

The second to last parameter allows us to specify any special features that we want the performance to use. We will just pass in DMUS_AUDIOF_ALL to indicate that we want all of the features available. This is the most common setting that will suffice in the majority of situations. Finally, the last parameter allows you to pass in the pointer to a DMUS_AUDIOPARAMS structure to allow you to specify parameters for the synthesizer. It also allows you to receive the settings the synthesizer is using. We do not need any of this functionality so we can just leave the last parameter set to NULL. That completes the initialization of the performance ready to play sounds. To facilitate the playback of 3D sounds, however, we need access to a DirectSound 3D listener, which is what we do next.

```
IDirectMusicAudioPath8 *audioPath3D;
m_performance->CreateStandardAudioPath( DMUS_APATH_DYNAMIC_3D,
                                        1, true, &audioPath3D );
audioPath3D->GetObjectInPath( 0, DMUS_PATH_PRIMARY_BUFFER, 0,
                              GUID_All_Objects, 0,
                              IID_IDirectSound3DListener,
                              (void**)&m_listener );
SAFE_RELEASE( audioPath3D );
```

The DirectSound 3D listener is represented by the IDirectSound3DListener8 interface. The best way to think of the listener is like a microphone placed in 3D space. You can position, orient, and apply velocity to this imaginary microphone. DirectSound will use the listener microphone to calculate everything needed to play back the 3D sounds correctly, taking into account the position, orientation, and velocity of both the microphone and each sound. DirectSound also uses the velocities to apply phenomena such as Doppler shift, which is the change of pitch that a sound produces when it moves past you at great speed, such as a car at a race track.

To create our listener, we first need to create a 3D audio path, and then from the 3D audio path we can get a pointer to the listener used by the audio path. This is the same listener used by all audio paths as it is inherently linked to the instance of DirectSound that is created by our performance. There is only one instance of the listener so it doesn't matter which audio path we use to request a pointer to it. For this reason, we just create a temporary 3D audio path, request the listener from it, and then destroy the audio path. We then have a pointer to the listener that is valid for the lifetime of our sound system.

We won't go into the details of creating the audio path as we will be covering that later in this chapter when we implement our AudioPath3D class. From the code here you can see how simple it is to create an audio path. Once we have our 3D audio path, the next step is to get the pointer to the listener from the audio path by calling GetObjectInPath, which is exposed by the IDirectMusicAudioPath8 interface. This function allows us to access a number of components in the audio path, and it is not limited to audio paths. Segments and sound buffers also expose their own version of this function, which allows you to access components from them, too. The prototype for this function (as exposed by IDirectMusicAudioPath8) is shown here:

```
RESULT GetObjectInPath
(
    DWORD dwPChannel,      // The performance channel to search.
    DWORD dwStage,         // The stage within the audio path.
    DWORD dwBuffer,        // Index of the buffer.
    REFGUID guidObject,    // Class identifier of the object to get.
    DWORD dwIndex,         // Index identifier for multiple matches.
    REFGUID iidInterface,  // Desired interface identifier.
    void ** ppObject       // Address to store the interface pointer.
);
```

The first four parameters are fairly uninteresting and we can just pass default values for them. The default settings indicate that we want to search all the objects on the first performance channel of the primary buffer used by the audio path. The only two parameters we really need to worry about are the last two. We need to specify IID_IDirectSound3DListener to indicate that we are only interested in the 3D sound listener interface. In the final parameter, we pass in the address of our m_listener pointer, which will store the pointer to the listener interface when the function call returns. Now that we have our listener, we no longer need the temporary 3D audio path, so we can release it.

```
    m_scale = scale;
    m_listener->SetDistanceFactor( m_scale, DS3D_IMMEDIATE );
}
```

The final step is to set the scale that our listener will use, which is called the *distance factor*. We first store the scale in our own member variable so that we can access it later on. We then call the SetDistanceFactor function on our listener and pass in the scale to use. We also pass in the DS3D_IMMEDIATE flag to indicate to DirectSound that we want the change to take effect immediately. The other flag you can set is DS3D_DEFERRED, which means that the change will not take effect until you call the CommitDeferredSettings function on the listener. Every time you change something the system needs to recalculate internally, which can take time.

During performance critical code (such as in the game loop) you want to minimize these time-consuming events. If you have to make a number of changes such as setting the listener's position, velocity, and orientation all at the same time, it is often best to use the DS3D_DEFERRED parameter and then call CommitDeferredSettings when you are done.

That is the end of the constructor. At this point the sound system is all set up and ready to use. Before we delve any deeper we should make note of the destructor, which will shut down the sound system and free all the allocated memory. All we need to do is call the `CloseDown` function on our performance to shut it down. After that, we can safely release the performance and the loader as shown here:

```
SoundSystem::~SoundSystem()
{
  m_performance->CloseDown();
  SAFE_RELEASE( m_performance );

  SAFE_RELEASE( m_loader );
}
```

There are a number of other functions exposed by our `SoundSystem` class, and they are all pretty straightforward. The `SetVolume` function allows you to set the overall volume of the sound system, which will affect all sounds played through it. `GetLoader` and `GetPerformance` return pointers to the loader object and the performance object, respectively. The `GarbageCollection` function is an interesting one. By default, the loader uses what is called *automatic caching*, which means that whenever an object is loaded in by the loader, it and any other objects that it references are cached in memory by the loader for quick and easy access. Over time the cache can fill up if you are loading a lot of objects, however, not all of the cached objects may be in use. To alleviate the pressure on the cache, you can call `GarbageCollection` function, which in turn calls the loader's `CollectGarbage` function. This will allow the loader to clear any objects from the cache that are not being used. Since this is an expensive operation it is best not to do it during performance critical code. In the engine, we will set it up so that the loader clears the cache whenever there is a state change as this is the most likely time when a lot of cached objects will lose their usefulness.

The last function in the `SoundSystem` class that we have not yet covered is the `UpdateListener` function, which is shown here:

```
void SoundSystem::UpdateListener( D3DXVECTOR3 forward,
                                  D3DXVECTOR3 position,
                                  D3DXVECTOR3 velocity )
{
  m_listener->SetOrientation( forward.x, forward.y, forward.z,
                              0.0f, 1.0f, 0.0f, DS3D_DEFERRED );

  position *= m_scale;
  m_listener->SetPosition( position.x, position.y, position.z,
                           DS3D_DEFERRED );
```

```
    velocity *= m_scale;
    m_listener->SetVelocity( velocity.x, velocity.y, velocity.z,
                            DS3D_DEFERRED );

    m_listener->CommitDeferredSettings();
}
```

The function takes as input three vectors that indicate the listener's forward vector, position, and velocity in 3D space. If you are unfamiliar with vectors, we will have a little primer after we have finished discussing the SoundSystem class. Assuming you have an understanding of them, you can see how the UpdateListener function works. It first sets the orientation of the listener, then the position, and finally the velocity. For both the position and the velocity we multiply it by our scale so that the value is in scale with the sound system. You will also notice that we use the DS3D_DEFERRED flag so that once we have finished setting all the parameters we just call CommitDeferredSettings to make it all happen.

3D VECTORS

As promised, we will have a quick 3D vector primer since it is a core fundamental of 3D math. You may be wondering why we are talking about 3D math now when we are supposed to be discussing our new sound system. If you think back to Chapter 4, you will remember that right in the middle of our great scripting discussion we took a bit of a detour to discuss encapsulation and automation. We did this because they were important topics that we were about to use in practice, and you needed to understand them before we moved on. In the same fashion here with 3D vectors, we could have discussed them earlier (before we started using them), however, the benefit of discussing them now is that we are starting to use them and we can learn about them with real examples rather than hypothetical ones. Sometimes we will take these little sidetracks when necessary. With that said, let's move on to discussing 3D vectors.

3D vectors are usually referred to as a quantity that has both a magnitude (a length) and a direction, such as a force like acceleration or velocity, or even just a displacement. For example, you could look at a car that is traveling north and say that the car has a velocity vector of *60 kph north*. If this car was in a game, you may say that it has a velocity vector of 60 units along the z-axis (assuming positive z pointed north). The most common vectors that you will see are 3D vectors that have x, y, and z components. D3DX provides a 3D vector that we will make use of throughout the book—D3DXVECTOR3. If we go back to our car example, we could write the velocity vector like this (0.0, 0.0, 60.0), which just says that the car is mov-ing 60 units in the positive z-axis direction. How often the car makes this move (i.e., every frame, every second, every hour) is up to you and depends largely on the scale that you are working with.

You should also note that not all vectors have to be treated as a magnitude and a direction. You can also treat them as absolute coordinates in 3D space. So, if we were to use our car example again, we could say that the car is positioned at (10.0, 0.0, −32.5), which means that the car is located at positive 10.0 along the x-axis, centered on the y-axis, and at negative 32.5 along the z-axis. In this case it does not mean that the car is moving 10 units along the x-axis and −32.5 units along the z-axis. This may seem a little confusing, but it really is quite simple to understand once you begin using vectors. It is often a good idea to name your vector variables after what they store. So, a vector that stores only a magnitude (i.e., 3D coordinates) would be called something like *position*, while a vector that is used for both magni-tude and direction should be called something like *velocity*.

Just when you thought it was over, it actually becomes even more confusing, because there is a third type of vector that we will use. In fact, it is very much related to a vector that you used in the last chapter when we talked about 3D geometry and lighting—the *normal vector*, or more appropriately called the *unit vector*, as it is not always used for a normal like the face or vertex normal you have previously seen (also a normal vector does not have to be of length 1, whereas a unit vector does). As already discussed, you can see that we have a type of vector that handles both magnitude and direction, which we can call a *force*. We also have a type of vector that just handles a magnitude, ignoring the direction, which we can call a *position* or *translation*. Our new type of vector handles the direction while ignoring the magnitude, which we can call a *facing* (i.e., the direction the vector is pointing). The best way to understand this is to look at an example. If we had the unit vector, or a facing (0.0, 0.0, 1.0), we would say that the vector is pointing toward the positive z-axis. Because this vector is a facing, we do not read it as if it were a force that is pushing 1 unit in the positive z-axis. We also do not read it as if it were a transla-tion that is centered on the x-axis and y-axis, and 1 unit along the z-axis.

There is one final point that you should be aware of when dealing with unit vectors. Any vector can become a unit vector by going through the process of *nor-malization*. Simply put, normalization means that you remove the magnitude from a vector. In other words, each component of the vector is proportionally scaled so that it is in the range of 0.0 to 1.0, ignoring the sign. This is achieved by dividing the vector by its magnitude, which is a common practice in 3D math, and allows you to quickly determine the facing or direction of a force. For example, let's say we had a car with a velocity vector of (20.0, 0.0, −10.0). We could calculate the car's facing by calculating its unit vector. In other words, we normalize the car's velocity vector. After normalization the velocity vector would become approximately (0.89, 0.0, –0.44). This means that we end up with a vector that points in the same direction that the car is traveling, but it is 1 unit in length. You may wonder what the point is to normalizing the vector. You can already determine the direction the car is facing by looking at the velocity vector, which indicates not only the magnitude of the velocity but also its direction. There are two reasons why we will often need to create unit vectors:

- It is easier to compare to vectors when they have been normalized. For example, it is far easier to calculate things like the angle between two unit vectors.
- It is easy to apply a force to a unit vector. After normalizing the vector you can then multiply it by a scalar value (such as 18, for example) and a magnitude of that length is applied to the vector.

In closing, take a look at Figure 6.2, which gives a visual representation of the three types of 3D vectors that we will be using through the rest of this book.

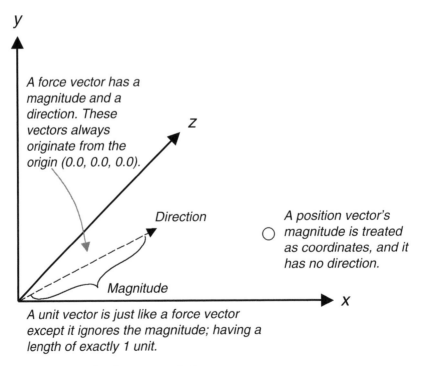

FIGURE 6.2 The three types of 3D vectors.

SOUND RESOURCE

We now have the main SoundSystem class implemented, ready to load, and play sounds. The next step is to implement a class that we can use to store individual sounds. For this we will create the Sound class. This class is not entirely necessary as all it will do is wrap itself around the IDirectMusicSegment8 interface that stores the sound data. Technically, we could just work directly with the IDirectMusicSegment8 interface, using it to store and play all our sounds. However, we will implement the Sound class for completeness and to facilitate usability. It will give us a higher level interface that will make the easy process of handling sounds even easier! So, let's have a look at the definition of the Sound class, which can also be found in SoundSystem.h.

```
class Sound
{
public:
  Sound( char *filename );
  virtual ~Sound();

  void Play( bool loop = false,
             unsigned long flags = DMUS_SEGF_AUTOTRANSITION );

  IDirectMusicSegment8 *GetSegment();

private:
  IDirectMusicSegment8 *m_segment;
};
```

If you haven't picked up on it yet you will notice that our Sound class does not inherit from the Resource class. This is because, as you probably remember, our sound resources are loaded and managed by the DirectMusic loader. Therefore, they do not need to be supported by our resource management system. Other than that little point, this class is almost self-explanatory, but worth a look at the constructor, at least.

```
Sound::Sound( char *filename )
{
  WCHAR *wideFilename = new WCHAR[strlen( filename ) + 1];
  MultiByteToWideChar( CP_ACP, 0, filename, -1, wideFilename,
                       strlen( filename ) + 1 );
  wideFilename[strlen( filename )] = 0;
```

```
g_engine->GetSoundSystem()->GetLoader()->LoadObjectFromFile(
        CLSID_DirectMusicSegment, IID_IDirectMusicSegment8,
        wideFilename, (void**)&m_segment );
SAFE_DELETE( wideFilename );

m_segment->Download(
        g_engine->GetSoundSystem()->GetPerformance() );
}
```

There are no prizes for guessing what the constructor takes as input, however, you should note that this must be the complete filename including the path. First, the filename is converted into a wide character (Unicode) string, as that is what the LoadObjectFromFile function accepts, which is the next step. The prototype for the LoadObjectFromFile function is shown here:

```
HRESULT LoadObjectFromFile
(
  REFGUID rguidClassID,  // Class object identifier.
  REFIID iidInterfaceID, // Interface identifier.
  WCHAR *pwzFilePath,    // Fully qualified filename and path.
  void ** ppObject       // Address that stores interface pointer.
);
```

For the first and second parameters, we pass in the unique identifiers for the class, and the interface of the object that we are creating, which in this instance is a segment. So, we pass in CLSID_DirectMusicSegment for the class and IID_IDirectMusicSegment8 for the interface. In the third parameter, we pass in the filename of the sound that we want to load into the segment. The final parameter is the address of the variable that will store the pointer to our new interface, which will be m_segment. The final step is to load the segment's data into the performance so that it can be played. This is achieved with a call to Download, passing in a pointer to the performance into which you want to load the data.

When the sound is destroyed, the destructor will unload the segment's data from the performance. It will also remove the segment object from the loader and finally release the segment. The destructor is shown here:

```
Sound::~Sound()
{
  m_segment->Unload(
      g_engine->GetSoundSystem()->GetPerformance() );
```

```
g_engine->GetSoundSystem()->GetLoader()->ReleaseObjectByUnknown(
    m_segment );
SAFE_RELEASE( m_segment );
}
```

The last function that is of interest is the Play function, which allows us to play a sound segment on the default audio path that we created for the performance. The implementation of the Play function is shown here:

```
void Sound::Play( bool loop, unsigned long flags )
{
  if( loop == true )
    m_segment->SetRepeats( DMUS_SEG_REPEAT_INFINITE );
  else
    m_segment->SetRepeats( 0 );

  g_engine->GetSoundSystem()->GetPerformance()->PlaySegment(
      m_segment, flags, 0, NULL );
}
```

The Play function takes as input a flag to indicate if the sound should be looped or not. The second parameter allows you to specify a number of optional flags that modify the sound's playback. There are far too many optional flags to list here, however, you can see the complete list by looking up DMUS_SEGF_FLAGS in the DirectX SDK documentation. Once in the function, we check the loop flag. If it is set to true, we set the number of repeats to infinite on the segment; otherwise, we set it to 0 so that the segment only plays once. This is achieved with a call to the SetRepeats function. Finally, we just need to call PlaySegment, which is exposed by the performance in the SoundSystem class. We pass in our segment to be played as the first parameter and the optional flags for the second parameter. We set the third parameter to 0, which indicates that we want to play the segment from the beginning. The last parameter is used for receiving a pointer to the segment state of this instance of the playing segment. This allows you to adjust the parameters for this instance of the playing segment, while it is playing. We don't need to do that so we can leave it set to NULL.

That basically wraps up the whole Sound class. There was, however, one last function that we didn't cover, which is GetSegment. All this function does is return a pointer to m_segment, which we will need when we try to play our sounds through the 3D audio paths that we are about to implement. Now we almost have our sound system completely implemented. There is one more class that we need to look at, which is the AudioPath3D. This class will allow us to create 3D audio paths so that we can play our sounds in 3D, which is really cool.

AUDIO PATHS

By now you should have a pretty good understanding of how the audio path works and what a 3D audio path does. If not, dissecting the AudioPath3D class should help you. Remember that the best way to learn code is to get in and play with it. We could talk about theory all day and you wouldn't learn half as much as what you would if we just looked at some real code. This is why the theory is kept to a minimum and we focus mainly on the actual implementation. So let's do just that with the AudioPath3D class, as its definition is shown here (which can also be found in SoundSystem.h).

```
class AudioPath3D
{
public:
  AudioPath3D();
  virtual ~AudioPath3D();

  void SetPosition( D3DXVECTOR3 position );
  void SetVelocity( D3DXVECTOR3 velocity );
  void SetMode( unsigned long mode );

  void Play( IDirectMusicSegment8 *segment, bool loop = false,
             unsigned long flags = DMUS_SEGF_SECONDARY );

private:
  IDirectMusicAudioPath8 *m_audioPath;
  IDirectSound3DBuffer8 *m_soundBuffer;
};
```

As with most classes, we have a constructor and a destructor, but note that this constructor has no parameters, which makes life even easier for us. The class also exposes a few functions that allow us to set some properties of the audio path, such as its position and the velocity in 3D space. Now this does not mean that the audio path is located in 3D space and can move around. It means that DirectSound will conduct its calculations on any sound played through this audio path, based on the position and velocity set in the audio path. You should also note that it is not the internal IDirectMusicAudioPath8 interface that stores the position and velocity, but the IDirectSound3DBuffer8 interface instead. We acquire this sound buffer once we have created the audio path, as you will see when we look at the implementation for the constructor. Finally, we have one more function that is used to play sounds on this audio path.

Remember that an audio path can be used to play any sound you want. It is often best to create one audio path per sound playing object rather than per sound. For example, if you had a weapon that could use one of three different sounds when it is fired, rather than creating an audio path for each sound, just create one for the weapon. That way you can set the audio path's position and velocity based on the position and velocity of the weapon in 3D space. Then you just play the appropriate sound on the audio path, which means that any one of the three sounds can be playing on it at any one time. It doesn't matter which sound you play as they will all be affected by the same position and velocity set on the audio path.

Let's start by having a look at what is going on inside the constructor, as shown here:

```
AudioPath3D::AudioPath3D()
{
  g_engine->GetSoundSystem()->GetPerformance()
          ->CreateStandardAudioPath( DMUS_APATH_DYNAMIC_3D, 1,
                                      true, &m_audioPath );

  m_audioPath->GetObjectInPath( DMUS_PCHANNEL_ALL,
                                DMUS_PATH_BUFFER, 0, GUID_NULL, 0,
                                IID_IDirectSound3DBuffer,
                                (void**)&m_soundBuffer );
}
```

The constructor is just a measly two lines of code, but that's all that it takes to set up a 3D audio path—it's just that easy. First we call the CreateStandardAudioPath function that is exposed by the performance in our SoundSystem class. You have already seen this function in use once before, back in the SoundSystem class constructor, however, we didn't go into details about the function. So let's have a look at its prototype here:

```
HRESULT  CreateStandardAudioPath
(
  DWORD dwType,                      // Type of path to create.
  DWORD dwPChannelCount,             // Number of channels.
  BOOL  fActivate,                   // Activate on creation.
  IDirectMusicAudioPath **ppNewPath  // Address of the variable to
                                     // hold the interface pointer.
);
```

For the first parameter, we can choose any of the audio path types that were shown in Table 6.1 earlier in this chapter. Since we want a 3D audio path we will choose the DMUS_APATH_DYNAMIC_3D option. For the second parameter, we will indicate that we just want the audio path to use one performance channel, as we will only be playing one sound at a time through the audio path. The third parameter allows you to indicate if you want the audio channel to be active as soon as it is created. This is a given as we will generally create audio paths when they are likely to be used, so we will set this value to true. The last parameter is just the address of the pointer that will store the interface pointer of our new audio path. For this parameter, we pass in the member variable m_audioPath.

Now that we have created our 3D audio path, we need to get the 3D sound buffer out of it so that we can set the various properties, such as the position and velocity. We do this with a call to GetObjectInPath on our new audio path. Just like CreateStandardAudioPath, we have also used the GetObjectInPath function once before back in the SoundSystem class constructor. If you remember, the last time we used the function to get a pointer to the global 3D listener. This time we are using it to get a pointer to the 3D sound buffer associated with this particular audio path. We use the function in exactly the same manner, except we just need to change a few of the parameters. First, we only want to search the first performance channel for the desired object (by specifying 0 for the first parameter) since our audio path only has one performance channel. Second, we are interested in searching for a sound buffer so we must specify DMUS_PATH_BUFFER for the second parameter. We leave the two index parameters (parameters three and five) set to 0 per usual, but this time we pass in GUID_NULL for the fourth parameter. This is because we are not interested in a complete object, just an interface. We want the interface to the 3D sound buffer that is being used by this audio path. To specify that, we pass in IID_IDirectSound3DBuffer through the second to last parameter—this is the interface identifier. Finally, the last parameter is the address of the pointer that will store the interface pointer of the 3D sound buffer, which will be our member variable m_soundBuffer.

As with everything else, when we are finished with our audio paths we must always remember to destroy them to free the memory that they have allocated for themselves. When you destroy an audio path, the `AudioPath3D` class destructor will be called, which just releases the sound buffer interface and the actual audio path itself. The implementation of the destructor is shown here:

```
AudioPath3D::~AudioPath3D()
{
  SAFE_RELEASE( m_soundBuffer );
  SAFE_RELEASE( m_audioPath );
}
```

Our `AudioPath3D` class also has a `SetPosition` and a `SetVelocity` function. Both of these functions operate in virtually the same manner. The only differences are that one accepts a position vector and the other accepts a velocity vector. Additionally, one calls `SetPosition` on the audio path's 3D sound buffer, while the other calls `SetVelocity` on the audio path's 3D sound buffer. Have a look at the implementation of both functions and you will see the similarities.

```
void AudioPath3D::SetPosition( D3DXVECTOR3 position )
{
  position *= g_engine->GetScale();
  m_soundBuffer->SetPosition( position.x, position.y, position.z,
                              DS3D_IMMEDIATE );
}

void AudioPath3D::SetVelocity( D3DXVECTOR3 velocity )
{
  velocity *= g_engine->GetScale();
  m_soundBuffer->SetVelocity( velocity.x, velocity.y, velocity.z,
                              DS3D_IMMEDIATE );
}
```

You can see that both the position and the velocity are adjusted by the scale to ensure that they are in scale with the sound system. You are expected to pass unscaled values to both of these functions. You will also note that both of the calls on the sound buffer use the DS3D_IMMEDIATE flag rather than the DS3D_DEFERRED flag. This is because the DS3D_DEFERRED flag is really only necessary when you are setting multiple properties at once. Since each function is only setting one property, and we have no guarantee that they will both be called together, it is best to apply their settings immediately.

The next function is a very small but very interesting function that we will make use of within our game as you will see in Part II. This function is the `SetMode` function, and its implementation is shown here:

```
void AudioPath3D::SetMode( unsigned long mode )
{
m_soundBuffer->  SetMode( mode, DS3D_IMMEDIATE );
}
```

So the question you may ask is: how can this tiny, almost insignificant function be so interesting? The answer is that it allows us to set how the audio path's sound buffer processes 3D sound, which you specify as the only parameter of the function. The `SetMode` function is then called on the sound buffer and your specified mode is passed to it. Once again, we use the `DS3D_IMMEDIATE` flag to make the setting take effect immediately. There are three different modes that you can choose from, which are shown in Table 6.2.

TABLE 6.2 Sound Buffer 3D Processing Modes

`DS3DMODE_DISABLE`	3D sound processing is disabled. Sounds played through this buffer do not have any 3D properties.
`DS3DMODE_HEADRELATIVE`	3D sound properties such as position and velocity are all relative to the 3D listener (the microphone). In other words, specifying a position of (5.0, 0.0, 0.0) means that the sound is 5.0 units away from the listener along the x-axis, regardless of where the listener is positioned.
`DS3DMODE_NORMAL`	Normal 3D sound processing. So a position of (5.0, 0.0, 0.0) means that the sound is played at that absolute position in 3D space. This is the default processing mode.

The first mode in Table 6.2 is pretty self-explanatory, but the second and third may take a little more explaining if you haven't grasped how they work. Let's work with a quick example. Say the listener is positioned at (10.0, 0.0, −5.0) in 3D space, and we have two 3D sounds—which we will call A and B. Sound A will use `DS3DMODE_HEADRELATIVE` mode, while sound B will use `DS3DMODE_NORMAL` mode. If we position sound A at (−1.0, 0.0, 2.0), then it would actually exist at (9.0, 0.0, −3.0) in

3D space. This is because the position of sound A is relative to the position of the listener. If we give sound B the same position of (–1.0, 0.0, 2.0), then it would be positioned at this absolute coordinate in 3D space as it is not relative to the listener. If the listener moved along the x-axis by –4 units, its new position would be (6.0, 0.0, –5.0). This means that sound A would now be positioned at (5.0, 0.0, –3.0), as it moves with the listener therefore it too is moved –4 units along the x-axis. Sound B however would still remain at (–1.0, 0.0, 2.0) in 3D space as it does not care where the listener moves. Figure 6.3 gives a visual representation of how these two 3D sound processing modes work.

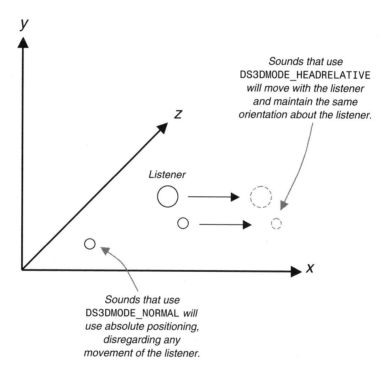

FIGURE 6.3 The difference between DS3DMODE_HEADRELATIVE and DS3DMODE_NORMAL.

The last but not least function is the Play function, which allows you to play a sound segment on the audio path. This function accepts as input a pointer to the sound segment to be played. This is why the Sound class has a GetSegment function. We could just pass in a pointer to a Sound class instance, but then we would not be able to use the AudioPath3D class with segments that were loaded through other means (i.e., not using the Sound class). This would reduce the flexibility of the AudioPath3D class. Just like the Play function on the Sound class, this one also accepts a flag for looping, and the last parameter allows you to specify any optional flags to modify the sound's playback. The implementation of the Play function is shown here:

```
void AudioPath3D::Play( IDirectMusicSegment8 *segment, bool loop,
                        unsigned long flags )
{
  if( loop == true )
    segment->SetRepeats( DMUS_SEG_REPEAT_INFINITE );
  else
    segment->SetRepeats( 0 );

  g_engine->GetSoundSystem()->GetPerformance()->PlaySegmentEx(
          segment, NULL, NULL, flags, 0, NULL, NULL, m_audioPath );
}
```

You can see that it looks very similar to the Play function used by the Sound class. In fact, this function operates almost identically. The only difference is that we use PlaySegmentEx on the performance instead of PlaySegment. The reason for this is that PlaySegmentEx allows us to pass in an audio path that we want to play the segment on as the last parameter of the function call. Whereas PlaySegment does not; any segments played using that function will play through the performance's default audio path.

We have now come to the end of the AudioPath3D class, and with that, the end of our entire sound system. You can see that it really isn't that complicated and very soon you are going to see just how easy it is to use. However, before we can test it we need to integrate it into our engine.

INTEGRATING THE SOUND SYSTEM

First, as with every new addition, we have to ensure that we link the files together by placing the appropriate #include statements in the correct files. We have done this so many times now with previous files, you should have a pretty good idea of what needs to be done. Just have a look in Engine.h and SoundSystem.cpp if you need to jog your memory.

There aren't really many changes that need to be made to the Engine class in order to use our new sound system. The most obvious, though, is that we need to add a member variable for the SoundSystem class, and a function for retrieving a pointer to the sound system, which is shown here:

```
public:
  SoundSystem *GetSoundSystem();

private:
  SoundSystem *m_soundSystem;
```

In the Engine class constructor we need to create our sound system with the following line of code:

```
m_soundSystem = new SoundSystem( m_setup->scale );
```

Then in the destructor we need to remember to destroy the sound system so that we do not leave any memory leaks behind. This is achieved by using the SAFE_DELETE macro on our m_soundSystem pointer. Finally, the last change to the Engine class is to add one more line of code to the ChangeState function, which is shown here:

```
m_soundSystem->GarbageCollection();
```

Remember when we talked about garbage collection so that the sound system can clean up unused objects to free memory? If so, then you will also remember that we said we would do it every time the engine changed states, which is exactly what is happening here. Now we are ready to test out our new sound system.

TESTING THE SOUND SYSTEM

ON THE CD
Let's wrap up another chapter with a quick test of our engine—this time with sound! You can find the test application in the Test project of the workspace for this chapter. This test is actually very quick and the only points we need to look at are a few lines of code in the TestState class.

First, you can see that the TestState class has a member variable called m_sound, which is just a pointer to a Sound class instance. We will use this to create and play a sound. First, we load the sound in the Load function of the TestState class, which is shown here:

```
m_sound = new Sound( "./Assets/Sound.wav" );
```

Remember that the name of the sound has to include the complete path to the sound; however, the path can be relative to the current working directory, which will be the directory where the executable exists. We also must not forget to destroy the sound in the Close function by using the SAFE_DELETE macro on the m_sound pointer. Finally, we want to play the sound. To make it a little more interesting we will link the sound to the pressing of the spacebar. We do this in the Update function and the code is shown here:

```
if( g_engine->GetInput()->GetKeyPress( DIK_SPACE ) )
  m_sound->Play();
```

Now every time the spacebar is pressed the sound will play. You should note that since we are not using our class, the sound will play on the default audio path provided by the performance. When we created the default audio path, we specified that we didn't want it to use 3D sound processing. So any sounds that you play this way will not have any 3D capabilities.

SUMMARY

Gradually our engine is beginning to take form as we add more features and flesh it out. In this chapter, we looked at how DirectMusic works, including Direct-Sound in regard to 3D sound playback. We then went on to discuss and implement the three classes that make up our sound system—SoundSystem, Sound, and AudioPath3D. After integrating the new sound system into our engine we ran another test on our engine, this time playing a short sound to test our new sound system. When we build our game in Part II, we will make use of the AudioPath3D class so you will see the 3D sounds in action. But, before we can do that we still have a lot more work to do on our engine.

Before our engine becomes any larger we must consider the impacts of multiplayer gaming. Adding network support for a game is not something that can be done at the end when you get around to it. It needs to be well thought out and considered early in the piece. Therefore, it has now come time for us to implement a networking system into our engine, which is exactly what we will do in Chapter 7. Once implemented, our engine will be able to communicate with other instances of the engine running on different computers over a network. This truly opens up a whole new game play experience.

7 Networking

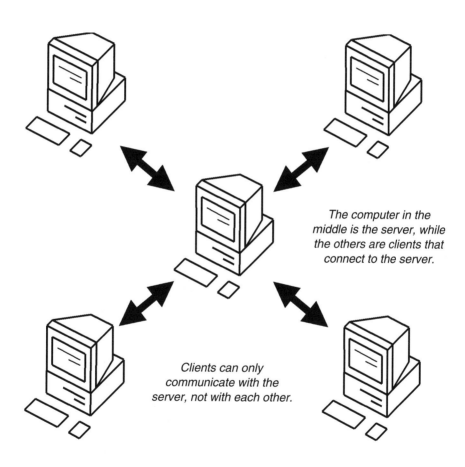

The computer in the middle is the server, while the others are clients that connect to the server.

Clients can only communicate with the server, not with each other.

In This Chapter

- Talk about networking and how DirectX handles it using DirectPlay.
- Look at the different network architectures and discuss the design of our networking system.
- Implement our networking system and integrate it into the engine.

Our engine is starting to resemble an engine, but it is missing a key ingredient if we ever hope to use it to create multiplayer games that can play across a network—it needs networking support. By the end of this chapter our engine will be capable of managing a network session (sending and receiving data; communicating with other instances of the engine running on the network). You can find the workspace for this chapter in the /Source/Chapter 7/ directory on the CD-ROM.

As with many of the topics in this book, networking is very in-depth and a proper discussion on the topic could easily fill an entire book, if not more. For this reason, you need to bear in mind that we cannot possibly cover everything. In addition to this, there will be some seemingly important topics that we may only gloss over. In fact, the implementation of our network system is quite long and perhaps a little overwhelming at first. We will try to keep everything as simple and straightforward as possible—we will discuss only the most important topics.

WORDS OF WARNING

In the previous chapters, we have discussed fairly basic topics that had simple implementations. This allowed us to look at almost every line of code and dissect everything. Of course, we have left the best until last so you'll find that as you progress the material gradually becomes more difficult. This chapter presents the first step up in the difficulty ladder and the next chapter will step up further. From here on we won't be able to always look at all of a particular topic's implementation. Instead, we will cover only the relevant code and leave the supporting material for you to pursue at your own leisure.

Keep in mind that just because it is in the book does not mean that the presented code is complete. Therefore, it is strongly advisable to have the code from the CD-ROM open in front of you on your screen. You will then be able to see how everything fits in relation to what we are discussing at the time.

When you finish this chapter you will have a complete DirectX networking system to handle virtually all of your multiplayer requirements. As with any chap-

ON THE CD

ter, if by the end the material has gone straight over your head and you cannot seem to understand any of it, the best thing to do is to read through the chapter one more time using the code on the CD-ROM as a reference. If after that you are still struggling, just carry on. Remember that we are here to learn how to make a game, not an engine. It is often easier to work backwards, which means that when we begin using the networking system in Part II, you will learn more about how to use it. Subsequently, you will then learn more about how it works by seeing it in a real working game. You must have patience and persistence. You will find that the easiest way to learn how something works is to use it and play with it, despite the fact that you may have no idea what you are doing. Gradually you will begin to understand what everything does, and you will soon learn what questions you should ask. At that point, do not forget about two of the most valuable resources that you have at your disposal: the DirectX SDK documentation and the Internet—you can find the answers to almost any question you have from these two resources.

One of the best Web sites that every game developer should visit on a regular basis is *www.GameDev.net*. Here you will find many articles on specific topics written by people who have been down the same path you are going down. Remember that everyone who knows something had to learn it first. Additionally, if you have never used the forums there, become familiar with them as there are a lot of talented people available who can answer many of your questions. Always remember to search the forum for your question before asking; chances are, someone else has already asked the same question and received an informed answer.

Additionally, you can visit my Web site at *www.coderedgames.com* for specific details regarding this book and its source code. There is also a forum for you to discuss any issues you may have. You can also visit *www.charlesriver.com* for the same information and updates.

NETWORKING WITH DIRECTPLAY

Now it is time to get very comfortable and prepare yourself for a whirlwind tour of networking with DirectX. There is one component of DirectX that is specifically designed for networking—DirectPlay. This component can manage virtually everything about a network session, which is a connection instance between one or more computers communicating data for the same specific purpose. In other words, if you host a multiplayer game, you are creating a session. Other players can then join your session when they play the same game. DirectPlay is the interface that allows you to create and join sessions, as well as search for sessions across a network. Once connected to a session, DirectPlay can then be used to send and receive data among clients of the same session. A client is anyone who joins the session; the session creator is referred to as the host, or server.

These are the main functions of DirectPlay; however, it can do a whole lot more than this. We will only cover what's necessary to create and join a session, locate sessions on the network, and send and receive data. To find out more about additional DirectPlay features, read through the *DirectPlay* section of the DirectX SDK documentation.

When we talk about a network, it can be any type of network, such as a local area network (LAN), a wide area network (WAN), or the entire Internet (which is just a large network). For the purpose of this book and to keep everything simple, we will focus on the LAN. This means that you have two or more computers connected together on the same network in a localized area (generally in the same room, or building, often connected through a hub or switch).

Before we move on to our specific network implementation, let's have a general look at how DirectPlay works. DirectPlay can operate using either a peer-to-peer or a client-server architecture, which we will discuss a little later in this chapter. Once you have decided which architecture your application will use, you then invoke DirectPlay's functionality using the appropriate interface. Additionally, you must decide which transport protocol DirectPlay is to operate under. The transport protocol is used by DirectPlay for all messaging (i.e., send/receiving network messages) and allows you to be abstracted away from the underlying complications of each service provider. The service provider is the technology that allows DirectPlay to communicate via the transport protocol. At the moment, DirectPlay supports the following service providers:

■ Transmission Control Protocol/Internet Protocol (TCP/IP)
■ Internetwork Packet Exchange (IPX)
■ Modem
■ Serial Link

TCP/IP is the most commonly used service provider for developing DirectPlay-supported applications. The benefit of using TCP/IP is that it is specifically designed for Internet communication. If you think about it, a LAN is just a miniature version of the Internet. If you design your network system to operate on a LAN, it makes it far easier to operate it across the Internet. For this reason we will use TCP/IP, so we will focus any further discussion on this service provider. Remember that you can always refer to the DirectX SDK documentation, which can give you many more details about each of the service providers.

To communicate across a network, DirectPlay uses what is called *addresses*, which are unique ways of identifying computers on a network. Every participant in a multiplayer game has a unique address that is used by DirectPlay to send messages and to identify where messages came from. A DirectPlay address comes in the form of a URL string, with a scheme, scheme separator, and a data string. The data string has all of the required information for DirectPlay to allow communication between the sender and the receiver. This may sound a little complicated, but fortunately, DirectPlay has an address object that wraps up the address in a simple little interface. The address object is an important part of network communication that you need to be aware of. You will see how it is used later when we develop our networking system.

Finally, you should also know a little bit of theory about how DirectPlay handles messages. A message is sent using a structure of data called a *packet*. Each packet has a header that contains information about the type of message it is and where it came from. The packet also contains the actual data that is being sent, which is appended to the end of the message. To communicate with your application, DirectPlay uses a call-back function just like the call-back functions used by windows and dialogs. The idea is that you implement a call-back function within your application to which DirectPlay can pass received messages. Whenever the call-back function is called by DirectPlay, it means that your application has received a message. All you need to do is check the message identifier to determine what type of message it is. Once you know the message type, you can then process the message's data appropriately.

That should be about enough theory for now. As previously mentioned, we cannot cover everything, so there are still a lot of holes in our theory, and you probably have a number of questions. Hopefully, as we discuss our network system, many of your questions will be answered as we progress. So let's move on to the actual architecture of our network system.

NETWORK ARCHITECTURE

As discussed earlier, DirectPlay uses two types of network architecture, or models. You must decide which one is best suited to your application and then develop specifically for that architecture. DirectPlay can use either peer-to-peer (supported by the `IDirectPlay8Peer` interface) or client-server (supported by the `IDirectPlay8Client` interface and the `IDirectPlay8Server` interface), with each having advantages and disadvantages.

The peer-to-peer model works by having a direct link between every computer in the session. There is still a host that controls the session, however, each client (or peer) can communicate directly with each other, without the host's permission. The idea is that each client keeps track of the game's state and the state of everyone in the game. Whenever a client needs to update itself, it sends a message to every other client to inform them of the changes. Additionally, one client (usually the one that created the session) is designated as the host. This client is responsible for managing logistics such as players joining and leaving the session, as well as game logic such as AI processing. Table 7.1 shows the advantages and disadvantages of the peer-to-peer model.

TABLE 7.1 Peer-to-Peer Advantages and Disadvantages

Advantages	Simpler model and easier to understand. No need for separate client-side and server-side code. Every client is identical and can perform the tasks of a host.
Disadvantages	Easy to implement poorly, which can result in increased network activity. Lack of scalability means that as the number of players increases, the number of messages increases significantly. Inappropriate when security is an issue as each client will receive most messages.

Despite the shortcomings of the model, it is actually a very good choice for a simple game that will not exceed 20–30 players (the typical maximum number of players as stated in the DirectX SDK documentation). Due to its advantages of simplicity, we will use this model for our engine. Figure 7.1 shows how a peer-to-peer model looks.

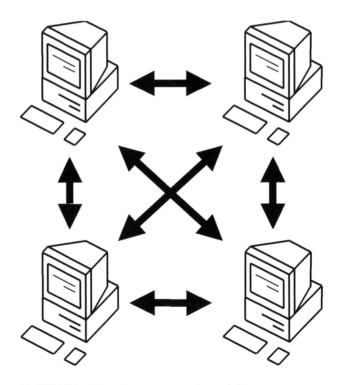

FIGURE 7.1 Peer-to-peer network model.

We have already decided which model we will use, but just for completeness, we will have a quick look at the client-server model as well. The client-server model is probably the most popular model used among commercial games, especially games that can be played over the Internet. Once you have mastered the peer-to-peer model, upgrading to the client-server model will be a walk in the park, but you have to start out simple. So let's see how the client-server model works.

In the client-server model, one computer (or sometimes more for the large scale online games) acts as a server, and all the other computers (or clients) are required to connect to the server in order to play. The clients can only communicate with the server—not with each other—while the server can communicate with each client. The server is usually a specially designed application that is optimized for handling the game's logistics and lacks all of the features that make a game playable, such as graphics and sound. The server manages everything about the game and the clients are just portals (or windows) into the game world. Whenever a player requires some sort of update, a message is sent to the server and the server broadcasts the result as necessary. Table 7.1 shows the advantages and disadvantages of the client-server model.

TABLE 7.2 Client-Server Advantages and Disadvantages

Advantages	The most efficient model in terms of network usage. As the number of players increases, network traffic increases linearly. The server can handle much of the logic processing, freeing the game clients to focus on better game play, graphics, sound, etc. Easier to manage the game world and apply changes or bug fixes to it when it is running on a central server. Much better model for security, as messages intended for a particular client go to that client only. Additionally, clients do not maintain the state of the game world.
Disadvantages	This model is a little more complicated to understand and implement as opposed to the peer-to-peer model. Separate client-side and server-side code needs to be developed.

The client-server model has many more benefits than the peer-to-peer model. However, the key difference is that the peer-to-peer model is a lot simpler to understand, implement, and work with. As previously mentioned, it is best to start simple. Once you have learned the peer-to-peer model, then you should upgrade to the client-server model. We will finish our discussion of the client-server model by looking at Figure 7.2, which shows how a client-server model looks.

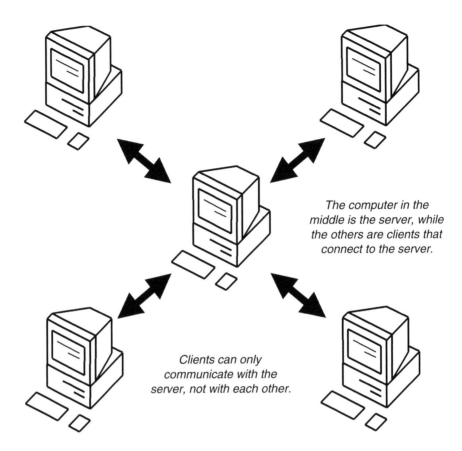

The computer in the middle is the server, while the others are clients that connect to the server.

Clients can only communicate with the server, not with each other.

FIGURE 7.2 Client-server network model.

Before we move on to any sort of implementation, we need to discuss one more important topic that affects our network architecture—network message processing. We already talked a little about this topic earlier, when you learned about packets. Now we need to go a little deeper and actually look at the method that we will use to process network messages. You already know that every time our application receives a network message, it enters a call-back function that checks the message's type and then processes the data in the message appropriately. The problem is that during a fast-paced action game such as a FPS, there are a lot of network messages flying around. Processing them takes time. What happens if an instance of our game client is suddenly flooded with thousands of messages from other players? If we don't use any sort of controlling mechanism to process these messages, the game client could easily bog down to an absolute crawl, becoming completely unplayable. On the flipside, we also need to ensure that the network system on the game client is not starved of processing time. If this happens then the game can easily fall out of sync with the other game clients as data will not be updated frequently enough.

To solve this problem, we will use a linked list and a timer. The discerning reader will immediately make the connection and see where we are headed, but let's step through our solution to this problem. In fact, this is actually a fairly common solution. Additionally, this solution makes up part of our engine control that we discussed in Chapter 3.

What we will do is every time a user-defined game message is received by our call-back function we will just add it to a linked list. Then, every frame we call a function on our network object that will allow it to process the messages in the linked list for a certain amount of time, which is where the timer comes in. It will continue to process messages from this linked list in a first-in first-out fashion until the timer has expired. At that point, the networking system will yield control back to the engine. Any messages left in the linked list that were not processed will be done in the next frame. Processing messages this way allows the clients to process enough messages per frame to remain in sync and maintain a playable game, while also preventing the client from being flooded with more messages than it can handle.

It may sound a bit perplexing, but it is very simple once you see it implemented, which we will do a little later in the chapter. We will start by looking at network messages and implementing the structures used to handle them.

MESSAGES

By now you should know what network messages are, and have a pretty good idea of what they are used for and how we will process them. If not, let's quickly recap. A network message is a packet that contains a header and the actual data being transferred in the message. The header identifies the message type and where it came from. Imagine a message like a letter and an envelope. The header is like the information on the envelope. It tells you everything you need to know in order to get the letter to the right person so that it can be processed appropriately. The letter inside the envelope is like the data, which is only read by the final person that the letter was addressed to.

Finally, as network messages are sent among the different players in a session, they are received by each client's network message handler, which is a call-back function used for processing the network messages. Whenever a user-defined message is received, it is placed into the network messages linked list. Every frame, the network system processes as many messages from this linked list as it can within an allotted amount of time. Each message is then sent to the appropriate place based on its type so that its data can be processed, which wraps up the life cycle of a network message.

You have probably noticed that we have mentioned *user-defined* messages a couple of times and you may be wondering what that means. In general, there are two types of messages that can be sent: system messages and user-defined messages. System messages are those that are defined and used by DirectPlay, such as messages for creating and joining a session, as well as messages for leaving and terminating sessions. These messages are already defined for you by DirectPlay, and each one has a set data structure that you must work with. User-defined messages on the other hand are those that you define. You create the data structure and you decide what they are used for and how they are processed. These types of messages are typically used for in-game messages such as updating player data.

We won't worry about putting system messages through our whole message processing system. Instead, we will just process them as soon as they arrive. There are two reasons for this. First, system messages are very rare in comparison to user-defined messages (i.e., they only occur when events such as a player joining or leaving the session happen), and second they often affect any user-defined messages waiting to be processed. For example, if you had a player leave the game but your client still had messages about that player waiting to be processed, then your client may try to process messages on a player it thinks is still in the game. To prevent this we need to process system messages immediately so that any user-defined messages about that player are handled appropriately.

Let's have a look at the structures that we will use to implement our network messages. We will use two structures—the `NetworkMessage` structure and the `ReceivedMessage` structure (found at the beginning of `Network.h`).

```
struct NetworkMessage
{
  unsigned long msgid;
  DPNID dpnid;
};

struct ReceivedMessage : public NetworkMessage
{
  char data[32];
};
```

The `NetworkMessage` structure acts like the header of a network message. It tells you what the message is (`msgid`) and who sent it (`dpnid`). The message identifier is just a unique number that you give to each message. You will see how we do that when we create our own user-defined messages when we build our game. The `dpnid` is a unique player identifier used to identify individual players in a session. Direct-Play manages the assignment of these identifiers for you. All you need to worry about is that every time a player joins a session, DirectPlay assigns them a unique identifier, which you can use to reference that player.

The `ReceivedMessage` structure is actually derived from our `NetworkMessage` structure. This new structure resembles the letter and envelope example that you saw recently. The `ReceivedMessage` structure is used for storing received messages in our linked list to be processed later. When a new message arrives, its header is copied over (which matches the `NetworkMessage` structure) and the data in the message is copied into the `data char` array. When the message is finally processed, we can extract the data from this buffer based on its type, so that we can process the data appropriately.

You can see in the `ReceivedMessage` structure that we have only allocated 32 bytes for network message data, which means that if a message has more than 32 bytes of data in it, then it will overrun the buffer. To prevent this you should allocate a large buffer at testing, and once you have optimized your network messages and finalized the largest size message you will be using, then reduce this buffer down to around that size. Remember that the smaller your network messages are the faster they are sent and processed, and the less memory they consume.

PLAYERS

So we have had a thorough look at network messages, but that is not the only data that the network system needs to operate. It also needs players (or clients) to send messages to and receive messages from. Although the information about a given player is very game specific, the network system still needs a few basic details about each player in the game for communication purposes. For this reason, the network system will maintain a definitive list of players in the game at any point. However, the game itself should still maintain a separate list of players that has all of the game specific data in it about each player.

Note: it is important to remember that any game specific player list needs to be constantly updated to match the network system's player list as it can change without warning if a new player joins the game, or an old player leaves the game.

With that said, let's introduce the `PlayerInfo` structure, which is used by the network system to store the basic details of each player in the game. The network system will achieve this by using a linked list of `PlayerInfo` structures. The linked list class we built in Chapter 1 is really coming in handy for a lot of things.

```
struct PlayerInfo
{
  DPNID dpnid;
  char *name;
  void *data;
  unsigned long size;

  PlayerInfo()
  {
    dpnid = 0;
    name = NULL;
    data = NULL;
    size = 0;
  }

  ~PlayerInfo()
  {
    SAFE_DELETE( name );
    SAFE_DELETE( data );
  }
};
```

The `PlayerInfo` structure is very basic, which is all we need as it only has to hold the essential player details. Basically, the `PlayerInfo` structure keeps a copy of the player's unique identifier assigned to it by DirectPlay. It also keeps a copy of the player's name, as well as a copy of the player's data and the size of the data. Now the `data` member is the interesting one. It is actually the application specific data that is passed when the player is created. DirectPlay allows you to pass an application specific data block that can be interpreted on the other end (i.e., when the message is received).

Let's look at an example to make it a little clearer. Say you were making a FPS that had some sort of team style game play. Before a new player can join the game they must select which team they want to be on. Once they have selected a team they can join the game and a network message is sent to every other game client informing them that a new player has joined the session. Each game client will then need to create a local instance of this new player so that they can manage the new player in the game. Within the message to create the new player, DirectPlay passes you three important pieces of information. The unique identifier assigned to the player by DirectPlay, the name of the player, and the application specific data block set by the new player. We can use this application specific data block to pass a flag that indicates which team the new player has chosen. That way, all of the game clients can just open up the application specific data block, read the flag, and then assign the local instance of the player to the correct team.

When we implement our FPS game we will use this application specific data block to pass information such as which character the player has chosen and which map was chosen by the host. The rest of the `PlayerInfo` structure should be fairly self-explanatory by now if you have been following right from the start. So let's stop here and move on to the next important topic, which will bring us another step closer to implementing our network system.

CRITICAL SECTIONS

What are *critical sections*, you may ask? To understand them, we must look at the way our application works with DirectPlay. In addition, you will need to learn a little about multithreading.

Every time you run an application on your computer, one or more processes are started for that application. You can view all of the processes running on your computer by opening up the Windows Task Manager. The vast majority of applications, such as the games we will be making, only use one process. A process has what is called a *thread*, which is like a single chain of instructions that is executed by the operating system. Often (especially when writing applications with networking) a process will have more than one thread. When this happens, the operating system must switch between the threads to allow each one to process. This is called *multithreading*.

DirectPlay makes use of multithreading to perform its networking in conjunction with your application. In other words, your application has one or more threads that process the game and a second thread that processes incoming network messages. Now you may be wondering where your application gets this extra thread from, as we never explicitly specify anything for it. What you don't realize is that when you implement the network message handler call-back function, you are in fact creating your second thread. Fortunately, DirectPlay handles the thread's management for us, so it is transparent to us, to a degree. You see, the network message handler (which acts in exactly the same way as the call-back functions for windows and dialogs) actually belongs to DirectPlay in a strange sort of way. Even though you implement it, you never call it. DirectPlay calls it whenever a network message is sent to your application. Because a network message can be received at any time (even while your application is in the middle of some other task like rendering, for example) the call-back function has to be run on its own thread, which still exists inside your application's process and resides in the same memory. This way, your application can receive network messages without having to drop what it is doing.

To give you a better example, think about how the postal service works. If you are outside mowing your lawn, for example, and a letter it sent to you, you don't have to immediately drop the lawn mower and tend to the incoming mail. Instead, the post office collects the mail and delivers it to your home, despite the fact that you are off doing something else completely unrelated. Then when you are ready, you can go and check your mailbox to receive any letters that have arrived.

Now that you understand what multithreading is, let's have a look at the biggest problem it faces, which caused the invention of the critical section and other mutex (mutual exclusion) devices. Because multiple threads exist in the same process, they also exist in the same memory, as previously mentioned. What this means is that they have to share resources in this memory. Say you had two threads and a variable that the two threads need to use. Because the two threads and the variable exist in the same memory, the threads have to share the variable. So what's the big deal, you ask? Well, what happens when both threads want to use the variable at the same time?

If one thread tried to read a variable while another one was trying to write data to that same variable, you could end up with some unexpected results. We have already decided earlier that whenever DirectPlay calls our application's network message handler, we will take the incoming message and add it to a linked list, so that later on when our application is ready it can handle any messages that are waiting to be processed. This causes a problem with mutual exclusion though. If a new network message arrives at the same time we are processing messages from the list we could have a problem. The network message handler's thread will attempt to add the new network message to the linked list while we are trying to read messages from the list.

To solve the problem, we use the critical section. The critical section bears its name from the fact that the code it protects is literally a critical section of code. In other words, if this section of code is not protected, then it can cause problems with mutual exclusion. Whenever we are about to process some questionable code, we lock the critical section that is assigned to that portion of code. Then when we are finished, we simply unlock the critical section. If another process attempts to lock the same critical section, it has to wait until the critical section is unlocked before it can proceed. The idea is that you wrap access to shared memory inside a critical section. It really is as simple as that. Figure 7.3 shows how the critical section works.

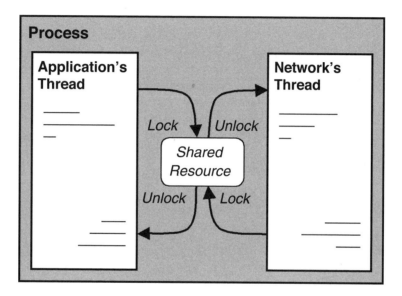

FIGURE 7.3 How critical sections work.

To enter a critical section we use the EnterCriticalSection statement and to leave a critical section we use the LeaveCriticalSection statement. Any code between these two statements is protected by this critical section, as shown in this example:

```
EnterCriticalSection( &myCS );

// Any code in here is protected.

LeaveCriticalSection( &myCS );
```

The code between the EnterCriticalSection *and the* LeaveCriticalSection *statements should be kept to a bare minimum. Remember that if a thread tries to enter a critical section that has already been entered by another thread, it will stall there until the critical section is free. This can be disastrous if the stalling thread is your main game thread; the player's game will appear to freeze while it waits. Additionally, you should never enter a critical section within another critical section. In other words, do not embed critical sections within each other.*

You should not embed critical sections within each other as shown in this example:

```
EnterCriticalSection( &firstCS );

EnterCriticalSection( &secondCS );

// The critical section "secondCS" is embedded inside the critical
// section "firstCS". This can lead to a major problem—deadlock!

LeaveCriticalSection( &secondCS );

LeaveCriticalSection( &firstCS );
```

This can cause a major problem called *deadlock*, which means the two or more threads have permanently stalled as they are each trying to enter a critical section that is locked by another thread. For example, thread A may try to enter secondCS, which has already been entered by thread B. At the same time, thread B is trying to enter firstCS, but it has already been entered by thread A. Both threads are deadlocked.

Other than that, critical sections are painless to use so long as you don't make any silly mistakes. You should now have a pretty good understanding of critical sections, so it is time now to look at one last topic before we begin developing our network system.

GLOBALLY UNIQUE IDENTIFIERS

Throughout the network code you will stumble across a type called a GUID (Globally Unique Identifier). Without going into too much detail, the basic premise of a GUID is that it is a string of alphanumeric characters that is unique, globally. In other words, you can never generate two of the same, in theory. So if you generate a new GUID, you are guaranteed that nobody else will ever generate the same one.

You can generate a GUID at runtime, but we won't go into that as it's unnecessary. We only need to generate a new GUID when we create a new application with networking features because the GUID is used by DirectPlay to identify different applications. To generate a new GUID you can use the GUIDGEN tool included with Visual Studio. You can find it in the ..\Common\Tools directory where Visual Studio is installed.

THE NETWORK SYSTEM

Much of the necessary groundwork is in place so we can begin looking at our actual network system. Of course, we could spend another whole chapter just discussing the theory of networking and DirectPlay, but that really isn't necessary. Instead, we will jump straight into the deep end. Throughout the remainder of this chapter, you will be introduced to the most significant part of the network system. We cannot possibly dissect it line-by-line, so you are encouraged to have the source code from the CD-ROM close at hand for reference. Once you have finished reading this chapter, you may want to consider reading through the source code in both the Network.h and the Network.cpp files to help you grasp how it all works.

ON THE CD

So with that out of the way, let's begin by looking at the massive class definition for the Network class, as shown here:

```
class Network
{
public:
  Network( GUID guid, void (*HandleNetworkMessageFunction)(
          ReceivedMessage *msg ) );
  virtual ~Network();

  void Update();

  void EnumerateSessions();

  bool Host( char *name, char *session, int players = 0,
          void *playerData = NULL, unsigned long dataSize = 0 );
  bool Join( char *name, int session = 0, void *playerData = NULL,
          unsigned long dataSize = 0 );
  void Terminate();
```

```
    void SetReceiveAllowed( bool allowed );

    SessionInfo *GetNextSession( bool restart = false );
    PlayerInfo *GetPlayer( DPNID dpnid );

    DPNID GetLocalID();
    DPNID GetHostID();
    bool IsHost();

    void Send( void *data, long size,
            DPNID dpnid = DPNID_ALL_PLAYERS_GROUP, long flags = 0 );
private:
    static HRESULT WINAPI NetworkMessageHandler( PVOID context,
            DWORD msgid, PVOID data );

private:
    GUID m_guid;
    IDirectPlay8Peer *m_dpp;
    IDirectPlay8Address *m_device;

    unsigned long m_port;
    unsigned long m_sendTimeOut;
    unsigned long m_processingTime;

    DPNID m_dpnidLocal;
    DPNID m_dpnidHost;

    CRITICAL_SECTION m_sessionCS;
    LinkedList< SessionInfo > *m_sessions;

    CRITICAL_SECTION m_playerCS;
    LinkedList< PlayerInfo > *m_players;

    bool m_receiveAllowed;
    CRITICAL_SECTION m_messageCS;
    LinkedList< ReceivedMessage > *m_messages;
    void (*HandleNetworkMessage)( ReceivedMessage *msg );
};
```

As you look through it, hopefully you will be able to recognize bits and pieces of it based on what we have already discussed. The class exposes a whole host of functions that allow you to enumerate, create, and join sessions, as well as send and receive network messages among other things. We will look at the most important functions a little later in the chapter, and ignore the basic functions such as GetPlayer and IsHost as they are very simple in comparison to some of the other functions that we really need to look at. You can pick up the working of these basic functions quite easily by simply looking at the source code for them.

A lot of the member variables are also fairly obvious as to what they are used for just by their names. You should be able to pick out the three major linked lists and their critical sections. Yes, that's right; we will be using three critical sections that you will learn about later. We will discuss the important member variables as we progress through the rest of this chapter, so don't worry if there is something you don't understand yet.

Let's move on to the class constructor, which takes two parameters as input. The first parameter is the application GUID that is used to uniquely identify this application on the network. The second parameter is a pointer to an application specific network message handler call-back function. This allows the application to create a call-back that the engine will call to process the user-defined network messages. When we integrate the network system we will add a new member to our EngineSetup structure that will allow us to specify a call-back function to be used here.

```
Network::Network( GUID guid,
    void (*HandleNetworkMessageFunction)( ReceivedMessage *msg ) )
{
  InitializeCriticalSection( &m_sessionCS );
  InitializeCriticalSection( &m_playerCS );
  InitializeCriticalSection( &m_messageCS );

  m_dpp = NULL;
  m_device = NULL;

  memcpy( &m_guid, &guid, sizeof( GUID ) );
```

Once inside the constructor, the first step is to initialize the three critical sections. We have one critical section for each of our linked lists, as they are all used by both our application's thread and the network message handler's thread. We then go on to clear our DirectPlay peer interface pointer and our device address pointer. If you think back to Chapter 5, we used a device there as well, but it was used to refer to the display adapter hardware. Here we also have a device, but this device refers to the local address on the network (i.e., the address of this application instance). After that, we need to make a copy of the application's GUID, which we will store in m_guid.

```
m_sessions = new LinkedList< SessionInfo >;

m_players = new LinkedList< PlayerInfo >;

m_messages = new LinkedList< ReceivedMessage >;
```

Next, we need to create our linked lists, of which there are three. m_sessions is used to store the sessions that we enumerate, m_players is used to store the list of players in the current session, and m_messages is used to store the list of received messages that need to be processed.

```
Script *settings = new Script( "NetworkSettings.txt" );
if( settings->GetNumberData( "processing_time" ) == NULL )
{
  m_port = 2509;
  m_sendTimeOut = 100;
  m_processingTime = 100;
}
else
{
  m_port = *settings->GetNumberData( "port" );
  m_sendTimeOut = *settings->GetNumberData( "send_time_out" );
  m_processingTime =
                  *settings->GetNumberData( "processing_time" );
}
SAFE_DELETE( settings );
```

Now this step is an interesting one. Here we read a script called Network-Settings.txt, and use it to load in the port that we will use to communicate across the network, the time out for sending messages and the time allowed for processing messages each frame. This settings script works in the same way as the one we used for the graphics settings. The only difference is that we don't have a nifty little dialog for it. Instead, we just leave it as a text file that the end user can open and alter directly. The reason for this is that these settings will probably never need to be changed. Only those who experience technical difficulties with the network may need to modify one of these settings. You will see what each of these settings are used for later in this chapter.

```
m_receiveAllowed = false;

HandleNetworkMessage = HandleNetworkMessageFunction;
```

We are almost done with the constructor. The next step is a very simple one that involves setting a flag called m_receiveAllowed to false. This flag tells the network system whether or not it is allowed to receive user-defined messages. This is used to prevent the application from receiving messages about a session before it is ready to start processing them. After setting this flag, we then store the pointer to the application-specific network message handler function.

```
CoCreateInstance( CLSID_DirectPlay8Peer, NULL, CLSCTX_INPROC,
                  IID_IDirectPlay8Peer, (void**)&m_dpp );
m_dpp->Initialize( (PVOID)this, NetworkMessageHandler,
                  DPNINITIALIZE_HINT_LANSESSION );

CoCreateInstance( CLSID_DirectPlay8Address, NULL, CLSCTX_INPROC,
                  IID_IDirectPlay8Address, (LPVOID*) &m_device );
m_device->SetSP( &CLSID_DP8SP_TCPIP );
m_device->AddComponent( DPNA_KEY_PORT, &m_port, sizeof(DWORD),
                  DPNA_DATATYPE_DWORD );
}
```

The final two steps involve creating the DirectPlay peer interface pointer and the device address. We use the CoCreateInstance function to create both of these interfaces as they are both COM objects. You have already seen this function used a number of times so it should be fairly straightforward now. You just need to note the class identifiers and the interface references that we use.

Once we have created our DirectPlay peer interface we need to initialize it with a call to Initialize. This function takes three parameters. The first one is the context of our class, which is passed to the network message handler by DirectPlay. This parameter is set to the this pointer in virtually all circumstances. The second parameter is a pointer to our network message handler call-back function. (This is the engine's internal network message handler, not the application specific handler. That one will be called by the engine to process user-defined messages, which the engine cannot handle). The final parameter allows you to specify several flags. There is only one flag we are interested in: DPNINITIALIZE_HINT_LANSESSION.

This hints to DirectPlay that we will be running over a LAN and not over the Internet. This allows DirectPlay to make certain assumptions that will give us increased network performance.

The last thing left to do in the constructor is to finish setting up the device address once it has been created. This is just a matter of selecting the service provider we want to use and setting the port that we want to communicate through. We set the service provider by calling SetSP and passing in CLSID_DP8SP_TCPIP for TCP/IP. The port is set by calling AddComponent, which allows us to add various components to an address, such as a port. To do that we just need to pass in DPNA_KEY_PORT to indicate a port component and then the actual port, which is stored in our member variable m_port. The last two parameters are used to tell the function what type of data we are passing in, and the size of it.

As usual, wherever a constructor is found allocating memory, an equivalent destructor must be found freeing that memory. So let's have a look at the Network class destructor.

```
Network::~Network()
{
  Script *settings = new Script( "NetworkSettings.txt" );
  if( settings->GetNumberData( "processing_time" ) == NULL )
  {
    settings->AddVariable( "port", VARIABLE_NUMBER, &m_port );
    settings->AddVariable( "send_time_out", VARIABLE_NUMBER,
                           &m_sendTimeOut );
    settings->AddVariable( "processing_time", VARIABLE_NUMBER,
                           &m_processingTime );
  }
  else
  {
    settings->SetVariable( "port", &m_port );
    settings->SetVariable( "send_time_out", &m_sendTimeOut );
    settings->SetVariable( "processing_time", &m_processingTime );
  }
  settings->SaveScript();
  SAFE_DELETE( settings );

  SAFE_RELEASE( m_device );

  if( m_dpp != NULL )
    m_dpp->Close( DPNCLOSE_IMMEDIATE );
  SAFE_RELEASE( m_dpp );
```

```
        SAFE_DELETE( m_sessions );

        SAFE_DELETE( m_players );

        SAFE_DELETE( m_messages );

        DeleteCriticalSection( &m_sessionCS );
        DeleteCriticalSection( &m_playerCS );
        DeleteCriticalSection( &m_messageCS );
    }
```

The first step is to save our network settings script. If the script does not exist (which it won't the first time the application is run), then the script variables are added; otherwise, they are updated in case they were changed during runtime. After that we call SaveScript and then destroy the script.

The next step is to release both our device address and our DirectPlay peer interface. However, before the DirectPlay peer interface is released, it should be closed if it exists. This ensures a graceful disconnection from the connected session, if there is one. After this we can destroy each of our linked lists, and finally delete our critical sections.

ENUMERATING SESSIONS

After you have created an instance of the Network class, one of the first things you will probably want to use it for is to enumerate the network for any sessions that are currently in progress. When you enumerate the network, your application broadcasts an enumeration message to every other DirectPlay equipped application on the network. When the remote application receives the message, DirectPlay checks to make sure that both the remote and the local applications are in fact the same application. This is done by comparing the GUID set by our local application's network component with the GUID set in the remote application's network component. If they match, we know that the two applications are the same and we can proceed with the enumeration. The next step is to check if the remote application is actually hosting a session. If so, the remote application sends a message to our local application with the address and name of the session so we can join it if we choose to.

DirectPlay handles this whole process; all we have to do is manage the replies that come back to us from each host. These replies are collected through our application's network message handler (in the form of DPN_MSGID_ENUM_HOSTS_RESPONSE messages) and we place them into a linked list specifically for storing the enumerated sessions, called m_sessions. Sessions are stored in a SessionInfo structure, which is defined in Network.h, and is shown here:

```
struct SessionInfo
{
  IDirectPlay8Address *address;     // Session network address.
  DPN_APPLICATION_DESC description; // Application description.
};
```

As you can see, a session has two pieces of information: an address and an application description. We have already discussed addresses earlier in this chapter. This address is the session host's address, which we need if we want to connect to this session. It describes where the session exists on the network. The description is a DPN_APPLICATION_DESC structure that stores all of the details about the DirectPlay application that is hosting this session. The definition of the structure is shown here:

```
typedef struct _DPN_APPLICATION_DESC {
  // Size of the structure.
  DWORD dwSize;

  // Flags to describe the application's behavior.
  DWORD dwFlags;

  // GUID generated by DirectPlay at start up.
  GUID guidInstance;

  // GUID of the application.
  GUID guidApplication;

  // Maximum number of players allowed in the game.
  DWORD dwMaxPlayers;

  // Number of players currently connected.
  DWORD dwCurrentPlayers;

  // Name of the session.
  WCHAR *pwszSessionName;

  // Password required to connect to the session.
  WCHAR *pwszPassword;
```

```
    // Reserved data, which must not be modified.
    PVOID pvReservedData;
    DWORD dwReservedDataSize;

    // Application specific data.
    PVOID pvApplicationReservedData;
    DWORD dwApplicationReservedDataSize;
} DPN_APPLICATION_DESC, *PDPN_APPLICATION_DESC;
```

You can see that there are quite a number of members in this structure. Most of them we don't need to concern ourselves with; the ones that we do need to worry about will be explained as we use them. When you want to enumerate the sessions on the network you just need to call the EnumerateSessions function, which is shown here:

```
void Network::EnumerateSessions()
{
  m_players->Empty();
  m_messages->Empty();
  m_sessions->Empty();

  DPN_APPLICATION_DESC description;
  ZeroMemory( &description, sizeof( DPN_APPLICATION_DESC ) );
  description.dwSize = sizeof( DPN_APPLICATION_DESC );
  description.guidApplication = m_guid;

  m_dpp->EnumHosts( &description, NULL, m_device, NULL, 0, 1, 0,
                    0, NULL, NULL, DPNENUMHOSTS_SYNC );
}
```

As soon as we enter the function we empty the three linked lists. The fact that you have called EnumerateSessions indicates that you are not connected to a session, nor hosting one. So we start with a clean slate. The next step is to fill in a basic DPN_APPLICATION_DESC structure. We need to zero the structure's memory and then set the application's GUID. This is the GUID that will be used by DirectPlay to compare the remote application and the local application. This comparison will be performed by DirectPlay running on the remote application when the enumeration message is received. Finally, we call the EnumHosts function, which is exposed by our DirectPlay interface. This function has quite a few parameters, so take a look at the function's prototype:

```
EnumHosts
(
  PDPN_APPLICATION_DESC const pApplicationDesc,
  IDirectPlay8Address *const pdpaddrHost,
  IDirectPlay8Address *const pdpaddrDeviceInfo,
  PVOID const pvUserEnumData,
  const DWORD dwUserEnumDataSize,
  const DWORD dwEnumCount,
  const DWORD dwRetryInterval,
  const DWORD dwTimeOut,
  PVOID const pvUserContext,
  HANDLE *const pAsyncHandle,
  const DWORD dwFlags
);
```

The first parameter is a pointer to a DPN_APPLICATION_DESC structure. We just created one for this, so we pass a pointer to the structure we just created. We ignore the second parameter as we do not know who the host is; that is what we are searching for. The third parameter, however, we do not ignore and we pass in the pointer to our device address. We set dwEnumCount to 1 to indicate that we want the enumeration broadcast to occur once only. All of the other parameters we can ignore except for the last one, where we pass in the DPNENUMHOSTS_SYNC flag. This tells DirectPlay to perform the enumeration synchronously. What this means is that the function call will not return until it has finished enumeration. This is fairly common among multiplayer games that allow you to search the network for active sessions. Often you will be able to click on a refresh button somewhere on the interface that will update the list of sessions. When you do this, the interface will appear to pause for a second or two. This is because the enumeration is happening synchronously and does not return until it is complete.

You can also perform the enumeration (and many other DirectPlay operations) asynchronously. This means that control returns back to your application immediately after calling the operation rather than waiting for the operation to complete. Therefore, you can allow your application to perform other tasks such as accepting user input while DirectPlay processes your requested operation in the background.

We won't go into the technical details of asynchronous operations; however, you will see an example later when we look at sending network messages. Synchronous operations are easier to understand so we will use them wherever possible. If you want to learn more about asynchronous operations simply take a look at the DirectPlay section of the DirectX SDK documentation. More specifically, have a look at the `CancelAsyncOperation` function in the `IDirectPlay8Peer` interface.

When the enumeration replies come back to your application, the network message handler will be invoked for each reply. The message has the `DPN_MSGID_ ENUM_HOSTS_RESPONSE` identifier and contains the details of the host (and its session) that replied. The following code snippet shows how we handle a host response. Assume `response` points to the data contained within the message.

```
SessionInfo *sessionInfo = new SessionInfo;
response->pAddressSender->Duplicate( &sessionInfo->address );
memcpy( &sessionInfo->description,
        response->pApplicationDescription,
        sizeof( DPN_APPLICATION_DESC ) );

EnterCriticalSection( &network->m_sessionCS );
network->m_sessions->Add( sessionInfo );
LeaveCriticalSection( &network->m_sessionCS );
```

First, we use the `Duplicate` function on the host's address information to create a copy of the host's address that we store in the `SessionInfo` structure. Second, we make a copy of the application description and also store that in the same `SessionInfo` structure. Then we enter the critical section for our session's linked list. We add the new session to the linked list and leave the critical section.

HOSTING AND JOINING SESSIONS

You now know how to enumerate sessions and how to handle the responses. However, all of that is worthless if you don't know how to create the sessions to be enumerated, or join the sessions that we do enumerate. So let's have a look at that right now. The `Network` class has two functions, appropriately call `Host` and `Join`— no prizes for guessing what they do. Both functions have a number of similarities, but we will start by looking at the `Host` function. Then we will be able to run through the `Join` function, just focusing on what it does differently from the `Host` function.

The `Host` function accepts five parameters as input. The first parameter is the name of the player who is hosting the session and the second one is the name of the session. The third parameter is used to specify the maximum number of players that are allowed to be connected to the session at any one time, including the host. The last two parameters are used for passing in any player-specific data that we want to be associated with the creation of the local player. Remember earlier in this chapter when we talked about how a player can have data associated with him to assist in creating the player? This is where that data is passed in.

```
bool Network::Host( char *name, char *session, int players,
                    void *playerData, unsigned long dataSize )
{
  WCHAR wide[MAX_PATH];

  DPN_PLAYER_INFO player;
  ZeroMemory( &player, sizeof( DPN_PLAYER_INFO ) );
  player.dwSize = sizeof( DPN_PLAYER_INFO );
  player.pvData = playerData;
  player.dwDataSize = dataSize;
  player.dwInfoFlags = DPNINFO_NAME | DPNINFO_DATA;
  mbstowcs( wide, name, MAX_PATH );
  player.pwszName = wide;
  if( FAILED( m_dpp->SetPeerInfo( &player, NULL, NULL,
                                  DPNSETPEERINFO_SYNC ) ) )
    return false;
```

The step in the Host function is to set up a DPN_PLAYER_INFO structure for the local player. The information that we put into this structure is what is passed to every other client in the session so that each client can create and maintain a local copy of every player in the game. The definition for the DPN_PLAYER_INFO structure is shown here:

```
typedef struct _DPN_PLAYER_INFO {
  DWORD dwSize;         // Size of the structure.
  DWORD dwInfoFlags;    // Identifies the structures contents.
  PWSTR pwszName;       // Name of the player.
  PVOID pvData;         // Player specific data.
  DWORD dwDataSize;     // Size of the player specific data.
  DWORD dwPlayerFlags;  // Identifies the host and local player.
} DPN_PLAYER_INFO, *PDPN_PLAYER_INFO;
```

First, we clear the structure and set its size. Then we set the player-specific data and the size of that data, as well as specifying the DPNINFO_NAME flag and the

`DPNINFO_DATA` flag, indicating that the structure contains both the player's name and player-specific data. Finally, we simply set the player's name and we're all done.

You will notice that we did not set the dwPlayerFlags. This is because DirectPlay sets this flag for you. Whenever your application receives a network message about a new player who has joined the session, you can check this flag. If it contains the `DPNPLAYER_LOCAL` *flag, it means that the new player is the local player (i.e., it belongs to the local application). If it contains the* `DPNPLAYER_HOST` *flag, then it means that the new player is the host of the session.*

The last step in setting the local player's information is to call `SetPeerInfo`, which is exposed by the DirectPlay peer interface. This assigns the `DPN_PLAYER_INFO` structure (that we just filled in) to our DirectPlay peer. We just pass the structure in as our first parameter, and then pass `DPNSETPEERINFO_SYNC` as the last parameter, to indicate that we want the function to process synchronously.

```
DPN_APPLICATION_DESC description;
ZeroMemory( &description, sizeof( DPN_APPLICATION_DESC ) );
description.dwSize = sizeof( DPN_APPLICATION_DESC );
description.guidApplication = m_guid;
description.dwMaxPlayers = players;
mbstowcs( wide, session, MAX_PATH );
description.pwszSessionName = wide;
```

The next step in hosting a session is to set up a `DPN_APPLICATION_DESC` structure. The details you set in this structure are used to define the application and the session. First, we need to set the GUID for the application. This is used when we enumerate sessions to ensure that we do not enumerate sessions from applications that do not match. Then we set the maximum number of players allowed to connect, and finally we set the session's name.

```
if( FAILED( m_dpp->Host( &description, &m_device, 1, NULL, NULL,
                         NULL, 0 ) ) )
   return false;


   return true;
}
```

The last step to host a session is to call the `Host` function on the DirectPlay peer interface; its prototype is shown here:

```
HRESULT Host
(
  const DPN_APPLICATION_DESC *const pdnAppDesc,
  IDirectPlay8Address **const prgpDeviceInfo,
  const DWORD cDeviceInfo,
  const DPN_SECURITY_DESC *const pdpSecurity,
  const DPN_SECURITY_CREDENTIALS *const pdpCredentials,
  VOID *const pvPlayerContext,
  const DWORD dwFlags
);
```

In the first parameter, we pass in a pointer to the DPN_APPLICATION_DESC structure that we just created. For the second parameter, we pass in the device address
that we want to host the session on. The rest of the parameters we can ignore and
just set them to their default values. We wrap the call up in an if statement to check
if it fails. If so, we return false; otherwise, we return true. The application can use
this return value to determine if the session hosting was successful.

If you have understood how to host a session, then you shouldn't have any
problem understanding how to join one, as this follows a similar path. Let's have a
look at the Join function in the Network class shown in the following code. You will
notice that it takes four parameters. The first parameter is the name of the local
player, just the same as the first parameter of the Host function. The second parameter is the index of the session (from the m_sessions linked list) that we want to
join. The last two parameters are used for specifying the player-specific data and its
size, just like in the Host function.

```
bool Network::Join( char *name, int session, void *playerData,
                    unsigned long dataSize )
{
  WCHAR wide[MAX_PATH];

  m_players->Empty();
  m_messages->Empty();

  if( session < 0 )
    return false;

  DPN_PLAYER_INFO player;
  ZeroMemory( &player, sizeof( DPN_PLAYER_INFO ) );
  player.dwSize = sizeof( DPN_PLAYER_INFO );
```

```
player.pvData = playerData;
player.dwDataSize = dataSize;
player.dwInfoFlags = DPNINFO_NAME | DPNINFO_DATA;
mbstowcs( wide, name, MAX_PATH );
player.pwszName = wide;
if( FAILED( m_dpp->SetPeerInfo( &player, NULL, NULL,
                                DPNSETPEERINFO_SYNC ) ) )
   return false;
```

First, we clear the player's linked list and the message's linked list, just in case they have anything left in them from a previous session. We also need to check the session index that has been passed in to ensure it is valid. An index of 0 indicates the first session in the linked list, while n-1 is the last session in the link list. If the session index is less than 0 then it is not valid and we return false. Finally, we set the player information for the local player. This is exactly the same as how we did it back in the Host function.

```
EnterCriticalSection( &m_sessionCS );

m_sessions->Iterate( true );
for( int s = 0; s < session + 1; s++ )
{
  if( m_sessions->Iterate() ==  NULL )
  {
    LeaveCriticalSection( &m_sessionCS );
    return false;
  }
}
```

The next step is to find the session that we want to join in the session's linked list. To do this we need to enter the m_sessionCS critical section to prevent the network message handler from trying to alter the session's linked list while we are reading from it. We then iterate through the linked list of sessions until we reach the index of the session we want to join, at which point we drop out from the iteration loop.

```
if( FAILED( m_dpp->Connect(
         &m_sessions->GetCurrent()->description,
          m_sessions->GetCurrent()->address, m_device, NULL,
         NULL, NULL, 0, NULL, NULL, NULL, DPNCONNECT_SYNC ) ) )
```

```
  {
    LeaveCriticalSection( &m_sessionCS );
    return false;
  }
  LeaveCriticalSection( &m_sessionCS );

  return true;
}
```

Now we have everything we need to join the session, so we call the `Connect` function exposed by our DirectPlay peer interface. The prototype for the `Connect` function is shown here:

```
HRESULT Connect
(
  const DPN_APPLICATION_DESC *const pdnAppDesc,
  IDirectPlay8Address *const pHostAddr,
  IDirectPlay8Address *const pDeviceInfo,
  const DPN_SECURITY_DESC *const pdnSecurity,
  const DPN_SECURITY_CREDENTIALS *const pdnCredentials,
  const void *const pvUserConnectData,
  const DWORD dwUserConnectDataSize,
  void *const pvPlayerContext,
  void *const pvAsyncContext,
  DPNHANDLE *const phAsyncHandle,
  const DWORD dwFlags
);
```

In the first parameter, we pass in the application description of the session we want to join, and the address of the session's host in the second parameter. For the third parameter we just need to pass in the local device address. That's about it. We can ignore the rest of the parameters as we do not need them (so we just set them to NULL), except for the last one, which we set to DPNCONNECT_SYNC. This will instruct DirectPlay to perform a synchronous connect, which means the function call will not return until the connection attempt either succeeds or fails. We wrap the call up in an `if` statement so that we can catch a failed attempt and return false. If the connection succeeds, then we can return true. The application can use this return value to determine if the connection succeeded. Finally, we must always remember to leave any critical sections that we have entered to prevent other threads from stalling.

SENDING AND RECEIVING MESSAGES

We can now create and join sessions as well as enumerate them, so the next logical step is to implement the messaging into our network system. It would be useless if we could not send or receive network messages. So let's begin by looking at the `Send` function of our `Network` class, as shown here:

```
void Network::Send( void *data, long size, DPNID dpnid,
                    long flags )
{
  DPNHANDLE hAsync;
  DPN_BUFFER_DESC dpbd;

  if( ( dpbd.dwBufferSize = size ) == 0 )
    return;
  dpbd.pBufferData = (BYTE*)data;

  m_dpp->SendTo( dpnid, &dpbd, 1, m_sendTimeOut, NULL, &hAsync,
                 flags | DPNSEND_NOCOMPLETE | DPNSEND_COALESCE );
}
```

The function accepts four parameters as input. First, you must pass in a pointer to the data that you want to send, along with the size of the data. Then you need to specify who you want to send the data to and what flags you want to use when you send it. The function checks the data size, and then copies the data into a `DPN_BUFFER_DESC` structure, which is used to send the data. Sending is achieved by calling the `SendTo` function that is exposed by the DirectPlay peer interface. The prototype for this function is shown here:

```
HRESULT SendTo
(
  const DPNID dpnid,
  const DPN_BUFFER_DESC *const pBufferDesc,
  const DWORD cBufferDesc,
  const DWORD dwTimeOut,
  void *const pvAsyncContext,
  DPNHANDLE *const phAsyncHandle,
  const DWORD dwFlags
);
```

In the first parameter, we pass in the DPNID of the player to whom we want to send the message. To send the message to every player connected to the session, we need to specify DPNID_ALL_PLAYERS_GROUP for this parameter. The next two parameters are used to pass in a pointer to our DPN_BUFFER_DESC structure that we just copied the data into. We specify 1 for cBufferDesc to indicate that there is just one DPN_BUFFER_DESC structure. For dwTimeOut we pass in m_sendTimeOut, which we read in from our network settings script back in the constructor. This is the number of milliseconds that DirectPlay should wait for the message to be sent. If the message is not sent after this time has expired, it is deleted. This prevents messages from backing up when they are not sending for some reason.

The next two parameters are used for sending messages asynchronously, which we want to do. This means that the function will return immediately without waiting for the message to be sent. We do not need to provide a context so we can set pvAsyncContext to NULL, however, we do need a handle for the call. So we need to pass in our hAsync handle to phAsyncHandle, even though we will never use it. The handle acts like a tangible receipt for the call that allows you to track the call later with functions such as CancelAsyncOperation, which allows you to cancel the operation later if you decide you do not want it to complete. In other words, you could stop the message from being sent if it hasn't already been sent.

The last parameter of the SendTo function is used to specify a number of flags that control how the message is sent. We pass in the flags, which were passed into the Send function as well as two of our own flags—DPNSEND_NOCOMPLETE and DPNSEND_COALESCE. Table 7.3 shows the different flags we can set.

Once a message has been sent, it will be received by the target application's network message handler. Our Network class has an internal message handler that can process all of the system messages for us, and store all of the user-defined messages so that the application can process them when it is ready. We cannot look at the entire message handler in the Network class as it is extremely long. You can find it in Network.cpp if you want to see its implementation. Here is a snippet that shows how the call-back function is structured:

ON THE CD

```
HRESULT WINAPI Network::NetworkMessageHandler( PVOID context,
                                               DWORD msgid, PVOID data )
{
  Network *network = (Network*)context;

  switch( msgid )
  {
    // Handle network messages in here. System messages are
    // processed immediately, while user-defined messages are
    // stored for later processing when the application is ready.
  }
}
```

TABLE 7.3 Message Sending Flags

DPNSEND_SYNC	Send the message synchronously.
DPNSEND_NOCOPY	Do not make a copy of the DPN_BUFFER_DESC structure to be sent. Although this can be more efficient, it is less robust because modifying the data in the DPN_BUFFER_DESC structure before receiving the DPN_MSGID_SEND_COMPLETE message can cause problems, therefore, you cannot combine this flag with DPNSEND_NOCOMPLETE.
DPNSEND_NOCOMPLETE	The DPN_MSGID_SEND_COMPLETE is not sent back to your application. You cannot combine this flag with DPNSEND_NOCOPY or DPNSEND_GUARANTEED, and pvAsyncContext must be NULL.
DPNSEND_COMPLETEONPROCESS	The DPN_MSGID_SEND_COMPLETE message is sent to your application when the sent message has been delivered to the target. This flag can slow the message transmission process, and you must also set the DPNSEND_GUARANTEED flag.
DPNSEND_GUARANTEED	Guarantees the message will be delivered to the target. This can slow down the message transmission process.
DPNSEND_PRIORITY_HIGH	Gives the message a high priority, and cannot be combined with the DPNSEND_PRIORITY_LOW flag.
DPNSEND_PRIORITY_LOW	Gives the message a low priority, and cannot be combined with the DPNSEND_PRIORITY_HIGH flag.
DPNSEND_NONSEQUENTIAL	This flag allows the target application to receive messages as soon as they arrive. If this flag is not set, DirectPlay will ensure messages are received by the target application in the order that they were sent.
DPNSEND_NOLOOPBACK	Prevents the message from being sent to yourself when you are broadcasting to a group that includes the sender, such as sending the message to every player in the session.
DPNSEND_COALESCE	Allows DirectPlay to combine packets when sending.

When DirectPlay calls the function, it will pass in the context, which is the pointer that we set back in the constructor when we initialized the DirectPlay peer interface. If you remember, we set it to the this pointer, which means that DirectPlay will pass us a pointer to our Network class instance. All we need to do is cast the context into a Network class instance pointer. Remember that the message handler is a separate thread, so this will allow us to use our Network class within the message handle. The next step is to enter a switch statement that checks the msgid, which is passed to us by DirectPlay. We can then process the message appropriately based on its msgid. The data pointer points to the address in memory where the message data is.

If you have a look at the implementation of the call-back function you will be able to see how it handles all the messages. The code has been commented to assist you in understanding how it works.

Fortunately, you never need to worry about how the system messages are processed, you really only need to concern yourself with handling the user-defined messages in your application. Let's have a quick look at what the Network class message handler does when a user-defined message arrives.

```
case DPN_MSGID_RECEIVE:
{
  if( network->HandleNetworkMessage == NULL )
    break;

  if( network->m_receiveAllowed == false )
    break;

  ReceivedMessage *message = new ReceivedMessage;
  memcpy( message, ( (PDPNMSG_RECEIVE)data )->pReceiveData,
        ( (PDPNMSG_RECEIVE)data )->dwReceiveDataSize );

  EnterCriticalSection( &network->m_messageCS );
  network->m_messages->Add( message );
  LeaveCriticalSection( &network->m_messageCS );

  break;
}
```

DirectPlay gives all user-defined messages the DPN_MSGID_RECEIVE message identifier, which is checked for by the switch statement in the message handler. First, we check if an application-specific network message handler was specified back when the Network class was instanced. If not, then we don't have any way of processing user-defined messages, so we can ignore it. We also need to check the m_receiveAllowed flag to make sure the network system is allowed to receive user-defined messages.

Assuming we pass these two checks, we then create an instance of the ReceivedMessage structure and copy the message data into it. Finally, we enter the m_messageCS critical section, add the received message to our m_messages linked list, and leave the critical section. The user-defined message is now stored and ready to be processed by the application.

PROCESSING NETWORK MESSAGES

When the application is ready it can call the Update function exposed by our Network class. This function will process any user-defined messages by passing them to the application-specific message handler. Let's have a look at how the function works.

```
void Network::Update()
{
  EnterCriticalSection( &m_messageCS );

  ReceivedMessage *message = m_messages->GetFirst();

  unsigned long endTime = timeGetTime() + m_processingTime;
  while( endTime > timeGetTime() && message != NULL )
  {
    HandleNetworkMessage( message );
    m_messages->Remove( &message );
    message = m_messages->GetFirst();
  }

  LeaveCriticalSection( &m_messageCS );
}
```

As soon as we enter the function we also enter the m_messageCS critical section. This prevents the network message handler from trying to add new messages to the m_messages linked list while we are processing messages from it. The next step is to get a pointer to the first message in the linked list. This will be the first message that we process. Remember that new messages are added to the end of the list, so the oldest messages will be at the front of the list.

Now we are ready to enter the `while` loop, which is controlled by a timer. The timer works by taking the current system time (using `timeGetTime`) and adding the processing time to it (which is taken from the network settings script). This gives us the end time where we want to stop processing messages (in milliseconds). Then, every iteration of the `while` loop we just check the system time against this end time. As soon as the system time goes past the end time, then the timer has expired and we stop processing network messages for this frame. We also check the pointer to the current network message to make sure it is not `NULL`. If it is, we have reached the end of the `m_messages` linked list, which means there are no more messages to be processed. As soon as either the timer expires or we reach the end of the linked list, we drop out of the `while` loop.

Inside the `while` loop we pass the current network message to the application-specific message handler. After that returns, we can safely delete the message from the `m_messages` linked list as it has been handled by the application. Then we move on to the next message in the linked list and the process repeats. Once we drop out of the `while` loop for whatever reason, we must remember to leave the critical section so that the network message handler can continue adding new messages.

CAUTION

Be careful when adjusting the network message processing time. If you set it too long, then you may spend too much time processing network messages, which will slow the application down and possibly stall the network message handler while it waits for the critical section to free up. On the other hand, if you don't set it long enough, then the application may not be able to process network messages fast enough; they will begin to back up and lag will gradually creep in as messages are processed much later than they should be.

INTEGRATING THE NETWORK SYSTEM

We have pretty much wrapped up the coverage of the new networking system. Although we could not cover everything, we have looked at the most important topics, so now it is time to integrate it into our engine. By now you should know what the first step is: linking the files correctly using the `#include` statement. You can look in `Engine.h` and `Network.cpp` to see how they are linked. Now let's have a look at the new members that have been added to the EngineSetup structure, as shown here:

```
GUID guid;
void (*HandleNetworkMessage)( ReceivedMessage *msg );
```

The first new member allows you to specify the GUID that the application will be identified by. If you do not specify one, then it is set to the default GUID in the structure's constructor. However, this is not advisable as it will cause confusion when you try to perform tasks such as enumerating sessions. You will find that if two applications have the same GUID, then DirectPlay will consider them to be the same even if they are not.

The second new member in the EngineSetup structure allows us to specify an application specific network message handler for processing user-defined messages. By default this is set to NULL in the structure's constructor. If you leave it set to NULL, your application will not be able to receive user-defined network messages.

In the Engine class we need to add a new private member called m_network, which will hold an instance of our Network class. We also need to add the GetNetwork function, which returns a pointer to our Network class instance. This allows the application to access the networking features to perform tasks such as creating and joining sessions, as well as sending messages.

If you have a look in the Engine class constructor we have added a new line of code that creates an instance of our network class, as shown here:

```
m_network = new Network( m_setup->guid,
                         m_setup->HandleNetworkMessage );
```

If you think back to when we looked at the constructor for our Network class, you will remember that we need to pass in the application's GUID and the application-specific, user-defined network messages handler. The new Network class instance is assigned to our m_network pointer. We also cannot forget to put the SAFE_DELETE(m_network) statement in the constructor to destroy the Network class instance.

Now if you have a look in the Run function of the Engine class you will see that in every frame we are calling the Update function on our Network class instance so that the user-defined network messages can be processed. That is the last change in our Engine class, so now the networking system is fully integrated and ready to use.

TESTING THE NETWORK SYSTEM

We have finally rolled around to that exciting part of the chapter where we test the engine again to see the results of all our hard labor. You can find the test application in the Test project of the workspace for this chapter. We have made some major changes to the TestState to test our networking. You should also note in the WinMain function that we are setting the GUID for the application. However, we are not setting an application-specific network message handler. This is because we won't be using user-defined messages just yet. You will see them in use when we implement the game in the Part II.

If you have a look at the TestState, you will see that all the good stuff is in the Update function. What we are doing in a nutshell is displaying some menu options to the user and then reading the user's input with the keyboard. If the user presses the H key, a new session will be hosted. If the E key is pressed the network will be enumerated for any active sessions. If any sessions are found through enumeration, they will be displayed in the menu and you will be able to join them by pressing the numerical key associated with the session. This sample only allows you to join the first three sessions displayed, however, it can easily be extended to support more.

Below the menu, a status read-out is displayed, showing your connection status. If you are not connected to a session it will read, NOT CONNECTED. If you are hosting a session it will read, CONNECTED–HOST, or if you have joined a session it will read, CONNECTED-CLIENT. Once connected to a session you cannot do anything other than disconnect. We know that the network message handler is work as you are able to host, join, and enumerate sessions. However, we are not testing the user-defined messages, as previously mentioned; these will be used when we make our FPS.

To test the networking system, you will need to run two separate instances of this test application across a LAN. In other words, you need at least two computers networked together in order to run the test.

SUMMARY

Chapter 7 has been a real journey. As you discovered at the beginning, networking is a very in-depth topic, so it is difficult to discuss everything in a short amount of time. We talked about DirectPlay and how it handles networking, as well as the different networking architectures you can use. We then discussed how our networking system will work and covered the supporting material, such as critical sections, before moving on to the long implementation of the system. Finally, we rounded it off with another test of our engine, this time with network support!

Due to the complexity of this topic, you should reread any areas that didn't make complete sense, as well as peruse the source code, which will give you the complete picture rather than just the snippets we looked at. Don't be afraid of the source code; it can actually be a better learning tool than all the descriptive text in the world. Also, do not forget about the DirectX SDK documentation, which can give detailed explanations of many of the topics that we could only lightly touch on.

Get ready for some real excitement in the next chapter when we implement our material and mesh systems. Finally, we will be able to render something other than plain old text. By the end of Chapter 8 we will have full 3D animated meshes complete with textures!

8 Materials and Meshes

In This Chapter

- Implement a script-driven material system.
- Discuss meshes and look at the mesh system we will use.
- Cover some other utility classes to aid us with handling and rendering 3D geometry.

It is time to implement everything our engine needs in order to render a 3D mesh with a texture applied to it. Keep in mind that we are stepping up the difficulty again; there is a lot of information to cover in this chapter, so we will move briskly. For the most effective learning experience, have the DirectX SDK documentation and the source code from the CD-ROM close at hand. You can find the workspace for this chapter in the /Source/Chapter 8/ directory on the CD-ROM.

ON THE CD

MATERIALS

Normally, we start a new chapter with several pages of theory. So to break up the monotony—and because we have so much to implement in this chapter—we will go straight to the fun. We will begin by implementing our material system.

In Chapter 5, we discussed textures and how they are rendered onto a face. So you already have an understanding of how textures are used, but what is a material? A material is something that you can apply to a face in 3D space. The material not only defines the texture that is applied to the face, but also defines a number of other properties about the face.

Before we go any further, we should clarify something. Direct3D also uses materials in the form of the D3DMATERIAL9 *structure. This structure is used by Direct3D to define how a face handles lighting in a 3D scene. It can define how the face reflects different types of lighting, as well as how the face appears to emit light. Although our materials will use the* D3DMATERIAL9 *structure for their lighting properties, our materials will define more than just this. Therefore, from now on when we refer to a material, we mean one of our custom materials, not Direct3D's* D3DMATERIAL9 *structure. We will refer to this structure as a material's lighting properties from now on.*

NOTE

With that clarification out of the way, we can continue to discuss our materials. The next logical question is: what is the purpose of these materials? Why can't we just apply a texture to a face and be done with it? The reason is that there are a lot more details about the face that we need to define than just the texture that is applied to it. This additional information is needed by our engine in order to process the face correctly. In addition, our game may have special requirements for different types of textures, so it is easy just to wrap it up in a material. If all this is confusing, let's have a look at an example that may make it a little easier to understand.

Say that in your FPS you wanted to play a footstep sound effect every time the player moves. Not only that, but you want the footstep sound effect to simulate the sound of the actual surface that the player is stepping on. If we were to just apply a texture to each face and leave it at that, then it would make it very difficult to play the correct footstep sound effect based on what the player is walking on. For example, the player may be walking on a face that has a texture applied to it that looks like concrete. However, how does our game know that this face is supposed to represent concrete? It doesn't. Therefore, we need to hardcode the game so that whenever the player walks on a face that has the concrete texture on it, the game plays the concrete footstep sound effect. However, if later on the player steps on a face with a grass texture, what happens then? We need to hardcode the game again to check this type of texture too, and change the footstep sound effect appropriately.

You can probably begin to see the problem here. Every time we add a new texture we need to hardcode into our game some sort of check so that it can play the correct footstep sound effect to simulate that texture. Wouldn't it be so much easier if we could just define a material that has all the information in it about the surface properties, such as the texture to use, the lighting properties, the sound effect to play when it is stepped on, and so forth?

In addition to this, it would be great if we could use materials in our game dynamically. In other words, we want to be able to add and remove materials without having to recompile the code. Fortunately, this is easy for us to achieve, so it is exactly what we will do, through the use of our scripting system that we implemented earlier. We will create a material system that allows us to define a small script for each material we use. Then when the game loads up a 3D scene, it just reads each material's script and loads in the appropriate details for each material. Take a look at Figure 8.1, which shows how this works.

You should be able to see how everything will work with our new material system. So as promised, let's keep moving on with the fun stuff and keep the theory to a minimum.

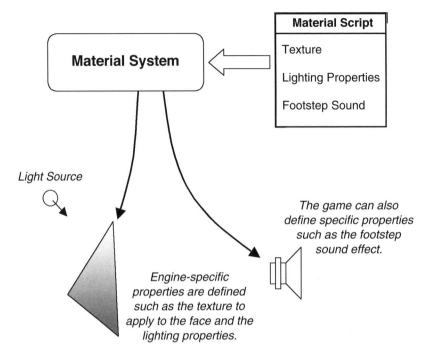

FIGURE 8.1   How the material system works.

MATERIAL SCRIPTS

Before we can actually implement our material system, we are going to need to define the material scripts. This doesn't mean that we need to write up a script now for every material we are going to use. Instead, we will just define the template that we will use to later create our material scripts. The material script template is shown here:

```
#begin

texture       string
ignore_face   bool
ignore_fog    bool
ignore_ray    bool

transparency colour

diffuse       colour
ambient       colour
specular      colour
```

```
emissive      colour
power         float


#end
```

This is the base script used for any new material. It defines all the basic properties that our engine needs in order to process a material correctly. Of course, you can add your own properties to the script for game-specific functionality, such as playing the appropriate sound effect when the player steps on a face with this material. We will cover that in the Part II when we develop our actual game.

Let's go though each of the properties in the script. First, we have the `texture` property, which is a `string`. This is where we enter the name of the texture file that is associated with the material. This should also include the path to the texture and it should be relative to the location of the script file. The next three properties are flags that define how the engine handles any faces that have this material applied to them. `ignore_face` tells the engine whether or not to render faces with this material. This is useful for placing faces in the scene that you do not want the player to see. `ignore_fog` tells the engine whether or not to apply fog effects to faces with this material. The last one, `ignore_ray`, is used to tell the engine whether or not faces with this material should be used for collisions. In other words, if this is set to true, then any faces with this material assigned to them will not be used during collision detection. You will see how this works when we add collision detection to our engine.

The next property is `transparency`. This is used to define the transparent color in the texture. Direct3D allows you to specify one color as the *color key*. The color key is a 32-bit ARGB (alpha, red, green, blue) color value, and tells Direct3D to ignore any pixels that match that color, which means they will not be rendered (see Figure 8.2). This allows you to render faces that have imaginary holes in them. Although the face is still there, Direct3D does not render the pixels with that matching color key. It is important to remember that the alpha component must always be 1.0, while the others can be any value between 0.0 and 1.0 inclusive. A `transparency` value of 1.0 0.0 0.0 0.0, would indicate a color key of opaque black. Therefore, any black pixels in the texture would not be rendered.

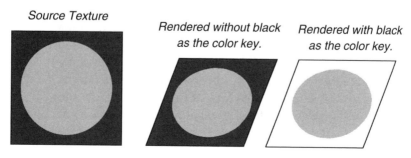

FIGURE 8.2   How transparency works with the color key.

The last five properties are used for defining the lighting properties of the material. They map directly onto the D3DMATERIAL9 structure. Let's have a look at the definition of the D3DMATERIAL9 structure, which is shown here:

```
typedef struct _D3DMATERIAL9 {
    D3DCOLORVALUE Diffuse;
    D3DCOLORVALUE Ambient;
    D3DCOLORVALUE Specular;
    D3DCOLORVALUE Emissive;
    float Power;
} D3DMATERIAL9;
```

From this definition, you can see how the properties map straight across. Each material has an internal D3DMATERIAL9 structure. The values you place in the script are then stored in this structure, which is set into Direct3D before the faces using the material are rendered. As previously mentioned, these properties allow Direct3D to calculate lighting on the faces. If you do not specify these properties, all your faces will render completely black when lighting is switched on. We won't be using lights for a while yet, but we will briefly look at how these properties work.

The first three are used to define how much of that particular light is reflected by the material. Just like in the real world, when light is reflected off objects, the object absorbs certain color spectrums while reflecting others, which gives the object its color; Direct3D works in a similar way. The Diffuse color is used to reflect light from the light sources you place in the scene. If you set a material's Diffuse to 0.0, 0.0, 1.0, 1.0 (red, green, blue, alpha), the material will reflect 100% of the blue component and 0% of the red and green components. Therefore, any faces rendered with this material will appear blue.

NOTE

The color key uses the ARGB component ordering while the D3DMATERIAL9 structure uses the RGBA component ordering for its members. Be careful not to confuse them or you will end up with all sorts of strange colors. If you want to make it consistent, DirectX provides you with a number of macros that allow you to specify color values using different component ordering.

The second type of lighting is called ambient light. A material's reflection of the ambient light is defined by the Ambient color property. Ambient light is the low intensity lighting that persists throughout the entire scene. It represents the darkest a face can be when it does not have direct light shining on it. The best way to visualize ambient light is to look at the lighting of a shadow. If a building casts a shadow on the ground from the sunlight, the shadow is not completely black. This is due to the ambient light, which (in real life) is just light that has reflected off many surfaces and no longer has a definitive source.

The next lighting property is called `Specular`, which is a specular reflection, and is used to apply highlights to the face. Specular highlights are used to make objects appear shiny, like metal, for example. The `Specular` property allows you to specify the color of the highlights on this material, with the most common being white or some shade of gray. Additionally, you need to set the `Power` property, which controls how sharp the highlights appear. The greater the value, the sharper the highlight, while lower values increase the area of effect. This is great for creating large, dull areas of highlight.

There is one more property that we need to mention, that is the `Emissive` property. This property is not used to reflect light; instead, it is used to generate fake light. This property allows you to make a material appear as though it is self-luminous. In other words, the material will appear to emit light of the set color. This is ideal for creating materials that seem to glow in the dark, for example. You have to keep in mind though that emissive light is not real light, it is just an illusion. The light emitted by the material will only light faces that the material is applied to, and will not affect any other face in the scene.

That's all the properties in our material script. As previously mentioned, you will see how to extend this so that you can add game-specific properties later when we develop our game. For now, let's just take what we have got here and implement this actual material system for loading and managing our materials.

THE MATERIAL SYSTEM

A material is really just a resource that we can run through our resource management system. In fact, it is a bit of a complex resource really as it is made up of a script and a texture, which are resources in themselves. Fortunately, we can wrap it all up in a single class called `Material` and just process it as one single resource. So let's have a look at the `Material` class definition, which is shown below and can also be found in the `Material.h` file.

```
class Material : public Resource< Material >
{
public:
  Material( char *name, char *path = "./" );
  virtual ~Material();
```

```
IDirect3DTexture9 *GetTexture();
D3DMATERIAL9 *GetLighting();
unsigned long GetWidth();
unsigned long GetHeight();
bool GetIgnoreFace();
bool GetIgnoreFog();
bool GetIgnoreRay();

private:
  IDirect3DTexture9 *m_texture;
  D3DMATERIAL9 m_lighting;
  unsigned long m_width;
  unsigned long m_height;
  bool m_ignoreFace;
  bool m_ignoreFog;
  bool m_ignoreRay;
};
```

Rather than dissecting the class definition, let's just take a look at the actual implementation, and discuss the class as we go. We will start with the class constructor, as shown here (the implementation can be found in `Material.cpp`):

```
Material::Material( char *name, char *path )
        : Resource< Material >( name, path )
{
  D3DXIMAGE_INFO info;

  Script *script = new Script( name, path );
```

Like any resource, the `Material` resource accepts two parameters in its class constructor, the name of the resource, and the path to it. This information is then passed to the `Resource` class, which the `Material` class is derived from. The `D3DXIMAGE_INFO` structure will be used later for retrieving information about the texture used by this material, which you will see put to use shortly. The next step is to load the script for the material. This is just a matter of creating a new script using the `name` and `path` that are passed in to the `Material` class constructor. Once the script is loaded, the first thing we need to do is check if the material is using any transparency (i.e., does it have a color key?). We need to check this because it will affect the way we load the texture for the material, as shown here:

```
if( script->GetColourData( "transparency" )->a == 0.0f )
{
  D3DXCreateTextureFromFileEx( g_engine->GetDevice(),
    script->GetStringData( "texture" ), D3DX_DEFAULT,
    D3DX_DEFAULT, D3DX_DEFAULT, 0, D3DFMT_UNKNOWN,
    D3DPOOL_MANAGED, D3DX_FILTER_TRIANGLE, D3DX_FILTER_TRIANGLE,
    0, &info, NULL, &m_texture );
}
else
{
  D3DCOLORVALUE *colour = script->GetColourData(
                          "transparency" );
  D3DCOLOR transparency = D3DCOLOR_COLORVALUE( colour->r,
                          colour->g, colour->b, colour->a );
  D3DXCreateTextureFromFileEx( g_engine->GetDevice(),
    script->GetStringData( "texture" ), D3DX_DEFAULT,
    D3DX_DEFAULT, D3DX_DEFAULT, 0, D3DFMT_UNKNOWN,
    D3DPOOL_MANAGED, D3DX_FILTER_TRIANGLE, D3DX_FILTER_TRIANGLE,
    transparency, &info, NULL, &m_texture );
}
```

The steps we take to load a texture with or without the color key are almost identical. Let's first have a look at how we do it without the color key. To load a texture from file we use the D3DX function called D3DXCreateTextureFromFileEx. Its prototype is shown here:

```
HRESULT WINAPI D3DXCreateTextureFromFileEx
(
  // Pointer to a Direct3D device interface.
  LPDIRECT3DDEVICE9 pDevice,

  // Filename (name + path) of the texture to load.
  LPCTSTR pSrcFile,

  // Width and height of the source texture in pixels.
  UINT Width,
  UINT Height,

  // Number of mip levels. D3DX_DEFAULT creates a complete set.
  UINT MipLevels,
```

```
    // Resource usage flags.
    DWORD Usage,

    // Texture pixel format.
    D3DFORMAT Format,

    // Memory class where the texture should be stored.
    D3DPOOL Pool,

    // Texture filtering flags.
    DWORD Filter,

    // Mipmap texture filtering flags.
    DWORD MipFilter,

    // Transparent color key. 0 disables the color key.
    D3DCOLOR ColorKey,

    // Description of the data in the source texture.
    D3DXIMAGE_INFO *pSrcInfo,

    // The 256 color palette.
    PALETTEENTRY *pPalette,

    // Address of a pointer to store the new texture.
    LPDIRECT3DTEXTURE9 *ppTexture
);
```

That is one long function, but the good news is that we can set many of the parameters to a default value, and let the function work everything out for us. For the first parameter, we just need to pass in a pointer to a Direct3D device, which we can request from the engine. In the second parameter, we pass in the filename of the texture we want to load, which we can access from our Resource base class. We set the Width and Height to D3DX_DEFAULT, as well as the MipLevels, which allows the function to take the dimensions from the source texture and create a full mipmap chain. We leave the Usage set to 0 as we do not want any special usage features and we allow the function to take the pixel format from the source texture by passing D3DFMT_UNKNOWN for the Format parameter.

The Pool parameter allows us to specify how we want the resource to be stored in memory. There are several options to choose from, and the most common are shown in Table 8.1.

TABLE 8.1 Common Resource Memory Pools

D3DPOOL_DEFAULT	The resource is placed in the most appropriate memory based on its usage. This is usually video memory. These resources need to be re-created when the current Direct3D device is lost.
D3DPOOL_MANAGED	Direct3D dynamically manages where the resource is stored. When it is being used it is promoted to device-accessible memory, and demoted back to system memory when not in use. These resources do not need to be re-created when the current Direct3D device is lost as Direct3D maintains a backup copy in system memory.
D3DPOOL_SYSTEMMEM	The resource is stored in system memory and therefore does not need to be re-created when the current Direct3D device is lost. System memory is not typically accessible by the 3D hardware.

For our texture resources we will use the D3DPOOL_MANAGED memory pool as it requires the least amount of our effort. We do not need to worry about moving resources between video and system memory, and we do not need to concern ourselves with re-creating the resource if the Direct3D device is lost. Moving on, the next two parameters allow us to adjust how the texture is filtered. The most common setting for these parameters is either D3DX_FILTER_POINT, D3DX_FILTER_LINEAR, or D3DX_FILTER_TRIANGLE. The first one is the poorest quality, but the least computationally expensive; and they increase in quality and processing overhead. D3DX_FILTER_TRIANGLE is the most computationally expensive; however, it provides the best texture filtering so that is what we will use.

We can ignore the next parameter, setting ColorKey to 0 as we have already determined that we do not need a color key. For pSrcInfo we pass in our D3DXIMAGE_INFO structure called info. When the function returns, this structure will be filled with various details about the texture, such as its dimensions, color depth, and pixel format. We will need some of these details shortly. The second to last parameter, pPalette, is only used when you are creating a palletized texture. In other words, the texture is a 256-color image that uses a palette. We won't be using these types of textures so we can just set this to NULL. Finally, we pass in m_texture in the last parameter, which is the address of a pointer that represents our new texture. That is the complete process of loading a texture from memory. However, we're not done. We also need to consider what happens when we want to use the color key.

You can see that we check the script for a transparency value, and if there is one, we process the else path of the check. The texture loading process is almost the same as what we did when we loaded a texture without the color key. In fact, we use all the same parameters, except for one. The ColorKey parameter needs to be changed to accept our transparent color key. The first step is to read the transparency from our script and store it in a D3DCOLORVALUE structure. The D3DXCreateTextureFromFileEx function accepts a D3DCOLOR value as the color key, which is just a DWORD value. So we use the D3DCOLOR_COLORVALUE macro to convert our D3DCOLORVALUE structure into a DWORD D3DCOLOR that we have called transparency. Then we just pass this variable into the D3DXCreateTextureFromFileEx function as the color key.

Fortunately, the hard part is over. We have now loaded the texture, either with or without the color key. The next step is just a matter of setting up our material based on the material's script, which is a very simple process. Let's have a look.

```
    m_width = info.Width;
    m_height = info.Height;

    m_lighting.Diffuse = *( script->GetColourData( "diffuse" ) );
    m_lighting.Ambient = *( script->GetColourData( "ambient" ) );
    m_lighting.Specular = *( script->GetColourData( "specular" ) );
    m_lighting.Emissive = *( script->GetColourData( "emissive" ) );
    m_lighting.Power = *( script->GetFloatData( "power" ) );

    m_ignoreFace = *( script->GetBoolData( "ignore_face" ) );

    m_ignoreFog = *( script->GetBoolData( "ignore_fog" ) );

    m_ignoreRay = *( script->GetBoolData( "ignore_ray" ) );

    SAFE_DELETE( script );
}
```

First, you can see that we are using the D3DXIMAGE_INFO structure (that was returned from the D3DXCreateTextureFromFileEx function) to store the width and height of our texture. The next step is to store all of the material's lighting properties in the D3DMATERIAL9 structure called m_lighting. We read each of these properties directly from the script. Then, we go through and set each of the material's flags, also taken straight from the script. Finally, we destroy the script as we have finished setting up the material.

The destructor for the `Material` class is extremely simple. It just releases our texture interface (that was created in the constructor) using the `SAFE_RELEASE` macro. The rest of the class is pretty straightforward, so we won't bother covering it. It just implements a whole lot of data accessing functions that allow you to retrieve any information about the material. You can have a look yourself in the `Material.cpp` file. For now, let's move on to integrating the new material system into our engine.

INTEGRATING THE MATERIAL SYSTEM

The first step is to link the files in correctly using the `#include` statements, which you should know by heart now. You will notice that we have added a new `ResourceManager` to our `Engine` class called `m_materialManager`, which is for managing all our materials. We have also added a new function called `GetMaterialManager`, which allows us to gain access to the material manager in order to load materials through it. You will be able to see how we create the material manager in the `Engine` class constructor, and then destroy it in the `Engine` class destructor. Have a look at the following line of code, which appears in the `Engine` class constructor, used to create our material manager:

```
m_materialManager = new ResourceManager< Material >
                    ( m_setup->CreateMaterialResource );
```

What's with the `CreateMaterialResource` tagged on the end like that? If you think about when we created the `ResourceManager` class in Chapter 2, you should remember that we gave the `ResourceManager` class a call-back function called `CreateResource`. This function is used by the `ResourceManager` class to allow you to specify a custom application-specific method to create the resource in question. In other words, every time one of these resources is created, the function from your application that you specified is called so that you can handle the way the resource is loaded. If you do not specify a function, like we did with the script resource manager, then the resource is just loaded per normal by the engine, using the specific resource's constructor.

For our materials, we want to allow the application to perform custom loading if it wants to. The reason for this is that we have already decided that we want to be able to add application specific properties to our materials. Since our generic

`Material` class has no way of handling custom material properties, the engine needs to allow the application to load these properties. To do this, we will allow the programmer to pass in an application-specific call-back function called `CreateMaterialResource` through the `EngineSetup` structure. If you have a look at the `EngineSetup` structure you will see it defined. Notice that it is set to NULL by default in the `EngineSetup` structure constructor.

You will see the material system put to use when we test the engine at the end of this chapter. As for the custom materials, you will have to wait until Part II when we develop the actual game. We will use the custom material loading to add a new property to our materials that will allow us to play different footstep sound effects based on which material the player is walking on. This brings us to the end of discussing our material system. Now it is time to move on to the next topic: bounding volumes.

BOUNDING VOLUMES

A bounding volume is a basic 3D shape that is used to enclose a given 3D area, usually a more complex shape. The most common bounding volumes are boxes and spheres as they are easy to manage and computationally inexpensive in a number of ways. However, you can really use any shape you like as a bounding volume; it really depends on its application. In fact, there is a third shape that is especially suited to enclosing the volume of a 3D humanoid shaped figure: an ellipsoid. As you know, a box has a width, length, and height, and a sphere has a radius. An ellipsoid, however, is like a cross between a box and a sphere as it actually has three radii—one for its width, one for its length, and one for its height. Figure 8.3 shows the three different bounding volumes.

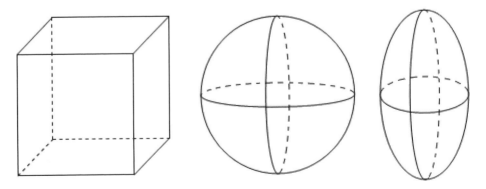

FIGURE 8.3 Three common bounding volumes from left to right: box, sphere, and ellipsoid.

One of the most common uses of bounding volumes in real-time computer games is to approximate the shape of a complex object for the purpose of collision detection. For example, if the player character is represented by a 3D human model consisting of several hundred faces, it can become difficult to perform accurate collision detection with that kind of data set and maintain a playable real-time frame rate. Instead, the character's volume is approximated by one of the previously mentioned primitive 3D shapes. Any collision detection is then performed using this approximated shape, rather than the complex character model. There are many uses for bounding volumes, which you will see later when we develop our game.

To facilitate the use of bounding volumes, we will add the BoundingVolume utility class to our engine. We won't bother looking at its implementation here; however, you can find it in the BoundingVolume.cpp file. Instead, we will just look at the definition of the class and quickly run through what the class can do.

```
class BoundingVolume
{
public:
  BoundingVolume();
  virtual ~BoundingVolume();

  void BoundingVolumeFromMesh( ID3DXMesh *mesh,
                      D3DXVECTOR3 ellipsoidRadius =
                      D3DXVECTOR3( 1.0f, 1.0f, 1.0f ) );
  void BoundingVolumeFromVertices( D3DXVECTOR3 *vertices,
                      unsigned long totalVertices,
                      unsigned long vertexStride,
                      D3DXVECTOR3 ellipsoidRadius =
                      D3DXVECTOR3( 1.0f, 1.0f, 1.0f ) );
  void CloneBoundingVolume( BoundingBox *box,
                      BoundingSphere *sphere,
                      D3DXVECTOR3 ellipsoidRadius =
                      D3DXVECTOR3( 1.0f, 1.0f, 1.0f ) );
  void RepositionBoundingVolume( D3DXMATRIX *location );

  void SetBoundingBox( D3DXVECTOR3 min, D3DXVECTOR3 max );
  BoundingBox *GetBoundingBox();

  void SetBoundingSphere( D3DXVECTOR3 centre, float radius,
                      D3DXVECTOR3 ellipsoidRadius =
                      D3DXVECTOR3( 1.0f, 1.0f, 1.0f ) );
  BoundingSphere *GetBoundingSphere();
```

```
      void SetEllipsoidRadius( D3DXVECTOR3 ellipsoidRadius );
      D3DXVECTOR3 GetEllipsoidRadius();

  private:
    BoundingBox *m_box;
    BoundingSphere *m_sphere;

    D3DXVECTOR3 m_originalMin;
    D3DXVECTOR3 m_originalMax;
    D3DXVECTOR3 m_originalCentre;

    D3DXVECTOR3 m_ellipsoidRadius;
  };
```

The BoundingVolume class is a complete solution capable of handling all three of the previously discussed bounding volumes. It uses two small structures called BoundingBox and BoundingSphere to store the data about the bounding box and bounding sphere, respectively. The bounding ellipsoid is simply a modified version of the bounding sphere. m_ellipsoidRadius stores the three ellipsoid radii, which are calculated as a percentage of the bounding sphere radius.

For example, you may have a bounding sphere radius of 10.0 units. If you were to set an ellipsoid radius (using the SetEllipsoidRadius function) of 0.53, 1.0, 0.4, then you are indicating that you want the ellipsoid to be 53% of the radius on the x-axis, 100% of the radius on the y-axis, and 40% of the radius on the z-axis. In other words, you would end up with an ellipsoid radius of 0.53×10.0, 1.0×10.0, 0.4×10.0, which would give you 5.3, 10.0, 4.0 as the ellipsoid radius.

The BoundingVolume class comes with a whole host of functions that allow you to create and manipulate the three different bounding volumes. Calling BoundingVolumeFromMesh allows you to build a bounding volume around the given mesh (from our Mesh class that we will be discussing shortly). BoundingVolume-FromVertices let's you build up a bounding volume from a list of vertices. This means that the smallest possible bounding volume (of both the bounding box and the bounding sphere) is created that encloses the given geometry, whether it is from a mesh or a list of vertices. You can also specify the percentages to use when creating the ellipsoid.

The RepositionBoundingVolume function allows you to reposition the bounding volume in 3D space. Having a bounding volume around an object is great, but if the object moves in 3D space, the bounding volume must also move with it, which is the purpose of this function. You will see it in use when we start using objects in our

3D scene. Finally, the `BoundingVolume` class provides you with a number of functions that let you manually set each of the three different bounding volume's dimensions, as well as retrieve them.

Since the `BoundingVolume` class is just an added utility class, we don't have the room to go through the very basic implementation. It is nothing more than some basic mathematics and a little help from the D3DX library, so you should have a brief look through `BoundingVolume.cpp` if you are interested in seeing how it works. Other than that, we are ready to move on to the real subject of this chapter—meshes, which is one of the best topics of 3D graphics. Let's get to it!

X FILE FORMAT

Before we can look at our `Mesh` class, which will handle our meshes, we must discuss a few of the basics. In terms of Direct3D, a mesh is an organized collection of faces that is treated as a single entity. DirectX comes with an excellent and extremely flexible file format called the *.x file* format, which allows you to create, save, and load 3D meshes to and from file. The .x file format is template driven, which is what gives it its flexibility and extendability features. What this means is that everything is defined within the file by a template. In terms of Direct3D, a template is much like our property scripts—it defines a number of internal variables that store the data for the template. Direct3D comes with a whole lot of standard templates that allow you to perform the most common tasks, such as storing mesh, animation, and texture data. However, you are free to create any type of template you like, storing whatever data you like. In fact, you don't even have to use the file format to store meshes only. It can theoretically store anything you like. Creating your own templates for .x file storage is beyond the scope of our discussion, and is not required for our purposes.

Creating a .x file to store a mesh properly can be a little tricky at first for the newcomer. Technically speaking, a .x file is really just a glorified text file (although it can be saved in a binary format), so if you really wanted to, you could open up your favorite text editor and write out the details of your mesh, then save it as a .x file. However, this is extremely tedious and error prone, not to mention virtually impossible if you try to create anything more complex than a simple cube. The easiest way to create a mesh is to use a 3D modeling package that can export to the .x file format. One of the most common packages is discreet® 3ds max®. You can download a trial version of 3ds max from the discreet Web site (*www.discreet.com*).

On the CD-ROM you can find the Panda DirectX Exporter, which is made by Andy Tather (more details can be found at *www.andytather.co.uk/Panda/ directxmax.htm*, including the latest version). It is an excellent .x file format exporter that plugs straight into 3ds max. You simply copy and paste the exporter file into the plugins directory where you installed 3ds max on your hard drive. When you run 3ds max, the exporter is automatically loaded and you will be able to select the .x file format from the file type drop-down list when you export your mesh creation.

Internally, a mesh is stored within the .x file using a hierarchy. If you use the mesh viewer that ships with the DirectX SDK, you can load any of the .x files on the CD-ROM and view its internal hierarchy. Once you have a mesh loaded in the mesh viewer, just select the Hierarchy option from the View menu. You will see a new window open that displays the top level of the hierarchy. You can imagine the hierarchy like a tree starting at the base and progressing up through the branches. Clicking on the little plus symbol next to any entry in the hierarchy expands that particular branch of the hierarchy, which in turn may reveal more branches that can be expanded. If you expand a branch of the hierarchy, and it is empty, it means you have reached the limits of that branch.

Each entry in the hierarchy is stored in what is called a *frame*. D3DX provides a structure called D3DXFRAME that is specifically designed for storing a frame in a hierarchy. Here is the definition of the D3DXFRAME structure:

```
typedef struct _D3DXFRAME {
  // Name of the frame.
  LPSTR Name;

  // A matrix that defines the transformation of the frame.
  D3DXMATRIX TransformationMatrix;

  // A pointer to a mesh container.
  LPD3DXMESHCONTAINER pMeshContainer;

  // Pointers to a sibling and child frame.
  struct _D3DXFRAME *pFrameSibling;
  struct _D3DXFRAME *pFrameFirstChild;
} D3DXFRAME, *LPD3DXFRAME;
```

The structure is perfect for storing the basic details of a frame such as its name, its transformation matrix (which is what Direct3D uses to define a position, rotation, and scale combined), and a mesh instance. The last two D3DXFRAME pointers are used to link the frame into the hierarchy, similar to how a linked list connects itself together. The only difference is that a linked list is linear with a single branch, while a hierarchy may have multiple branches.

The actual mesh data is stored in a D3DXMESHCONTAINER structure, which is also provided by the D3DX library. Meshes are stored within frames as you previously saw in the D3DXFRAME structure. Each frame can hold one or more meshes as the D3DXMESHCONTAINER can link itself to another mesh just like a singly linked list. Let's have a look at the definition of the D3DXMESHCONTAINER container:

```
typedef struct _D3DXMESHCONTAINER {
  // Name of the mesh.
  LPSTR Name;

  // Defines the type of mesh, and holds the mesh data.
  D3DXMESHDATA MeshData;

  // Array of materials used by the mesh (lighting properties).
  LPD3DXMATERIAL pMaterials;

  // An effect pointer, which we won't be using.
  LPD3DXEFFECTINSTANCE pEffects;

  // Total number of materials in the pMaterials array.
  DWORD NumMaterials;

  // Adjacency information about the faces in the mesh.
  DWORD *pAdjacency;

  // Skin information pointer used for skinned meshes.
  LPD3DXSKININFO pSkinInfo;

  // Pointer to the next mesh in the list.
  struct _D3DXMESHCONTAINER *pNextMeshContainer;
} D3DXMESHCONTAINER, *LPD3DXMESHCONTAINER;
```

As previously mentioned, when you create a mesh and save it to a .x file, it is stored in a frame within the hierarchy. If you were to create two separate cubes in 3ds max and export them out, you would end up with the left hierarchy shown in Figure 8.4. By combining the two cubes into one single mesh, you would end up with the hierarchy on the right, shown in Figure 8.4.

FIGURE 8.4   Two cube meshes produce the left hierarchy, while one produces the right hierarchy.

The true power of the hierarchy is not seen until we start doing animation. When you animate a mesh, you need to place *bones* throughout the mesh that are linked to the vertices in the mesh. The bones act just like the bones in your body (hence the name). When a bone moves, any vertices linked to the bone also move with it. Bones are built up using a hierarchy, similar to how the bones in your body are linked together. This is why the hierarchy structure the .x file uses is so ideal. Before we discuss this any further, let's continue by looking at two more structures, one of which will help to facilitate the discussion further.

As great as the D3DXFRAME and D3DXMESHCONTAINER structures are, they do not account for everything. There are still a number of properties about a frame or mesh that we need to store that these structures do not accommodate for. To resolve the issue, we will create two new structures that derive from the D3DXFRAME and D3DXMESHCONTAINER structures, respectively. So let's have a look at them now, starting with the Frame structure.

```
struct Frame : public D3DXFRAME
{
  D3DXMATRIX finalTransformationMatrix;

  D3DXVECTOR3 GetTranslation()
  {
    return D3DXVECTOR3( finalTransformationMatrix._41,
                        finalTransformationMatrix._42,
                        finalTransformationMatrix._43 );
  }
};
```

Since frames are linked using a hierarchy, it is inherent that some frames are going to have parents and others will have children—most likely both. What this means is that each frame can potentially have other frames higher than it in the hierarchy, and other frames lower than it in the hierarchy, within the same branch. You also know that each frame has a transformation matrix (called `TransformationMatrix`), which defines how the frame is positioned in 3D space. If you are unsure what a matrix is, don't worry as we will have a crash course in them shortly.

Now the question is what happens when a parent frame moves? What happens to all its children? This isn't something we need to worry about just yet, but it will become apparent when we start animating our meshes, so we will accommodate for it now. As previously mentioned, when you animate a mesh you use bones. The bones themselves are represented by frames within the hierarchy. In order to animate, a mesh's bones need to move, which means that each frame's transformation is moving in 3D space. If a parent frame moves, it has to move its children with it.

The best way to visualize this is to use your own body. Imagine the bones in your arm are the frames, and your physical arm is the mesh. Each bone is represented by a frame and is linked to a parent bone (higher in the arm), and may have one or more children (lower in the arm). If you move one of the bones in your arm, all of its children move proportionally with it. In other words, if you raise your upper arm up in the air you will find that your lower arm and your hand also raise up in the air, despite the fact that you did not move those bones. This is because each bone down the hierarchy takes on the movements of its parent bone, combining it with its own movement.

In order to calculate and store the transformation of a frame based on its parent's movements combined with its own movements, we need another variable where we can store this new positional information. So we derive a new structure from the `D3DXFRAME` structure and call it `Frame`. Then we define our new property within the `Frame` structure. Throughout the implementation of our `Mesh` class, rather than using the `D3DXFRAME` structure, we use the `Frame` structure. Additionally, we also add the `GetTranslation` function to the `Frame` class. This function extracts the actual x,y,z positional coordinates from the `finalTransformationMatrix` and returns it. This is useful when you want to know the position of a frame in 3D space.

Don't worry if this seems a little complicated, as we will be discussing animation further in Chapter 9, which may help you to understand how this all works. As already mentioned, if you don't know what all this matrix stuff is about, we will talk about that very shortly. For now we have one more structure left to look at—the

MeshContainer structure, which is what we will use instead of the D3DXMESHCONTAINER structure.

```
struct MeshContainer : public D3DXMESHCONTAINER
{
  char **materialNames;
  Material **materials;
  ID3DXMesh *originalMesh;
  D3DXATTRIBUTERANGE *attributeTable;
  unsigned long totalAttributeGroups;
  D3DXMATRIX **boneMatrixPointers;
};
```

The MeshContainer structure derives from the D3DXMESHCONTAINER structure, so it has all the same functionality; we have just added some new needed properties. First, we have added an array of material names and an array of actual materials, which are the materials used by these meshes. These are the same materials that we created earlier in this chapter. The originalMesh pointer allows us to store an original, unmodified copy of our mesh as a reference point. The attributeTable and the totalAttributeGroups are used for rendering the mesh, and the boneMatrixPointers is used for animating the mesh. You will see these in use later when we implement our Mesh class.

MATRICES

It is time again for one of those fun detours where we discuss something completely irrelevant to the topic at hand. This time we need to talk about matrices, as you have just been exposed to them, and we are going to start using them a whole lot more—especially in Chapter 9. We will keep this as light as possible, avoiding any of the scary mathematics behind matrices. The great part about using matrices with DirectX is that the D3DX library comes with numerous functions and structures specifically for handling and manipulating matrices, therefore, you don't need to worry about the underlying works, at least to begin with. Before we look at how D3DX can help us, let's quickly talk about what matrices are.

Matrices are used by Direct3D to perform what is called a *transformation*. More specifically, these transformations occur in 3D, which means that a transformation can be applied to a 3D position or vector, for example. 3D transformations are used to perform a number of tasks, such as expressing a position relative to a point in 3D space, rotating or scaling in 3D, or altering the player's view of the 3D scene. This is synonymous to changing the position, direction, and perspective of the virtual camera in 3D space. A single matrix is defined by a number of columns and a number of rows. The most common matrix you will come across (and the one we will be working with) is the 4×4 matrix, which means that the matrix has 4 rows and 4 columns as shown in Figure 8.5.

$$\begin{bmatrix} M_{11} & M_{12} & M_{13} & M_{14} \\ M_{21} & M_{22} & M_{23} & M_{24} \\ M_{31} & M_{32} & M_{33} & M_{34} \\ M_{41} & M_{42} & M_{43} & M_{44} \end{bmatrix}$$

FIGURE 8.5 A 4×4 matrix.

As previously mentioned, D3DX provides a structure designed for storing 4×4 matrices. The definition of this structure, which identifies each component in the matrix, is shown here. If you wanted to access the value in the second row, third column, you would use _23.

```
typedef struct D3DXMATRIX {
   FLOAT _11, FLOAT _12, FLOAT _13, FLOAT _14,
   FLOAT _21, FLOAT _22, FLOAT _23, FLOAT _24,
   FLOAT _31, FLOAT _32, FLOAT _33, FLOAT _34,
   FLOAT _41, FLOAT _42, FLOAT _43, FLOAT _44;
} D3DXMATRIX;
```

The most common use of matrices in 3D math is to transform a 3D object from one position in 3D space to another. This can involve the use of a translation matrix, a rotation matrix, and/or a scaling matrix. The translation matrix simply moves an object from one point to another in 3D space. The rotation matrix obviously rotates an object around a point, such as its center. Finally, the scaling matrix is used to scale the object; in other words, increase or decrease its size. So in order to move an object from one point to another, you would build a translation matrix specifically for the movement and then apply it to the object's position. If you then wanted to turn the object around on the spot, you would build a rotation matrix and apply it to the object's rotation.

An advantage of using matrices is that the effects of two or more matrices can be combined to produce a single output by simply multiplying the matrices together—this is called *matrix concatenation*. For example, in our previous example we translated and rotated our imaginary object using two matrices: a translation matrix and a rotation matrix. We can achieve the same result by combining the rotation matrix with the translation matrix into a new matrix. If we then apply this new matrix to our object, we end up with the same result as before when we used two matrices.

CAUTION

When combining matrices, always remember that matrix concatenation is not commutative. This means that the order in which you multiply the matrices together is crucial. The best way to remember this is to use the left-to-right rule. What this means is that the effects of the matrices will be applied in a left-to-right order. Take a look at the following formula which concatenates three matrices together: a rotation matrix, a translation matrix, and a scaling matrix.

$$M = M_R \cdot M_T \cdot M_S$$

This concatenation has the effect of first rotating the object, then translating it, and finally scaling it. If you swap the order the matrices are concatenated, you swap the order in which they are applied to the object.

This has been a very quick lesson in matrices and you may still have questions. Fortunately, you do not need to know much about the underlying workings of matrices or the mathematics involved in order to use them. However, to fully appreciate them you should have a quick look at the Transforms section of the DirectX Graphics Programming Guide in the DirectX SDK documentation. If you are struggling with this topic, you will be able to better understand how matrices work by perusing this section. Throughout the rest of this book you will see matrices put to good use, and you will learn far more about them as you see them in practice.

LOADING THE MESH HIERARCHY

Before we go any further, you should be aware that like networking (from Chapter 7), the whole topic of meshes is extremely detailed. Therefore, it is impossible for us to cover everything. Instead, we will cover an overview of how meshes work and look at the important parts of the implementation. You are strongly encouraged to have the source code from the CD-ROM for this chapter available for reference as we cannot list all of the code in the book. Additionally, if there are any specific topics that you do not feel comfortable with, you should always look them up in the DirectX SDK documentation as it can often give a much more thorough explanation. After our little crash course in matrices, we can carry on with discussing our meshes. It is now time to look at the process of loading the hierarchy from a .x file.

ON THE CD

Once you have created your mesh and saved it to a .x file, the first step is to load the .x file, reading and storing the mesh hierarchy. As you already know, when we load a .x file, the hierarchy is made up of frames, each of which will be stored using our `Frame` structure that you saw earlier. The actual mesh data will be contained within one or more frames, and stored using our `MeshContainer` structure, which you also saw earlier. Fortunately, D3DX provides the `ID3DXAllocateHierarchy` interface, which is used to facilitate the loading and allocating of a .x file hierarchy. The interface exposes four functions that each work in a very similar way to a call-back function. The idea is that you derive a new class from this interface and override each of the four functions with your application-specific code. When you load the .x file, your overridden functions are called to allow you to load the frames and meshes, while D3DX worries about creating the actual hierarchy for you. It may sound a little complicated, but it is quite simple once you see it in practice. Let's start by looking at the `AllocateHierarchy` class that we derive from the `ID3DXAllocateHierarchy` interface.

```
class AllocateHierarchy : public ID3DXAllocateHierarchy
{
  STDMETHOD( CreateFrame )( THIS_ LPCSTR Name,
                            LPD3DXFRAME *ppNewFrame );
  STDMETHOD( CreateMeshContainer )( THIS_ LPCSTR Name,
                    CONST D3DXMESHDATA *pMeshData,
                    CONST D3DXMATERIAL *pMaterials,
                    CONST D3DXEFFECTINSTANCE *pEffectInstances,
                    DWORD NumMaterials, CONST DWORD *pAdjacency,
                    LPD3DXSKININFO pSkinInfo,
                    LPD3DXMESHCONTAINER *ppNewMeshContainer );
```

```
STDMETHOD( DestroyFrame )( THIS_ LPD3DXFRAME pFrameToFree );
STDMETHOD( DestroyMeshContainer )( THIS_ LPD3DXMESHCONTAINER
                                    pMeshContainerToFree );
};
```

As you can see, the four functions exposed by ID3DXAllocateHierarchy that we have overridden are CreateFrame, CreateMeshContainer, DestroyFrame, and DestroyMeshContainer. It should be fairly obvious as to what each function actually does, with the first two being used to create frames and mesh containers, respectively, and the last two used to destroy (or free) frames and mesh containers, respectively. There are also quite a few parameters being passed to these functions, especially the CreateMeshContainer function. You do not need to concern yourself with passing the correct data through these parameters as that is all handled for you by D3DX when you load the .x file. Remember that we use D3DX to load the .x file and create the hierarchy. These functions are called by D3DX to give us the opportunity to load our frames and mesh containers as the hierarchy is being created. All of the information we need to load a frame or mesh container will be provided by D3DX, so don't worry about that either.

Now let's have a brief look at how each function works before we move on to discussing our main Mesh class. We won't look at the actual implementation of each function, as it is either very straightforward (such as the CreateFrame and DestroyFrame functions), or a little too complicated for us to be talking about here, such as the CreateMeshContainer function. Instead, we will simply look at how they work and then you can peruse the source code on the CD-ROM.

Remember that this type of code is underlying utility code intended to support a higher level class; in this case, the Mesh class, which we will cover shortly. If you do not quite understand how this all works, don't worry about it, just move on. When you start developing the game you will see that we will never directly interact with this code. In fact, if you don't care about how a mesh is loaded and stored, then you can effectively skip this entire section and still be able to create a game using this code without any problem. Once this code is written, it never needs to be touched again unless you want to modify the way the mesh is loaded, or add a new feature to the loading process.

With that said, we can start by looking at how our AllocateHierarchy class handles the creation and destruction of a single frame using the Frame structure. When the .x file is being loaded, every time a new frame in the hierarchy is encountered during the loading process, D3DX calls our CreateFrame function. This gives us the opportunity to create, fill out, and return a `Frame` structure that stores the details of the new frame. When the function is called, D3DX passes in the name of the new frame (which it reads in from the .x file) and the address of a pointer to a `D3DXFRAME`, which is the structure that D3DX works with. Since our `Frame` structure is derived from the `D3DXFRAME` structure, we can create a new `Frame` structure, assign the name to it, and then return a pointer to it. D3DX will handle the rest and link it into the hierarchy correctly for us.

When it comes time to destroy the frame (such as when you are shutting the application down), D3DX will call the `DestroyFrame` function passing in a pointer to the frame that needs to be destroyed. Destroying the frame is even easier than creating it. Basically, it is just a matter of freeing all the memory that we allocated in the `CreateFrame` function. We just use the `SAFE_DELETE` macro, passing in the same pointer of the frame we want to destroy, and it's as simple as that. In fact, the `DestroyMeshContainer` function works in exactly the same way. A pointer to the mesh container that needs to be destroyed is passed to you. All you need to do is perform the reverse of what is done in the `CreateMeshContainer` function, freeing all the memory that was allocated. Have a look at the code to the `DestroyFrame` and the `DestroyMeshContainer` functions and you will see that their operation is really quite simple.

The last function we need to look at is `CreateMeshContainer`. This function is the most complex of the four, mainly because it has so many parameters that you need to attend to, which makes it a very busy function. The main priority of this function is to create a new `MeshContainer` structure and return a pointer to it, just like how the `CreateFrame` function creates a new `Frame` structure and returns a pointer to that. However, it also has to perform a number of other actions as well, such as storing the details of the actual mesh data and the materials used by the mesh.

If you take a look at the code where we store the details of the materials, you will notice that we are actually just storing the texture names, which are the names of our material scripts. Normally, you would load the textures here and store them; however, at this point we have no idea where the material scripts are located. In other words, we have the name of the material, but we don't know the path to it. So we store the name and then later we will load each material script using the same path as the mesh's .x file.

THE MESH SYSTEM

Although you are probably at a bit of a loss as to how the mesh hierarchy is loaded, don't be concerned. You should at least have a basic understanding of how it works by now. If not, perhaps you need to reread the previous sections, have a look through the source code, or consult the DirectX SDK documentation for additional clarification on any areas that you are still unsure about. At the end of this chapter, don't worry if you haven't fully understood everything. In fact don't be alarmed if you finish this chapter and have no idea how the mesh system works. You will completely understand it when you actually start using it. Although this has been mentioned before, it is important to repeat. The fact is the entire mesh system is one of the most complicated systems you will face in this book, and one of the few systems that we are just going to talk about rather than actually implement line by line. Remember that these topics (like networking from the last chapter), can fill an entire book in themselves, so we cannot cover everything. All you need to concern yourself with is learning an overview of how everything here works, and gaining enough understanding so that you can start using the code in your own projects. As time progresses, you will undoubtedly want to add new features and modify the behavior of the mesh system. It is at this point that you will really learn how meshes are loaded and handled internally—not now. So with that said, let's begin by looking at the Mesh class definition.

```cpp
class Mesh : public BoundingVolume, public Resource< Mesh >
{
public:
  Mesh( char *name, char *path = "./" );
  virtual ~Mesh();

  void Update();
  void Render();

  void CloneAnimationController(
              ID3DXAnimationController **animationController );

  MeshContainer *GetStaticMesh();
  Vertex *GetVertices();
  unsigned short *GetIndices();

  LinkedList< Frame > *GetFrameList();
  Frame *GetFrame( char *name );
  Frame *GetReferencePoint( char *name );

private:
  void PrepareFrame( Frame *frame );
  void UpdateFrame( Frame *frame,
              D3DXMATRIX *parentTransformationMatrix = NULL );
  void RenderFrame( Frame *frame );
```

```
private:
  Frame *m_firstFrame;
  ID3DXAnimationController *m_animationController;

  D3DXMATRIX *m_boneMatrices;
  unsigned long m_totalBoneMatrices;

  MeshContainer *m_staticMesh;
  Vertex *m_vertices;
  unsigned short *m_indices;

  LinkedList< Frame > *m_frames;
  LinkedList< Frame > *m_refPoints;
};
```

You have probably seen larger, more intimidating classes than this one, but don't be fooled—there is quite a bit going on behind each of those functions. Remember that when we are done, you will be able to use the class to load and handle all of your meshes very easily without having to touch the underlying code inside this class or any of its supporting classes and structure we previously looked at. This is perfect when you are learning, as you will be able to focus on developing your games without having to worry about how to load and process meshes with DirectX. Later on when you become more experienced (or if you are already experienced), you will probably want to learn how this is done. Between this text, the code on the CD-ROM, and the DirectX SDK, you should have all the resources you need to facilitate your learning.

We will start by running through the Mesh class definition, pointing out the highlights. First you will notice that the Mesh class derives from both the BoundingVolume class and the Resource class. The Resource class derivation is fairly obvious. A mesh's .x file has a name and a path to that file. These are traits of a resource, so we will treat it like one and allow it to be managed by our resource management system that we created earlier. The BoundingVolume class is a new one, however, and you have never seen it in use before. You should know what the BoundingVolume class does as we have already discussed it. The reason we want to derive our Mesh class from it is so that we can create a set of bounding volumes around the mesh. Remember that the BoundingVolume class is used to define a bounding box, sphere, and ellipsoid. By creating a set of these bounding volumes around the mesh when it is loaded, it will make it easier for us to later access the bounding volume information of an object that uses a mesh, without having to calculate it every time we need it.

The Mesh class supports all the standard functions, such as the constructor and the destructor, which are used to load and destroy the mesh, respectively. It also has the Update and Render functions, which are called whenever the mesh needs to be updated (for animation purposes), or rendered, respectively. The class also has a number of public utility functions, which are used for accessing various details about the mesh, such as the frames in the mesh. Finally, you will notice a few private functions, which are used internally within the class for preparing, updating, and rendering the mesh. These functions work in what's called a *recursive* manner, which you will see when we discuss them later.

The last highlight of the class is the many member variables it has. Most of them probably look pretty foreign to you, but once again, don't worry. You will learn about them in due course as we look at the different implementation snippets from the Mesh class, starting with the constructor, which is used to load the mesh.

LOADING A MESH

ON THE CD

When you create a new mesh, all of the loading takes place in the Mesh class constructor. You can find the complete implementation of the Mesh class constructor in the Mesh.cpp file in the workspace for this chapter. The code is well commented, so you can read it to get an overview of what is happening. To assist you, we will extract a few of the important points and have a look at them here. We will start with the mesh hierarchy from the .x file, which is achieved with the following two lines of code:

```
AllocateHierarchy ah;
D3DXLoadMeshHierarchyFromX( GetFilename(), D3DXMESH_MANAGED,
                            g_engine->GetDevice(), &ah, NULL,
                            (D3DXFRAME**)&m_firstFrame,
                            &m_animationController );
```

First, we need to create an instance of our AllocateHierarchy class. Remember that this is the class that is used to load and destroy the frames and mesh containers within the hierarchy. The next step is to call the D3DXLoadMeshHierarchyFromX function provided by the D3DX library. The prototype for the function is shown here:

```
HRESULT WINAPI D3DXLoadMeshHierarchyFromX
(
  // Filename (name + path) of the .x file to load.
  LPCSTR Filename,
```

```
    // Mesh creation option flags.
    DWORD MeshOptions,

    // Pointer to the Direct3D device to associate the mesh with.
    LPDIRECT3DDEVICE9 pDevice,

    // Pointer to an ID3DXAllocateHierarchy interface.
    LPD3DXALLOCATEHIERARCHY pAlloc,

    // Interface for loading application-specific data.
    LPD3DXLOADUSERDATA pUserDataLoader,

    // Returned pointer to the first frame in the loaded hierarchy.
    LPD3DXFRAME* ppFrameHeirarchy,

    // A returned animation controller for the mesh's animations.
    LPD3DXANIMATIONCONTROLLER* ppAnimController
);
```

The first parameter is fairly simple; it is just a matter of passing in the complete filename of the .x file, which is stored by our Mesh class within the base Resource class. For the second parameter, there are many options that you can pass in—far too many to list here. If you look up the D3DXMESH enumeration in the DirectX SDK documentation, you will receive a complete list of possible options, along with descriptions of each option. There is only one option that we are really interested in, which is D3DXMESH_MANAGED. This tells the function that we want the mesh resource to be managed by the device. If you recall, this allows the resource to exist in system memory, but is automatically copied to device-accessible memory when it is needed for rendering. This also means that the resource does not need to be re-created when the device is lost because a copy always exists in system memory.

In the third parameter, we pass in a pointer to our Direct3D device. This will associate the mesh with this device, which means that when the device is lost or destroyed, we can no longer render this instance of the loaded mesh. The fourth parameter allows us to pass in a pointer to our AllocateHierarchy class. You will notice that it actually requests an ID3DXAllocateHierarchy interface pointer, but since our AllocateHierarchy class derives from the ID3DXAllocateHierarchy interface, we can use our version. This means that our overridden functions in the AllocateHierarchy class will be called to create the frames and mesh containers when the mesh hierarchy is being constructed.

The next parameter can be ignored as it is used for loading your own custom-defined data that is saved in the .x file. We briefly touched on this back at the start of this chapter and also noted that we do not need this functionality. The final two parameters are just pointers that the function returns back to you. For the first one we pass in m_firstFrame, which is a pointer to a Frame structure. When the function returns, this points to the first frame in the loaded mesh's frame hierarchy. Later on you will see how we use this pointer along with recursive functions to traverse the hierarchy so that we can perform operations on each frame, such as updating or rendering. Finally, in the last parameter we pass in the m_animationController member variable, which is a pointer to an ID3DXAnimationController interface. This interface is used to control any animations built into the mesh that are saved in the .x file. You will learn more about this later, especially in Chapter 9 when we look at animated objects.

Assuming the function returns successfully, the .x file has been read and the mesh's frame hierarchy has been loaded. However, before we can start using the mesh, there are two more major steps we have to complete. The first of these steps is to prepare the frame hierarchy and the second step is to create a static version of the mesh, which is just a term used to define a mesh that cannot animate. Before we talk any further about static meshes, let's focus on preparing the mesh's frame hierarchy. To do this we call the private function PrepareFrame, which belongs to our Mesh class. This function accepts one parameter, which is a pointer to a Frame structure instance. In this call to PrepareFrame we pass in m_firstFrame.

You have already been introduced to the term, *recursive*, but you may not understand what that means. PrepareFrame is the first function we are going to look at that is a recursive function. What that means is that it calls itself; it's as simple as that. The function performs some tasks and then calls itself again to repeat those tasks. It continues doing this until it has performed the tasks a predefined number of times—like a glorified loop. What makes recursive functions amazing is that you can pass input to the function based on calculations from the previous recursion. Let's have a look at an oversimplified example.

```
void Count( int number, int CountTo )
{
  number++;

  printf( "%d\n", number );

  if( number < CountTo )
    Count( number, CountTo );
}
```

The above function is used to count from `number` to `CountTo`, and to print the numbers to a console prompt. You can test it by creating a new console application, placing this function before the main function, and calling it like this:

```
Count( 0, 10 );
```

In this example, you would see the numbers 1 through 10 displayed on the screen indicating that the recursive function is counting up to 10. This is a very basic recursive function that increments the number you start it at and then checks to see if it has reached the number you want it to count to. If it has not, then it calls itself again passing in the incremented number and the number you want to count to. The next recursion increments the number and checks again. If it still hasn't reached the number you want it to count to, then it performs another recursion and so on until it reaches the desired number. At that point it stops calling itself, and returns, which allows the previous recursion to return and so on down the line until each function call has returned.

You must always make sure that a recursive function has a guaranteed out. In other words, there must be some sort of check that allows the function to abort the recursion. In our previous example function, the check simply involved seeing if the count had reached the desired number. If you do not have such a check in, the function will continue to recur indefinitely. This may cause memory or processor intensive recursive functions to stop your application from responding, or even make it crash.

If you have a look at the implementation to the `PrepareFrame` function (found in `Mesh.cpp`), you will see how the function performs its recursion at the end of the function. The code is shown here:

```
if( frame->pFrameSibling != NULL )
  PrepareFrame( (Frame*)frame->pFrameSibling );

if( frame->pFrameFirstChild != NULL )
  PrepareFrame( (Frame*)frame->pFrameFirstChild );
```

The `Frame` structure has two members called `pFrameSibling` and `pFrameFirstChild` (these are inherited from `D3DXFRAME`), which are used to link the frame into the hierarchy. `pFrameSibling` links the frame with all the other frames on the same level in the hierarchy. In other words, they have the same parent. `pFrameFirstChild` is used to point to the frame's first child, which is actually the first frame of the next level in the hierarchy under this parent. To prepare the entire frame hierarchy we need to call the PrepareFrame function once for each frame in the hierarchy. Each time it is called we pass in a new frame. The recursion is started with the siblings of the current frame, if it has any. Once all the siblings have been processed, recursion then drops down to the first child of the last sibling. After this child has been processed, all of its siblings are processed, and so on. We then move back up the hierarchy processing the children of previous frames. Figure 8.6 shows how the frame hierarchy is traversed using a recursive function.

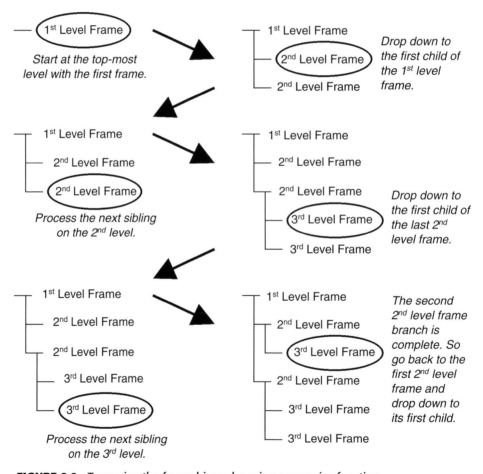

FIGURE 8.6 Traversing the frame hierarchy using a recursive function.

A recursion reaches the end of a branch in the hierarchy when both `pFrame-Sibling` and `pFrameFirstChild` equate to `NULL`. This means that there are no more siblings under the current parent, and the current frame has no children. At this point, the recursive function returns, which allows the previous recursion to return and so on. This continues back up the hierarchy until a frame is found that has an unprocessed child. We then enter a new recursion, pursuing the frames in this new branch. Eventually, that branch comes to an end and so too does every other branch in the hierarchy. When this happens, each remaining recursion returns back up the hierarchy until we reach the top where the whole process started. The last call to the recursive function (which is actually the first call we made to begin the process) returns and the hierarchy traversal is complete.

Now you should have a pretty good idea about how `PrepareFrame` traverses through the hierarchy processing every frame. If you have a look at the rest of the code in this function you will be able to see what it does to actually process each frame. The most important point here is that the function checks if the current frame has a mesh container. If it does, then it prepares the mesh container for rendering. There are two steps here: storing pointers to the bone matrices, and loading the mesh's materials.

The first step is probably a little too complicated for you to worry about right now, but we will touch on it anyway. If you recall, we discussed how a mesh uses bones for its animation, which function just like the bones in your body. Let's say you had a frame that enclosed your left leg, and this frame has a mesh container in it that houses all the mesh data for your left leg. In order for your left leg to move, you have to move the bones in that leg (technically, you move your muscles, not the bones, but we'll ignore that slight complication). The key here is that you only want your left leg to move when the bones in your left leg move. In other words, if the bones in your right leg start moving or the bones in your arms start moving, you don't want your left leg to move. To facilitate this, we maintain a list of pointers to the matrices for each of the bones that affect your left leg. Remember that each bone is just a frame that has a transformation matrix, which indicates the frame's position, rotation, and scale in 3D space. When these frames animate, the matrices change, and when these matrices are applied to the vertices in the mesh, they move—resulting in animation!

So back to the first step in preparing the mesh container, we need to find all of the bones that affect the mesh in the current frame. Then we store a pointer to the frame's transformation matrix for each of these bones. Later you will see how these bone matrices are used when we render the mesh. For now, let's look at the second step in preparing the mesh containers: loading the mesh's materials.

If you have an understanding of how our material system works with the re-source management system, then you should have no problem seeing how this works. All we do is go through the list of material names that we stored when we created the mesh container. For each valid material name, we invoke the engine's material manager so that it can load the material script. The material manager ensures that only one copy of the material exists at a time, and all the details for the material (such as its texture) are loaded the first time it is created. We store a pointer to each of the materials in the `materials` array, which is a member of the `MeshContainer` structure.

That's about all there is to preparing the mesh container, which concludes our discussion of the `PrepareFrame` function. Obviously, we didn't look at the function line by line, so there are a few minor details that we overlooked, but you should have the general idea about what is going on. The final step we need to discuss, which we mentioned some time ago, is the process of creating the static mesh. This is the last step of loading a mesh, and you can find the code to this in the `Mesh` class constructor.

As you should already be aware, a static mesh is just a mesh that has no ability to animate, which means it has no need for bones. This single assumption is very powerful as it allows us to completely remove the frame hierarchy from the static mesh. Instead of using a frame hierarchy, we collapse the mesh into a single mesh container inside a single frame. The advantage of this is that it greatly improves the efficiency of rendering the mesh. First, we do not need to traverse a hierarchy every time we need to render the mesh, and second, we can render the mesh in one call if it uses a single material. In other words, we can send all the mesh data to the video card once, rather than once for each mesh container in the frame hierarchy. This is perfect for meshes that do not need to animate, such as the majority (if not all) of the scenery and geometry that make up a typical scene.

Any mesh can be easily converted into a static mesh, even one that has bones and uses a frame hierarchy. To achieve this we use the `D3DXLoadMeshFromX` function, which is provided by the D3DX library and is extremely simple to use. Just like the `D3DXLoadMeshHierarchyFromX` function, `D3DXLoadMeshFromX` loads a mesh from a .x file. The only difference it that is does not use the `AllocateHierarchy` class. There-fore, it ignores the mesh's frame hierarchy and simply collapses the entire .x file into a single mesh. You can imagine this as though it is a mesh with one frame and one mesh container. Take a look at the code in the `Mesh` class constructor to see just how easy it is to load a static mesh from a .x file. The very last parameter of the function stores a pointer to your new mesh once the function returns.

Once the static mesh has been loaded, there are a few more things we need to do, which you can see in the code of the `Mesh` class constructor. The most important step is to load the mesh's materials. Fortunately, this is done in exactly the same manner as we did when we prepared the mesh frame hierarchy earlier. The mesh's materials are stored in the `MeshContainer` structure instance that houses our static mesh. Since we have already loaded the mesh using frames, all the mesh's materials should have already been loaded into memory when we prepared the frame hierarchy. Therefore, even though we are loading the materials again, nothing should be loaded into memory. Instead, the material manager recognizes that the materials already exist and just returns pointers to them.

The last step is to fill in the mesh's bounding volume details. If you recall, we derived the `Mesh` class from the `BoundingVolume` class so that we can create a set of bounding volumes around the mesh for reference purposes. Now it is time to create the bounding volumes using our new static mesh. To do this we simply call the `BoundingVolumeFromMesh` function, which is a member of the `BoundingVolume` class. We only need to worry about the first parameter of the function, which is a pointer to an `ID3DXMesh`. We pass in `m_staticMesh->originalMesh` (which is our static mesh pointer) and the function will calculate and store a bounding box, sphere, and ellipsoid around the mesh (you should be aware that the ellipsoid will be the same shape as the sphere because we did not specify an ellipsoid radius in the second parameter of the function).

The last few lines of code in the `Mesh` class constructor are used for creating a vertex and index buffer containing the mesh's vertices and indices, respectively. These will be used later by the scene manager to access the vertices of the geometry used in the scene. Don't concern yourself too much with this now as we haven't covered vertex or index buffers yet. We will talk about them in Chapter 10 when we start using them, so let's continue on with our `Mesh` class for now.

UPDATING AND RENDERING A MESH

The `Mesh` class has two functions that look like this:

```
void Mesh::Update()
{
  UpdateFrame( m_firstFrame );
}


void Mesh::Render()
{
  RenderFrame( m_firstFrame );
}
```

These two functions are used for updating and rendering the mesh's frame hierarchy, respectively. Both of them call one of the internal functions of the Mesh class that kicks off a recursive traversal of the frame hierarchy. In other words, the UpdateFrame and RenderFrame functions work just like the PrepareFrame function that we looked at earlier. They each accept a pointer to a Frame structure, which is then used to process the entire frame hierarchy starting with the first frame that we pass in here. These functions traverse the frame hierarchy in exactly the same manner as the PrepareFrame function so we won't bother going through that again. Instead, we will look at what each of the functions actually does internally.

First we have the UpdateFrame function, which looks like this:

```
void Mesh::UpdateFrame( Frame *frame,
                        D3DXMATRIX *parentTransformationMatrix )
{
  if( parentTransformationMatrix != NULL )
    D3DXMatrixMultiply( &frame->finalTransformationMatrix,
                        &frame->TransformationMatrix,
                         parentTransformationMatrix );
  else
    frame->finalTransformationMatrix =
                        frame->TransformationMatrix;

  if( frame->pFrameSibling != NULL )
    UpdateFrame( (Frame*)frame->pFrameSibling,
                         parentTransformationMatrix );

  if( frame->pFrameFirstChild != NULL )
    UpdateFrame( (Frame*)frame->pFrameFirstChild,
                         &frame->finalTransformationMatrix );
}
```

As you can see by the last few lines of code, the function traverses the frame hierarchy using a recursive approach. All we are really interested in is the first few lines of code, which build up the frame's final transformation matrix. Each frame stores a transformation matrix—in TransformationMatrix—that indicates the position, rotation, and scale of the frame. If you think back to when we discussed how the frame hierarchy works with animation, you will remember that when a parent frame moves, all of its children move with it. For this reason, we need to maintain another transformation matrix for each frame, which is the frame's transformation matrix combined with its parent's transformation matrix—this is stored in finalTransformationMatrix.

If you look at the code you can see that if a parent's transformation matrix has been passed in, then we combine it with the frame's transformation matrix using the D3DXMatrixMultiply function. Then when we traverse the frame hierarchy, we pass the appropriate parent's transformation matrix. If we are going to a sibling, we pass in the same parent transformation matrix. If we are going to a child, we pass in the current frame's final transformation matrix, which includes the transformation of its parent, grandparent, and so on. Figure 8.7 shows how the process works through the frame hierarchy.

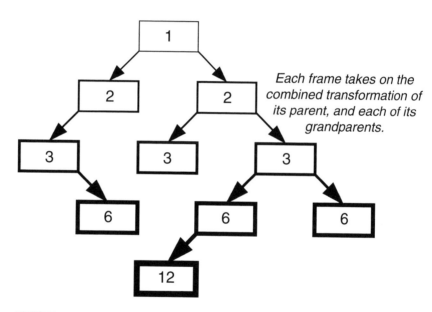

FIGURE 8.7 Frame transformation matrices combined through the frame hierarchy.

Finally, we have the RenderFrame function, with a major portion of it shown here:

```
if( meshContainer->pSkinInfo != NULL )
{
  for( unsigned long b = 0;
       b < meshContainer->pSkinInfo->GetNumBones(); ++b )
    D3DXMatrixMultiply( &m_boneMatrices[b],
              meshContainer->pSkinInfo->GetBoneOffsetMatrix( b ),
              meshContainer->boneMatrixPointers[b] );
```

```
PBYTE sourceVertices, destinationVertices;
meshContainer->originalMesh->LockVertexBuffer( D3DLOCK_READONLY,
                                (void**)&sourceVertices );
meshContainer->MeshData.pMesh->LockVertexBuffer( 0,
                                (void**)&destinationVertices );
meshContainer->pSkinInfo->UpdateSkinnedMesh( m_boneMatrices,
                    NULL, sourceVertices, destinationVertices );
meshContainer->originalMesh->UnlockVertexBuffer();
meshContainer->MeshData.pMesh->UnlockVertexBuffer();

for( unsigned long a = 0;
     a < meshContainer->totalAttributeGroups; a++ )
{
  g_engine->GetDevice()->SetMaterial(
    meshContainer->materials[
    meshContainer->attributeTable[a].AttribId]->GetLighting() );
  g_engine->GetDevice()->SetTexture( 0,
    meshContainer->materials[
    meshContainer->attributeTable[a].AttribId]->GetTexture() );
  meshContainer->MeshData.pMesh->DrawSubset(
    meshContainer->attributeTable[a].AttribId );
  }
}
else
{
  for( unsigned long m = 0; m < meshContainer->NumMaterials; m++)
  {
    if( meshContainer->materials[m] )
    {
      g_engine->GetDevice()->SetMaterial(
                  meshContainer->materials[m]->GetLighting() );
      g_engine->GetDevice()->SetTexture( 0,
                  meshContainer->materials[m]->GetTexture() );
    }
    else
      g_engine->GetDevice()->SetTexture( 0, NULL );

    meshContainer->MeshData.pMesh->DrawSubset( m );
  }
}
```

The above code is a snippet from the function showing how the rendering works. It assumes that the frame has a valid `MeshContainer` instance with a valid mesh in it. The first step is to check if the mesh container has any skin information, which will indicate if the mesh is a skinned mesh or not (i.e., does it have bones that can be animated?). When a mesh that uses bones is loaded (through the use of the `D3DXLoadMeshHierarchyFromX` function), an `ID3DXSkinInfo` interface instance is created for that mesh. This interface is used to handle and manipulate the bone matrices (that we discussed earlier), as you will see in a moment.

The first step when rendering a skinned mesh is to create the bone transformations using the transformation matrices stored by the mesh container. You should be able to remember when we prepared the mesh containers we stored pointers to the bones (frames) that affected each mesh container. Once we have the transformation matrix for each bone that affects the mesh container, we can apply them to the mesh's vertices in order to transform them. This is achieved by locking the mesh's internal vertex buffer and calling the `UpdateSkinnedMesh` function (exposed by the `ID3DXSkinInfo` interface); passing in the bone transformation matrices and the mesh's vertices.

Don't get caught up with the details now (especially with the vertex buffers as they will be discussed later); just try to understand the overall picture. It may appear complicated, and if you let yourself become bogged down in the details you may become frustrated. Instead, just remember that this is implemented here for you; you do not need to touch it now if you don't want to. When you have completed this book and you are more confident in your skills, you can come back and tinker with it. You will find that it will become much clearer with practical hands-on experience.

The final step is to render the mesh based on its attribute groups. A single mesh is divided into one or more attribute groups, with each face in the mesh belonging to one of these attribute groups. An attribute group defines the details of how the faces that belong to it should be rendered. For example, you may have a mesh that has two different materials applied to it. All of the faces that have the first material applied to them will be part of attribute group one, while all the other faces (with the other material applied to them) will be part of attribute group two. When we render the mesh, we go through each of the attribute groups and set up the device so it is prepared to render the faces that belong to the current attribute group. After we have rendered the faces, we move to the next attribute group, prepare the device to render these faces, and finally render the faces. This process continues until we have gone through all of the attribute groups, therefore rendering all of the faces in the mesh.

As you can see from the code, we set the texture and the Direct3D material (lighting properties) for each attribute group before we call the DrawSubset function on the mesh. We pass in the ID of the actual attribute group that we are rendering to the DrawSubset function. This instructs the function to render only the faces that belong to the given attribute group. Once we have gone through all the attribute groups, our mesh (in the current mesh container) will be completely rendered, with the appropriate material applied to each face.

From the code you can see what happens when we try to render a mesh that does not have any skin information (i.e., it is not a skinned mesh). In other words, this is like a static mesh that does not have any bone transformations applied to its vertices. We render this mesh in virtually exactly the same way as a skinned mesh. The only difference is we do not need to calculate the bone transformation matrices, or apply them to the mesh's vertices. All we need to do is go through each material in the mesh (i.e., each attribute group) and render the faces that use each material separately—using the DrawSubset function, just like we did before.

That's all there is to updating and rendering a mesh. As you can see, we didn't go into too many details, nor did we cover every single line of code. As previously stressed (a number of times), just focus on learning the overall picture and start using the code in your projects. Later on, when you are a confident programmer, you will find that there will be areas you may want to modify. At this point, you will find it much easier to understand the inner works, and before too long you will be able to rewrite the entire system yourself. If this is all new to you, then just stay focused on the big picture for now. At the end of this chapter, we will run a quick test to show the mesh loading and rendering at work. In Part II you will see all this code in action when we develop our actual game.

INTEGRATING THE MESH SYSTEM

By now you should understand exactly how to integrate a new component into the engine, and you should find that the Mesh class is extremely simple. All we need to do is link the Mesh.h and Mesh.cpp files by using the appropriate #include statements, which you should know by heart by now. Other than that, the only addition to the Engine class is the introduction of the mesh manager, which is a resource manager for handling our new mesh resource. You can see the new resource manager in the Engine class definition, as well as a public function for accessing it outside of the engine. Just like all the other resource managers, we create it in the Engine class constructor, and destroy it in the Engine class destructor.

Those are all the changes necessary in order to start using the meshes within the engine and have them managed by a resource manager. Before we test it, let's look at one more class that is loosely related to meshes (it is used for rendering so we'll squeeze it in here).

THE RENDER CACHE

The RenderCache class is a nifty little utility class that we will add to the engine. We won't bother implementing it as it's really small and basic in its operation. Instead, we will talk about what it does and how it works, without getting too technical. Let's start with a brief explanation of how the RenderCache class fits in to the greater scheme of things.

Although we haven't talked about vertex or index buffers yet, the RenderCache class revolves around them. You should know (as we lightly touched on it in Chapter 5) that a vertex buffer contains the vertices of any faces that you want to render. An index buffer is a different (yet related) type of buffer that compliments a vertex buffer. It works by storing a list of indices that point to the vertices in a vertex buffer. The main purpose of storing these indices is to facilitate the rendering of the vertices in the vertex buffer. Let's have a quick look at how vertex buffers and index buffers are used for rendering.

Let's say you have 10 faces that you could render (with each face being made up of three vertices) on any given frame, but you don't necessarily render all of them every frame. To do this you would create a vertex buffer that had room for 30 vertices, enough to hold all 10 faces. Each frame you would put the vertices of the faces you wanted to render in the vertex buffer and then send the vertex buffer to the video card to be rendered. This is a perfectly viable situation, however, it creates one problem. Although you wouldn't notice it with such a small number of faces, if you were doing this with a real scene containing thousands of faces, you would notice a performance hit. The problem is that every frame the vertex buffer is being filled (which is computationally expensive), and is then being copied to device-accessible memory (which is also computationally expensive). Moving anything between video memory and system memory every frame is inefficient and should always be avoided. This is sometimes referred to as *thrashing*.

To reduce the amount of data copied to and from device-accessible memory, we use an index buffer. Here's how it works. At the start you create one static vertex buffer that holds all of the vertices that you will need in your scene, and you place it in device-accessible memory on the video card (this may not always be possible if you have many faces and little video memory, but we will ignore that fact for now). Then you create an index buffer, which is used to store the indices of vertices in the vertex buffer. In other words, each index refers to one vertex in the vertex buffer, just like an array. Each frame you decide which vertices you want to render and place their indices in the index buffer. Then, rather than sending the entire vertex buffer to the video card, you just send a small index buffer that contains the indices of the vertices to be rendered.

To illustrate this, let's use an example we like to call the *restaurant example*. Imagine you go into a restaurant to have a meal. The restaurant has a menu with every possible item that you may want to order (the menu is like the vertex buffer). The waiter comes and takes your order as you point out the items that you would like to have. Obviously, you don't want everything on the menu, so you pick a select few and the waiter (who acts like the index buffer) jots down a reference to each item you selected, perhaps a number that is next to each item on the menu. Once you are done, you instruct the waiter that you are finished and send him back to the kitchen with your order. This is just like sending the completed index buffer back to the video card with just the indices of the vertices you want rendered. The cook in the kitchen then creates the items you have chosen from the menu based on the references the waiter noted on the order. Finally, the waiter brings the items you ordered and presents them on your table. In the same way, the video card processes only those vertices that are referenced by the index buffer and presents them to you on the screen by rendering them.

Hopefully, you should have a good understanding of the role of the index buffer and we can take a look at the actual RenderCache class now. The idea behind using the RenderCache class is that you create a vertex buffer that holds all of the vertices for all of the faces you may want to render. For each material used by the faces represented by these vertices, you create one render cache. This means that a single render cache is responsible for all of the vertices whose faces use the same material defined by the render cache. Each render cache maintains an index buffer that you fill with the indices of the vertices you want rendered every frame. Once you are done, each render cache takes its turn to set its material and then passes its indices of the vertices to be rendered from the vertex buffer that you created. Let's have a look at the RenderCache class definition, which can be found in RenderCache.h and shown here:

```
class RenderCache
{
public:
  RenderCache( IDirect3DDevice9 *device, Material *material );
  virtual ~RenderCache();
```

```
    void AddFace();
    void Prepare( unsigned long totalVertices );

    void Begin();
    void RenderFace( unsigned short vertex0, unsigned short vertex1,
                     unsigned short vertex2 );
    void End();

    Material *GetMaterial();

private:
  IDirect3DDevice9 *m_device;
  Material *m_material;

  IDirect3DIndexBuffer9 *m_indexBuffer;
  unsigned short *m_indexPointer;
  unsigned long m_totalIndices;
  unsigned long m_faces;

  unsigned long m_totalVertices;
};
```

We won't bother looking at the implementation of the RenderCache class as much, as it is very straightforward. In addition to this, we do not have any practical use for it just yet, so we will hold off any further discussion until Chapter 10 when we start using vertex buffers, index buffers, and the RenderCache class for rendering our scene. If you want to have a peek at the implementation, take a look at RenderCache.cpp. Other than that, we will quickly touch on how the class works.

When you create an instance of the RenderCache class you must set the device and material that it uses. We set the device so that it does not have to be continually requested from the engine, and we set the material so it knows which material to use when rendering. When you are creating the vertex buffer that this render cache will work with you must call AddFace for each face that the render cache must manage. This will increase the size of the render cache by three vertices. Once you have the render cache to the size you want, you must call Prepare, which will create the internal index buffer.

It is important that you create your render caches big enough (through the use of AddFace) to hold all of the vertices they will ever need to render before you call Prepare. Once you call Prepare, the size of the render cache is set and can only be changed by destroying and re-creating it. You do not want to risk overrunning the buffer.

The render cache is now ready to use. All you need to do is set the vertex buffer to be rendered (don't worry about how to do that for now, we will cover that later) and then use the render cache to render the faces. To do this you must call `Begin`, which locks the index buffer so that you can add indices to it. Every time you find a face in the vertex buffer that you want to render (which has the same material as used by this render cache), you call `RenderFace`, passing in the indices of the three vertices that make up the face. These indices are then stored in the index buffer. Once you are done you call `End`, which unlocks the index buffer and renders all the vertices pointed to by this render cache's index buffer.

In order to use the render cache in the engine, all we need to do is link in the `RenderCache.h` and `RenderCache.cpp` files using the `#include` statements. There are no changes required to the Engine class. The `RenderCache` class is ready to go. All you need is a vertex buffer full of vertices to render and you're all set, which you will see in Chapter 10.

TESTING THE MATERIALS AND MESHES

ON THE CD

Finally, after a complex chapter, we are rewarded with the most visually exciting test so far. For the first time we are producing something on the screen that looks a whole lot better than the plain old text that we have become complacent with. You can find the test application in the `Test` project of the workspace for this chapter. If you have a look at the code in our `TestState` class you will see that it is really quite easy to load and render a mesh with our new class. Not only that, but also our script-driven material system is shown in action here as the texture applied to the mesh is a material recognized by our system.

In the `Load` function of our `TestState` class we create our mesh with the following line of code:

```
m_mesh = new Mesh( "Gun.x", "./Assets/" );
```

This loads our mesh in the same way that we load any other resource. You should be aware though that for this simple test we are ignoring the mesh manager. This means that we are loading and destroying the mesh ourselves. If we used the mesh manager to load our mesh then we wouldn't need the `SAFE_DELETE( m_mesh )` in the `Close` function of our `TestState` class as the mesh manager would clean up after us. In addition to this, we wouldn't need to worry about accidentally loading two or more of these mesh instances into memory. So you can see that in a real application it is extremely valuable to use the various resource managers.

You will notice that in the `RequestViewer` function, we specify that we want both the render target and the z buffer to be cleared because we are now rendering in 3D. Finally, in the `Render` function of our `TestState` class you can see that we call `Render` on our mesh, which—you guessed it—renders our mesh each frame. It really cannot get any easier than this. Figure 8.8 shows the output of our test application.

FIGURE 8.8 Our test application rendering a mesh.

You will probably notice a few lines of code in the `Load` function of our `TestState` class, which look like this:

```
D3DXMATRIX view;
D3DXMatrixLookAtLH( &view, &D3DXVECTOR3( -50.0f, 50.0f, -150.0f ),
                           &D3DXVECTOR3( 0.0f, 0.0f, 0.0f ),
                           &D3DXVECTOR3( 0.0f, 1.0f, 0.0f ) );
g_engine->GetDevice()->SetTransform( D3DTS_VIEW, &view );
```

Don't worry too much about this as we will cover it in Chapter 9. As a quick introduction, it is just creating a view matrix, which is what Direct3D uses to position and orient the virtual eye (or camera) in 3D space. In other words, it defines what you are looking at. Here we are setting up a camera to view our mesh. We are placing the camera −50.0 units along the x-axis, 50.0 units up the y-axis, and −150.0 units along the z-axis. The second vector (the one with all the 0.0's) defines what we are looking at (which in this case is the origin of 3D space—where our mesh happens to be placed). The last vector defines which way is up. By setting the y-axis to 1.0 we are telling Direct3D that we want the positive y-axis to point up. Additionally, remember that we are using a left-handed Cartesian coordinate system, so the positive z-axis will point into the screen.

You can try adjusting the values in the first vector to move the camera around. You will notice that no matter where you put the virtual camera, it will always point to the position set in the second vector. If you adjust the second vector, you can change what you look at. As for the third vector, try changing the 1.0 to −1.0 and see what happens. The whole view flips upside down. This is because you are telling Direct3D that the negative y-axis points up, which flips the whole coordinate system.

EXERCISE

Before we conclude this chapter, it is time for a quick exercise to test your knowledge so far. Your mission, should you choose to accept it, is to modify the test application for this chapter so that it can do the following:

1. Connect the camera to some keys on the keyboard so that it can be moved around.
2. Load a script that can be used to position the camera in 3D space.

Both of these tasks are not too difficult, and you have already learned everything you need to complete them, so give it a try before you read any further as the following contains some spoilers. If you are having trouble with either of these tasks, try looking up the information in the appropriate chapters that cover user input and scripts. If you still cannot figure it out, then read on to see one possible solution for each of these tasks.

To move the camera around with the keyboard, one of the quickest (but probably least robust) methods is shown here and is completely implemented in the `pdate` function of the `TestState` class. In fact, you can copy and paste this code straight in without any further modification to the class.

```
virtual void Update( float elapsed )
{
  static D3DXVECTOR3 pos = D3DXVECTOR3( -50.0f, 50.0f, -150.0f );

  if( g_engine->GetInput()->GetKeyPress( DIK_W, true ) == true )
    pos.z += 0.5f;
  if( g_engine->GetInput()->GetKeyPress( DIK_S, true ) == true )
    pos.z -= 0.5f;
  if( g_engine->GetInput()->GetKeyPress( DIK_A, true ) == true )
    pos.x -= 0.5f;
  if( g_engine->GetInput()->GetKeyPress( DIK_D, true ) == true )
    pos.x += 0.5f;

  D3DXMATRIX view;
  D3DXMatrixLookAtLH( &view, &pos, &D3DXVECTOR3( pos.x + 50.0f,
                                 pos.y - 50.0f, pos.z + 150.0f ),
                                 &D3DXVECTOR3( 0.0f, 1.0f, 0.0f ) );
  g_engine->GetDevice()->SetTransform( D3DTS_VIEW, &view );
};
```

This allows you to use the w,a,s,d keys to move the view around on the x-axis and the z-axis. The point that the view looks at is kept the same distance away and moves with it. Finally, here is a simple method of positioning the view using a script. All you have to do is replace the code in the Load function that creates the view matrix with this code.

```
Script *script = new Script( "Camera.txt", "./Assets/" );

D3DXMATRIX view;
D3DXMatrixLookAtLH( &view,
                &D3DXVECTOR3( script->GetVectorData( "pos" )->x,
                              script->GetVectorData( "pos" )->y,
                              script->GetVectorData( "pos" )->z ),
                &D3DXVECTOR3( script->GetVectorData( "at" )->x,
                              script->GetVectorData( "at" )->y,
                              script->GetVectorData( "at" )->z ),
                &D3DXVECTOR3( script->GetVectorData( "up" )->x,
                              script->GetVectorData( "up" )->y,
                              script->GetVectorData( "up" )->z ) );
g_engine->GetDevice()->SetTransform( D3DTS_VIEW, &view );

SAFE_DELETE( script );
```

ON THE CD

This allows you to adjust the position, look at point, and the up vector of the virtual camera using a script called `Camera.txt`, which you can find in the `Assets` directory that accompanies this chapter's workspace.

As you can see, it is very simple to add extra functionality like this. Don't be afraid to experiment; that is how you learn. If that was a breeze for you, then maybe you want to try something a little tougher. You could try to make the view's look at point move with the mouse so that you can look around by moving the mouse. You could also read up about the *world matrix* in the DirectX SDK documentation, which is used to position objects such as meshes in 3D space. If you figure out how that works, you could try repositioning the mesh or even connecting it to keys so that you can move it around. If all that sounds too daunting, then don't worry about it, we will cover it together in due course.

SUMMARY

This has probably been the most complex chapter so far, packed full of complicated details! However, it has definitely been the most rewarding too, as we finally saw some real 3D rendering on the screen for the first time. We developed a great little script-driven material system and a powerful mesh system that can handle all of our meshes—both animated and static. We also added a couple of utility classes for handling bounding volumes and render caches. Finally, we looked at another engine test, which showed off our mesh and material systems in action.

NOTE

Remember that if you are new to this, then don't worry too much about trying to understand every detail. Just focus on the big picture and start using the code; later you can go though the details when you are more confident. If you are experienced, then you may want to take the time now to go through the code on the CD-ROM, specifically looking at the details we did not cover thoroughly. Everything is commented and you can always refer to the book to guide you. Don't forget about the DirectX SDK documentation too as it can often give more technical details in place of the lighter discussions provided in this book.

In the next chapter, we will take our new meshes and encapsulate them inside what we call objects. An object is a clean and easy to use interface that allows you to manage a renderable entity in 3D space. You will see how we create objects that can be positioned and moved around in 3D space. We will also create two other special objects, one of which has the ability to animate any mesh associated with it. So if you thought the test application for this chapter was exciting, then wait until you see what we will do in Chapter 9!

9 ▪ Objects

In This Chapter

- Learn about game objects and how they are used.
- Cover topics such as object movement using vectors and the world matrix.
- Add three different types of base objects to our engine to support a typical FPS.

In the last chapter, we implemented a mesh system that allowed us to load and render 3D meshes on the screen. As exciting as this might be, there is one problem—we cannot move them around. What is a 3D game such as a FPS if all the meshes are static and never move or animate. We want player meshes that can run around, and weapon meshes that spawn into our game, rotating on the spot until they are collected by a player. Throughout this chapter, we will put the necessary infrastructure in place to support these features, and make our meshes come to life. You can find the workspace for this chapter in the /Source/Chapter 9/ directory on the CD-ROM.

ON THE CD

USING OBJECTS

In most computer games there are things moving around that the player can interact with. In fact, the player is usually represented by something that can also move around within the game environment. For example, the player might be a small spaceship that can fly around destroying other spaceships. There might also be various power-ups floating around that the player can collect. In addition to this, there may even be obstacles moving around that the player may have to avoid, for example. All of these "things" have a few common elements. First, they are all (most likely) represented by some sort of graphic or mesh, and second, they all have some physical properties that allow them to move around and collide with one another. In other words, at a fundamental level, they are all very similar. They are all what we call *game objects*, or just *objects* for short.

Creating objects for a game is usually an area where you can make great use of inheritance and polymorphism. If you haven't heard of either of these terms, they are simply just a couple of object-oriented programming buzzwords. You probably don't realize it, but you have already been using the techniques defined by these two buzzwords. Inheritance simply means that you derive a class from another base class so that you inherit its functionality. Polymorphism defines the process of calling a function on a base class that has been overridden by a derived class. Let's take a look at a quick example. Say you had a class that had a virtual function in it. You could then create a new class that derives from the first class; therefore, your first class becomes your base class. In your new derived class you can override the virtual function so that when that function is later called, the derived version of the function will be used in place of the base class implementation.

These two techniques are extremely valuable when defining the objects in your game. They allow you to create a base object that supports all of the common functionality found in any type of object. For example, you may identify that all of your objects must have a position in 3D space. Rather than adding a positional vector to each of your object classes, it is far easier to create a base object class with the positional vector in it. Then you just derive any new objects from this base class. All your new objects will inherit the positional vector, and therefore be able to use it. We will use this principle for our objects, too. We will define a base object that has all of the properties in it that are common to all of our game objects. Whenever we create a new object, we will derive a new class from the base object class so that we inherit its functionality in the new object. In fact, the process doesn't have to stop there. You can create another type of object that derives again from the new object that derives from the base object. Figure 9.1 shows an example of deriving objects from one another.

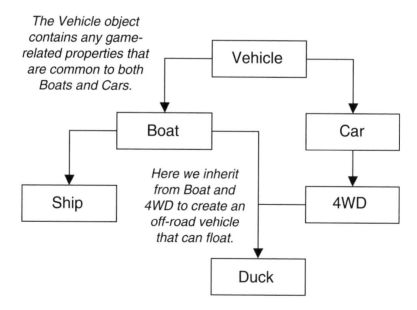

FIGURE 9.1   Deriving game objects.

The base object class that we will create will allow us to place basic objects in our 3D scene. These objects will be able to have a mesh assigned to them so that they have a tangible visible mass. Alternatively, you may not want to give the object a mesh; say if you were creating invisible way-point objects, for example. Through the use of vectors and a special type of matrix called the world matrix, we will be able to position, rotate, and move these objects around in 3D space. These are just a few of the abilities our base object will have. Once in place, we will be able to derive from it to create more complex objects that build off the basic functionality set in place by our base object.

Before we start implementing our base object, let's discuss a couple of important topics relating to positioning and moving our objects in 3D space. More specifically, we need to discuss this elusive world matrix in enough detail for you to understand how it works, as the placement of any object or mesh in 3D space relies on it.

OBJECT MOVEMENT

Since our objects will exist in 3D space, they must conform to the Cartesian coordinate system. In other words, an object must have a position in 3D space that is defined by an (x, y, z) coordinate. The easiest way to represent this coordinate is with a simple positional vector. This sufficees if we just want our objects to sit in one place for all of time, but obviously we are going to want to move some of them around. Moving an object really isn't that hard. It is just a matter of changing its position. If you had an object that was positioned 12.0 units along the x-axis and you wanted to move it 2 units further along the x-axis, you would simply change the object's x-axis position from 12.0 to 14.0. As you can see, it really isn't that hard to move an object around. The hard part is, keeping track of the movement.

Rather than trying to manage how far an object must move and how often it must move that distance, it is far easier to implement a simple physics-based movement system that is calculated over time. This sounds far more complicated than it actually is. Let's have a look at an example that should clarify the situation.

Let's say we are working in 3D space with a scale of one unit to one meter, which means that one meter in the real world is equal to one unit in our virtual world. Now let's pretend we have a car object that is traveling along the positive x-axis (in 3D space) at 10 meters per second (m/s). We can store the car's movement in another vector that we can call the velocity vector, which would look like this: (10.0, 0.0, 0.0). Now the key is to ensure that we move our car 10.0 units along the positive x-axis every second. This is a crucial point to understand. We do not want to move the car 10.0 units every frame. If we were running at 50 fps for example, and we moved the car 10.0 units every frame, then we would be moving it 500.0 units along the positive x-axis every second. This is equivalent to traveling at

500 m/s! The problem is that we want to be able to update our car every frame so that it doesn't appear to just jump 10.0 whole units every second because this would create very jerky movement.

So how do we move our car every frame, but ensure that it doesn't move more than 10.0 units along the positive x-axis each second? Well, it's quite simple really. If we need to spread the car's movement across 50 frames (assuming we are running at 50 fps), then we can simply divide our car's velocity by 50, which will give us the amount the car has to move each frame. In this case, we would need to move our car 0.2 units (since 10.0 divided by 50 equals 0.2) along the positive x-axis each frame. After 50 frames the car will have moved 10.0 units. Since we are running at 50 fps, we are therefore moving our car at 10.0 m/s (our original goal). Problem solved, right? Not quite. We have taken a step in the right direction, but there is one major flaw in our design. We cannot assume that our application will be running at 50 fps. What happens if this same application is run on a slower or a faster computer? It will run at a different frame rate and therefore throw our calculations off. If we ran it on a slower computer that could only achieve 25 fps, then we would only be moving the car 5.0 units each second as the number of frame updates have been halved, but we haven't doubled the distance we move the car each frame. A correct solution will need to take into account the fact that the frame rate can change; not only among computers, but even among frames on the same computer.

To solve this problem we must take into account the time between each frame and use this difference in time to calculate how far the car should move each frame. This is often referred to as *time-based movement*, and we already have the infrastructure in place to achieve this. If you recall in Chapter 2 when we implemented the Engine class, we calculated the elapsed time of each frame within the Run function. As you should already be aware, the elapsed time is simply the number of seconds that passed since the last frame. Since frames are processed so quickly, there will often be quite a few frames in a single second. This means that the elapsed time will often be a very small value such as 0.02 of a second (or 20 milliseconds). This is just what we need to calculate time-based movement.

Let's regress to our example with our newfound knowledge. If our application is running at 50 fps (therefore our car is updated 50 times each second), we would have an elapsed time of 0.02 (1 second divided by 50 frames equals 0.02 of a second for each frame). Imagine the elapsed time like a percentage—it is the percentage of a second that needs to be processed by the current frame. Therefore, at 50 fps each frame is responsible for processing 2% of an entire second's worth of movement (since multiplying 0.02 by 100 gives you the percentage of 2%). Each frame we just need to move the car by 2% of the car's velocity. To do this we take the 10.0 m/s and multiply it by our elapsed time of 0.02. This gives us a result of 0.2 m/s, which is how much we need to move the car each frame in order to achieve a total of 10.0 m/s across 50 frames.

It may look as though we have just done the same thing with time-based movement as we did before we used time-based movement, and to a degree it is the same. This is only because we used the same example running at 50 fps. If the frame rate were to change (which it will between every frame in a real test), you would find that the first method would yield inaccurate results meaning that the car would either move too slow or too fast. With time-based movement it doesn't matter if the frame rate fluctuates as it is calculated on a per frame basis and the elapsed time will change to reflect the time between the previous frame and the current frame.

WORLD MATRIX

At the end of the last chapter, you were introduced to the view matrix for the first time, and you probably remember in Chapter 5 where we discussed the projection matrix also. Well now it is time to learn about the third and final matrix that Direct3D uses: the world matrix. Let's quickly recap the first two matrices before we discuss the world matrix in detail.

The view matrix is used to position and orientate the viewer in 3D space. As you saw at the end of the last chapter, the D3DX library provides a few functions that can be used to build a view matrix. We won't be using any of those functions in our engine because we will calculate the view matrix a little differently as you will see later.

Next we have the projection matrix, which acts like the lenses in a camera. If you imagine the view matrix defining the position and orientation of our virtual camera, then the projection matrix adjusts the lenses of this virtual camera. The projection matrix allows you to set the viewing angle for the field of view, the near clipping plane, and the far clipping plane. In fact, you can even do little tricks with the projection matrix such as narrowing and widening the field of view to make the view appear as though it is zooming or focusing, especially if you adjust the view matrix, too. That's a story for another day, but maybe you can tinker with the projection matrix and see if you can figure it out.

The final of the three matrices is probably the most interesting because it is used to actually position your objects in 3D space. When you position the camera to view an object in 3D space, Direct3D needs to calculate where to render the object on your screen so that it appears as though you are viewing the object from the camera in 3D space. You can imagine your screen like a window into 3D space that is the position where the lens of the camera sits. To view the object correctly, Direct3D needs to project the 3D object onto your flat 2D screen. This whole process is achieved through the use of the three matrices. Let's look at the process in a little more detail.

A single mesh (which may be used as the mesh for an object in your scene) is located in what is called *model space*. What this means is that the mesh has its own local coordinate system, just like the Cartesian coordinate system that Direct3D uses. If you were to pick a point 2.0 units along the positive x-axis in the mesh's model space, then no matter where you move that mesh in 3D space (which is also called *world space*), the point you picked will remain the same in model space. See Figure 9.2 for the relation between model space and world space.

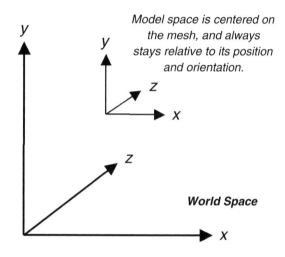

FIGURE 9.2   Model space compared to World Space.

Direct3D uses the world matrix to move a mesh from its own model space to world space, which puts it in the same space as all the other meshes in your scene (even though each has its own model space). Once in world space, Direct3D then uses the view matrix to transform (remember that matrices are used for transformations) the mesh into *camera space* so that it is relative to the camera's position and orientation. Next, the projection matrix is used to transform the mesh into *projection space*. This is where the vertices of the mesh are scaled and so forth to give the impression of 3D perspective. Finally, the mesh is clipped to the screen and projected into *screen space* so that it can be rendered on your screen. Obviously, there is a lot of behind-the-scenes work that goes on to perform all of this. Fortunately for us, Direct3D handles all of this and we only need to concern ourselves with setting the matrices appropriately, which is very easy to do.

You have already seen how to set the projection matrix in Chapter 5, and as mentioned there, once it is set you never need to touch it again unless you plan to change the projection for some reason. The view matrix needs to be calculated and set once per frame, assuming that the view changes each frame—which it most likely will in a fast-paced FPS. You will see how this is done later in this chapter.

As for the world matrix, you will probably want to store one for each object in your game. This will allow you to adjust each object's world matrix independent of each other. In other words, a separate world matrix needs to be calculated for each object in your scene. This doesn't mean you need to recalculate each object's world matrix every frame. You only need to recalculate an object's world matrix when it moves in any way. Therefore, if you have a tree that never moves, you only need to calculate its world matrix once. An object that is constantly moving, on the other hand, will probably need its world matrix recalculated every frame.

When it comes time to render your objects, you must first set the object's world matrix (i.e., register it with Direct3D) before rendering the object's mesh. This will tell Direct3D where to place the mesh in world space.

It is important to remember that Direct3D can only have one world matrix set at a time. This means that each frame you must set each object's world matrix before you render its mesh, and you must render the mesh before you set the next object's world matrix. This means that you cannot go through and set the world matrix for each of your objects, then go through and render each object's mesh. If you did this, all of the meshes would be rendered using the world matrix of the last object that you set.

You should now have a fairly good idea of how the world matrix works in relation to your objects and the other two matrices that Direct3D uses. We are not going to go into any more detail about the matrices here. Instead, we will move on to the actual implementation of our base object. There you will see how the world matrix is created and set before rendering.

SCENE OBJECTS

The base object is the lowest, most fundamental object that you can use. It contains all of the basic functionality that is common to every type of object you will later need. All new objects are derived from the base object so that they can inherit its common functionality. Since we call our 3D world a scene, it is only fitting that we call our base object a *scene object*. The scene object represents the most basic object that can exist in our scenes. Now it's about time we looked at something overwhelming again, so let's look at the huge SceneObject class definition, which can be found in SceneObject.h and is reproduced here:

```
class SceneObject : public BoundingVolume
{
public:
  SceneObject( unsigned long type = TYPE_SCENE_OBJECT,
               char *meshName = NULL, char *meshPath = "./",
```

```
                        bool sharedMesh = true );
virtual ~SceneObject();

virtual void Update( float elapsed, bool addVelocity = true );
virtual void Render( D3DXMATRIX *world = NULL );

virtual void CollisionOccurred( SceneObject *object,
                                unsigned long collisionStamp );

void Drive( float force, bool lockYAxis = true );
void Strafe( float force, bool lockYAxis = true );
void Stop();

void SetTranslation( float x, float y, float z );
void SetTranslation( D3DXVECTOR3 translation );
void AddTranslation( float x, float y, float z );
void AddTranslation( D3DXVECTOR3 translation );
D3DXVECTOR3 GetTranslation();

void SetRotation( float x, float y, float z );
void SetRotation( D3DXVECTOR3 rotation );
void AddRotation( float x, float y, float z );
void AddRotation( D3DXVECTOR3 rotation );
D3DXVECTOR3 GetRotation();

void SetVelocity( float x, float y, float z );
void SetVelocity( D3DXVECTOR3 velocity );
void AddVelocity( float x, float y, float z );
void AddVelocity( D3DXVECTOR3 velocity );
D3DXVECTOR3 GetVelocity();

void SetSpin( float x, float y, float z );
void SetSpin( D3DXVECTOR3 spin );
void AddSpin( float x, float y, float z );
void AddSpin( D3DXVECTOR3 spin );
D3DXVECTOR3 GetSpin();

D3DXVECTOR3 GetForwardVector();
D3DXVECTOR3 GetRightVector();

D3DXMATRIX *GetTranslationMatrix();
D3DXMATRIX *GetRotationMatrix();
D3DXMATRIX *GetWorldMatrix();
D3DXMATRIX *GetViewMatrix();
```

```
        void SetType( unsigned long type );
        unsigned long GetType();

        void SetFriction( float friction );

        unsigned long GetCollisionStamp();

        void SetVisible( bool visible );
        bool GetVisible();

        void SetEnabled( bool enabled );
        bool GetEnabled();

        void SetGhost( bool ghost );
        bool GetGhost();

        void SetIgnoreCollisions( bool ignoreCollisions );
        bool GetIgnoreCollisions();

        void SetTouchingGroundFlag( bool touchingGround );
        bool IsTouchingGround();

        void SetMesh( char *meshName = NULL, char *meshPath = "./",
                      bool sharedMesh = true );
        Mesh *GetMesh();

    protected:
      D3DXVECTOR3 m_forward;
      D3DXVECTOR3 m_right;

      D3DXMATRIX m_worldMatrix;
      D3DXMATRIX m_viewMatrix;

    private:
      D3DXVECTOR3 m_translation;
      D3DXVECTOR3 m_rotation;

      D3DXVECTOR3 m_velocity;
      D3DXVECTOR3 m_spin;

      D3DXMATRIX m_translationMatrix;
      D3DXMATRIX m_rotationMatrix;
```

```
    unsigned long m_type;
    float m_friction;
    unsigned long m_collisionStamp;
    bool m_visible;
    bool m_enabled;
    bool m_ghost;
    bool m_ignoreCollisions;
    bool m_touchingGround;
    bool m_sharedMesh;
    Mesh *m_mesh;
};
```

The SceneObject class is the largest of the three types of objects we are going to look at in this chapter. So if you can wade through this, the rest of this chapter should be all downhill. To begin with, you should note that the SceneObject class derives from the BoundingVolume class. This allows us to maintain a set of bounding volumes around our scene object for purposes such as collision detection. The SceneObject class also has the usual constructor, destructor, Update, and Render functions that we have come to depend on. We will discuss these more a little later.

You should also notice that the class comes with a multitude of functions that allow us to adjust its positional details, such as its translation, rotation, and velocity. Finally, there are many utility functions that give us the ability to retrieve the different matrices used by the objects as well as the various engine specific properties, which will be discussed as they come up. As for the long list of member variables, we will explain those too as they arise. So let's start with the class constructor.

```
    SceneObject::SceneObject( unsigned long type, char *meshName,
                              char *meshPath, bool sharedMesh )
{
  SetType( type );

  SetTranslation( 0.0f, 0.0f, 0.0f );
  SetRotation( 0.0f, 0.0f, 0.0f );

  SetVelocity( 0.0f, 0.0f, 0.0f );
  SetSpin( 0.0f, 0.0f, 0.0f );

  m_forward = D3DXVECTOR3( 0.0f, 0.0f, 1.0f );
  m_right = D3DXVECTOR3( 1.0f, 0.0f, 0.0f );

  m_friction = 0.0f;
```

```
    m_collisionStamp = -1;

    m_visible = true;
    m_enabled = true;
    m_ghost = false;
    m_ignoreCollisions = false;

    m_touchingGround = false;

    m_mesh = NULL;
    SetMesh( meshName, meshPath, sharedMesh );
}
```

Despite the size of the constructor it really doesn't do a whole lot. Its main purpose is to clear all of the necessary member variables to some default state ready to use. We will talk about the different member variables as we cover their use a little later. For now we will just talk about two main points of the constructor. You can see that the constructor takes a type as input, which is then set using the SetType function exposed by the class. If you jump back to the beginning of the SceneObject.h file for a moment you will see the following line of code:

```
#define TYPE_SCENE_OBJECT 0
```

This defines a type for the scene object. Any new scene object will have its type (which is stored in the m_type member variable) set based on the type that is passed in through the SceneObject class constructor. Later on when we create new types of objects we will define new types that can be set in this manner. We use these types as class identifiers so that we can identify what type of object we are working with. For example, you may have a linked list that stores pointers to all the objects in your game. To ensure the list is compatible with any type of object, it will need to store SceneObject pointers. In order to make complete use of an object's functionality you need to cast the SceneObject pointer into the appropriate class type. This is where the type identifier comes into play. If you checked the type of one of your objects and it returned TYPE_PLAYER_OBJECT, then you would know that this object is actually a PlayerObject, for example. Therefore, you would cast the SceneObject pointer into a PlayerObject pointer in order to access the functionality of the PlayerObject class. If you don't quite follow that, you will learn more about it when you see the different types of objects put to use as we build our game.

The second point you should be aware of in the constructor is how the object's mesh is handled. The constructor accepts the name of a mesh file and the path to the file as well as a third parameter called sharedMesh. The filename and path are used to load the mesh resource, but the sharedMesh flag is used to determine whether the mesh resource manager should be used to load the mesh. A shared mesh is one that is only loaded into memory once and the same instance is used by an object that requires the mesh. A non-shared mesh is one that is loaded specifically for this object. Therefore, if you create two objects that use the same mesh and you tell them to use a non-shared mesh, then they will load their own individual copies of the mesh into memory.

For static meshes you should always use shared meshes; however, for animated meshes this is not always possible. An animated mesh can change and if two or more objects are referencing it then they will all be affected by any changes made to the mesh by one of the objects. Therefore, for meshes such as the player's mesh (which animates) you will need to use non-shared meshes. Fortunately, you probably won't have more than a handful of players in the game at any one time so non-shared meshes in this respect should not prove to be a major problem.

You will see that at the end of the constructor we call the SetMesh function, which takes the last three parameters sent in through the constructor. This function will load the mesh and use the mesh manager when necessary for a shared mesh. The loaded mesh is destroyed in the class destructor when the object is destroyed. We won't bother looking at the destructor as it is only a few lines to destroy the mesh.

Now before we move on to the Update function, it is probably a good time to discuss some of those member variables that we have skirted around. We will skip the matrices and the positional vectors as we have already had a good discussion about those earlier. Instead, we will start with the m_forward and m_right vector. These two vectors are just unit vectors that contain nothing more than a direction. Quite simply, the m_forward vector is used to store the forward direction of the object. This is the direction the object is facing. The m_right vector is used to store the direction pointing to the object's right. If you extend your left arm out in front of you and your right arm out to your side (parallel with your body and perpendicular to your left arm), then you have simulated these two vectors. Your left arm acts as your forward vector while your right arm acts as your right vector. We maintain these two vectors for our objects so that we can make calculations based on the direction they are facing. You will notice that we set these two vectors in our class constructor. The default values state that the object is facing down the positive z-axis, and the right vector points down the positive x-axis. As the object rotates, these vectors will obviously change, however, they will always remain relative to one another and maintain a right angle between them. Later you will see how these vectors are calculated and used.

Next we will look at the `m_friction` member variable and what it is used for. As you know, our objects exist in 3D space, and therefore have a 3D coordinate position. In addition to this, their position can move over time as we discussed earlier. Sometimes we will move our objects manually. What this means is that we will physically enter in a coordinate in 3D space that we want the object to move to. At other times, we want an object's movement to be automated to a degree. What this means is that we want to tell the object to move in a particular direction at a particular speed—which we call a *velocity vector*. We have defined a velocity vector for our object called `m_velocity`. Each frame, the object should use time-based movement to move itself based on the velocity we give it.

Sometimes we don't want our objects to have limitless motion, sometimes we want them to slow down and stop by themselves. Imagine you were creating a car object and you wanted to give it a velocity that made it travel at a particular speed in the direction the car is facing as long as the player is holding down the forward key. When the player releases the forward key you want the car to start slowing down until it eventually comes to rest. How do you achieve this? You use a friction coefficient of course, which is exactly what `m_friction` is. The friction coefficient is applied to the velocity every frame in order to slow it down. As long as the player is holding the forward key down, a velocity force will be added to the car that will outweigh the friction force. Otherwise, when the velocity is multiplied by the friction (which might be something like 0.99) every frame, it will reduce the velocity, which will have the effect of slowing the car down. Figure 9.3 shows how friction works with velocity.

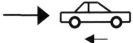

A small amount of friction is constantly applied to the car's velocity. If the car has no velocity it will have no effect.

If an acceleration force is applied that is too small, friction will prevent the car from moving.

A larger acceleration force will overcome the friction and increase the velocity of the car.

After the acceleration force stops, the car will roll to a stop as its velocity is reduced by friction.

FIGURE 9.3 How friction affects velocity.

Friction will always be applied to an object's velocity. Therefore, if you are making an object accelerate, you must ensure that the amount of force being applied is great enough to overcome the friction. Otherwise, the object will not move.

There are just a few more member variables from the SceneObject class that we need to discuss. First, we will look at the m_collisionStamp, which is used to store the latest frame that the object registered a collision. We have already discussed the notion of frame stamps before, and used them in our input system from Chapter 3, so we won't cover the topic again. We don't really have any need for frame stamps right now, but later you will see how we can use them to determine when an object last collided with something.

Finally, we will look at the different flags the SceneObject has, which will be used by the engine for various object management tasks. There are a total of five flags that can be set on an object, which are:

m_visible: The object is visible. Invisible objects are not rendered.

m_enabled: The object is enabled. Disabled objects are not updated.

m_ghost: The object is a ghost. Ghost objects cannot physically collide with anything.

m_ignoreCollisions: Should the object ignore collisions. The collisions can still occur, they are just not registered.

m_touchingGround: Indicates if the object is touching the ground.

The SceneObject class has all the necessary functions to set and retrieve each of these flags where applicable. Their implementation is extremely basic so we won't list it here, but you can find it yourself in the SceneObject.cpp file.

UPDATING AND RENDERING OBJECTS

Most of the supporting functions from the SceneObject class are very simple in their implementation and it is not necessary for us to go through them in any explicit detail. As previously mentioned, you can find the implementation to all of the functions in the SceneObject.cpp file. There are, however, two functions that are of particular interest and we should spend some time discussing them. The Update and the Render functions are probably the two most important functions of the entire SceneObject class. We will start with the Update function; its implementation is shown here:

```
void SceneObject::Update( float elapsed, bool addVelocity )
{
  float friction = 1.0f - m_friction * elapsed;

  m_velocity *= friction;
  if( addVelocity == true )
  {
    D3DXVECTOR3 velocity = m_velocity * elapsed;
    AddTranslation( velocity.x, velocity.y, velocity.z );
  }

  m_spin *= friction;
  D3DXVECTOR3 spin = m_spin * elapsed;
  AddRotation( spin.x, spin.y, spin.z );

  D3DXMatrixMultiply( &m_worldMatrix, &m_rotationMatrix,
                      &m_translationMatrix );

  D3DXMatrixInverse( &m_viewMatrix, NULL, &m_worldMatrix );

  m_forward.x = (float)sin( m_rotation.y );
  m_forward.y = (float)-tan( m_rotation.x );
  m_forward.z = (float)cos( m_rotation.y );
  D3DXVec3Normalize( &m_forward, &m_forward );

  m_right.x = (float)cos( m_rotation.y );
  m_right.y = (float)tan( m_rotation.z );
  m_right.z = (float)-sin( m_rotation.y );
  D3DXVec3Normalize( &m_right, &m_right );

  RepositionBoundingVolume( &m_translationMatrix );
}
```

Like any Update function, the first parameter is the elapsed time between the current frame and the last frame—this will come in handy for our time-based movement. The second parameter—addVelocity—is a flag that tells the function whether or not to apply the object's internal velocity. You should recall that we talked about having a velocity vector for our objects that will allow us to automate the process of moving our objects. This flag is used to switch that automated process on and off.

If you want to handle the movement of an object manually, then just pass in `false` through the `addVelocity` parameter. The object will then only move when you explicitly tell it to. Alternatively, you can give the object a velocity and then pass in `true` through the `addVelocity` parameter and the object will move by itself, taking friction into account. You can see how this works in the function where we check if the `addVelocity` flag equates to `true`. If so, we calculate the amount to move the object this frame based on the elapsed time and then add that to the object's translation. You can also see how the friction is taken into account by calculating the amount of friction to apply this frame based on the elapsed time. The velocity is then multiplied by this friction factor in order to reduce it before we apply it to the object's translation.

The `SceneObject` class has another vector that we have neglected to mention thus far called `m_spin`. This vector works in virtually the same way as the velocity vector, except rather than specifying how fast to move the object in a particular direction, it specifies how fast to spin the object around any of its axes. We will use this vector to make things like weapon pickups rotate on the spot in our game, waiting to be picked up by the player. You can see that the spin vector is treated in much the same way as the velocity vector. First the friction is applied to the spin, then the amount of spin to apply to the object in the current frame is calculated based on the elapsed time, and finally this spin is added to the object.

Once the object's translation and spin have been updated, the next step is to calculate the object's world matrix and view matrix. To calculate the object's world matrix we use the `D3DXMatrixMultiply` function, which allows us to multiply two matrices together. In other words, we can combine the effects of two matrices. To create the world matrix we need to combine the object's translation and rotation matrices. The translation matrix is used to keep track of the object's position in 3D space. In other words, it is a matrix representation of the object's translation vector. The rotation matrix is used to keep track of the object's rotation (or facing), and is a matrix representation of the object's rotation vector. By combining these two matrices we create a world matrix for this object that will transform the object's mesh (when rendered) from model space to world space so that it appears at the correct position with the correct rotation in 3D space.

If you are wondering where the translation and rotation matrices came from, don't worry, we will have a quick look at them now before we move on. Our objects use two 3D vectors to keep track of their translation and rotation at all times, which are appropriately named `m_translation` and `m_rotation`. You move an object by adjusting its translation vector, in the same way you rotate an object by adjusting is rotation vector. In order to create a world matrix, we need to create two more matrices first that represent the data stored in these two vectors. The translation matrix represents the translation of the object in a matrix, while the rotation matrix represents the rotation of the object in a matrix. Every time the translation vector changes the translation matrix must be updated. In the same way, the rotation matrix must be updated every time the rotation vector changes.

The translation matrix is created using the following line of code, which is called every time the translation vector changes:

```
D3DXMatrixTranslation( &m_translationMatrix, m_translation.x,
                        m_translation.y, m_translation.z );
```

The `D3DXMatrixTranslation` function (exposed by the D3DX library) is specifically used for creating a translation matrix from a 3D vector. The last three parameters allow you to enter the x, y, z coordinates, which are taken straight from the translation vector. The first parameter is the pointer to the matrix that will store the result of the operation when the function returns.

Creating the rotation matrix is a little trickier and is done using the following code, which is called every time the rotation vector changes.

```
D3DXMATRIX rotationX, rotationY;
D3DXMatrixRotationX( &rotationX, m_rotation.x );
D3DXMatrixRotationY( &rotationY, m_rotation.y );
D3DXMatrixRotationZ( &m_rotationMatrix, m_rotation.z );
D3DXMatrixMultiply( &m_rotationMatrix, &m_rotationMatrix,
                                        &rotationX );
D3DXMatrixMultiply( &m_rotationMatrix, &m_rotationMatrix,
                                        &rotationY );
```

The `D3DXMatrixRotationX`, `D3DXMatrixRotationY`, and `D3DXMatrixRotationZ` functions (also exposed by the D3DX library) are used to create a rotation matrix around their respective axis, which is the first step. Once we have a separate rotation matrix for each axis, we can combine them using the `D3DXMatrixMultiply` function a couple of times to get them all. Once the process is complete, we will have a rotation matrix that combines the rotations of all three axes.

So we can now combine our translation and rotation matrices to create a world matrix, but how do we create the view matrix? Creating the view matrix is actually quite simple and only requires a single line of code. The view matrix is simply the inverse of the world matrix, and is calculated using the `D3DXMatrixInverse` function (from the D3DX library) as you can see in the `Update` function of the `SceneObject` class. The function takes the world matrix, inverts it, and stores it in the view matrix that we supply. Now you may be wondering why we are calculating a view matrix for our objects anyway. When we discussed the view matrix earlier, you learned that you only need one view matrix set, which is the view that you want the player to see on their screen. So why are we creating a view matrix for all of our objects?

The simple answer is that later we will derive our player object from the base scene object. By incorporating the view matrix into the objects, we can easily view the world from the perspective of an object by using its view matrix. This is perfect considering that our players will be objects themselves. The added advantage is that we can view the 3D world from any of our objects in the scene. For example, if you created a security camera on the wall in your scene, you could switch to its view by simply using its view matrix. How cool is that?

We have almost finished dissecting the Update function. Once we have calculated our world and view matrix, the next step is to calculate the forward and right vectors of the object, which just requires a little trigonometry. If you look at the code you can see exactly how we use m_rotation to calculate our forward and right vectors, which are only affected by the rotation of the object. We won't go into the details of trigonometry here, but any good high school mathematics textbook will cover the basics of trigonometry, including sin, cos, and tan, which are what we are using. Once the vectors have been calculated, we must ensure they are unit vectors by normalizing them with the D3DXVec3Normalize function, exposed by the D3DX library. This will produce vectors with a magnitude of exactly one unit. In other words, the vectors will be purely directional vectors with no length, which is exactly what we want.

The final step is to reposition the object's bounding volume. As you know, the SceneObject class derives from the BoundingVolume class. This means that our objects have a set of bounding volumes (box, sphere, and ellipsoid) inherently built into them, which are based on the bounding volumes surrounding the object's mesh. The bounding volumes around the actual mesh are located in model space, but to ensure that they are positioned correctly in relation to the other objects in our scene (for purposes such as collision detection), we must transform the bounding volumes into world space.

By using the world matrix of the object, we can transform the bounding volumes into world space in the same way that the mesh is transformed into world space. The problem with this, however, is that the world matrix takes the object's rotation into account. This means that our bounding volumes would be rotated to the same facing as our objects. We do not want our bounding volumes to do this as it makes collision detection calculations harder. It is far easier to calculate collision detection between axis-aligned bounding volumes, which means they are positioned correctly in world space around the object; however, they are not rotated with the object. In other words, the objects can rotate freely inside their bounding volumes. To achieve this, rather than transforming our bounding volumes by the object's world matrix, we will only transform them by the object's translation matrix instead. Figure 9.4 illustrates the situation.

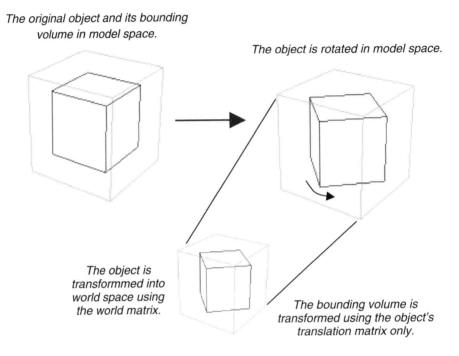

The original object and its bounding volume in model space.

The object is rotated in model space.

The object is transformmed into world space using the world matrix.

The bounding volume is transformed using the object's translation matrix only.

FIGURE 9.4 Axis-aligned bounding volumes transformed from model space to world space.

To perform this repositioning we just call RepositionBoundingVolume (which is exposed by the BoundingVolume class), and pass in the object's translation matrix. This ensures that the bounding volumes are physically located where the object exists in the world's rather than in the object's model space.

We have come to the end of the Update function and despite the long discussion, there really isn't anything too difficult taking place inside the function. If you did struggle with anything, chances are it is because you are probably struggling with understanding vectors or matrices. If this is the case, you should take the time to reread the section about vectors earlier in the book and the discussion on matrices earlier in this chapter. Hopefully, this will refresh your memory and help to back up our discussion of the Update function. Don't forget about the DirectX SDK documentation, too. It contains some great information about vectors and matrices (with an especially good introduction to the world, view, and projection matrices), so have a look at that too if need be.

Now it is time to look at the last function of interest in the SceneObject class—the Render function. Thankfully, this function isn't anywhere near the size or complexity of the Update function, so if you didn't have too many problems with that, then you are in for some pretty calm waters now. Like the Update function, you can find the implementation to the Render function in SceneObject.cpp. The implementation is also reproduced here:

```
void SceneObject::Render( D3DXMATRIX *world )
{
  if( m_mesh == NULL )
    return;

  if( world == NULL )
    g_engine->GetDevice()->SetTransform( D3DTS_WORLD,
                                         &m_worldMatrix );
  else
    g_engine->GetDevice()->SetTransform( D3DTS_WORLD, world );

  m_mesh->Render();
}
```

The first thing you should notice is that the function takes a pointer to a matrix as input. By its name you should realize that it is supposed to be a pointer to a world matrix. The reason why we take a pointer to a world matrix as input is simply for flexibility. Despite the fact that the SceneObject class has its own internal world matrix, sometimes you may want to override it and position the object using your own world matrix. You can see in the function how we check if the input world matrix pointer is NULL. If so, we know that an alternative world matrix was not passed in, so we set the object's internal world matrix instead. Setting the world matrix is achieved in the same manner as setting either of the other two matrices (the view or projection matrices), using the SetTransform function on the Direct3D device. The only difference is that we need to pass in D3DTS_WORLD as the first parameter to inform Direct3D that we want to set the world matrix.

After we have set the world matrix, the final step is to simply call the Render function on the object's mesh. We must bear in mind that an object does not have to have a mesh; therefore, it is possible for m_mesh to be NULL (if the object doesn't have a mesh). If you call a function on a NULL pointer it will cause an access violation error, so to prevent this we must check to make sure that the pointer is not NULL. This is done at the start of the function as you can see.

These kinds of checks only need to be made when there is a possibility of accessing a NULL *pointer, no matter how remote that possibility might be. Doing this will create more robust code and increase usability.*

You have been thoroughly introduced to the base SceneObject class, but do not forget to look through the implementation of the class on the CD-ROM to pick up on the minor details that we didn't cover. Next we will look at our first derived object class, the animated object.

ANIMATED OBJECTS

An animated object is simply an object with a mesh that can be animated. The base SceneObject class does not have support to animate a mesh, but that's okay as we can assume that the majority of meshes won't need to be animated. Remember that you only want to place common functionality in the base class. Since a small minority of meshes will actually have animations associated with them (such as the player's mesh), we can derive a new class from our base class called AnimatedObject that will specifically handle the animations of a mesh. Let's have a look at the class definition, which can also be found in AnimatedObject.h.

```
class AnimatedObject : public SceneObject,
                       public ID3DXAnimationCallbackHandler
{
public:
  AnimatedObject( char *meshName, char *meshPath = "./",
                  unsigned long type = TYPE_ANIMATED_OBJECT );
  virtual ~AnimatedObject();

  virtual void Update( float elapsed, bool addVelocity = true );

  void PlayAnimation( unsigned int animation,
                      float transitionTime, bool loop = true );
  ID3DXAnimationController *GetAnimationController();
```

```
private:
  virtual HRESULT CALLBACK HandleCallback( THIS_ UINT Track,
                                           LPVOID pCallbackData );

private:
  ID3DXAnimationController *m_animationController;
  unsigned int m_currentTrack;
  float m_currentTime;
};
```

As expected, the class derives from the SceneObject class. However, it also derives from the ID3DXAnimationCallbackHandler interface, which is exposed by the
D3DX library. This interface has a single function in it called HandleCallback
(which is a call-back function) that we need to override, which you can see in the
class definition. If you have a look at the implementation of this function (in
AnimatedObject.ccp), you will notice that the function does nothing at all. We do
not need to use the function in this class, but we do need to provide it as a virtual
function so that it can be overridden by other classes that we will later derive from
this class, such as the PlayerObject class. We will look at what this function is used
for in a moment, but let's continue discussing the AnimatedObject class first.

The next point of interest is in the constructor where we use the TYPE_
ANIMATED_OBJECT object type identifier. This is a new identifier that is defined in
AnimatedObject.h and is used by default whenever a new AnimatedObject instance is
created. A second point of interest is that the class has an Update function, which
simply overrides the SceneObject class implementation. This implementation is
used whenever Update is called on the object due to polymorphism. Finally, you
should note the PlayAnimation function, which is used to play one of the animations associated with the mesh assigned to the object.

Now let's have a look at the implementation of the class, which will clear up a
number of details. The implementation can be found in AnimatedObject.cpp, and
we will start with the class constructor as shown here:

```
AnimatedObject::AnimatedObject( char *meshName, char *meshPath,
                    unsigned long type ) : SceneObject( type,
                    meshName, meshPath, false )
{
  if( GetMesh() != NULL )
    GetMesh()->CloneAnimationController( &m_animationController );
  else
    m_animationController = NULL;
```

```
if( m_animationController != NULL )
{
  m_animationController->SetTrackSpeed( 0, 1.0f );
  m_animationController->SetTrackSpeed( 1, 1.0f );
}

m_currentTrack = 0;
m_currentTime = 0.0f;
}
```

When the class constructor is called, it first calls the SceneObject class constructor passing over the appropriate parameters. You will notice how the object type is passed through, which will be set with the base SceneObject class. Therefore, whenever the object is queried for its type, it will not return TYPE_SCENE_OBJECT. Instead, it will return TYPE_ANIMATED_OBJECT or whatever identifier you originally passed into the AnimatedObject class constructor. You should also notice that we pass in false for the last parameter to indicate that we do not want a shared mesh.

Once the base SceneObject class constructor returns, we know that the mesh has been loaded so we can begin processing the AnimatedObject class constructor. If a mesh was loaded (remember that an object does not have to have a mesh), then we need to take a copy of its animation controller. The animation controller is the heart of the AnimatedObject class and is the most crucial component. To take a copy of the animation controller interface—ID3DXAnimationController—we just need to call CloneAnimationController on the mesh. You can find the implementation to this function in Mesh.cpp, but all it does is call CloneAnimationController on the ID3DXAnimationController interface stored in the Mesh class. The animation controller is loaded when we create the mesh. The ID3DXAnimationController interface is used to control the animations that belong to the mesh (hence the name). It is also responsible for matching the animation data to the frames in the mesh so that the correct transformations are applied to the correct frames. The interface also has the ability to combine multiple animations and blend smoothly between them.

Once we have a valid animation controller we need to set the speed of the first and second tracks. By setting the track speed to 1.0, it ensures that any animations played on these tracks will play back at full speed. Don't worry about what this means for now as we will cover all of this very shortly. You will see how the animation controller is used in a moment, as well as the two member variables that we clear at the end of the constructor.

The next function that we need to look at in more detail is the Update function, which is shown below and can also be found in AnimatedObject.cpp:

```
void AnimatedObject::Update( float elapsed, bool addVelocity )
{
  SceneObject::Update( elapsed, addVelocity );

  if( m_animationController )
  {
    m_animationController->AdvanceTime( elapsed, this );

    m_currentTime += elapsed;
  }

  if( GetMesh() != NULL )
    GetMesh()->Update();
}
```

The Update function simply overrides the SceneObject class Update function. Since we still want our AnimatedObject to behave like any other object we must call Update on the base object so that it can be processed. Once the base SceneObject has been processed its Update function can then continue with the AnimatedObject class Update function. First, we ensure that a valid animation controller exists. If the object doesn't have a mesh, it won't have an animation controller either. If there is an animation controller, we can proceed to update it by calling its AdvanceTime function. The AdvanceTime function takes in two parameters, the amount of time to advance the animation controller (in seconds), and a pointer to a user-defined animation call-back handler interface.

Fortunately, our elapsed time is in seconds and it indicates the amount of time that has passed since the last time the animation controller was updated. Therefore, we will use our elapsed time (which is passed into the Update function) as the first parameter of the AdvanceTime function. For the second parameter, we just pass in the this pointer, to indicate that we want to use this class to be the user-defined animation call-back handler interface. If you recall, we derived the AnimatedObject class from the ID3DXAnimationCallbackHandler interface so that we can override the HandleCallback function. The AdvanceTime function is looking for a pointer to a user-defined ID3DXAnimationCallbackHandler interface, which is exactly what we have turned the AnimatedObject class into by deriving from the ID3DXAnimation-CallbackHandler interface.

When we start using the AnimatedObject class (when we create our game) you will see how we can add *keys* to our animation. A key can be set to trigger at a particular time within the animation. Whenever AdvanceTime is called, the animation controller checks if any of our user-defined keys have been triggered. If so, the animation controller will call our `HandleCallback` function so that we can handle the key. You will learn more about this when we actually use it to implement the footsteps in our player mesh's run animation.

After we have updated the animation controller there are only two more steps left. First, we need to increment our `m_currentTime` member variable by the elapsed time. This allows us to keep track of the global animation time. We will use this in the `PlayAnimation` function's various timing operations, which you will see very shortly. The second and last step is to update the object's mesh by calling `Update` (from the `Mesh` class).

NOTE

You will notice that we update the mesh in the `AnimatedObject` class rather than the `SceneObject` class. The reason for this is that the `Mesh` class `Update` function is used to update the frame hierarchy for animation purposes. Since we only want the `AnimatedObject` class to be able to handle animations, then we only need to update the mesh in this class.

The last function that we need to look at is the `PlayAnimation` function, which is the most complex and most important function of the whole class. Let's jump straight to going through its implementation, as shown here (which can also be found in `AnimatedObject.cpp`).

```
void AnimatedObject::PlayAnimation( unsigned int animation,
                                    float transitionTime, bool loop )
{
```

We will start by looking at the function's input parameters, of which there are three. The first parameter is an identifier of the animation that you want to play. Animations are referenced by the animation controller using a unique sequential number starting at 0. In other words, the first animation is identified by 0 and the second animation is identified by 1. So if you wanted to play animation four, then you would pass in 3 as the first parameter of this function.

TIP

You can even create an enumeration that gives each of these identifiers a meaningful name. This way, rather than passing in a value such as 3, you can pass in an identifier such as `ANIMATION_RUN`, which would correspond to animation 3 for example.

The second parameter of the function is the animation transition time. An animated mesh will always have an animation that it is currently playing (even if the animation has ended, it is still considered the current animation). What this means is that when you tell the animation controller to change to a different animation, the animation controller has to stop playing the current animation and start playing the new animation. The problem is that if you just stop the current animation and start the new one you will notice a significant jump when the mesh switches animation. You have probably seen it before in games you have played. The transition time is used to tell the animation controller how long you want to take to change from the current animation to the new animation (in seconds). While in transition, the animation controller will blend the two animations together as it reduces the playback weight of the current animation and increases the playback weight of the new one to take the current animation's place.

The final parameter is a simple flag that indicates whether the animation should loop or not. If you pass in true, then the animation will continue playing over and over again until you tell it otherwise. This is great for walk or idle animations. If, however, you pass in false, then the animation will only be played once. When the animation reaches its last frame it will stop there and the mesh will appear to be frozen in place. This is good for one-shot animations such as a death animation where you want the player to fall to the ground and then lay motionless.

```
if( m_animationController == NULL )
  return;

if( transitionTime <= 0.0f )
  transitionTime = 0.000001f;

unsigned int newTrack = ( m_currentTrack == 0 ? 1 : 0 );

ID3DXAnimationSet *as;
m_animationController->GetAnimationSet( animation, &as );
```

Once in the function, the first step is to ensure we have a valid animation controller. If not, then we simply drop out of the function. Assuming we have a valid animation controller, we then need to ensure the transitionTime is greater than zero simply because (as of the DirectX 9.0c, October 2004 update) the D3DX functions we are about to use do not like a transitionTime value of zero (or less of course). The reasoning behind this is not clear and the documentation does not mention anything about it. So to compensate for this, we will set a zero value to 0.000001f, which is so close to zero it is negligible.

The next step is to select which track we want to play the new animation on. The animation controller uses tracks to play the different animations. For example, you could have a walk animation playing on the first track and a shoot animation playing on the second track. The animation controller will blend these animations so that the mesh appears to walk and shoot at the same time. We use the m_currentTrack member variable to identify which track the current animation is playing on. By checking m_currentTrack, we can determine which track we need to use for our new animation. If the current animation is playing on the first track, then we will use the second track to blend in the new animation. In the same way, we will use the first track if the current animation is playing on the second track.

Once we have determined which track we want to play the new animation on, we then need to get a pointer to the actual animation that we want to play. The animation controller refers to a single complete animation as an *animation set*, and we use the ID3DXAnimationSet interface to manipulate them. We gain access to the animation set that we want to play by calling GetAnimationSet, exposed by the animation controller. In the first parameter we pass in the identifier of the animation that we want to use. This is just the identifier that is passed into the PlayAnimation function. The second parameter will be a pointer to the actual animation when the function returns.

```
m_animationController->SetTrackAnimationSet( newTrack, as );

m_animationController->UnkeyAllTrackEvents( m_currentTrack );
m_animationController->UnkeyAllTrackEvents( newTrack );
```

The next step is to set the new animation onto the track on which it should play. This is done by simply calling SetTrackAnimationSet on the animation controller, passing in the identifier of the track that the animation should play on as well as a pointer to the animation that should be played. Once set, we can proceed to clear the events on both tracks by calling UnkeyAllTrackEvents once for each track, passing in the identifier of the track to clear. The animation works by setting time-based events on the tracks, which controls how the tracks are processed and when to make changes to them. Table 9.1 shows a few of the common events that can be set on a track.

TABLE 9.1 Common Track Events

Enable	Event that enables or disables the track at a given time.
Speed	Event that changes the playback speed of the track at a given time.
Weight	Event that changes the blending weight of the track at a given time.

We are now ready to begin setting the events on the two tracks so that the animation controller can change from the current animation to the new animation. How we set up these events depends on one factor, whether or not the new animation needs to loop. In other words, should it continue playing over and over again, or should it play just once and the hold on the last frame of the animation. Have a look at the next code snippet before we continue discussing it.

```
if( loop == true )
{
   m_animationController->KeyTrackEnable( m_currentTrack, false,
                                        m_currentTime +
transitionTime );
   m_animationController->KeyTrackWeight( m_currentTrack, 0.0f,
m_currentTime,
                                        transitionTime,
D3DXTRANSITION_LINEAR );
   m_animationController->SetTrackEnable( newTrack, true );
   m_animationController->KeyTrackWeight( newTrack, 1.0f,
m_currentTime,
                                        transitionTime,
D3DXTRANSITION_LINEAR );
}
```

If the new animation should loop, then we want to smoothly transition from the current animation to the new animation. In order to achieve this smooth transition, we must gradually reduce the weight of the track with the current animation playing on it while we increase the weight of the track with the new animation playing on it. This is done by setting a weight event on each track using KeyTrackWeight. In the first parameter we pass in the identifier of the track we want to set the event on. For the second parameter we pass in the weight that we want the track to change to. For the old track we set it to 0.0 and for the new track we set it to 1.0 (like a percentage between 0% and 100%). The third parameter indicates when we want the transition to begin and the next parameter indicates how long we want the transition to take place. We set the start time to m_currentTime to indicate that we want the transition to begin immediately, and we set the transition time to transitionTime, which was passed into the PlayAnimation function. This means that throughout the period from m_currentTime to m_currentTime + transition-Time, the old track's weight will transition from 1.0 to 0.0 and the new track's weight will transition from 0.0 to 1.0. The final parameter controls how the transition takes place. This can be set to either D3DXTRANSITION_LINEAR or D3DXTRANSITION_EASEINEASEOUT. We will use D3DXTRANSITION_LINEAR as it uniformly changes the value over time. Figure 9.5 shows the difference between the two options.

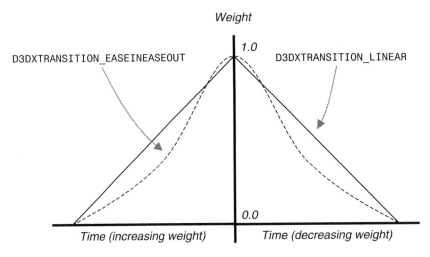

FIGURE 9.5 The difference between the two transition types.

We also need to enable the track with the new animation using the SetTrack-Enable function, passing in the identifier of the track and the enable flag (which is true in this case). This enables the track immediately. Finally, we need to disable the track with the current animation, however, we cannot do this immediately as we need to wait for its weight to transition to 0.0 before we disable it; otherwise, we will notice a jump in the animation. To do this we use the KeyTrackEnable function, which works in a similar way to the KeyTrackWeight function, except rather than setting a weight, we are setting the enable flag. Since disabling a track does not need to transition, we just need to indicate when we want the track to be disabled. We know how long the weight transition will take, so we need to time it so that the track is disabled when the weight transition completes. We can calculate this time by simply adding m_currentTime and transitionTime—this is when we want to disable the track.

```
else
{
  m_animationController->SetTrackEnable( m_currentTrack, false );
  m_animationController->SetTrackWeight( m_currentTrack, 0.0f );
  m_animationController->SetTrackEnable( newTrack, true );
  m_animationController->SetTrackWeight( newTrack, 1.0f );
  m_animationController->SetTrackPosition( newTrack, 0.0f );
```

```
    m_animationController->KeyTrackEnable( newTrack, false,
                                    m_currentTime + as-
>GetPeriod() );
    }
```

We are almost finished with this function, so hang in there. If the `loop` flag that is passed into the `PlayAnimation` function is set to `false`, then we need to adjust the track with the new animation on it so that it will only play once. Rather than transitioning to the new track, we will simply stop the current track and start the new one immediately. We do this by calling `SetTrackEnable` and `SetTrackWeight` on both the current track and the new track. For the current track we pass in `false` and `0.0f` to `SetTrackEnable` and `SetTrackWeight`, respectively. For the new track we pass in `true` and `1.0f`.

The next step is to set the track's position back to the start. We have no guarantee that an animation will play from the start, so we need to enforce it in this case to ensure we see the entire animation. In a looped animation this generally is not a problem. We then need to add an event to the track to disable the track when it is finished. This is exactly the same as what we just did to disable the track with the current animation for a looped animation. The only difference is that we need to use GetPeriod on the animation to determine how long the animation is. This will tell us how long we need to wait before disabling the track.

```
    as->Release();

    m_currentTrack = newTrack;
}
```

Finally, we can release the animation as we no longer need it, and we can set the current track to the new track. This means that next time the `PlayAnimation` function is called, the tracks will be switched.

This has brought us to the end of the `PlayAnimation` function, and the end of the `AnimatedObject` class. Be sure to have a look at the complete code for the `AnimatedObject` on the CD-ROM in order to pick up on the small details we have overlooked. Other than that, it is time to move on to our final object for the engine, which will also derive from the `SceneObject` class—the spawner object.

ON THE CD

SPAWNER OBJECTS

In essence, the spawner object is designed to "spawn" other objects into the game. For example, you may want a weapon pickup positioned somewhere in your scene.

All you do is place an object spawner there and tell it which object to spawn. It will then spawn the chosen weapon at that location. When the player collects the spawned object, the spawner can then spawn another one after a predetermined amount of time has passed. You will better understand how the spawner object works if we look at its implementation, so let's start with the SpawnerObject class definition, which can be found in SpawnerObject.h.

```
class SpawnerObject : public SceneObject
{
public:
  SpawnerObject( char *name, char *path = "./",
                 unsigned long type = TYPE_SPAWNER_OBJECT );
  virtual ~SpawnerObject();

  virtual void Update( float elapsed, bool addVelocity = true );

  virtual void CollisionOccurred( SceneObject *object,
                                  unsigned long collisionStamp );

  Script *GetObjectScript();

private:
  char *m_name;
  float m_frequency;
  float m_spawnTimer;
  Sound *m_sound;
  AudioPath3D *m_audioPath;
  Script *m_objectScript;
};
```

You can see that we have defined a new object type (TYPE_SPAWNER_OBJECT), which is passed in through the constructor by default. We also override the base SceneObject class Update and CollisionOccurred functions, which we will look at shortly. You should also notice that the spawner objects are script driven, which means that we will write scripts to control our spawner objects. Everything from the type of object they spawn, to the frequency they are spawned at, and the sound that is played when the spawned object is collected by a player, will be controlled by a script. There is not a lot to look at in the class definition, so let's move straight to the implementation, starting with the class constructor as shown here. It can also be found in SpawnerObject.cpp.

```cpp
SpawnerObject::SpawnerObject( char *name, char *path,
                             unsigned long type ) : SceneObject( type )
{
  SetGhost( true );

  Script *script = new Script( name, path );

  m_frequency = *script->GetFloatData( "frequency" );

  m_spawnTimer = 0.0f;

  if( script->GetStringData( "sound" ) != NULL )
  {
    m_sound = new Sound( script->GetStringData( "sound" ) );
    m_audioPath = new AudioPath3D;
  }
  else
  {
    m_sound = NULL;
    m_audioPath = NULL;
  }

  m_objectScript = g_engine->GetScriptManager()->Add(
                          script->GetStringData( "object" ),
                          script->GetStringData( "object_path" ) );

  m_name = new char[strlen( m_objectScript->GetStringData(
                          "name" ) ) + 1];
  strcpy( m_name, m_objectScript->GetStringData( "name" ) );

  SetMesh( m_objectScript->GetStringData( "mesh" ),
           m_objectScript->GetStringData( "mesh_path" ) );

  SetSpin( 0.0f, 1.0f, 0.0f );

  if( *script->GetFloatData( "radius" ) != 0.0f )
    SetBoundingSphere( D3DXVECTOR3( 0.0f, 0.0f, 0.0f ),
                       *script->GetFloatData( "radius" ) );
  else if( GetMesh() != NULL )
    SetEllipsoidRadius( *m_objectScript->GetVectorData(
                        "ellipse_radius" ) );

  SAFE_DELETE( script );
}
```

The constructor may look a little complicated, but all it is doing is preparing the object spawner based on the default settings and the settings in the script assigned to it. This includes setting the spawner object as a ghost, which means that it will register collisions but it won't physically block anything so that a player can walk through it.

In order to set up the spawner using its script, we must load the script based on the name and path passed into the constructor. From there we can access the various data needed to prepare the spawner, such as its frequency (i.e., its spawn delay) and the sound to play when the spawned object is collected. You can see that if there is a collection sound then we load it and create the 3D audio path to play the sound on. This way, we can position the sound in 3D space so that the players can hear each other collecting objects.

The next step in the constructor is to load the actual mesh of the object to spawn. This mesh will be used by the object spawner so that the players can see what object is spawned. First, we load the script of the object to be spawned (which is determined by the object spawner's script), then we set the object spawner's mesh to the mesh used by the spawned object. We then give the object spawner a slow spin around its y-axis so that the spawned object appears to rotate on the spot. Finally, we just set the spawner object's bounding volumes based on that of the script or the mesh. This bounding volume is used to detect when a player collides with the object spawner so that the spawned object can be collected by the player.

You should also remember that there is a destructor that destroys everything we have loaded, freeing its memory. We won't bother looking at this because you should be fairly familiar with destroying things by now. We only need to cover the creation of everything as that is usually the hard part. Nevertheless, you can find the implementation of the destructor in SpawnerObject.cpp if you want to look at it. Now, however, it is time to move on to the Update function, which is an overridden function from the base SceneObject class. The implementation of the function is shown here:

```
void SpawnerObject::Update( float elapsed, bool addVelocity )
{
  SceneObject::Update( elapsed, addVelocity );

  if( GetVisible() == false )
  {
    m_spawnTimer += elapsed;
    if( m_spawnTimer >= m_frequency )
    {
```

```
            SetVisible( true );
            SetIgnoreCollisions( false );
            m_spawnTimer = 0.0f;
        }
    }

    if( m_audioPath != NULL )
    {
      m_audioPath->SetPosition( GetTranslation() );
      m_audioPath->SetVelocity( GetVelocity() );
    }
}
```

Just like the animated object, since the spawner object is really a scene object at heart, it needs to update like one. To ensure that the spawner object behaves like a scene object we need to call the Update function on the base SceneObject class. After the base SceneObject class Update function returns, we can begin performing the spawner object specific update.

First, we check if the object is visible. The reason for this is that we will use the object's visible flag to determine if the spawned object has been collected. When a player collides with the object spawner, we will set its visible flag to false so that the engine stops rendering it. This way it will appear as though it has been collected. When it respawns, then we set the flag back to true so that it is rendered again. Therefore, if the object spawner's visible flag is false, we know that it is waiting to respawn so we need to calculate when to do this.

When the object spawner's object is collected, it will respawn after the frequency delay has passed (which is stored in m_frequency). To check this we just use a simple timer that updates m_spawnTimer using the elapsed time. When m_spawnTimer reaches m_frequency then the delay has passed and we can respawn the object. This involves making the object visible again and resetting the timer back to zero.

The last step in the Update function is to keep the 3D audio path updated with the spawner object. This is just a matter of ensuring that the audio path's position and velocity match the object's position and velocity. Usually, a spawner object is placed and never moves, but by updating them each frame like this you have the option of moving them at runtime. For example, you may create an object spawner on the back of a moving vehicle.

Finally, the last function that we need to look at in this class is the Collision-Occurred function, which is exposed by the SceneObject class. You have never seen it in use before and we will be overriding it here to give it an implementation specific to our spawner objects, as shown below. This implementation can also be found in SpawnerObject.cpp.

```
void SpawnerObject::CollisionOccurred( SceneObject *object,
                                        unsigned long collisionStamp )
{
  SceneObject::CollisionOccurred( object, collisionStamp );

  if( object->GetType() == TYPE_SCENE_OBJECT ||
      object->GetType() == TYPE_ANIMATED_OBJECT ||
      object->GetType() == TYPE_SPAWNER_OBJECT )
    return;

  SetVisible( false );
  SetIgnoreCollisions( true );

  if( m_audioPath != NULL && m_sound != NULL )
    m_audioPath->Play( m_sound->GetSegment() );
}
```

First, we need to call the base SceneObject class CollisionOccurred function so that the collisionStamp can be registered. Then we just check what type of object collided with the spawner object. Since we know that none of the objects we have created for the engine will have the ability to "collect" an object from an object spawner, we can safely return if the collision occurred with any of these objects. We determine what type of object we collided with by simply checking the object's type. If the object we collided with is not any of the standard types we have already created for the engine, we know that it must be a user-defined type such as the player object. Therefore, we will assume that the user-defined object can collect from the spawner object so we will proceed with that assumption.

CAUTION

Keep in mind that any type of user-defined object has the ability to trigger this collision code when it contacts the object spawner. This isn't a major problem for our game as the only user-defined object we will be creating that has the ability to move around and collide with object spawners is the player object. Therefore, it is safe to make the assumption we have made. You may later decide to add other types of user-defined objects that you do not want to be able to trigger an object spawner's collision code. To remedy this, you may consider adding a user-defined list of objects with which to ignore collisions, which you give to the spawner object when it is created.

Once we have determined that we have collided with a valid object, we then proceed to "collect" the object that is spawned by the object spawner. First, we set the object spawner's visible flag to `false` so that it is no longer rendered, and we set its ignore collisions flag to `true`. This prevents the object spawner from registering any more collisions while it is waiting to respawn its object. Then, we play the object collection sound, so that the players receive an audio cue indicating they have collected something.

We have started to discuss the results of object collisions, however, we have not discussed anything about how two objects collide with one another. You may wonder how we are going to handle this. Simply, we know that two objects have collided when their respective bounding volumes touch each other. Checking this can be as simple as testing two bounding boxes or two bounding spheres for contact, which is very easy to do. In fact, we already have the code to perform these checks, which can be found in `Geometry.h` *(a file we added to our engine in Chapter 2). We do, however, need to do a little more processing than just checking two bounding volumes. We will talk about this further in Chapter 10 when we implement our scene management.*

INTEGRATING THE OBJECTS

To integrate the three objects into the engine we must remember to link the files correctly with the appropriate `#include` statements. Then we can take a look at the changes we need to make to the engine, starting with the `EngineSetup` structure found in `Engine.h`.

As you can see, we have added a new member to the `EngineSetup` structure called `spawnerPath`, which is simply the path where the engine can find all of the object spawner scripts. We can store all of our object spawner scripts in an assets folder and just point the engine to it. Then we can reference an object spawner's script by its name, knowing that the engine will apply the correct path to find the script. The main reason we need to do this is that object spawners are application specific. The engine has no idea what object spawners we will create and where we will store them; therefore, we need to tell it beforehand so that they can be loaded on demand by the engine without our input, as you will see in Chapter 10 when we start using them.

The final change we need to make actually stems from the `ViewerSetup` structure in `State.h`. You can see that we have added the `SceneObject *viewer` member to the structure, which is used each frame to inform the engine which object is being used to view the scene. When the engine calls your `RequestViewer` implementation (from your derived state class), you can indicate which object you are using to view the scene, which will usually be your player object. Now that the engine has access to the viewing scene object, we can incorporate a few additions into the `Run` function of the `Engine` class, as shown here:

```
if( viewer.viewer != NULL )
{
  m_device->SetTransform( D3DTS_VIEW,
                          viewer.viewer->GetViewMatrix() );

  m_soundSystem->UpdateListener(
                          viewer.viewer->GetForwardVector(),
                          viewer.viewer->GetTranslation(),
                          viewer.viewer->GetVelocity() );
}
```

Assuming we have a valid viewer, we need to do two things. First, we need to set the view transformation matrix to that of the view scene object so that Direct3D can display the scene based on the view of the view object. The second step is to update the 3D sound listener by calling `UpdateListener` on our sound system. We simply need to pass in a few details about the listener (which is the view scene object), so that we can position the virtual microphone where the view object exists in 3D space. We use the object's forward vector so that we face the microphone in the correct direction.

TESTING THE OBJECTS

ON THE CD
For this test application we will create one of each type of object. You can find the test application in the `Test` project of the workspace for this chapter. If you take a look at the Load function of our `TestState` class, you can see how we create each of the three objects. The first is an animated object that will use a mesh with an animation. The second is a scene object that we will use as a virtual camera to fly around with. The final object is a spawner object that spawns the object detailed in its script. You can see how the mesh of the spawned object simply rotates on the spot where the object spawner is positioned. Figure 9.6 shows what this test application looks like.

FIGURE 9.6 The test application rendering the animated object and the spawner object.

Look inside the script file for the object spawner to see how it is set up—it is actu-ally very basic. It defines the spawning frequency (which is the delay between col-lection and respawn), the collision radius (a value of 0.0 indicates that it uses the mesh's radius), and the name and path of the object to spawn. You can also add a sound when the object is collected. It is not shown in this script because we are not using it in this sample, but you will see it in the scripts we use in our game.

If you look at the RequestViewer function, you can see how we set the scene ob-ject that we created to be the viewer. You can also see in the Update function how we move the virtual camera around using the w, a, s, d keys, and the mouse to look around.

EXERCISE

As we did in Chapter 8, let's run a little exercise using our test application. Here is what you can try to do with the test application:

1. Allow the view to switch between multiple objects such as the camera and the object spawner with a key press.
2. Allow the object spawner to register a collision with the camera object.

The first item should be pretty easy. All you need to do is add a couple of key press checks. When the user presses a particular key, change the `viewer` pointer in `RequestViewer` to point to `m_spawner`. Then when a different key is pressed (or even the same key again) the view changes back to the virtual camera `m_viewer`. You will notice that when the view is set to `m_spawner`, it will rotate as we made the object spawner spin slowly. Therefore, you will see the animated object go by in the view as the view is rotated with the object spawner.

The second exercise is a little more complicated. What you need to do is check the bounding sphere of the camera against the bounding sphere of the object spawner. The code to do this has already been provided for you in `Geometry.h` (included in Chapter 2), specifically the `IsSphereCollidingWithSphere` function. Then, when you determine a collision has occurred, you call the `CollisionOccurred` function on both the objects. The object spawner knows how to respond to the collision, so you just need to worry about determining when a collision takes place. If you have trouble figuring this out, then don't worry about it because we will cover these details in Chapter 10.

SUMMARY

This has been an exciting chapter as we have really increased the functionality of our engine by adding these objects. We had a good discussion about how the objects work and then proceeded to implement the three standard objects that our engine will support: the base scene object, the animated object, and the spawner object. Keep in mind that these objects are specifically geared toward developing a FPS. So if you were to try to create a different type of game using this engine, you may find that the objects will need modification.

Finally, after integrating the objects into our engine, we looked at a great little test application that showed off our three new object types. You were also given some exercises to modify the test application. As previously mentioned, if you had any problems with the exercises, don't worry about it. You will learn everything you need to completely solve them in the next chapter. In fact, the whole collision de-tection problem will be solved to the point that it is automated by the engine and you won't need to worry about it. When we create the game, we will be able to throw all sorts of objects into our scene, and they will all collide together properly (as long as they are derived from our base scene object).

So as you can probably guess, the next chapter will tie up a lot of loose ends. Well, we should hope so anyway, considering that it is the last chapter for develop-ing our engine. Even though we can see the light at the end of the tunnel, we still have quite a bit to do. We have saved the best, and some of the hardest, topics 'til last, so prepare yourself for a bit of a rough ride in the next chapter; but, we will try to keep it as smooth and straightforward as possible. The reward will definitely be worth it as we will have a completed engine that can manage and render a complete scene with all our game objects—so turn the page to the beginning of the end.

10 Scene Management

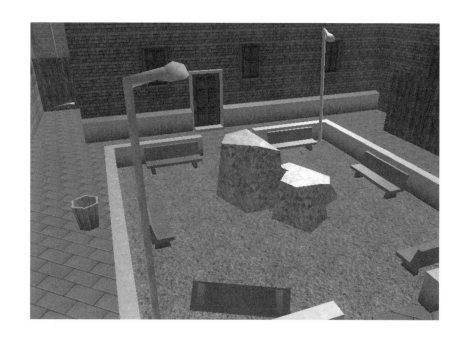

In This Chapter

- Learn about the different forms of culling, such as view frustum and occlusion culling.
- Cover topics such as collision detection, response, and gravity.
- Create an efficient rendering system using an octree.

Our engine is almost complete, and soon it will be ready for action. In this chapter, we will focus on implementing what we call *scene management* into our engine. You can find the workspace for this chapter in the /Source/ Chapter 10/ directory on the CD-ROM.

ON THE CD

WHAT IS SCENE MANAGEMENT?

You should already have a basic idea of what scene management entails, as we touched on it in Chapter 1. If you recall, a scene is simply a level or map in your game. It defines a complete 3D environment that is bounded in some way and is separated from the other scenes in your game, much like the scenes in a movie are separate environments.

The topic of scene management broadly covers everything to do with managing a scene within your game. The tasks required from one game to another to manage their scenes can vary greatly. However, there are a few common scene management elements found across most games, which are:

- The ability to load and destroy a scene properly.
- Management of scene data, such as the objects in the scene.
- Display of the scene to the player, which is most likely through rendering 3D geometry.

We can't stop there though, as we have to break it down further and look at specific tasks. In particular, we must identify the tasks that our game and engine require. Remember that the scene management tasks for one game (although similar) can be completely different in their method for another game. In addition to this, we also have the problem of determining what needs to be handled by the engine and which tasks we will leave for the game to handle. Fortunately, we know that our engine is designed specifically for a FPS so we can make a lot of assumptions and design our scene management specifically for that type of game. Note: this doesn't mean that our engine will be useless for handling other types of games, it just means that it probably won't be very good, and you will need to modify the engine for the new type of game.

Now let's look more specifically at the tasks that our engine must handle in order for it to manage a scene for our FPS game. First, we want our engine to be able to load a scene using a simple script. The script will define properties such as which mesh to use, how the lighting will look, and so forth. The engine should also be able to read our scene mesh hierarchy and identify certain types of frames that we will embed into the mesh hierarchy. This will allow us to store data such as player spawn point locations and object spawner locations directly into the mesh file for the scene. We cannot forget that our engine needs to be able to destroy our scene properly when we are done to prevent nasty memory leaks.

When it comes to managing scene data, we want the engine to be able to track all of the objects in the scene and keep them updated. It should be able to provide collision detection between the objects and the scene as well as allow the objects to interact with one another. We also want the engine to be able to render our scene for us, including all of the objects in it. The engine should be able to break the scene up and efficiently render the parts of the scene that are visible to the player each frame.

Once all of these features are implemented it will take a lot of the pressure off of us when it comes time to create our game. Don't stress out if this little wish list sounds like a lot of hard work. With this book, the information on the CD-ROM (which you will find out about later in this chapter), and the source code for this chapter, you have all the tools at your disposal not only to implement everything we just listed, but also to understand it. The key is to have patience and don't bite off more than you can chew. In other words, if this is all brand new to you, take it real slow, and study one bit at a time.

There is a very good chance that you will finish this chapter and have no idea what just happened or what you were supposed to learn. The reason for this is that this is a very intense chapter. In fact, this is where our project climaxes, and you will probably find that this chapter is the most complex of them all. So keep that in mind and don't let yourself become frustrated if you have trouble. Remember the big picture and come back to this chapter when you have finished the book. In time, as you play with the code more in your own projects, you will learn how everything works.

NOTE

ON THE CD

Beware that this chapter covers quite a bit of source code (much more than any other chapters). Therefore, it is physically impossible (and would be very boring) to list it all in the book. Most of the time, we will just look at the definitions and cover only the important snippets of the actual implementation. Keep this in mind and always refer to the complete source code provided on the CD-ROM to view the implementation in its proper context. The source code contains many comments, which can help you understand it.

CULLING

One of the most important aspects of scene management is rendering the scene. We are not going to discuss rendering the scene just yet; instead, we are going to discuss how to avoid rendering the scene. That's right, we want to look at methods that will allow our engine to avoid rendering as much of the scene as possible. Why do want to do this? Quite simply because the less we render, the less work our video card has to do, and the less work the video card has to do, the better.

A game's performance is often measured by how many frames per second it can achieve in a given situation. This is often referred to as a *benchmark*. We measure performance in this manner because it gives us an indication of how well the underlying engine is handling the scene. When the engine has to process and render a lot of data, the frame rate drops. On the other hand, when the engine processes and renders very little, you will notice an increased frame rate. Therefore, it makes sense to introduce techniques into the engine that minimize the amount of data that the engine has to process and render for each frame.

Measuring a game's performance by frame rate alone is technically inaccurate. The reason for this is that a drop in frame rate from 100 fps to 90 fps is not the same as a drop from 40 fps to 30 fps. Instead, you should look at the change in frame rate as a percentage. Therefore, changing from 100 fps to 90 fps is a 10% performance hit, whereas changing from 40 fps to 30 fps is in fact a 25% performance hit, which is much worse.

One of the most common methods of alleviating the strain on the video card is through *culling* (or sometimes called *hidden surface removal*), which is a general term used to define the filtering of faces that do not require rendering. What this means is that any face in the scene that does not need to be rendered in a particular frame, does not need to be pushed down the DirectX graphics pipeline. This does not mean that the face does not exist, or is removed from the scene. It simply means that the engine does not send the face to DirectX to be rendered. The real question is, how do we determine if a face needs to be culled?

There are a number of common methods we can use to perform culling, with some being more complicated than others. The most effective solution usually combines two or more methods to ensure the most accurate culling results. The reason for this is that each method has its strengths and weaknesses. Some methods are computationally fast, but are relatively inaccurate, while others are slower, but yield better precision. It is usually best practice to employ a fast and rough culling method to cull away most of the non-visible faces (i.e., faces that cannot be seen by the viewer in the current frame). Then we follow this up with a slower, more accurate method that removes the extra faces not culled away by the fast method.

Developing an effective culling algorithm is like a fine balancing act. Your computer has two processors (the CPU and the GPU) that you must keep busy at all times. However, you don't want to let one of them become overloaded, therefore creating a bottleneck. The more culling you perform, the more strain you put on the CPU. On the other hand, the less culling you do, the more strain you put on the GPU. Figure 10.1 shows the relationship between culling and performance. You can see that as we perform more culling on our scene, the better the performance, up to a point, after which performance begins to drop off. This happens because the CPU is causing a bottleneck due to the amount of processing involved with the elaborate culling algorithm. You should also notice from Figure 10.1 that culling is affected by diminishing returns. This means that the more you do, the less of a performance increase you gain. The idea is to find the perfect balance among the amount of culling the CPU performs, the amount of geometry the GPU renders, and the amount of work you have to do to achieve satisfactory results.

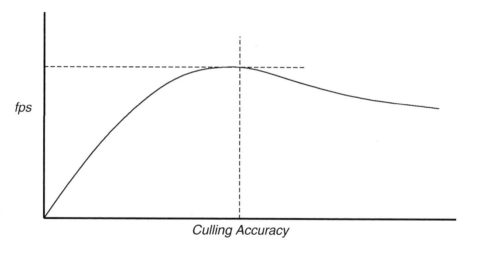

FIGURE 10.1 The relationship between culling and performance.

As previously mentioned, there are a number of common culling methods in use today. Table 10.1 shows three common methods used to cull hidden faces, as well as the advantages and disadvantages.

For our culling system, we will use all three of the methods shown in Table 10.1. We have already touched on back face culling in Chapter 5 so you should recall what that is. Fortunately for us, DirectX has back face culling built into it, and using it is as simple as switching it on. In fact, it is on by default, so that makes it even easier. The second two culling methods are new and they require a little discussion. We'll start with frustum culling.

TABLE 10.1   Culling Methods

Method	Advantages	Disadvantages
Back Face	DirectX can perform this for us. It is just a matter of switching it on.	None really. The performance gain justifies the addition of this extra step to the graphics pipeline.
Frustum	Relatively easy to implement. Can be quite computationally inexpensive.	Fairly inaccurate. Many faces close to the view will be rendered.
Occlusion	Perfect for removing surfaces in view that are hidden behind something.	Can be a significant burden on the CPU in complex scenes.

In the last chapter, we talked about the view and projection matrices. We know that the view matrix defines the virtual camera used to view the scene, and the projection matrix acts like the lenses of the camera to control the projection of the 3D scene onto your flat monitor screen. If you combine these two matrices (i.e., multiply them together), you can derive a new matrix that represents the *field of view* (FOV). The FOV simply defines what can be seen by the camera. To better understand this principle, you can look at the FOV of your own eyes. While keeping your head and eyes still, facing straight ahead, extend your right arm out to your side and move it back until you can no longer see it in your peripheral vision. This means that your arm is no longer in your FOV. If you move your arm back in slowly, it will eventually come back into your FOV when you can see it again in the corner of your eye.

We will use this exact principle to cull faces that are not in the camera's FOV. To achieve this we need to create what is called a *frustum* (or a *view frustum*) from the camera's FOV matrix. You can imagine a view frustum like a pyramid on its side, with its apex positioned at the camera and its base extended away in the direction of the camera's facing. Figure 10.2 shows what a view frustum looks like.

We won't look at the actual implementation details just yet as we will be covering all that later in the chapter. Instead, let's look at how the view frustum can be used to cull the scene. Once a view frustum has been calculated, we can define it using a set of *planes*. A plane (which is provided by the D3DX library through the use of the D3DXPLANE structure) is like a flat 2D surface, which extends infinitely through 3D space; it has no thickness and it has no boundaries. It has two sides (a positive side and a negative side), and every vertex in 3D space is located on either

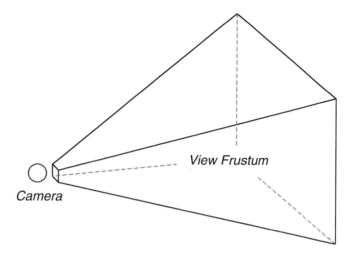

FIGURE 10.2   A view frustum, based on the virtual camera's field of view matrix.

one of these sides. Our view frustum can be defined using six of these planes (however, you can get away with only five if you ignore the near plane, which is what we will do in our implementation). If you look at Figure 10.2 again, you can see that we need a plane for each of the sides of the pyramid.

The planes are not enclosed by the actual shape of the sides of the view frustum pyramid, as they extend indefinitely along their axes. The shape of the view frustum is enforced by the fact that the planes intersect each other, therefore creating a pyramid-shaped box in 3D space. Once we have this box we can test if faces are visible by checking if they are on the inside or the outside of this box, which is quite easy to do. Figure 10.3 shows how planes are used to define a physical view frustum in 3D space.

Now that you understand how view frustum culling works, you shouldn't have too much trouble understanding how occlusion culling works as it relies on the same principle. Occlusion culling basically means to cull the scene that is hidden behind occluders. So what is an occluder? An occluder can be any object that has the ability to conceal parts of the scene from the viewer. A typical example is a large building or a solid wall. If the player is viewing the scene and a large solid wall hides a good portion of the player's view, then it makes sense to cull anything that is behind that wall. Figure 10.4 illustrates the example.

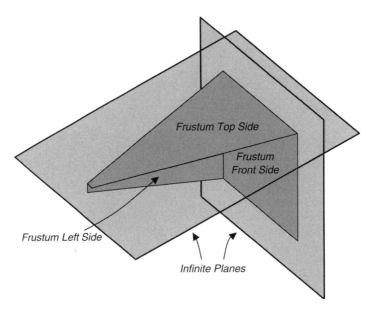

FIGURE 10.3 The top and front of a view frustum defined by infinite planes.

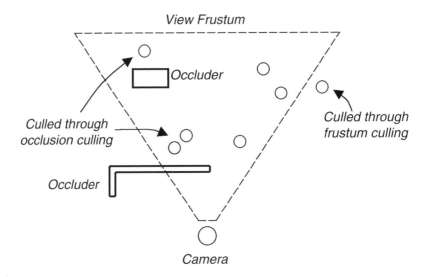

FIGURE 10.4 A scene that is partially hidden due to the occluders.

How do we determine if something is hidden by an occluder? We use the same principle as discussed for frustum culling. All we need to do is create a frustum that extends from the occluder, away from the viewer. Then, rather than culling everything that is outside the frustum, we cull everything that is inside the frustum. Figure 10.5 shows how frustums are used for occlusion culling.

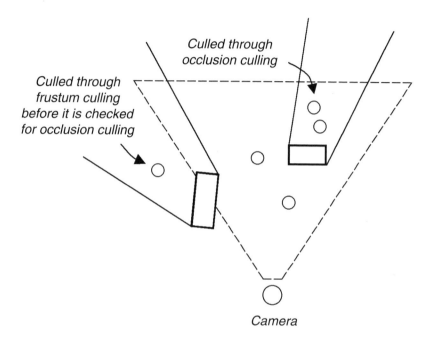

FIGURE 10.5   Shows how frustums are used for occlusion culling.

With these three culling methods we are able to cull a good portion of our scene and prevent many of the hidden surfaces from being sent through the DirectX graphics pipeline. You should be aware that this system is not perfect; there will still be a number of faces that are rendered each frame that don't need to be. However, it is not necessary to have a perfect system. We must keep the balance in mind and prevent our CPU from becoming a bottleneck from over culling. Figure 10.6 gives you an idea of the kind of returns each of the culling methods will give us. As you can see, the more culling we do, the less effective it is.

You should also note that the effectiveness of our culling methods is also strongly linked to the data set we give it to cull. In other words, what is the system trying to cull? Individual faces, groups of faces, whole objects? We haven't talked about this yet, but we will cover it later in this chapter.

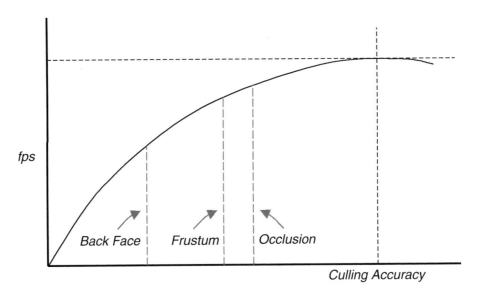

FIGURE 10.6   The effectiveness of our culling methods.

RENDERING A SCENE

As previously mentioned, rendering the scene is one of the most important aspects of scene management. We have already discussed how to avoid rendering the non-visible parts of the scene, however, there are still two loose ends that need to be tied up. The first loose end was presented when we brought up the topic of the data set, simply meaning how the geometry in the scene is arranged. The second loose end involves how we plan to actually render the visible parts of the scene after we have performed our culling. Let's start by looking at the data set.

Our scenes are comprised of a whole lot of static geometry. For example, in our scene we may have a building, some furniture, a parked car, some trees, and the actual ground surface that all this rests on. Despite the fact that they are logically separate objects, they collectively make up all the geometry in our scene. Our scenes are created (using a 3D modeling package) and stored as one large mesh file, which is exported to the .x file format, of course. Then we just need to load in one mesh and we have access to all the static geometry in our scene. The problem is, all this geometry is stored in one big vertex buffer (with one large index buffer to access it), which is what we call a *polygon soup*. In other words, all of the faces in our scene are just mashed together with no real coherency; only through the use of the index buffer can we even render them. So how do we perform culling on a big polygon soup?

The simply answer is, we don't. The only way we could possibly perform culling in something like this would be to check each face for visibility every frame, which would be completely infeasible. Yes, it would produce virtually perfect results, but the performance hit on the CPU to perform such accurate culling is far too great. So to alleviate the pressure on the CPU, rather than checking each face individually, we group them together and check them as groups. This may not be as accurate, but it is far more practical. Consider the case of a group which contains a dozen faces, for example. If half of the group was considered visible and the other half was not, we still render the whole group. The performance hit on the GPU to render a few non-visible faces is less than the performance hit on the CPU to accurately cull them.

By logically grouping our faces together, we can also approximate a shape around them, which means we can enclose them in a bounding volume. Then we simply need to check the bounding volume for culling, rather than the exact shapes of the faces. The degradation in accuracy by doing this is insignificant compared to the performance gained through culling in this fashion. The reason for this is that we only have to check a simple box or sphere against the view frustum and occlusion frustums, rather than the complex shape formed from tightly enclosing the group of faces. Figure 10.7 shows a 2D example of how groups can be culled.

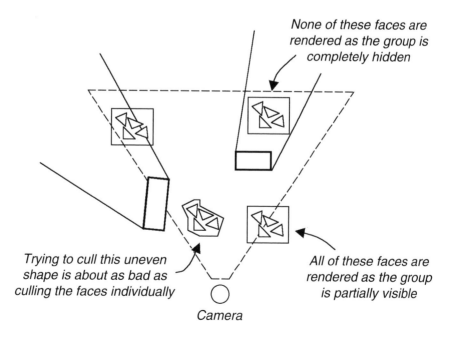

FIGURE 10.7 Culling groups of faces rather than individual faces.

This leaves us with one last glaring question: how do we go about grouping the faces in our scene? To do this we use an *octree*, a common approach that has been around for quite sometime. We won't go into too much detail about octrees just yet as we will talk about them more when we implement our system. However, we shall quickly touch on them in case you are unfamiliar with octrees. Basically, an octree is like an upside down tree, or perhaps the root system of a tree.

First, the entire scene is enclosed in one large bounding volume. This is divided into eight equal-sized bounding volumes (hence the name octree—oct meaning eight). Each of these smaller bounding volumes are then divided, each into eight smaller equal-sized bounding volumes. As the tree is created, each face is assigned to the bounding volume that encloses it (sometimes more than one for larger faces that span two bounding volumes). This process continues for a predetermined length of time, usually based on the depth of the tree, the size of the bounding volumes, or the number of faces enclosed by each bounding volume. Once complete, we are left with a hierarchy of bounding volumes (just like the hierarchy used in the .x files) that groups all of the faces in the scene. Then it is just a matter of traversing this hierarchy each frame (just like traversing the hierarchy of a .x file) and culling the non-visible groups. The beauty of this approach is that if one bounding volume is determined to be hidden, then you know that every bounding volume below it in the same branch of the hierarchy is also hidden. Therefore, there is no need to test those bounding volumes for culling. Figure 10.8 shows how a scene is divided using an octree approach. If this sounds a little complicated, don't worry as we will discuss it further when we look at the actual implementation later in the chapter.

For now, let's tie up our final loose end—how to render the scene. In Chapter 8, we implemented a RenderCache class, which has the sole purpose of rendering a batch of faces, meaning that it renders all the faces that belong to a particular material type. It is really quite simple how it works. Our entire scene is stored in one vertex buffer, which is fine because we can assume our scenes are not too large. We then create a render cache for each material type used by our scene. Each frame, we cull the scene based on the current view. When a face is found to be visible, we inform the render cache that it belongs to (based on the material used by the face) that we want that face rendered. Just like informing the waiter which dish we want from the menu, if you remember our restaurant example in Chapter 8. The render caches track the indices on the faces to be rendered in the current frame. Once we have finished culling the scene, we instruct the render caches to send their index buffers to DirectX to render the faces from the scene's vertex buffer. This completes the process, which is repeated again in the next frame.

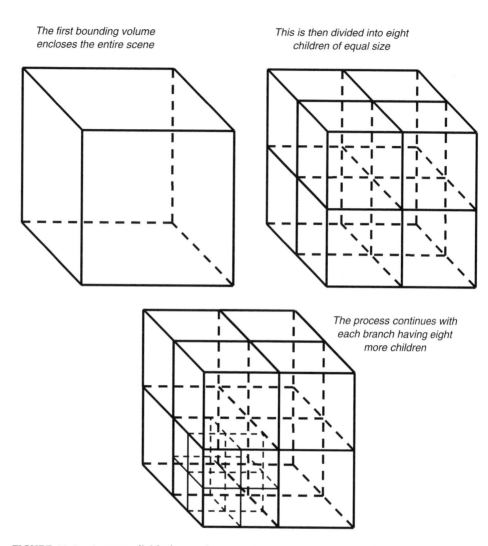

The first bounding volume encloses the entire scene

This is then divided into eight children of equal size

The process continues with each branch having eight more children

FIGURE 10.8 A scene divided up using an octree approach.

Don't stress out if this sounds overwhelming. Fortunately, we already have some of the infrastructure in place. In addition to this, once the culling system foundations are in place, everything will piece together nicely. The rendering process will become a lot clearer later when we look at the implementation of the scene management system. Until then, let's look at the final important aspect of scene management: collision detection.

COLLISION DETECTION

If you have ever tried writing the most basic of collision detection code, you will probably agree that it is almost a science of its own, and an extremely error-prone one at that. In fact, anything more complicated than making basic primitive objects (such as spheres and boxes) collide and respond properly in a 3D world is a real challenge. For a typical 3D FPS, we need a bit more than just simple primitive collision detection. We need a system that allows our players to move smoothly about inside a 3D environment. The system also needs to handle collision detection between objects such as players and object spawners, for example.

This is no easy feat, and the final implementation is long winded and complicated. In fact, it would take at least two chapters to cover it properly, and they would be tough chapters to comprehend (especially if you are not mathematically inclined). We will have our collision detection and response; we just aren't going to go through the details of its implementation. This brings us to an important concept found in the game development industry—*don't do what you don't have to*, or more commonly put, *don't reinvent the wheel.* You have probably heard that phrase before, and it is a very important phrase to remember if you hope to build the game of your dreams.

The fact of the matter is you probably cannot do everything. Not many people are brilliant artists, crack programmers, and master designers all rolled into one. Take programming, for example. Generally, you will find that most programmers are experts in one or two topics, such as network programming, sound programming, or AI programming. They have specialized in an area that they are interested in. You have probably specialized (or will specialize) in an area that you are interested in. Say you decide to specialize in network programming and you develop a great networking system for your next game, but then realize you need a professional sound system. You will probably find yourself at a bit of a loss. You can spend the next few months struggling to develop a sound system that is probably half as good as what you intended, or you can harness the expertise of someone who specializes in sound programming. You simply find a low cost (or possibly free) sound system that does what you need and then license it for your project.

With the Internet so accessible, it is very easy to find the answer to almost any problem. You can often find a lot of free resources for your projects on the Internet. Admittedly, the free resources may not be up to the same standard of a commercial endeavor, but for a little cash there are low cost solutions that are quite good. Whenever you begin a new project you should always think about what your project will need. Then decide what you can do and how much time you are prepared to invest—for everything that you cannot do (whether it is due to lack of knowledge or lack of time), research alternative solutions. Before you know it, you will build a game that uses your networking code, someone else's sound library, another person's rendering engine, and somebody else's AI code. All that matters is that you will have your game.

The final note about using other people's work is credit—always give credit when credit is due. If you were to develop a code library that you allowed someone to use, you would want the credit for your work, so always return the same courtesy. Most importantly, always seek written permission for anything you plan to use in a commercial project. In other words if you intend to make money from your project, which uses somebody else's work, you must always have their written permission first. Not only is this a courtesy, but it can also prevent legal complications.

So why all the advice about using other people's work? Well, let's move on and see why we had this little discussion.

For our collision detection system (which will be integrated into our scene management system) we will use the algorithm presented in the "Improved Collision Detection and Response" article written by Kasper Fauerby. The actual algorithm is a little complicated, which is why we won't look at it specifically in this book. Instead, you will be presented with the working code of a modified version of the algorithm, specifically written for our engine so that it fits perfectly with our scene management system. The actual article that presents the original algorithm is provided on the CD-ROM in the /Article/ directory. Mr. Fauerby has done a great job of presenting the algorithm, and you are strongly encouraged to read his article if you are interested in learning more about collision detection and response, as well as the inner workings of the algorithm.

ON THE CD

The algorithm is designed to allow an approximated mesh to move smoothly through a 3D environment. What we mean by an approximated mesh is that the mesh representing the colliding object is approximated by a bounding volume. It is far too difficult to have a 3D character walk through a 3D environment with perfect collision detection, due to the many faces that make up a typical 3D character. To simplify this, we simply enclose the 3D character inside a bounding volume. Then we use the bounding volume to perform the collision detection. This allows the object to move through the scene with smooth collision detection, while maintaining a realistic experience for the player.

We already have the BoundingVolume class, which is used to enclose all of our objects. In addition to this, the actual collision detection algorithm works using ellipsoids, which is already supported by our BoundingVolume class. You have already learned about ellipsoids in Chapter 8, so we won't go over them again here. However, you should note that the reason why we use ellipsoids is that they are far better for approximating complex meshes than other types of bounding volumes such as spheres or boxes. Take a human character that is standing upright, for example. A sphere that is stretched along its y-axis (which creates an ellipsoid) is perfect for approximating the human mesh. Take a look at Figure 10.9, which shows how an ellipsoid compares to a sphere or a box. Notice how the ellipsoid has the least amount of wasted space between its boundaries and the object it encloses.

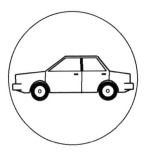
There is a lot of wasted space when using a sphere.

A box is better, however, the sharp edges make it harder to move smoothly through a 3D environment.

An ellipsoid provides the best of both worlds. The least wasted space without the sharp edges.

FIGURE 10.9 Ellipsoids compared to spheres and boxes for accurate bounding volumes.

You can find our implementation of the algorithm in the `CollisionDetection.h` file found in the workspace for this chapter. Our implementation of the algorithm has had a number of modifications made to it so that it is compatible with our scene management system. Most importantly, it has been modified so that it can register collisions between objects, allowing players to collect objects from object spawners. The algorithm will call the `CollisionOccurred` function on objects whenever they collide with one another. This allows the colliding objects to perform their collision response based on what they collide with. The beauty of this system is that it works with any object you give it, just as long as the object is derived from the base SceneObject class. This means that you can create your own objects for your game and process custom collision response for them by overriding the object's CollisionOccurred function.

The collision detection algorithm will be completely integrated into our scene management system. Therefore, once we have implemented our scene management system you should never have to worry about the collision detection code again. In preparation for this, let's have a look at how our collision detection system works. If you have a look in CollisionDetection.h you will see the Collision-Data structure, which is used to track the details of an object moving through our scene. Its definition is shown here:

```
struct CollisionData
{
  float scale;
  float elapsed;
  unsigned long frameStamp;

  SceneObject *object;

  D3DXVECTOR3 translation;
  D3DXVECTOR3 velocity;
  D3DXVECTOR3 normalizedVelocity;

  D3DXVECTOR3 gravity;

  bool collisionFound;
  float distance;
  D3DXVECTOR3 intersection;
};
```

The first few parameters are filled in by our scene management system. They equate to the scale used by the scene management system, the current elapsed time, and the current frame stamp (which is just a numerical value that is incremented each frame). You can see that the structure also takes a pointer to the object that is being tested for collision, as well as some vectors. The rest of the members are all used internally by the collision detection system, so we don't need to worry about them. All except the gravity vector that is, which we do need to set. This allows us to give the system a vector that is used to apply gravity to the object. Generally speaking you will want to pass in a vector that has a negative value for the y-axis.

A gravity vector set to (0.0, -9.81, 0.0) *will give you a gravity of roughly the same as that here on Earth.*

The idea is to iterate through all the objects in the scene each frame and build a `CollisionData` structure for each object. Then you pass the structure to the collision detection system using the `PerformCollisionDetection` function and the collision detection system takes it from there. The prototype for this function is shown here:

```
inline void PerformCollisionDetection( CollisionData *data,
    Vertex *vertices, SceneFace *faces, unsigned long totalFaces,
    LinkedList< SceneObject > *dynamicObjects )
```

You can see that the function takes in our `CollisionData` structure as well as pointers to two arrays: one that contains all of the vertices in our scene and the other that contains all of the faces made up by the vertices in our scene (we will discuss this further later in the chapter). The function also takes in the total number of faces in the scene as well as the list of objects in the scene. All of this data is used to perform the collision detection and response for the single object in the current frame.

After the `PerformCollisionDetection` function has returned, the object you passed in (through the `CollisionData` structure) will have been moved appropriately for that frame based on its movement vectors and any collisions that may have happened in that frame. Once this is done, the final step is to call the `Update` function on the object. However, it is important to pass in `false` for the `addVelocity` parameter (the second parameter) to ensure that the object does not move itself using its own velocity vector. Remember that the collision detection system has already moved the object for this frame. The following code example shows how the whole process works:

```
void FrameUpdate( float elapsed )
{
  static unsigned long frameStamp = 0;
  frameStamp++;

  m_objects->Iterate( true );
  while( m_objects->Iterate() )
  {
```

```
static CollisionData collisionData;
collisionData.scale = 1.0f;
collisionData.elapsed = elapsed;
collisionData.frameStamp = frameStamp;
collisionData.object = m_objects->GetCurrent();
collisionData.gravity = D3DXVECTOR3( 0.0f, -9.81f ,0.0f )
                             * elapsed;

PerformCollisionDetection( &collisionData,
                    (Vertex*)m_vertices, m_faces,
                          m_totalFaces, m_objects );

    m_objects->GetCurrent()->Update( elapsed, false );
  }
}
```

You will just have to imagine that the `FrameUpdate` function is part of a larger system and therefore has access to members that have already been defined, such as `m_objects` and `m_vertices`.

You should be able to see how to use the collision detection system now; if not, you will see it put to use later when we implement our scene management system. If this material is a little beyond you at the moment, don't be concerned. It will be integrated into our scene management system and you will never need to touch it. Just focus on the big picture for now. When you are confident, you can read the article on the CD-ROM and peruse the code in `CollisionDetection.h`. If you are ready now, read the article and look at the code before continuing. If you cannot understand it, just remember that it will come in time. Most people have no idea how a car works under the hood, but they still know how to drive the car. You will probably feel this way for a while, but the more you "drive" your code, the sooner you will understand how it works.

ON THE CD

THE VIEW FRUSTUM

If you recall earlier in this chapter when we talked about culling, we looked at the concept of frustum culling or more specifically, view frustum culling. You learned that each frame the view frustum is calculated using the view and projection matrices. To facilitate the management of a dynamic view frustum (i.e., one that can change every frame with the movement of the player), we will use the `ViewFrustum` class, which can be found in `ViewFrustum.h`. The class definition is also shown here:

```
class ViewFrustum
{
public:
  void Update( D3DXMATRIX *view );

  void SetProjectionMatrix( D3DXMATRIX projection );

  bool IsBoxInside( D3DXVECTOR3 min, D3DXVECTOR3 max );
  bool IsBoxInside( D3DXVECTOR3 translation, D3DXVECTOR3 min,
                    D3DXVECTOR3 max );
  bool IsSphereInside( D3DXVECTOR3 translation, float radius );

private:
  D3DXMATRIX m_projection;
  D3DXPLANE m_planes[5];
};
```

The class has an Update function, which is used to update the view frustum each frame. The SetProjectionMatrix function must be called every time the projection matrix changes to ensure the view frustum is calculated correctly. Since the projection matrix is usually set once at load time, you should only have to call this function once. The final three functions are used for checking if a bounding box or a bounding sphere is inside the view frustum. You will notice that there are two IsBoxInside functions, which essentially do the same thing, they just accept different input. The two member variables are used for storing the projection matrix and the planes that make up the view frustum, respectively. You will notice that there are only five planes despite the fact that a view frustum has six sides. This is because we are going to ignore the near plane. Since it is usually so close to the viewer (and the apex of the frustum), there is no sense in tracking such a small plane.

Let's have a look at the most important function of the ViewFrustum class, the Update function. You can find the implementation for this function in ViewFrustum.cpp.

```
void ViewFrustum::Update( D3DXMATRIX *view )
{
  D3DXMATRIX fov;
  D3DXMatrixMultiply( &fov, view, &m_projection );

  m_planes[0].a = fov._14 - fov._11;
  m_planes[0].b = fov._24 - fov._21;
  m_planes[0].c = fov._34 - fov._31;
  m_planes[0].d = fov._44 - fov._41;
```

```
    m_planes[1].a = fov._14 + fov._11;
    m_planes[1].b = fov._24 + fov._21;
    m_planes[1].c = fov._34 + fov._31;
    m_planes[1].d = fov._44 + fov._41;

    m_planes[2].a = fov._14 - fov._12;
    m_planes[2].b = fov._24 - fov._22;
    m_planes[2].c = fov._34 - fov._32;
    m_planes[2].d = fov._44 - fov._42;

    m_planes[3].a = fov._14 + fov._12;
    m_planes[3].b = fov._24 + fov._22;
    m_planes[3].c = fov._34 + fov._32;
    m_planes[3].d = fov._44 + fov._42;

    m_planes[4].a = fov._14 - fov._13;
    m_planes[4].b = fov._24 - fov._23;
    m_planes[4].c = fov._34 - fov._33;
    m_planes[4].d = fov._44 - fov._43;

    D3DXPlaneNormalize( &m_planes[0], &m_planes[0] );
    D3DXPlaneNormalize( &m_planes[1], &m_planes[1] );
    D3DXPlaneNormalize( &m_planes[2], &m_planes[2] );
    D3DXPlaneNormalize( &m_planes[3], &m_planes[3] );
    D3DXPlaneNormalize( &m_planes[4], &m_planes[4] );
}
```

The function may look a little long, but it really just repeats itself if you look closely at what it is doing. First, it creates the FOV matrix using the passed in view matrix and the stored projection matrix. It then creates each of the view frustum's planes (except the near plane of course) using the FOV matrix, and finally normalizes the planes. If you recall from Chapter 8 what a 4 × 4 matrix looks like, you should be able to see that to create each plane we just need to access the appropriate components of the FOV matrix. The plane is represented by a point in 3D space, which is defined by the (a, b, c) members of the D3DXPLANE structure. The d member defines the plane's distance from the world origin.

The last few functions are very simple, so there is really no need to look at them here. You should take a look at their implementation in ViewFrustum.cpp, especially the first IsBoxInside function, as we will make great use of it later on.

You should be aware that functions like IsBoxInside *do not require the entire box (or sphere) to be enclosed by the view frustum. As long as just part of the bounding volume is within the view frustum's planes, the function will return true.*

We have finished discussing and implementing the utilities required by our scene management system. All we need to do now is lay down some foundational structures (almost literally), and we are ready to implement our long awaited scene manager.

SCENE FACE

The first foundational structure we are going to look at is the SceneFace structure. You have already seen how the PerformCollisionDetection function takes as input a pointer to an array of these. So let's discuss exactly what this structure will be used for. The definition of the structure is shown here, and you can also find it in SceneManager.h.

```
struct SceneFace : public IndexedFace
{
  RenderCache *renderCache;
  unsigned long renderStamp;
};
```

As you can see there really isn't all that much to the structure. It is actually derived from IndexedFace, which we defined in Geometry.h (if you recall from Chapter 2). This structure allows us to track each and every face in our scene. The renderCache member stores a pointer to the render cache that the face belongs to, and renderStamp is just like a frame stamp. The only difference is that rather than being incremented each frame, it is actually set to the current frame stamp of the frame in which the face was rendered. By tracking when each face was lasted rendered, we can ensure that each face is not rendered more than once in the same frame.

It is important to remember that these faces are in fact indexed faces. This means that they do not store the physical vertices that define them, but instead store the indices of those vertices.

SCENE LEAF

The second foundational structure we need to look at is the `SceneLeaf` structure. As you already know, the faces in our scene will be divided up like an octree. This allows us to group our faces into logical bounding volumes, so that these bounding volumes can be tested for culling rather than the individual faces. We will call each of these bounding volumes a scene leaf. In other words, they are like leaves on our octree. The definition for the `SceneLeaf` structure is shown here, and it can also be found in `SceneManager.h`.

```
struct SceneLeaf : public BoundingVolume
{
  SceneLeaf *children[8];
  unsigned long visibleStamp;
  LinkedList< SceneOccluder > *occluders;
  unsigned long totalFaces;
  unsigned long *faces;

  SceneLeaf()
  {
    for( char c = 0; c < 8; c++ )
      children[c] = NULL;
    occluders = new LinkedList< SceneOccluder >;
    totalFaces = 0;
    faces = NULL;
  }

  virtual ~SceneLeaf()
  {
    for( char c = 0; c < 8; c++ )
      SAFE_DELETE( children[c] );
    occluders->ClearPointers();
    SAFE_DELETE( occluders );
    SAFE_DELETE_ARRAY( faces );
  }
};
```

The `SceneLeaf` structure derives from the `BoundingVolume` class as it is essentially just a bounding volume that happens to be a box, which our `BoundingVolume` class supports. The structure also comes packed with the standard constructor and destructor to initialize and destroy everything, respectively. You can see that the structure maintains an array of pointers to its children to facilitate the creation, traversal, and destruction of the hierarchy of bounding volumes that the scene will be divided up into. We also have the `visibleStamp`, which works in exactly the same fashion as the `renderStamp` from `SceneFace`. However, this stamp is used to track when the `SceneLeaf` was last visible. Finally, the `SceneLeaf` structure also maintains a list of scene occluders and scene faces. In other words, it tracks which occluders and which faces in the scene are actually physically located (in 3D space) within the bounding volume of the scene leaf.

That's about all there is to this structure. It may appear fairly useless at the moment, but wait until our scene manager gets its hands on it. Then you will see the true power of this little structure as it is used as the building blocks of the entire hierarchy that divides the scene for efficient rendering. Before we get too carried away, let's just look at the last foundational structure that our scene manager will use. In fact, the `SceneLeaf` structure uses it too, so you can probably pick it.

SCENE OCCLUDER

The last of our three foundational structures is, of course, the `SceneOccluder` structure, which is the largest and most complicated of the three structures. You should be able to remember earlier in this chapter when we talked about culling our scene using occluders (i.e., objects that have the ability to hide parts of the scene). This is the structure that will be used to track and manage a single occluding object in our scene. In other words, for each occluding object in the scene, we will need a single instance of this structure to manage that occluder. The definition of the structure is shown below and can also be found in `SceneManager.h`.

```
struct SceneOccluder : public BoundingVolume
{
  unsigned long visibleStamp;
  D3DXVECTOR3 translation;
  unsigned long totalFaces;
  Vertex *vertices;
  unsigned short *indices;
  LinkedList< D3DXPLANE > *planes;
  float distance;

  SceneOccluder( D3DXVECTOR3 t, ID3DXMesh *mesh,
                 D3DXMATRIX *world )
  {
    visibleStamp = -1;
```

```
      translation = t;

      totalFaces = mesh->GetNumFaces();
      vertices = new Vertex[mesh->GetNumVertices()];
      indices = new unsigned short[totalFaces * 3];

      Vertex* verticesPtr;
      mesh->LockVertexBuffer( 0, (void**)&verticesPtr );
      unsigned short *indicesPtr;
      mesh->LockIndexBuffer( 0, (void**)&indicesPtr );

      memcpy( vertices, verticesPtr,
              VERTEX_FVF_SIZE * mesh->GetNumVertices() );
      memcpy( indices, indicesPtr,
              sizeof( unsigned short ) * totalFaces * 3 );

      mesh->UnlockVertexBuffer();
      mesh->UnlockIndexBuffer();

      for( unsigned long v = 0; v < mesh->GetNumVertices(); v++ )
        D3DXVec3TransformCoord( &vertices[v].translation,
                                &vertices[v].translation, world );

      planes = new LinkedList< D3DXPLANE >;

      BoundingVolumeFromMesh( mesh );

      D3DXMATRIX location;
      D3DXMatrixTranslation( &location, t.x, t.y, t.z );
      RepositionBoundingVolume( &location );
    }

  virtual ~SceneOccluder()
  {
    SAFE_DELETE_ARRAY( vertices );
    SAFE_DELETE_ARRAY( indices );

    SAFE_DELETE( planes );
  }
};
```

First, you should notice that the structure derives from the `BoundingVolume` class. The reason for this is that our occluders are surrounded by a bounding box that is used to determine which scene leaves the occluder belongs to. This allows us to determine if an occluder is visible each frame, and therefore avoid processing the ones that are not visible in the current frame. You should also see that the structure contains a `visibleStamp`, just like the one in the `SceneLeaf` structure, and it is used in exactly the same manner to track when the occluder is visible.

Continuing through the member variables, the next on the list is `translation`, which stores the location of the occluder in 3D space. We also have a list of vertices and a list of indices as well as the total number of faces that make up the occluder. We need to store the vertices and the indices because our occluders can be any arbitrary shape. What this means is that we may have one occluder in the shape of a house and the next in the shape of a large truck. Both of these objects will have different faces that make the object. Therefore, we cannot assume that an occluder will be a simple box shape. You must be careful when defining occluders as they can be computationally expensive when they have a lot of faces. The best occluders are large objects with very few faces, such as large box shapes. We will further discuss this later in the chapter.

Finally, you should see that the structure maintains a linked list of planes and a `distance` member. Remember that our scene occluders work in much the same way as our view frustum for culling. The only difference is that instead of culling everything outside the frustum, we want to cull everything inside the frustum. To achieve this we obviously need to build a frustum each frame that extends from the occluder away from the viewer as shown in Figure 10.10. Just like the view frustum, we use planes to define the walls of our frustum. However, unlike the view frustum which has at most six planes, we do not know how many planes are required for our occluding frustum. This is due to the possibility of our occluders being arbitrary shapes, with many edges that a plane can protrude from, also shown in Figure 10.10.

So what is the `distance` member for? The simple answer is that it is used to maintain the distance between the occluder and the viewer each frame. Why is that important? Well, imagine if we have multiple occluders visible each frame and we want to ensure that we process as few of them as possible. To do this, we need to take into account the situation where one occluder completely conceals another. For example, say you had a large building in front of you and a smaller one behind it. If the large building completely occludes the smaller building from your sight, there is no point in processing the smaller building if it were an occluder. The reason being, that anything the smaller building can occlude is guaranteed to be occluded by the larger building, therefore we only need to process the larger building

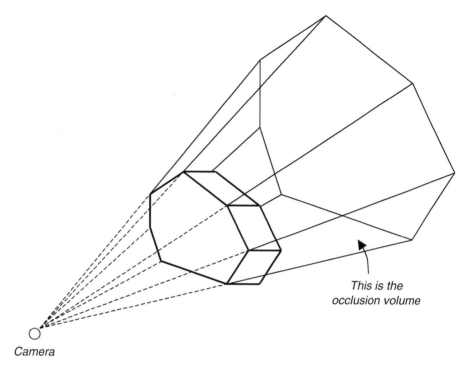

This is the occlusion volume

Camera

FIGURE 10.10 An occlusion volume built from an arbitrary 3D shape.

as an occluder. The best why to handle this is to process the occluders in a front to back order. Therefore, we process the occluder that is closest to the viewer first, then the next closest, and so on. By doing this we can check if any of the visible occluders that are further away are in fact completely occluded. If so we can ignore them.

The last point of interest is the constructor and the destructor for the structure. The destructor is pretty plain; however, the constructor is quite busy. It stores the vertices and indices of a mesh that you pass to it, and then transforms the vertices based on a world matrix that you also pass in. This moves the vertices from model space to world space so that they are ready for use in our 3D scene. The final step in the constructor is to build (and position) the bounding volume based on the scene occluder's mesh.

This pretty much wraps up our discussion of the `SceneOccluder` structure for now. We will soon look at the implementation of our scene manager, which will put all three of the foundational classes to good use. In doing this, you will see how they are used and gain an understanding of how they work, which should help clear up any questionable areas, if there are any.

SCENE SCRIPTS

You may not have noticed yet, but there is something severely lacking that we must address before we implement our scene manager. We haven't talked about scene assets, which cover the necessary resources for our scene manager to render a 3D environment. Other than textures, spawner objects, and sound effects, there are two main resources that we should look at that form the basis of our scene: the scene script and the scene mesh. Let's have a look at the scene script first, and then we will cover the scene mesh in the next section.

ON THE CD

If you take a look in the `Assets` directory where this chapter's test application is located on the CD-ROM you will find a file called `Abandoned City.txt`. The content (excluding the initial comments) of the script is shown here:

```
#begin

name          string "Abandoned City"
gravity       vector 0.0 -9.81 0.0

ambient_light color 0.5 0.5 0.5 1.0
sun_direction vector -0.6 -0.3 0.4

fog_colour    colour 0.8 0.8 0.8 1.0
fog_density   float  0.02

mesh          string "Abandoned City.x"
mesh_path     string ./Assets/

max_faces     number 32
max_half_size float  16.0

#end
```

The first six variables are used for setting up the scene. They are fairly self-explanatory and they are accompanied by a description in the actual script. The `mesh` and `mesh_path` variables allow you to define the .x file that will be used for the scene. The last two variables are used for managing the subdivision of the scene's faces. They define the maximum number of faces allowed in each scene leaf, and the maximum half size of each scene leaf. The half size of a scene leaf is simply its size along any axis (since it is the same size along all three axes, making a square box) divided by two. If a scene leaf contains too many faces and it is too large, then it will be divided up.

When you run the test application for this chapter, try playing around with the different values to see the effects on the scene. However, before you can do that we are going to need a mesh for our scene. So let's have a look at how to create one.

SCENE MESH

Creating a scene mesh is really not too difficult if you have had a little practice with a 3D modeling package such as 3ds max. If you do not have 3ds max the first thing you should do is go to the discreet® Web site (*www.discreet.com*) where you can download a trial version. Once you have the software installed, don't forget to install the exporter provided on the CD-ROM. There are other programs that you can model a scene in such as MilkShape 3D® for example, which is also supported by the exporter on the CD-ROM. You can download a trial version from the chUmbaLum sOft® Web site (*www.swissquake.ch/chumbalum-soft*). In fact, you can use just about any 3D modeler you wish. Just as long as you can save your creation to a .x file and you can name the frames in the mesh hierarchy. You'll see why this is important shortly.

ON THE CD

Assuming you have 3ds max installed and you are familiar with it, you should load the scene file called Abandoned City.max, which is included on the CD-ROM. The file can be found in the Assets directory where this chapter's test application is located on the CD-ROM. This is a typical scene and it contains everything our engine is capable of handling. We will now discuss the various aspects of building a scene in a 3D modeling package such as 3ds max. Everything we discuss is exhibited in this sample scene, so use this as a reference point.

All the geometry in the scene is made up of faces that have each been textured with one of the .dds texture files that you will find in the same directory as the scene file you just loaded. You can easily create your own scenes by modeling your scene and applying materials to each of the faces. You then just need to export your creation out to a .x file and load it into the engine using a script file. However, if you want to see the true potential of the engine, then you need to learn a few more things about scene creation.

This is where the part about being able to name the frames in the .x file becomes important. As you should remember from Chapter 8, a .x file is internally made up of frames, which are organized into a hierarchy. Each frame can contain data used by our scene, such as a mesh or even just a reference point (i.e., a point located in 3D space). When the .x file is loaded by our engine, we want the scene manager to be able to read these frames and then act upon the data inside the frame based on the name of the frame. This allows us to virtually use our 3D modeling package as a level editor.

For example, we can create a point in 3D space and call it `player_spawn_point`. We can save this point into its own frame (within the .x file frame hierarchy), which we call `player_spawn_point`. Then we just need to tell our scene manager to place a player spawn point at the same translation as specified by the frame called `player_spawn_point`. In fact, we can make our scene manager search through the frame hierarchy and place a player spawn point for each frame that is found that matches that name. To ensure that this works properly and remains consistent between scenes, we need to develop some sort of standard or naming convention. However, before we can come up with a standard or naming convention we need to look at what we can place in our scene. Table 10.2 shows a list of things that can be placed into a scene.

From Table 10.2 we can see that there are three special items that we can place in our scene, so we need some sort of standard for placing and identifying them. Let's go through each of them starting with the occluders.

TABLE 10.2 Scene Items

Occluders	An occluder is defined by a section of geometry that has the ability to hide parts of the scene. To ensure that our scene manager can identify our occluders, we need to make sure that each occluder is separated into its own frame. In other words, the occluder must be a separate piece of geometry that is not attached in any way to the rest of the geometry in our scene.
Object Spawners	An object spawner is not represented by any geometry in our scene; instead, it is just a point in 3D space. How you define that point doesn't matter. All that matters is that a separate frame (in the scene's .x file frame hierarchy) exists for each object spawner. The frame's internal transformation matrix must be able to position the object spawner at the correct location in 3D space.
Player Spawners	A player spawner is just like an object spawner. There must be a separate frame for each player spawner, which can be used to position the player spawner in 3D space. Like an object spawner, a player spawner can be represented by anything you like such as an invisible piece of geometry or a single point in 3D space, which is what we will use in 3ds max. You should also be aware that a player spawner has a second point that identifies a radius around the player spawner. You will learn more about this later.

To place an occluder in our scene, it is just a matter of placing a separate piece of geometry into the scene that is not attached to the rest of the scene. To give you an example using 3ds max, if you were to select the Box object type and draw a 3D box in your scene, it would be classified as a separate piece of geometry as it is not attached to anything else and you can select it. You can see that it is named something like "Box01" if you select it. This tells you that the geometry (i.e., the faces) that makes up this box is enclosed within its own frame, which would have the same name within the exported .x file's frame hierarchy. If you save the entire scene to a .x file and then take a look at the frame hierarchy within the .x file, you would be able to find this frame with the box's geometry contained within it. The frame would also contain a translation matrix that is used to position the box's geometry in 3D space. Figure 10.11 shows three boxes in 3ds max. Each box is a separate piece of geometry within the scene and therefore would be saved as separate frames. If we saved this scene to a .x file we would have three frames called "Box01," "Box02," and "Box03."

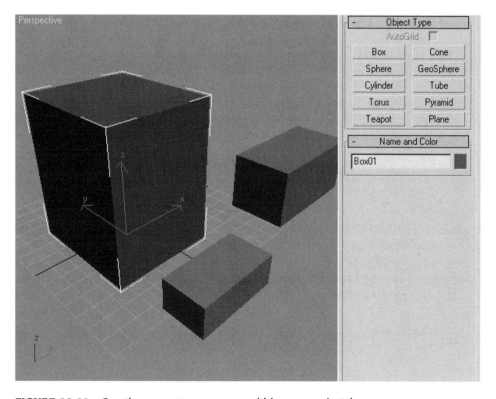

FIGURE 10.11   Creating separate geometry within a scene in 3ds max.

So the key to creating scene occluders is to create a separate piece of geometry in the scene and then name it something that our engine can identify. It is important that each occluder has a unique name so that our engine can identify them. To name an occluder we will use the prefix "oc_" followed by the name of the occluder. Then to ensure the names are unique we will add an underscore and a number postfix to the end of the name. For example, if we wanted to name the three boxes in Figure 10.11 so that the engine would identify them as occluders we would call the first one "oc_box_01," the second one "oc_box_02," and the third one "oc_box_03." The basic rule of thumb is that you can put whatever you like between the two underscores, just make sure you have the "oc_" prefix and a unique number postfix.

Now we need to look at placing object spawners, which is actually very similar to placing occluders. The only difference is that we can use whatever we want to create a new frame. All we really care about in the frame is the transformation matrix that is used to position the object spawner in 3D space. In 3ds max we can use a point to represent an object spawner as it will be contained within its own frame and the engine will not render it; it is just an invisible point in 3D space. For object spawners we will use the "sp_" prefix in front of the name and the unique number postfix.

What you place between the two underscores matters now. The name between the two underscores needs to match up to the name of the script that is used for the object spawner. Let's look at an example. Say you had an object spawner script called `rifle.txt` and you wanted to create an object spawner in your scene that can spawn a rifle weapon. You would call the object spawner "sp_rifle_01." If you wanted to add a second rifle spawner to your scene you would call it "sp_rifle_02," and so on. When the scene manager loads the scene's .x file and it finds these frames, it creates a rifle object spawner at the locations specified by the transformation matrices in these frames. You don't need to add the `.txt` extension to the name as the scene manager does that for you when it loads the object spawner's script.

The final item that we need to look at is the player spawn point. This is actually just like an object spawner and it is created and named in exactly the same manner. The only difference is that you do not need to match the name to a script as the scene manager already knows what a player spawner is and how it works. So all you need to do is place a point in your scene and call it "sp_player_01" and the scene manager will place a player spawn point there. If you want more than one player spawn point, just name them consecutively. So the second one would be called "sp_player_02" and the third would be called "sp_player_03," and so on.

There is one more point we need to add to our player spawn points, literally. Each of our player spawn points must be accompanied by a second matching point that is used to determine a radius around the spawn point. These new points are named exactly the same except they do not have the "sp_" prefix, but instead have a "_radius" postfix. So our radius point for the first player spawn point would be called "player_01_radius," and the second one would be called "player_02_radius," and so on. When the scene manger loads the player spawn points, it will calculate the distance between each player spawn point and its respective radius point. This radius is then used to create a bounding sphere around the player spawn point.

The reason that we want to do this is to prevent what's called *spawn point camping*, which you are probably familiar with. If not, it is the name given to the activity of waiting for new players to spawn so that you can shoot them immediately before they have a chance to prepare themselves, which is very unfair. Later on you will see how we will use this bounding sphere around the spawn points to prevent this activity. Basically all we do is prevent players from spawning at a point that has other players within its bounding sphere.

When you design your own scenes it is important that you give the spawn points a large enough radius so that other players cannot camp nearby. However, do not make the radius too big or it will constantly register other players even when they are not camping. This prevents the spawn point from ever being used. Take a look at Figure 10.12 for some examples.

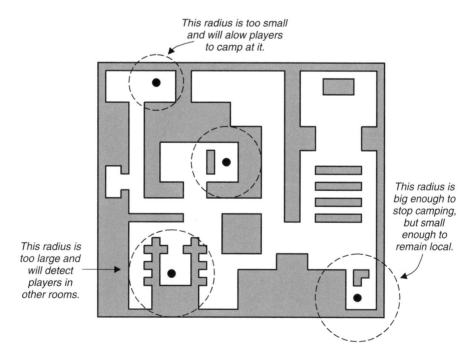

FIGURE 10.12 Some examples of placing player spawn points.

That's about all there is to building your own scenes; you can see it is not that complicated. Once you have built one, the process becomes very easy. Now that we have the foundational structures in place and we have covered the two main assets that are needed to build a scene, we are now ready to look at the implementation of the actual scene manager, which we have been building up to.

SCENE MANAGEMENT SYSTEM

Welcome to the end . . . seems like a fitting opening for your worst nightmare. Definitely, the largest and seemingly most complex class is now upon us. The shadow of this class has loomed over us, only to reveal itself to be a mouse cleverly disguised as a tiger. In fact, you've probably seen cartoons where a large terrifying shadow is cast on a wall, but then when you see what is casting the shadow, you realize it is just a small mouse with a close light projecting its shadow. We can use the same analogy with the SceneManager class that we are about to dissect. Yes, it is the largest class in our engine, and at first glance it looks quite terrifying. However, after we have slowly stepped through it, you have read through all the source code, and practiced using the class a little, you will realize it is really not that bad.

Having said that, here is the class definition, which is shown below and can also be found in SceneManager.h. If you have a close look at it, you will realize that there really isn't a lot here that you haven't seen before. We have a few functions, some variables, a few linked lists, and a couple of things about vertices—all the usual suspects. So take a look at it and then laugh at its simplicity!

```
class SceneManager
{
public:
  SceneManager( float scale, char *spawnerPath );
  virtual ~SceneManager();

  void LoadScene( char *name, char *path = "./" );
  void DestroyScene();
  bool IsLoaded();

  void Update( float elapsed, D3DXMATRIX *view = NULL );
  void Render( float elapsed, D3DXVECTOR3 viewer );

  SceneObject *AddObject( SceneObject *object );
  void RemoveObject( SceneObject **object );
```

```
      SceneObject *GetRandomPlayerSpawnPoint();
      SceneObject *GetSpawnPointByID( long id );
      long GetSpawnPointID( SceneObject *point );

      LinkedList< SpawnerObject > *GetSpawnerObjectList();

      bool RayIntersectScene( RayIntersectionResult *result,
              D3DXVECTOR3 rayPosition, D3DXVECTOR3 rayDirection,
              bool checkScene = true, SceneObject *thisObject = NULL,
              bool checkObjects = false );

private:
    void BuildOcclusionVolume( SceneOccluder *occluder,
                               D3DXVECTOR3 viewer );

    void RecursiveSceneBuild( SceneLeaf *leaf,
            D3DXVECTOR3 translation, float halfSize );
    bool RecursiveSceneFrustumCheck( SceneLeaf *leaf,
            D3DXVECTOR3 viewer );
    void RecursiveSceneOcclusionCheck( SceneLeaf *leaf );

private:
    char *m_name;
    float m_scale;
    ViewFrustum m_viewFrustum;
    D3DXVECTOR3 m_gravity;
    bool m_loaded;
    Mesh *m_mesh;
    unsigned long m_maxFaces;
    float m_maxHalfSize;
    unsigned long m_frameStamp;

    LinkedList< SceneObject > *m_dynamicObjects;
    LinkedList< SceneOccluder > *m_occludingObjects;
    LinkedList< SceneOccluder > *m_visibleOccluders;
    LinkedList< SceneObject > *m_playerSpawnPoints;
    LinkedList< SpawnerObject > *m_objectSpawners;
    char *m_spawnerPath;

    SceneLeaf *m_firstLeaf;
```

```
        IDirect3DVertexBuffer9 *m_sceneVertexBuffer;
        Vertex *m_vertices;
        unsigned long m_totalVertices;

        LinkedList< RenderCache > *m_renderCaches;

        unsigned long m_totalFaces;
        SceneFace *m_faces;
    };
```

Since this is such a long class definition, rather than discussing each individual item in it, let's move straight to the implementation of the important functions. That way we can discuss the functions in more detail, and you can learn about the member variables as we discuss the implementation of the class. You should note that we will focus on the most important parts of the class. For example, the constructor and destructor do not really do much in this class, so we won't bother looking at them. For the complete implementation be sure to reference `SceneManager.cpp`.

LOADING THE SCENE

The first function that we will look at is the `LoadScene` function. Once the scene manager class has been instanced you can call this function with the name of (and path to) the scene script that you want to load. Let's step through the implementation of this function.

```
    void SceneManager::LoadScene( char *name, char *path )
    {
      m_occludingObjects = new LinkedList< SceneOccluder >;
      m_visibleOccluders = new LinkedList< SceneOccluder >;
      m_playerSpawnPoints = new LinkedList< SceneObject >;
      m_objectSpawners = new LinkedList< SpawnerObject >;
```

The `SceneManager` class maintains four linked lists for managing the various items in a scene. There is a list that tracks all of the occluder objects and a list that tracks which occluder objects are visible each frame. We also have a list that tracks all of the player spawn points in the scene, and finally a list that tracks all the object spawners in the scene. At this point all we need to do with these lists is create an instance of each so they are ready to use.

```
Script *script = new Script( name, path );

m_name = new char[strlen( script->GetStringData( "name" ) ) +1];
memcpy( m_name, script->GetStringData( "name" ), ( strlen(
    script->GetStringData( "name" ) ) + 1 ) * sizeof( char ) );


m_gravity = *script->GetVectorData( "gravity" ) / m_scale;
```

Now we need to load the scene's script using the name and path that were passed into the LoadScene function. Once loaded, we just create a char buffer that we copy the name of the scene into. Then we set the m_gravity member vector based on the gravity set in the script.

```
D3DLIGHT9 sun;
sun.Type = D3DLIGHT_DIRECTIONAL;
sun.Diffuse.r = 1.0f;
sun.Diffuse.g = 1.0f;
sun.Diffuse.b = 1.0f;
sun.Diffuse.a = 1.0f;
sun.Specular = sun.Diffuse;
sun.Ambient.r = script->GetColourData( "ambient_light" )->r;
sun.Ambient.g = script->GetColourData( "ambient_light" )->g;
sun.Ambient.b = script->GetColourData( "ambient_light" )->b;
sun.Ambient.a = script->GetColourData( "ambient_light" )->a;
sun.Direction = D3DXVECTOR3(
                    script->GetVectorData( "sun_direction" )->x,
                    script->GetVectorData( "sun_direction" )->y,
                    script->GetVectorData( "sun_direction" )->z );
sun.Range = 0.0f;
g_engine->GetDevice()->SetRenderState( D3DRS_LIGHTING, true );
g_engine->GetDevice()->SetLight( 0, &sun );
g_engine->GetDevice()->LightEnable( 0, true );
g_engine->GetDevice()->SetRenderState( D3DRS_SPECULARENABLE,
                                        true );
```

The next step is to set up the lighting for the scene. This is actually quite simple as we are just going to use the DirectX fixed function vertex lighting, and we are only going to have one light source—the sun (or moon for night time). To create a light in DirectX you need to fill in a D3DLIGHT9 structure. The definition of this structure is shown here:

```
typedef struct _D3DLIGHT9
{
  // The type of light, D3DLIGHT_POINT, D3DLIGHT_SPOT or
  // D3DLIGHT_DIRECTIONAL.
  D3DLIGHTTYPE Type;

  // The diffuse, specular, and ambient color of the light.
  D3DCOLORVALUE Diffuse;
  D3DCOLORVALUE Specular;
  D3DCOLORVALUE Ambient;

  // The position and direction of the light.
  D3DVECTOR Position;
  D3DVECTOR Direction;

  // The range affects how far the light can travel.
  float Range;

  // This is used by spotlights, which we won't be using.
  float Falloff;

  // The attenuation affects how the light fades over distance.
  float Attenuation0;
  float Attenuation1;
  float Attenuation2;

  // Like Falloff, these are used by spotlights. You can find
  // more information in the DirectX SDK documentation.
  float Theta;
  float Phi;
} D3DLIGHT9;
```

For our sunlight we set it up as a directional light. What this means is that it has no position in 3D space, just a direction. So the light is applied to everything in the entire scene. For the lighting levels we set the diffuse and specular to full bright. You may consider adding another variable to the scene script that allows you to change the color of the light just like we do with the ambient light. As you can see, we set the ambient light by taking the four components from the script. Finally, we set the direction of the light based on the direction in the script. The rest of the values we don't need to worry about as they do not apply to directional lighting. If you were creating a point light you would also need to set the position and range of the light, perhaps even adjusting the attenuation to achieve the desired effect.

Now that we have our sun set up we only have a couple of things to do before lighting works properly. First, we need to set two render states to true;

D3DRS_LIGHTING and D3DRS_SPECULARENABLE, which switches lighting on and enables specular highlights, respectively. Finally, we need to set our light using a call to SetLight on the device and then enable the light by calling LightEnable, also on the device.

You will notice how for both of those functions we pass in 0 as the first parameter. This means that we are storing our light in the first index. If we wanted to use a second light, we would reference it by passing 1 into both of these functions. The number of simultaneous lights that you can use depends on your video card, but it is usually about eight.

```
float density = *script->GetFloatData( "fog_density" ) *m_scale;
g_engine->GetDevice()->SetRenderState( D3DRS_FOGENABLE, true );
g_engine->GetDevice()->SetRenderState( D3DRS_FOGCOLOR,
   D3DCOLOR_COLORVALUE( script->GetColourData( "fog_colour" )->r,
                 script->GetColourData( "fog_colour" )->g,
                 script->GetColourData( "fog_colour" )->b,
                 script->GetColourData( "fog_colour" )->a ) );
g_engine->GetDevice()->SetRenderState( D3DRS_FOGVERTEXMODE,
                                       D3DFOG_EXP2 );
g_engine->GetDevice()->SetRenderState( D3DRS_FOGDENSITY,
                               *(unsigned long*)&density );
```

Now that we have lighting in our scene, the next step is to set up the fog based on the settings in the scene script file. You can see we take the fog density setting from our script file and multiply it by our scale to ensure that it fits in with the scale we are using. After we enable the fog using the D3DRS_FOGENABLE render state, we need to set the color of the fog based on the color set in the script file, which is done using the D3DRS_FOGCOLOR render state. Finally, we need to set the fog density using the D3DRS_FOGDENSITY render state, and the way in which DirectX applies the fog using the D3DRS_FOGVERTEXMODE render state. There are a number of options you can use for this render state, which are shown in Table 10.3. We will use D3DFOG_EXP2 for now, but you should experiment to see the different effects.

TABLE 10.3 Fog Vertex Modes

D3DFOG_NONE	Effectively switches fog off.
D3DFOG_EXP	Thickens fog exponentially based on density across distance.
D3DFOG_EXP2	Thickens fog exponentially based on the square of density across distance.
D3DFOG_LINEAR	Thickens fog linearly based on density between the start and end points.

If you want to use D3DFOG_LINEAR, *you will need to adjust the* D3DRS_FOGSTART *and* D3DRS_FOGEND *render states in order for the fog to work correctly.*

```
m_maxFaces = *script->GetNumberData( "max_faces" );
m_maxHalfSize = *script->GetFloatData( "max_half_size" );

m_mesh = g_engine->GetMeshManager()->Add( script->GetStringData(
              "mesh" ), script->GetStringData( "mesh_path" ) );

SAFE_DELETE( script );
```

Before we finish with the scene script we must do a few more things. First, we need to store the rules for dividing the scene leaves. The scene is divided until the scene leaves are small enough and there aren't too many faces in them. Finally, we just need to load the actual .x file mesh that will be used for our scene. We do this by grabbing the name and path of the file from the script and passing it to our mesh manager.

```
D3DDISPLAYMODE *display;
display = g_engine->GetDisplayMode();
D3DXMATRIX projection;
D3DXMatrixPerspectiveFovLH( &projection, D3DX_PI / 4,
  (float)display->Width / (float)display->Height, 0.1f / m_scale,
   m_mesh->GetBoundingSphere()->radius * 2.0f );
g_engine->GetDevice()->SetTransform( D3DTS_PROJECTION,
                                     &projection );

m_viewFrustum.SetProjectionMatrix( projection );
```

Now we need to adjust our projection matrix so that it is large enough for our scene. You can see how we adjust it for scale and adjust it based on the size of the scene. This ensures that the player can view the entire scene from any angle. Once adjusted, we need to set it with the device and also set it with our view frustum, which is built into our scene manager.

You have to be careful with large scenes as this method will allow the projection matrix to view the entire scene from one side to the other. This can lead to significant performance penalties, especially on open scenes with little occlusion culling. You may want to try experimenting with the fog and the far clipping plane of the projection matrix so that the scene is clipped away just beyond the point the fog becomes solid. This is a common approach used in most FPS and can easily be achieved by thickening up the fog and bringing the far clipping plane in. By using either D3DFOG_EXP *or* D3DFOG_EXP2 *you can ensure that the fog thickens faster over distance, but still gives you a clear image at close range.*

```
m_renderCaches = new LinkedList< RenderCache >;

for( unsigned long m = 0; m < m_mesh->GetStaticMesh()
                                    ->NumMaterials; m++ )
{
  bool found = false;

  if( m_mesh->GetStaticMesh()->materials[m] == NULL )
    continue;

  m_renderCaches->Iterate( true );
  while( m_renderCaches->Iterate() )
  {
    if( m_renderCaches->GetCurrent()->GetMaterial()
        == m_mesh->GetStaticMesh()->materials[m] )
    {
      found = true;
      break;
    }
  }

  if( found == false && m_mesh->GetStaticMesh()->materials[m]
                            ->GetIgnoreFace() == false )
    m_renderCaches->Add( new RenderCache( g_engine->GetDevice(),
                    m_mesh->GetStaticMesh()->materials[m] ) );
}
```

This step involves preparing a list of render caches to render the scene's faces. All we are doing is creating a linked list of render caches and then iterating through the list of materials in the scene's mesh. For each new material we find, we add a new render cache to the linked list that handles that material. We also check if each material is set to ignore faces by using the GetIgnoreFace function on the material. This is one of the flags that you can set in the material script. If this is set to true then we don't bother creating a render cache for this material as faces with this material are not supposed to be rendered.

Once this is done, we are ready to start checking the frames of the scene's mesh. Remember that we are looking for frames that contain occluders, object spawners, or player spawn points. This is a long step, so have a look at the code, and then we will discuss it.

```
LinkedList< Frame > *frames = m_mesh->GetFrameList();
```

```
frames->Iterate( true );
while( frames->Iterate() != NULL )
{
  if( strncmp( "oc_", frames->GetCurrent()->Name, 3 ) == 0 )
  {
    m_occludingObjects->Add( new SceneOccluder(
            frames->GetCurrent()->GetTranslation(),
        ( (MeshContainer*)frames->GetCurrent()->pMeshContainer )
                                        ->originalMesh,
          &frames->GetCurrent()->finalTransformationMatrix ) );
    continue;
  }

  if( strncmp( "sp_", frames->GetCurrent()->Name, 3 ) == 0 )
  {
    char *firstDash = strpbrk( frames->GetCurrent()->Name, "_" );
    firstDash++;
    char *lastDash = strrchr( firstDash, '_' );
    unsigned long length = lastDash - firstDash;
    char *name = new char[length + 5];
    ZeroMemory( name, sizeof( char ) * ( length + 5 ) );
    strncpy( name, firstDash, length );
    strcat( name, ".txt" );

    if( stricmp( name, "player.txt" ) == 0 )
    {
      char *radiusName = new char[strlen( firstDash ) + 8];
      ZeroMemory( radiusName, sizeof( char ) *
                            ( strlen( firstDash ) + 8 ) );
      strncpy( radiusName, firstDash, strlen( firstDash ) );
      strcat( radiusName, "_radius" );

      Frame *radiusFrame = frames->GetFirst();
      while( radiusFrame != NULL )
      {
        if( stricmp( radiusFrame->Name, radiusName ) == 0 )
          break;

        radiusFrame = frames->GetNext( radiusFrame );
      }

      SAFE_DELETE_ARRAY( radiusName );
```

```
              float radius = 0.0f;
              if( radiusFrame != NULL )
                radius = D3DXVec3Length( &(radiusFrame->GetTranslation()
                          - frames->GetCurrent()->GetTranslation() ) );

              SceneObject *point = new SceneObject( NULL, NULL );
              point->SetTranslation(
                        frames->GetCurrent()->GetTranslation() );
              point->SetBoundingSphere( D3DXVECTOR3( 0.0f, 0.0f, 0.0f ),
                                          radius );
              point->SetVisible( false );
              point->SetGhost( true );
              point->Update( 0.0f );
              m_dynamicObjects->Add( m_playerSpawnPoints->Add( point ));
           }
           else
           {
              SpawnerObject *spawner = new SpawnerObject( name,
                                                          m_spawnerPath );
              spawner->SetTranslation(
                        frames->GetCurrent()->GetTranslation() );
              spawner->Update( 0.0f );
              m_dynamicObjects->Add( m_objectSpawners->Add( spawner ) );
           }

           SAFE_DELETE_ARRAY( name );
        }
     }
```

You can see that we grab a pointer to the linked list of frames stored by our scene's mesh. The frame hierarchy is not actually stored in a linked list within the .x file, but our Mesh class builds a linked list for us to make it easy to traverse through the hierarchy without putting any importance on ordering (refer to the Mesh class implementation in Mesh.cpp to see how this linked list is built). Once we have this list, we can start to iterate through the list of frames.

We first check if the frame has the "oc_" prefix. If so, we know it contains an occluder so we add a new occluder to the linked list of occluding objects. These are stored using the SceneOccluder structure, and the new occluder is built using the structure's constructor, which we looked at earlier. We just need to pass in the appropriate parameters, which includes the mesh stored in the frame as well as the frame's translation and transformation matrix.

If the frame is not an occluder, we check if it has the "sp_" prefix, which indicates that the frame contains a spawner. If it is a spawner, we need to get the actual name of the spawner, which can be found between the two underscores in the frame's name. By adding the .txt extension to the name, we will arrive at the name of the script used for this spawner. If that script's name happens to be player.txt, then we know that this is a player spawn point, which is predefined in our engine. We then proceed with setting up the player spawn point, which isn't all that complicated; you should be able to see exactly what is happening by just looking at the code. The only interesting aspect is how we search the frame list for the frame that contains the player spawn point's radius point. This is then used to calculate the bounding sphere around the player spawn point as we previously discussed.

If the spawner is not a player spawn point, we know that it is an object spawner and there must be a user-defined script for it. So we proceed with creating a new SpawnerObject and add it to our list of dynamic objects. When we create a new SpawnerObject, we pass in the name of the object spawner's script as well as the global object spawner script path, which is passed to the engine through the EngineSetup structure. The object spawner then sets itself up based on its script as we discussed by in Chapter 9.

TIP

You should notice that our object spawners are also added to a special list called m_objectSpawners, *while our player spawn points are added to their own list called* m_playerSpawnPoints. *This allows you to iterate through just the object spawners, or just the player spawners. Alternatively, you can iterate through the dynamic objects' list to process everything.*

```
bool *validFaces = new bool[
        m_mesh->GetStaticMesh()->originalMesh->GetNumFaces()];
ZeroMemory( validFaces, sizeof( bool ) *
        m_mesh->GetStaticMesh()->originalMesh->GetNumFaces() );

Vertex *vertices = NULL;
unsigned short *indices = NULL;
unsigned long *attributes = NULL;

m_mesh->GetStaticMesh()->originalMesh->LockVertexBuffer(
                        D3DLOCK_READONLY, (void**)&vertices );
m_mesh->GetStaticMesh()->originalMesh->LockIndexBuffer(
                        D3DLOCK_READONLY, (void**)&indices );
m_mesh->GetStaticMesh()->originalMesh->LockAttributeBuffer(
                        D3DLOCK_READONLY, &attributes );
```

The next step involves preparing the scene's vertices and faces for rendering. Before we can begin we need to lock the scene mesh's vertex, index, and attribute buffers. This allows us to access these buffers as you will soon see. You will also notice that we have created an array called validFaces. This is used to flag each face in the scene as either valid or invalid, which we are about to do. A face is considered valid if it uses a material that is supported by one of our render caches. If you recall, we create a render cache for each material that was not set to ignore faces. Therefore, any face that uses a material that ignores faces will not belong to any of the render caches, and therefore will not be rendered. Take a look at the code below, which flags the faces as valid or not.

```
for( unsigned long f = 0; f < m_mesh->GetStaticMesh()
                           ->originalMesh->GetNumFaces(); f++ )
{
  m_renderCaches->Iterate( true );
  while( m_renderCaches->Iterate() )
  {
    if( m_renderCaches->GetCurrent()->GetMaterial()
        == m_mesh->GetStaticMesh()->materials[attributes[f]] )
    {
      m_totalFaces++;
      validFaces[f] = true;
      break;
    }
  }
}


m_faces = new SceneFace[m_totalFaces];

m_totalVertices = m_totalFaces * 3;

g_engine->GetDevice()->CreateVertexBuffer( m_totalVertices *
            VERTEX_FVF_SIZE, D3DUSAGE_WRITEONLY, VERTEX_FVF,
            D3DPOOL_MANAGED, &m_sceneVertexBuffer, NULL );

Vertex *tempVertices = new Vertex[m_totalVertices];
```

After we have flagged all of the faces, the next step is to create one large vertex buffer that stores all of the vertices used only by the faces flagged as being valid. You can see that we create an array of faces called m_faces, which has enough room in it for only our valid faces. After we have created the vertex buffer, we also create an array of vertices that will be used to filter out only the vertices that are used by the valid faces.

```
m_sceneVertexBuffer->Lock( 0, 0, (void**)&m_vertices, 0);

for( f = 0; f < m_totalFaces; f++ )
{
  if( validFaces[f] == false )
  {
    indices += 3;
    continue;
  }

  m_faces[f].vertex0 = *indices++;
  m_faces[f].vertex1 = *indices++;
  m_faces[f].vertex2 = *indices++;

  m_renderCaches->Iterate( true );
  while( m_renderCaches->Iterate() )
  {
    if( m_renderCaches->GetCurrent()->GetMaterial()
        == m_mesh->GetStaticMesh()->materials[attributes[f]] )
    {
      m_faces[f].renderCache = m_renderCaches->GetCurrent();
      m_renderCaches->GetCurrent()->AddFace();
      break;
    }
  }

  tempVertices[m_faces[f].vertex0] =
              vertices[m_faces[f].vertex0];
  tempVertices[m_faces[f].vertex1] =
              vertices[m_faces[f].vertex1];
  tempVertices[m_faces[f].vertex2] =
              vertices[m_faces[f].vertex2];
}
```

We first lock the vertex buffer, and then we begin checking every face in the mesh. If the face is not valid, we simply skip it. If it is valid, we store its indices, allocate it to the render cache that handles its material, and finally store its vertices.

```
memcpy( m_vertices, tempVertices,
        m_totalVertices * VERTEX_FVF_SIZE );


m_sceneVertexBuffer->Unlock();

SAFE_DELETE_ARRAY( tempVertices );


m_mesh->GetStaticMesh()->originalMesh->UnlockAttributeBuffer();
m_mesh->GetStaticMesh()->originalMesh->UnlockIndexBuffer();
m_mesh->GetStaticMesh()->originalMesh->UnlockVertexBuffer();

SAFE_DELETE_ARRAY( validFaces );
```

Once we have all of the valid faces stored properly we can then copy all of the vertices to the vertex buffer using memcpy. Remember that this will only copy the vertices used by the valid faces, as these are the only ones we stored. With that complete, we can unlock our vertex buffer, delete the array of vertices and the array of valid faces, and unlock all the buffers on the scene's mesh.

```
  m_firstLeaf = new SceneLeaf();

  RecursiveSceneBuild( m_firstLeaf,
                       m_mesh->GetBoundingSphere()->center,
                       m_mesh->GetBoundingBox()->halfSize );

  m_renderCaches->Iterate( true );
  while( m_renderCaches->Iterate() )
    m_renderCaches->GetCurrent()->Prepare( m_totalVertices );

  m_loaded = true;
}
```

The final step is to divide our scene up for efficient rendering. We do this by using the RecursiveSceneBuild function. We pass the first leaf to the function, which is the leaf that encloses the entire scene. This function then recursively (i.e., it calls itself) divides the leaves up until the entire scene is broken up into a hierarchy of bounding volumes. Each volume contains a handful of faces that will allow for efficient rendering, as whole sections of the scene can be easily culled away each frame.

Despite the power of the `RecursiveSceneBuild` function, we won't cover it in the book as it is very simple in its implementation. Just take a look at it in `SceneManager.cpp`, and read through the comments. In a nutshell, it creates a `BoundingVolume` for the current leaf, and then creates child leaves as necessary. Once this is done, pointers to the faces and occluders are stored within the leaves that contain them. This is achieved with functions from `Geometry.h` that you were presented with in Chapter 2, so it is only a few lines of code.

Once this is complete, all that is left is to prepare the render caches with a call to `Prepare` on each one. This sets them up ready for rendering. Refer back to Chapter 8 for more details about the render caches.

This completes the code for loading a scene with the scene manager. Look at the actual source code for this as it contains further comments that may help you clear up any gray areas. Other than that, let's move on to updating and rendering the scene.

UPDATING AND RENDERING THE SCENE

We will start by looking at the implementation of the `Update` function of our scene manager, which is shown below. We won't discuss it in detail as you should already be familiar with its workings, to a degree, after the discussion we had about collision detection earlier. If you can remember the example `FrameUpdate` function that we looked at, then you shouldn't have too much trouble understanding this function because it does virtually the same thing.

```
void SceneManager::Update( float elapsed, D3DXMATRIX *view )
{
  if( m_firstLeaf == NULL )
    return;

  m_frameStamp++;

  m_viewFrustum.Update( view );

  m_dynamicObjects->Iterate( true );
  while( m_dynamicObjects->Iterate() )
  {
    if( m_dynamicObjects->GetCurrent()->GetEnabled() == false )
      continue;
```

```
if( m_dynamicObjects->GetCurrent()->GetGhost() == true )
{
  m_dynamicObjects->GetCurrent()->Update( elapsed );
  continue;
}

if( m_dynamicObjects->GetCurrent()->GetEllipsoidRadius().x +
    m_dynamicObjects->GetCurrent()->GetEllipsoidRadius().y,
    m_dynamicObjects->GetCurrent()->GetEllipsoidRadius().z
    <= 0.0f )
{
  m_dynamicObjects->GetCurrent()->Update( elapsed );
  continue;
}

static CollisionData collisionData;
collisionData.scale = m_scale;
collisionData.elapsed = elapsed;
collisionData.frameStamp = m_frameStamp;
collisionData.object = m_dynamicObjects->GetCurrent();
collisionData.gravity = m_gravity * elapsed;

PerformCollisionDetection( &collisionData,
                  (Vertex*)m_vertices, m_faces, m_totalFaces,
                           m_dynamicObjects );

  m_dynamicObjects->GetCurrent()->Update( elapsed, false );
  }
}
```

You can see how the frame stamp is incremented and the view frustum is updated each frame. Other than that, the only step is to update all of the objects in the scene. This is just a matter of iterating through the list of dynamic objects and performing collision detection on each one where necessary.

Objects that are not enabled are skipped entirely, and objects that are set as ghosts are updated but do not have any collision detection performed on them. We also avoid performing collision detection on any objects that do not have an ellipsoid bounding volume around them. Obviously, without a bounding volume the object cannot collide with anything, so we can skip the processing entirely. If the object passes all of these tests, we then proceed with the collision detection and update it accordingly. This is virtually the same as what we looked at earlier when we discussed collision detection. You should be able to pick up the similarities immediately.

As you can see this is not too exciting. However, a much more exciting function is the render function. This is where it all happens—where we bring our scene to life! Let's step through the implementation of the render function.

```
void SceneManager::Render( float elapsed, D3DXVECTOR3 viewer )
{
  if( m_firstLeaf == NULL )
    return;

  m_visibleOccluders->ClearPointers();

  RecursiveSceneFrustumCheck( m_firstLeaf, viewer );
```

First, we need to ensure that there is a scene leaf hierarchy to process. If not, we cannot render the scene. If so, we can proceed by clearing the list of pointers to the visible occluders. This list is populated each frame with pointers to any occluders that are visible in the current frame. Since we are at the start of a new rendering frame, this list will contain the pointers to the visible occluders from the last frame, so we need to clear it now. Once that is done we can begin the first step of culling, which is to perform view frustum culling on the scene using the RecursiveScene-FrustumCheck function. This is a recursive function that descends through the scene leaf hierarchy culling away the leaves that fall outside the view frustum. We will look at this function in more detail later in this chapter.

```
  m_visibleOccluders->Iterate( true );
  while( m_visibleOccluders->Iterate() )
  {
    if( m_visibleOccluders->GetCurrent()->visibleStamp
        != m_frameStamp )
      continue;

    BuildOcclusionVolume( m_visibleOccluders->GetCurrent(),
                          viewer );

    SceneOccluder *occludee = m_visibleOccluders->GetNext(
                        m_visibleOccluders->GetCurrent() );
    while( occludee != NULL )
    {
      if( IsSphereOverlappingVolume(
              m_visibleOccluders->GetCurrent()->planes,
              occludee->translation,
              occludee->GetBoundingSphere()->radius ) == true )
```

```
    if( IsBoxEnclosedByVolume(
                m_visibleOccluders->GetCurrent()->planes,
                occludee->GetBoundingBox()->min,
                occludee->GetBoundingBox()->max ) == true )
        occludee->visibleStamp--;

    occludee = m_visibleOccluders->GetNext( occludee );
  }
 }
```

The next step is to build up the occlusion volumes for any occluders that were found to be visible after performing the view frustum culling. During view frustum culling, m_visibleOccluders will have been populated with pointers to all of the occluders found to be visible in the current frame. We can now iterate through this list, building occlusion volumes for each one using the BuildOcclusionVolume function, which will be covered later in this chapter.

After an occluder's occlusion volume has been built, we can then use that occlusion volume to check if any of the other visible occluders are hidden inside the occlusion volume. If you can recall, we keep track of the distance that each occluder is from the viewer, which is used to sort the visible occluders from front to back (i.e., closest to the viewer first). This is all done inside the RecursiveSceneFrustumCheck function, so the m_visibleOccluders list is sorted. This means that we can iterate through the rest of the list (from the current visible occluder) and check if any of the distant occluders are concealed, which is exactly what we are doing in the previous code snippet. To do this, we just use a couple of the utility functions provided in Geometry.h.

You will notice that we first use IsSphereOverlappingVolume, then IsBox-EnclosedByVolume. The reason for this is that it is computationally cheaper to test a bounding sphere than a bounding box. Since the bounding sphere test catches most of the hidden occluders, we don't have to check the bounding box very often. The performance improvement gained by checking the bounding sphere first outweighs the performance penalty of having to check both bounding volumes in the relatively small number of cases.

```
m_renderCaches->Iterate( true );
while( m_renderCaches->Iterate() )
  m_renderCaches->GetCurrent()->Begin();

RecursiveSceneOcclusionCheck( m_firstLeaf );
```

Now that we have identified exactly which occluders are visible, we can proceed to check the rest of the scene leaves (i.e., those that passed the view frustum check) against the occlusion volumes of the visible occluders. This is achieved with a call to the RecursiveSceneOcclusionCheck function. This is another recursive function, which we will further discuss later in this chapter.

You will also notice that we instruct each of our render caches to prepare for rendering with a call to Begin. This allows the render caches to accept the indices of faces that are flagged as visible this frame. The RecursiveSceneOcclusionCheck function takes care of this, as it is the last visibility test performed on the scene. Therefore, any faces that pass this test are likely to be visible.

```
D3DXMATRIX world;
D3DXMatrixIdentity( &world );
g_engine->GetDevice()->SetTransform( D3DTS_WORLD, &world );

g_engine->GetDevice()->SetStreamSource( 0, m_sceneVertexBuffer,
                                        0, VERTEX_FVF_SIZE );
g_engine->GetDevice()->SetFVF( VERTEX_FVF );

m_renderCaches->Iterate( true );
while( m_renderCaches->Iterate() )
  m_renderCaches->GetCurrent()->End();
```

To render the scene, we first need to set the world matrix to the identity matrix, which enures that our scene is rendered at the origin of 3D space (0.0, 0.0, 0.0). We then need to tell DirectX where to get the vertices from by setting the stream source to the scene's vertex buffer using the SetStreamSource function on the device. This gives DirectX access to the vertices that are used by the valid faces in our scene's mesh. In addition, we also need to set the flexible vertex format used by the vertices by calling SetFVF on the device. This tells DirectX how each vertex is structured so they can be read correctly.

To complete the rendering, we need to call End on each of our render caches. This causes each render cache in turn to set its material and texture and then send its indices to DirectX to be rendered. DirectX then uses these indices to reference the vertices in the vertex buffer that we just set. In theory, once this is complete, all of the faces that were deemed to be visible this frame are rendered to the render target and ready to be displayed to the screen.

Now it is time to go through and render any of the dynamic objects in the scene that are visible. This is just a matter of iterating through the m_dynamicObjects linked list and checking each object for visibility. If an object is found to be visible then it is rendered.

```
    m_dynamicObjects->Iterate( true );
    while( m_dynamicObjects->Iterate() )
    {
      if( m_dynamicObjects->GetCurrent()->GetVisible() == false )
        continue;

      if( m_viewFrustum.IsSphereInside( m_dynamicObjects
              ->GetCurrent()->GetBoundingSphere()->centre,
                m_dynamicObjects->GetCurrent()->GetBoundingSphere()
              ->radius ) == false )
        continue;

      bool occluded = false;
      m_visibleOccluders->Iterate( true );
      while( m_visibleOccluders->Iterate() )
      {
        if( m_visibleOccluders->GetCurrent()->visibleStamp
            != m_frameStamp )
          continue;

        occluded = true;

        m_visibleOccluders->GetCurrent()->planes->Iterate( true );
        while( m_visibleOccluders->GetCurrent()->planes->Iterate() )
        {
          if( D3DXPlaneDotCoord( m_visibleOccluders->GetCurrent()
            ->planes->GetCurrent(), &m_dynamicObjects->GetCurrent()
            ->GetBoundingSphere()->center ) < m_dynamicObjects
            ->GetCurrent()->GetBoundingSphere()->radius )
          {
            occluded = false;
            break;
          }
        }

        if( occluded == true )
          break;
      }

      if( occluded == true )
        continue;

      m_dynamicObjects->GetCurrent()->Render();
    }
}
```

As you can see, we first check the bounding sphere of the object against the view frustum. If it passes this test, we then need to iterate through the list of visible occluders and check if the object's bounding sphere falls outside any of the planes that make up each occluder. If it does, it is not concealed by the occluder. Once we find an occluder that completely conceals the object, we can skip it. Otherwise, the object needs to be rendered.

We have now covered the three main functions of the scene manager that you are going to interact with when writing the game in Part II. However, there are a few internal functions that we still need to look at, which we previously used.

BUILDING OCCLUSION VOLUMES

When we were rendering the scene we used a function called BuildOcclusionVolume, which is used to build an occlusion volume from an occluder based on the viewer's location in 3D space. So let's have a look at this function and see how it works.

```
void SceneManager::BuildOcclusionVolume( SceneOccluder *occluder,
                                         D3DXVECTOR3 viewer )
{
   LinkedList< Edge > *edges = new LinkedList< Edge >;
```

The function takes as input a point to the SceneOccluder that we want to build an occlusion volume for, as well as the location of the viewer (or camera) in 3D space. The first step in the function is to create a linked list of edges. This list is used to build up a list of edges around the extent or border of the occluder from the viewer's point of view. An example is shown in Figure 10.13.

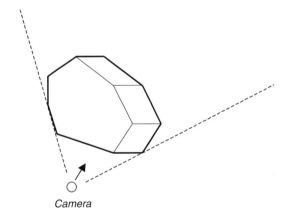

Camera

FIGURE 10.13 The edges of an occluder object from the viewer's point of view.

```
for( unsigned long f = 0; f < occluder->totalFaces; f++ )
{
  unsigned short index0 = occluder->indices[3 * f + 0];
  unsigned short index1 = occluder->indices[3 * f + 1];
  unsigned short index2 = occluder->indices[3 * f + 2];

  if( D3DXVec3Dot( &occluder->vertices[index0].normal,
      &( occluder->vertices[index0].translation - viewer ) )
      < 0.0f )
  {
    if( edges->GetTotalElements() == 0 )
    {
      edges->Add( new Edge( &occluder->vertices[index0],
                            &occluder->vertices[index1] ) );
      edges->Add( new Edge( &occluder->vertices[index1],
                            &occluder->vertices[index2] ) );
      edges->Add( new Edge( &occluder->vertices[index2],
                            &occluder->vertices[index0] ) );
    }
    else
    {
      Edge *found0 = NULL;
      Edge *found1 = NULL;
      Edge *found2 = NULL;

      edges->Iterate( true );
      while( edges->Iterate() != NULL )
      {
        if( ( edges->GetCurrent()->vertex0->translation ==
                occluder->vertices[index0].translation &&
                edges->GetCurrent()->vertex1->translation ==
                occluder->vertices[index1].translation ) ||
              ( edges->GetCurrent()->vertex0->translation ==
                occluder->vertices[index1].translation &&
                edges->GetCurrent()->vertex1->translation ==
                occluder->vertices[index0].translation ) )
          found0 = edges->GetCurrent();

        if( ( edges->GetCurrent()->vertex0->translation ==
                occluder->vertices[index1].translation &&
                edges->GetCurrent()->vertex1->translation ==
                occluder->vertices[index2].translation ) ||
              ( edges->GetCurrent()->vertex0->translation ==
                occluder->vertices[index2].translation &&
```

```
                        edges->GetCurrent()->vertex1->translation ==
                        occluder->vertices[index1].translation ) )
              found1 = edges->GetCurrent();

          if( ( edges->GetCurrent()->vertex0->translation ==
                  occluder->vertices[index2].translation &&
                  edges->GetCurrent()->vertex1->translation ==
                  occluder->vertices[index0].translation ) ||
                ( edges->GetCurrent()->vertex0->translation ==
                  occluder->vertices[index0].translation &&
                  edges->GetCurrent()->vertex1->translation ==
                  occluder->vertices[index2].translation ) )
              found2 = edges->GetCurrent();
        }

        if( found0 != NULL )
          edges->Remove( &found0 );
        else
          edges->Add( new Edge( &occluder->vertices[index0],
                                &occluder->vertices[index1] ) );

        if( found1 != NULL )
          edges->Remove( &found1 );
        else
          edges->Add( new Edge( &occluder->vertices[index1],
                                &occluder->vertices[index2] ) );

        if( found2 != NULL )
          edges->Remove( &found2 );
        else
          edges->Add( new Edge( &occluder->vertices[index2],
                                &occluder->vertices[index0] ) );
      }
    }
  }
```

We iterate through each face in the occluding object and check if the face is directed toward the viewer. Faces on the back side of the object are considered to be facing away from the viewer and therefore are ignored. Whenever a visible face is found, we need to add its edges to the edge list, so long as they are the only instance of the edge. In other words, we check all of the other edges already in the edge list to see if the new edges are already in the list. If they are, then we remove the edge from the list, otherwise we add it to the list.

The reason we need to remove duplicate edges is because only unique edges can form the boundary of the object. Since an edge is shared by two faces, then if both faces are visible, the shared edge registers twice. This means that the edge is an internal edge and therefore does not constitute the boundary of the object from the viewer's point of view. Figure 10.14 illustrates the situation.

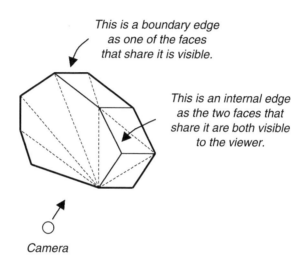

FIGURE 10.14 The difference between an internal edge and a boundary edge.

```
occluder->planes->Empty();

D3DXPLANE *plane = new D3DXPLANE;
D3DXPlaneFromPointNormal( plane, &occluder->translation,
                          &( occluder->translation - viewer ) );
occluder->planes->Add( plane );
```

We now empty the list of planes for this occluder as those planes are from a previous frame and are no longer valid. We then create the front plane for the occlusion volume. This is the plane that faces the viewer and is positioned where the occluder is. It prevents objects in front of the occluder (those between the viewer and the occluder) from being occluded. To create the plane we use the `D3DXPlane-FromPointNormal` function provided by the D3DX library. We use the position of the occluder to position the plane, and then the normal between the occluder's position and the viewer's position in order to derive the correct orientation for the plane.

Specifying a normal that goes from the viewer to the plane would give you a backward-facing plane that would result in incorrect occlusion tests.

```
edges->Iterate( true );
while( edges->Iterate() != NULL )
{
    D3DXVECTOR3 vertex1 = edges->GetCurrent()->vertex0
                                        ->translation;
    D3DXVECTOR3 vertex2 = edges->GetCurrent()->vertex1
                                        ->translation;

    D3DXVECTOR3 dir = vertex1 - viewer;
    D3DXVec3Normalize( &dir, &dir );
    D3DXVECTOR3 vertex3 = vertex1 + dir;

    plane = new D3DXPLANE;
    D3DXPlaneFromPoints( plane, &vertex1, &vertex2, &vertex3 );
    occluder->planes->Add( plane );
}

SAFE_DELETE( edges );
}
```

Once the front plane is created, we can then iterate through the list of edges, which will only contain the actual boundary edges from the viewer's point of view. For each edge we create a plane is positioned where the edge is and has the same orientation as the edge. This gives us an enclosed volume that extends away from the occluding object indefinitely. In other words, the volume is not capped with a far plane like the view frustum is.

We are almost at the end now and you have probably had just about enough of this scene manager. Hang in there just a little longer as we only have two more functions to look at. Actually, there are a few more than that, but we won't cover them all in the book as they are relatively easy. We are only looking at the complex ones, which means if you can follow along with these then you will have no trouble understanding the others.

PERFORMING CULLING

Now we are hitting the real workhorse of the scene manager. The next two functions that we are about to look at provide all of the culling for our scene manager. They are both recursive functions, which operate in exactly the same manner. The only difference is one culls the scene based on the view frustum while the other culls the scene based on the occlusion frustums or volumes. So let's go through the first of the two—the RecursiveSceneFrustumCheck function.

```
bool SceneManager::RecursiveSceneFrustumCheck( SceneLeaf *leaf,
                                               D3DXVECTOR3 viewer )
{
  if( m_viewFrustum.IsSphereInside(
                    leaf->GetBoundingSphere()->center,
                    leaf->GetBoundingSphere()->radius ) == false )
    return false;

  if( m_viewFrustum.IsBoxInside( leaf->GetBoundingBox()->min,
                        leaf->GetBoundingBox()->max ) == false )
    return false;

  leaf->visibleStamp = m_frameStamp;
```

These first few lines are all that are needed to perform the actual frustum check for a single leaf in the scene. We first check the bounding sphere of the leaf that was passed into the function and then we check its bounding box. Once again we do this for performance reasons, and if the leaf passes both tests we can set its visible stamp. Then we move on to its children to see if any of them are visible, which is where the recursive side of the function comes into play.

The beauty of this approach is that if a leaf fails (in other words it is not visible), then we are assured that none of its children are visible. This means we can effectively cut out an entire branch of the tree by just checking one leaf.

```
    char visibleChildren = 0;
    for( char c = 0; c < 8; c++ )
      if( leaf->children[c] != NULL )
        if( RecursiveSceneFrustumCheck( leaf->children[c], viewer ))
          visibleChildren++;

    if( visibleChildren > 0 )
      return false;
```

Here you can see how we go through all eight of the leaf's children, checking each one with a recursive check. This in turn checks their children and so on down the tree. This recursive process stops when you reach the end of a branch, or you find a leaf that has no visible children. It then returns to a previous leaf with an unexplored branch and continues down that new branch. This process continues until the entire hierarchy is processed.

```
leaf->occluders->Iterate( true );
while( leaf->occluders->Iterate() )
{
  if( m_viewFrustum.IsSphereInside(
            leaf->occluders->GetCurrent()->translation,
            leaf->occluders->GetCurrent()->GetBoundingSphere()
                                        ->radius ) == false )
    continue;

  if( m_viewFrustum.IsBoxInside(
          leaf->occluders->GetCurrent()->GetBoundingBox()->min,
          leaf->occluders->GetCurrent()->GetBoundingBox()->max )
          == false )
    continue;

  leaf->occluders->GetCurrent()->distance =
  D3DXVec3Length( &( leaf->occluders->GetCurrent()->translation
  - viewer ) );
```

Once we have reached the end of a branch we can then begin to check the occluders that are stored in the leaf at the end of the branch, since this data is only stored in the end leaves. The leaves that contain children do not store occluders.

We go through each occluder that is stored in this leaf and check if it is visible. Once again, we determine this by first checking the bounding sphere and then the bounding box around the occluder. If the occluder is visible we then calculate the distance between the viewer and the occluder so that it can be sorted in the list.

```
m_visibleOccluders->Iterate( true );
while( m_visibleOccluders->Iterate() )
{
  if( leaf->occluders->GetCurrent()
      == m_visibleOccluders->GetCurrent() )
    break;

  if( leaf->occluders->GetCurrent()->distance
      < m_visibleOccluders->GetCurrent()->distance )
  {
```

```
            m_visibleOccluders->InsertBefore( leaf->occluders
                ->GetCurrent(), m_visibleOccluders->GetCompleteElement
                ( m_visibleOccluders->GetCurrent() ) );
            leaf->occluders->GetCurrent()->visibleStamp
                                                = m_frameStamp;
            break;
        }
    }
}
```

We then need to iterate through the list of visible occluders to ensure that this occluder is not already in the list. If it is not, we insert it into the list just before the occluder that is the next closest to the viewer. Since the list is sorted, we are guaranteed to find the occluder in the list (if it already exists) before we add it to the list. This prevents us from adding the same occluder twice.

```
    if( leaf->occluders->GetCurrent()->visibleStamp
        != m_frameStamp )
    {
      m_visibleOccluders->Add( leaf->occluders->GetCurrent() );
      leaf->occluders->GetCurrent()->visibleStamp = m_frameStamp;
    }
  }


  return true;
}
```

Finally, we need to check if the occluder was not added to the list. This will occur if the occluder is further away from the viewer than any of the other occluders already in the list. If this occurs we then need to add the occluder to the end of the list.

That wraps up the view frustum culling algorithm. Any scene leaf that was determined visible this frame will have its visible stamp set to the current frame stamp. This information is then used in the next function that we are going to look at, which performs the occlusion culling—the RecursiveSceneOcclusionCheck function.

```
    void SceneManager::RecursiveSceneOcclusionCheck( SceneLeaf *leaf )
    {
      if( leaf->visibleStamp != m_frameStamp )
        return;

      m_visibleOccluders->Iterate( true );
      while( m_visibleOccluders->Iterate() )
      {
```

```
    if( m_visibleOccluders->GetCurrent()->visibleStamp
        != m_frameStamp )
      continue;

    if( IsSphereOverlappingVolume(
                    m_visibleOccluders->GetCurrent()->planes,
                    leaf->GetBoundingSphere()->centre,
                    leaf->GetBoundingSphere()->radius ) == true )
      if( IsBoxEnclosedByVolume(
                    m_visibleOccluders->GetCurrent()->planes,
                    leaf->GetBoundingBox()->min,
                    leaf->GetBoundingBox()->max ) == true )
        return;
  }
```

As soon as we enter the function we check if the visible stamp of the passed-in scene leaf is set to the current frame stamp. If not, we know that it was culled by the view frustum so we don't need to bother checking it here as it is already deemed to be hidden. If the leaf is visible, we need to iterate through the list of visible occluders to test the scene leaf against their occlusion volumes. As usual, this is just a matter of checking the bounding sphere of the scene leaf against the occlusion volume then the bounding box of the scene leaf. If either of these tests fails, we know that the scene leaf was occluded and we can skip it.

```
    for( char c = 0; c < 8; c++ )
      if( leaf->children[c] != NULL )
        RecursiveSceneOcclusionCheck( leaf->children[c] );
```

If the scene leaf is visible, we then move on to checking each of its children. This is recursive in nature just like the last function, so it will check the entire scene leaf hierarchy for us. Once a leaf's children have been processed, the next step is to register any faces that are stored in this leaf for rendering.

```
    for( unsigned long f = 0; f < leaf->totalFaces; f++ )
    {
      if( m_faces[leaf->faces[f]].renderStamp == m_frameStamp )
        continue;

      m_faces[leaf->faces[f]].renderStamp = m_frameStamp;

      m_faces[leaf->faces[f]].renderCache->RenderFace(
                              m_faces[leaf->faces[f]].vertex0,
                              m_faces[leaf->faces[f]].vertex1,
                              m_faces[leaf->faces[f]].vertex2 );
```

```
        }
    }
```

You can see that we loop through each face stored in this leaf and check if it has already been registered for rendering. A face can be stored in more than one leaf if it spans across multiple leaves. Therefore, we need to avoid rendering the face multiple times when multiple leaves are visible that all contain the same face. To achieve this we use another stamp: this time a render stamp. This stamp is set to the current frame stamp when the face is registered with its render cache. By skipping faces that have their render stamp set to the current frame stamp, we can prevent them from being registered twice with their render cache.

To register a face for rendering, we call the RenderFace function on the render cache that the face belongs to. This will be the render cache that handles the same material that is applied to the face. All we have to pass to the function are the three indices that make up the face. This way, DirectX knows which vertices from the vertex buffer are used to render this face.

There is a one small problem with our occlusion culling method. That's right, there is a flaw, which has been largely avoided up until now. Rather than trying to explain it, take a look at Figure 10.15 and see if you can spot the problem.

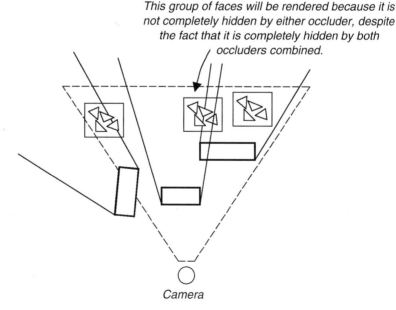

FIGURE 10.15 The flaw in our occlusion culling method exhibited.

As you can see, if something is not completely hidden by a single occluder, it will be rendered. Unfortunately, there is not a lot we can do about it. You can modify the system to take overlap into account, however, this is beyond the scope of our simple engine. The best thing you can do is to try to ensure that you use large objects as occluders. If you have multiple objects next to one another in a scene, then simply create a large invisible occluder that spans all of the smaller objects. If you load up the sample scene (on the CD-ROM) in 3ds max you can see several examples of this. It is next to impossible to achieve the perfect culling system, so don't worry about it too much. As long as it culls most of the hidden surfaces, it will be fine.

ON THE CD

Finally, we have come to the end of one grueling class. You are encouraged to read through the source code with its comments, which will help you to better understand the material we covered. Additionally, there are a number of smaller functions that we didn't touch on, which perform game-related tasks. You will learn more about these as we develop the game, beginning in the next chapter. Finally, we will start with some real fun stuff, but before we get too carried away, we still have a bit more work to do before we can use our new scene manager. Besides, you are probably curious to see the demo for this chapter if you haven't already looked at it.

INTEGRATING THE SCENE MANAGEMENT SYSTEM

The scene manager needs to be integrated into our engine before it is fully functional so let's do that now. Besides the usually linking, there are a few additions to the Engine class. If you look at the Engine class definition in Engine.h you will see that we have added a SceneManager member variable as well as a function for external access of the scene manager.

If you go over to Engine.cpp you can see that we create the scene manager in the Engine class constructor and destroy it in the destructor, per usual. When the scene manager is created, we need to give it a scale to work with and the path to locate the user-defined object spawner scripts, as shown here:

```
m_sceneManager = new SceneManager( m_setup->scale,
                                   m_setup->spawnerPath )
```

If you take a look at the Run function in the Engine class you can see that we now update the scene manager like this:

```
m_sceneManager->Update( elapsed, viewer.viewer->GetViewMatrix() );
```

We also allow the scene manager to render the scene by calling its `Render` function between the calls to `BeginScene` and `EndScene` on the device, as shown here:

```
if( viewer.viewer != NULL )
  m_sceneManager->Render( elapsed,
                          viewer.viewer->GetTranslation() );
```

The scene manager is now fully integrated into our engine and ready for us to load in a scene. This completes our engine, so let's have a look at the test application for this chapter, which will show off pretty much everything our engine can do.

TESTING THE SCENE MANAGEMENT SYSTEM

Now comes the exciting part, the test application, which is the best so far. You can find the test application in the `Test` project of the workspace for this chapter. Despite the fact that it is the most impressive test application you have seen so far, there really isn't all that much to it. This is because we have made several key assumptions about the type of game we will build with this engine so we can automate a lot of the tasks within the engine that would normally have to be handled by the game. In addition, we are using scripts to handle our scene and the objects within it, which takes a lot of pressure off the need to hard code everything. This results in smaller, easier to understand code.

If you take a look at the `Load` function of our `TestState` class, you can see that we only need one line of code to load our scene and a few lines of code to set up a camera that we can fly around the scene, as shown here:

```
g_engine->GetSceneManager()->LoadScene( "Abandoned City.txt",
                                        "./Assets/" );

g_engine->GetSceneManager()->AddObject( m_viewer
                                        = new SceneObject );
m_viewer->SetTranslation( 0.0f, 0.0f, 0.0f );
m_viewer->SetFriction( 5.0f );
```

In the `Update` function of our `TestState` class, we just have a few lines of code that allow us to move our virtual camera around the scene using the mouse to look around and the w, a, s, d keys to move. Figure 10.16 shows a screen shot from the test application.

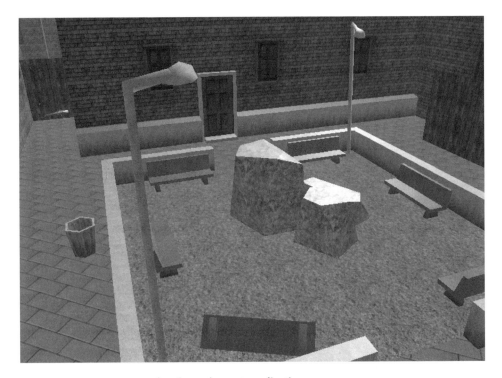

FIGURE 10.16 A screen shot from the test application.

EXERCISES

Before you complete this part of the book and move on to developing the game, take a minute or two to try these short exercises that will help you understand how the system works.

■ See if you can make the camera object you control be affected by collision detection and gravity.
■ Try to alter the scene to create a nighttime effect.

Employing collision detection really isn't that hard; all you need to do is register the object with the scene manager so that it has control over the object, and ensure the object has a bounding volume. You already have the first base covered, as the camera object is registered with the scene manager. You simply give it a bounding volume and the scene manager immediately applies collision detection and gravity to the object, as shown in this example:

```
m_viewer->SetBoundingSphere( D3DXVECTOR3( 0.0f, 0.0f, 0.0f ),
                 60.0f, D3DXVECTOR3( 1.0f, 1.0f, 1.0f ) );
```

Altering the scene to achieve a nighttime effect isn't difficult either. All you need to do is adjust the lighting and fog effects in the scene script. With these properties in the scene script, you can create everything from a moonlit night scene to a Martian planet scene with red lighting and thick green fog. Go ahead and try it.

SUMMARY

We have come to the end of this long chapter and with that, the end of Part I. In this chapter, we covered many important topics about scene management, including culling, collision detection, and scene rendering. This completes our engine with which we can build our game. So without wasting any more time, let's move on to Part II where we will begin to build our game.

Part

II

The Game

We have come a long way and our engine is finally mature enough to use in the development of our very own FPS. This part of the book is relatively short (only three chapters). Despite the fact that there is a lot of information crammed into the upcoming chapters, the main reason for so few chapters is simply because building our game is not that difficult. There really isn't a lot that needs to be done.

Due to the design decisions we made with the engine, it turns out that the engine is capable of handling most of the basic tasks for us. In fact, it automates so much that even some of the complex tasks appear mundane. Take a look at the test application for Chapter 10. You can see from there that with just a few lines of code we can have a complete 3D scene running, with object spawners and collision detection. We can even move around this 3D scene like we are playing a game. The amazing part is that all of this is running within the engine. So just think of all the exciting game features we can spend time on, knowing that the engine will take care of the basics for us.

Finally, bear in mind that the design and implementation we will use for our game is one of countless possible scenarios. Therefore, it will have its strengths and it will also have its weaknesses. The bottom line is, if you reach the end of the book and realize that you don't like the way we did something, then just change it. In fact, you can scrap the whole game and start again with the engine as your foundation. With that said, let's begin with Chapter 11 where we will lay down the foundations for our new game.

11 Foundations

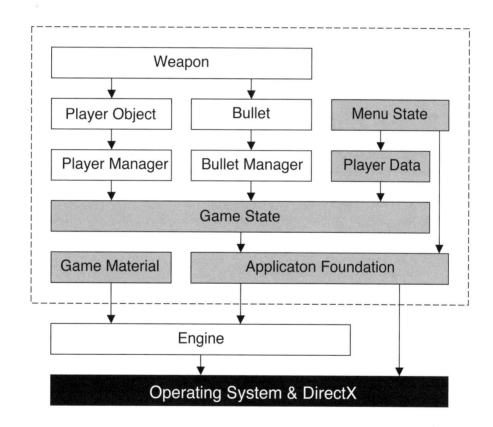

In This Chapter

■ Cover the basic design of our FPS game.

■ Look at some of the foundational data for our game, such as the custom game material.

■ Implement the two states that will control our game: the menu state and the game state.

ON THE CD

If you have followed through all of Part I then congratulations on completing the engine that we are about to use to build our own FPS. If you struggled to understand the workings of the engine, this part of the book should help clarify many aspects of the engine as we flex all of its muscles. You can find the workspace for this chapter in the /Source/Chapter 11/ directory on the CD-ROM.

GAME DESIGN

You are probably eager to start building something you can actually play with. So far we have been implementing underlying engine functionality, which can sometimes become a little mundane, especially when there is no real visual payoff. Now it is time to begin working on a playable game; but before we do that we need to lay out what we have in mind. In other words, we need to do a little design. We aren't going to spend an entire chapter on it, but we should at least identify what we are trying to achieve.

Obviously, we are creating a FPS, so we are going to need many of the basic elements that you find in a typical FPS game, which include:

■ A simple game-play experience where players fight each other individually to score frags, while trying to stay alive. This is often referred to as a *deathmatch* game.

■ An environment for the game to take place in. This is usually called a map or level (or scene as we refer to it).

■ A movable object for each player to control in the game, which is sometimes called a *character* or *player*. A typical FPS represents the players as animated human characters.

■ Multiple weapons, which are used by the players to score frags on one another. Guns are the most typical weapons found in a FPS and come in various shapes and sizes, each firing some sort of projectile.

■ Collectible objects, allowing players to move around and collect better weapons. When a player collects more than one weapon, the player should be able to change between them.

These represent the most fundamental building blocks for any FPS; of course, there are many other features we can add, but the emphasis is on the word *features*. This means that from the above list, we can create a simple game whereby two or more players can move around a 3D environment, collecting weapons, and fighting each other in an effort to increase their frag count while avoiding being fragged themselves. As you can see, this is the basis of any typical FPS. Although it may not be the most exciting of game play as is, it is playable and that's a start. Once this basic game is done, it will be quite easy to add any new *features*, which will increase the enjoyment of the game.

Before we discuss adding new features to the game, let's take a look at the fundamental components in a little more detail. If we review our short requirements list, we can identify three key areas of functionality:

1. Game play or game logic
2. Players
3. Weapons

We will begin our discussion with game play. The best way to think of game play (or game logic) is to imagine it like the rules of the game. Take a typical board game for example. It has a board, some playing pieces, and a rule book. The board and the pieces are there to facilitate the game play and are akin to our later areas of functionality (i.e., the players and the weapons). The rule book represents the game play as it outlines the rules of play and guides the players through the game. Of course, the rule book cannot create game play on its own; it also needs players to carry out actions in the game. The rule book merely provides boundaries for the players and maintains the structure and integrity of the game play.

Implementing game play into a computer game is not straightforward. It is not as easy as just creating a new class called `GameLogic` (or something like that), which contains all the rules of the game. The game logic has to permeate through the entire game in order to work properly. For example, you wouldn't create a `Players` class that contains all of the functionality for the players and then create a separate class that dictates how a player works in the game. Instead, you would implement the game logic for players directly into the `Players` class, which allows the `Players` class to manage a player in its entirety. This approach allows you to build a modular game with greater flexibility.

If you decide that you don't like the way the players work, rather than having to filter all the player-related game logic out of the game, you can simply scrap the `Players` class and rebuild a new one without severely affecting the rest of the game. You will see how we will build our game using this approach, which means that we will have no single point in the implementation that defines the game logic. It will be spread through the game's implementation and each component will manage its related area of game logic. There will, however, be a foundational level that will support the game logic, which is what we will implement later in this chapter. Before we do, let's have a look at the other two primary areas of functionality.

The second fundamental area of functionality is the players. In terms of the game's implementation, the players are handled by four separate entities. The first is the player's mesh, which is just a simple animated mesh of a human character. The second entity is the character script, which is a very short script that gives the game some basic information about the character mesh. The third entity is a class to manage a single player in the game. It stores all the data for a single player, which means that if there are four players in the game, then there are four instances of this class. The final entity is a player management class, which tracks each player in the game and manages the interactions between them. We will leave the discussion of this topic for now, as the next chapter will cover it in much more detail.

The final primary area of implementation is the weapons. What fun would a FPS be without weapons? The weapons are probably the most complex aspect of the game's implementation, which is why we will leave that topic until the last chapter. But to quickly touch on it, the weapons are made up of several entities, just like the players. The first entity consists of the weapon meshes—that's right, there is more than one per weapon. Each weapon has two meshes, one is used for the first person view and the other is used for the third person view (i.e., what the other players see when you run past them). The second entity is the script, which is used to define the properties of the weapon such as how fast it shoots and how much damage it does. The third entity is the class that manages a single weapon, and the final entity consists of two classes for managing the projectiles (or bullets) that are fired from the weapons. Combined, these classes allow a player to hold and fire a weapon, and have a bullet fly through the scene until it hits something.

From this discussion you should have a clear understanding of the fundamental building blocks of a basic FPS, which makes it quite obvious as to what our game must do. Before we move on though, take a look at Figure 11.1 that shows how each of the key components fit together. Although all of the components theoretically have the ability to communicate with each other (and most do in one small way or another), the arrows on the diagram indicate the major flow of information among the components. The area inside the dotted square bounds the implementation of our game and the lightly shaded components indicate what we will implement in this chapter. It may seem like a large slice of the pie, but it really isn't, as you will soon see. So let's move to the next step and learn how to integrate our engine into the new project so that we can build a game using it.

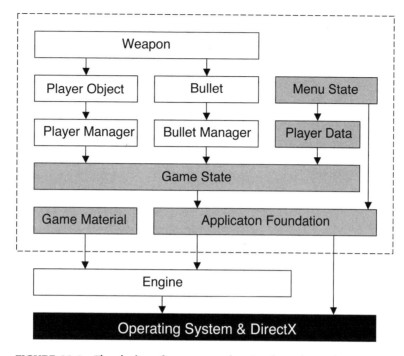

FIGURE 11.1 The design of our game, showing how the major components fit together.

INTEGRATING THE ENGINE

Before we can begin to implement our game and make use of the various classes and functions created in our engine, we need to include the engine into our project so that the compiler can link everything correctly.

In order to use our engine, we need to include two files in our project. The first of these files is the library (.lib) file that is created when we compile our engine. This gives the complier access to the functionality of our engine, which is compiled into this library file. The second file that we need is the header file. In fact, we need all the header files used by our engine as they constitute the interfaces between our game and our engine. In other words, the interfaces allow our game to communicate with the engine. Fortunately, we made a decision early in the engine's conception that we wanted a single point of contact. This means that we only have to include one header file in our project, and it does the rest.

If you recall, we used the `Engine.h` file as our single point of contact. Whenever we created a new header file, we immediately included it in `Engine.h`. One benefit of this is that the header files contained in `Engine.h` are accessible by the entire engine, as every component included `Engine.h`. An added benefit is that now we only have to include this one header file in our game project, and the compiler automatically includes all the rest for us, as they are included inside `Engine.h`.

The following shows the code for including the engine's header file and the library file into the game project. You can also find this code in `Main.h` in the workspace for this chapter.

```
#include "..\Engine\Engine.h"
#pragma comment( lib, "../Engine/Engine.lib" )
```

That's it! With those two lines of code we have successfully linked our new game project to our engine. Now we are ready to begin to implement our game and make use of all the features of our engine.

NOTE

Although we are not including any of the other header files used by our engine, they are still being indirectly included through `Engine.h`. Therefore, our game project needs access to all of them along with the library file. If you look in the /`Source`/ `Chapter 11`/ directory on the CD-ROM you will see another directory called `Engine`. This is where the library file and all the header files have been placed for use by our game. If you modify the engine and recompile a new library file (or modify any of the header files) and you want the changes to be included in your project, then you will need to update the files in this directory. This is as easy as copying the new library and/or header files into the directory and overwriting the old ones.

INITIALIZING THE ENGINE

The first function you are likely to write when starting any new project is the `WinMain` function, which you know is the entry point to the application. Now that our game project is linked to our engine, we can proceed with writing the `WinMain` function, which initializes and runs our engine. In essence, we are just filling out an `EngineSetup` structure, creating an instance of the `Engine` class, and then calling `Run` on that instance. Throughout the past 10 chapters, you have seen this done a number of times in the test applications; it should be familiar to you now, so we won't bother discussing it any further. Take a look at the code for the `WinMain` function, which can be found in `Main.cpp`.

```
int WINAPI WinMain( HINSTANCE instance, HINSTANCE prev,
                    LPSTR cmdLine, int cmdShow )
{
  GUID guid = { 0xd6c55c78, 0x5030, 0x43b7,
              { 0x85, 0xa9, 0xc, 0x8b, 0xbe, 0x77, 0x5a, 0x62 } };

  EngineSetup setup;
  setup.instance = instance;
  setup.guid = guid;
  setup.name = "Cityscape";
  setup.scale = 0.01f;
  setup.totalBackBuffers = 1;
  setup.HandleNetworkMessage = HandleNetworkMessage;
  setup.StateSetup = StateSetup;
  setup.CreateMaterialResource = CreateMaterialResource;
  setup.spawnerPath = "./Assets/Objects/";

  new Engine( &setup );
  g_engine->Run();

  return true;
}
```

As previously mentioned, if you have followed along through the entire book so far, you should have no problems identifying each of the EngineSetup structure properties. You will notice that we are using the three call-back function pointers, HandleNetworkMessage, StateSetup, and CreateMaterialResource. Let's look at the first two now. The last one we will discuss a little later.

When we implemented our networking system in Chapter 7, we introduced the HandleNetworkMessage property to the EngineSetup structure. You learned how this property is used to give the engine a pointer to a function that can be called whenever a user-defined network message arrives for processing. In other words, if a network message arrives that the engine cannot identify and handle, it passes it to your application using this call-back function pointer to give you an opportunity to handle the message. The following code shows what our call-back function actually does when the engine calls it:

```
void HandleNetworkMessage( ReceivedMessage *msg )
{
  if( g_engine->GetCurrentState()->GetID() != STATE_GAME )
    return;
```

```
    ( (Game*)g_engine->GetCurrentState() )
                    ->HandleNetworkMessage( msg );
}
```

Our game is going to use two states (which we will implement soon): a menu state and a game state. Although there can be network activity during the menu state (such as enumerating, hosting, or joining sessions), none of it is actually user-defined; they are just system messages that the engine can handle. The only time we will ever need a user-defined message is during game play, which means that the engine must be in the game state. To prevent our game from accidentally processing game-related messages when it is not in a game, we first check which state the engine is in. If it is in the game state, then we proceed to process the incoming user-defined network message by calling HandleNetworkMessage on our game state.

CAUTION

The HandleNetworkMessage function will be specifically implemented into our game state, therefore removing the check for the game state will cause the application to crash when it attempts to access the HandleNetworkMessage function on a state that does not have it.

The second call-back function pointer is StateSetup, which we have seen many times before. The only real difference is that we are adding two states to our engine rather than just one as we did when we were using our traditional test state. The code for the StateSetup function is shown here:

```
void StateSetup()
{
  g_engine->AddState( new Menu, true );
  g_engine->AddState( new Game, false );
}
```

It's really straightforward. You can see that we are adding a Menu class state and a Game class state (both of which will be implemented later in this chapter). You will notice that in the second parameter we pass in true for the menu state and false for the game state. If you remember how our state system works, then you will know that when we add a new state to the engine, we have the option of telling the engine to change to that state immediately. In this case, we have told the engine to switch to the menu state as soon as it is added. The game state is added, but the engine will not change to it—this state will wait quietly until activated. Therefore, the engine will be in the menu state as soon as it processes its first frame.

This completes the initialization of our engine. If it were possible to run the application at this point (we still need to create the state classes that are added to the engine before we can compile and run the application), you would be presented with the Graphics Settings dialog followed by the actual application window that is created based on the settings in the Graphics Settings dialog. Once running, the engine would process frames from the menu state and the only thing you could do is press F12 to exit. This is our blank canvas on which we are going to build our FPS, so let's get on with it.

CUSTOM GAME MATERIAL

The first game-specific component that we are going to implement is our custom game material. If you recall from Chapter 8, we implemented a material system that allows us to create materials that consist of a texture and a script. The script is used to specify properties of the material, such as how it handles lighting. You should also remember that a material is a resource, and in our `Resource` class we implemented a call-back function that allows the engine to query the application for user-defined or custom resource loading.

This means that although our engine supports basic materials, the presence of the call-back resource creation allows us to specify custom material creation within our application. In other words, we can override the engine's basic material loading implementation and replace it with our own version that is specific to the application we are building with the engine—but why would we want to do this? The simple answer is that our engine cannot foresee all the possible ways that we may want to use materials in the future; therefore, it has to be flexible enough to allow us to add to the material system, just like any other resource. The best way to understand this is to look at an example, and the best example to look at is the actual game that we are building.

Currently, our engine can load a material from a material script (which prepares the material in the engine with the correct texture and engine specific properties), which is fine if all we need from the material system is the ability to paint textures on the faces in our scene and have them reflect light correctly. However, in our FPS game we need a little more from our material system; the materials must have the ability to store a sound effect, more specifically a footstep sound effect. When we run around in our scene we want to hear footsteps and we want them to sound like the material that we are stepping on. In other words, if we are running on gravel, we want it to sound like we are running on gravel. If we then step off the gravel and on to a concrete footpath, we want our footsteps to change to reflect that fact that we are now stepping on concrete. We will implement the actual footstep sound playback in the next chapter, but for now we need to implement the infrastructure that will support the footstep sound effects.

To achieve the desired result, we could simply check what material the player is stepping on and then play a sound effect that is appropriate to the material, as shown in the following pseudo code:

```
check material under player
if( material == gravel )
{
  play gravel footstep sound effect
}
else if( material == concrete )
{
  play concrete footstep sound effect
}
```

The problem with this solution is that it is highly inflexible. If we later decide to add a new material, add a new footstep sound effect, or change an existing material or footstep sound effect, we would have to modify and recompile the code every time we made a little change. A far more effective approach is to implement the footstep sound effects directly into the material system. To achieve this we need to add a new optional variable to our material scripts that stores the path and name of a footstep sound effect to play every time that material is stepped on. In fact, we won't stop with just one; we will allow as many footstep sound effects to be added to a material as desired, by simply incrementing a number that is appended to the end of the variable name, as shown in the following example.

```
step_sound0   string ./Assets/Sounds/gravel_footstep0.wav
step_sound1   string ./Assets/Sounds/gravel_footstep1.wav
step_sound2   string ./Assets/Sounds/gravel_footstep2.wav
```

You can see we have a hypothetical gravel material that has three footstep sound effects added to its material script. Since this is optional, you do not have to add any footstep sound effects to a material at all if you do not want the material to play a sound when stepped on (or if you know it will never be stepped on). To handle the loading of our new variable, we need a new class that derives from the engine's Material class. This new class will have the ability to load and store the data for our new footstep sound effects, while still allowing the engine to load the rest of the material (such as its texture and lighting properties). The definition of our new GameMaterial class is shown here, and can also be found in GameMaterial.h:

```
class GameMaterial : public Material
{
public:
  GameMaterial( char *name, char *path = "./" );
  virtual ~GameMaterial();

  Sound *GetStepSound();
```

```
private:
  LinkedList< Sound > *m_stepSounds;
};
```

You can immediately see that the new class has a linked list of Sound resources, which is used to store the sound effects when they are loaded from the script. Now take a look at the constructor for our GameMaterial class, which is shown here and can also be found in GameMaterial.cpp.

```
GameMaterial::GameMaterial( char *name, char *path )
             : Material( name, path )
{
  Script *script = new Script( name, path );

  m_stepSounds = new LinkedList< Sound >;
  char stepSound[16] = { "step_sound0" };
  while( script->GetStringData( stepSound ) != NULL )
  {
    m_stepSounds->Add( new Sound(
                       script->GetStringData( stepSound ) ) );
    sprintf( stepSound, "step_sound%d",
             m_stepSounds->GetTotalElements() );
  }

  SAFE_DELETE( script );
}
```

First, the name and path of the material script is passed through to the Material class, which is essential to allow the base Material class to load the material resource properly. Once that returns, we can proceed with loading the game-specific content from the material script (i.e., the footstep sound effects). This is just a matter of going through the footstep sound effect variables starting with step_sound0, then step_sound1, and so on until the last one is reached. With each new variable we load the sound effect that it points to and store it in the m_stepSounds linked list.

Once this is done, our new game-specific material is loaded and ready to use. Remember that you can add any sort of game-specific data to your material scripts and then load it in the same manner as illustrated here. Some examples include a ricochet sound effect that is played when the material is shot, or a spark sprite (i.e., a small image) that can be rendered when the material is shot. If you use your imagination, you will soon come up with a number of material-related effects you can create with the material system.

There is one last point that we need to cover before we can close this topic—how do we initiate the loading of our game specific materials? This is where the callback resource creation function comes into play, which we discussed earlier. In our

EngineSetup structure we have a member called CreateMaterialResource, which allows us to specify a function in our application that is called by the engine's internal material system every time a new material is created. When the engine's material system calls this function, it passes to it a pointer to the address in memory of the new material that is about to be created, as well as the name and path to the material's script. Your job is to fill the memory of the new material with your own custom material. In other words, this is where you initiate the loading of our game-specific material. You can look at the implementation of this function here, which can also be found in Main.cpp.

```
void CreateMaterialResource( Material **resource, char *name,
                             char *path = "./" )
{
  *resource = new GameMaterial( name, path );
}
```

As you can see it is quite basic. All we do is create a new GameMaterial at the address in memory specified by the engine. The engine will always treat the material as if it is an instance of the Material class, but you will know that it is in fact an instance of the GameMaterial class. The beauty of this is that you can query the material system for a pointer to any material and then cast it into a pointer to a GameMaterial instance, which allows you to make use of the extra data stored by the GameMaterial class, in addition to that stored by the Material class.

Don't worry too much about how the footstep system will work, as we will implement it in the next chapter. For now, let's move on and add the menu state to our game, which in effect is the entry point to our game for the player.

THE MENU STATE

The menu state is really very basic and its only purpose is to house the menu system that we will use to allow the player to enter details such as their name, and perform tasks such as hosting and joining sessions. The menu state is created by overriding the engine's State class, as shown here and can also be found in Menu.h:

```
class Menu : public State
{
public:
  Menu();

  virtual void Update( float elapsed );
};
```

The implementation of our Menu class is very plain indeed. The actual menu itself it represented by a dialog window just like the one we used for our graphics settings dialog. The Update function in the Menu class serves only to display this dialog window. Once displayed, it functions using the MenuDialogProc function, which is a procedure call-back function just like the one used for the graphics settings dialog. If you followed the implementation of the graphics settings dialog, then you will have no trouble understanding the implementation of this dialog, as there are so many similarities. For this reason we won't bother covering it here, but you can have a look at the MenuDialogProc function in Menu.cpp.

Figure 11.2 shows what our menu dialog looks like. As previously mentioned, it is just another dialog like the one used for our graphics settings. Since we need to add the resource file that stores our graphics settings dialog to our new game project (as it is used by our engine), we will add our new menu dialog directly to this same resource file. In the workspace for this chapter, you will see the resource file (which contains the graphics settings dialog and our new menu dialog) has been added to our game project.

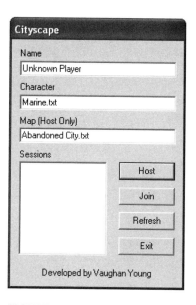

FIGURE 11.2 Our menu dialog.

Before we wrap up this short coverage of the menu state, there is one function that we should look at, which can be found in Menu.cpp. It is the UpdateSessionsList function, which is used to enumerate the network for active sessions and then populate the list box control (on the menu dialog) with the results so that the user can choose a session to join. The implementation of this function is shown here:

```
void UpdateSessionsList( HWND window )
{
  g_engine->GetNetwork()->EnumerateSessions();

  SessionInfo *selectedSession;
  int selected = (int)SendMessage( GetDlgItem( window,
                    IDC_SESSIONS ), LB_GETCURSEL, 0, 0 );
  if( selected != LB_ERR )
    selectedSession = (SessionInfo*)SendMessage( GetDlgItem(
            window, IDC_SESSIONS ), LB_GETITEMDATA, selected, 0 );

  SendMessage( GetDlgItem( window, IDC_SESSIONS ), WM_SETREDRAW,
              false, 0 );

  SendMessage( GetDlgItem( window, IDC_SESSIONS ),
              LB_RESETCONTENT, 0, 0 );

  char name[MAX_PATH];
  SessionInfo *session = g_engine->GetNetwork()->GetNextSession(
                        true );
  while( session != NULL )
  {
    wcstombs( name, session->description.pwszSessionName,
              MAX_PATH );

    int index = (int)SendMessage( GetDlgItem( window,
                IDC_SESSIONS ), LB_ADDSTRING, 0, (LPARAM)name );
    SendMessage( GetDlgItem( window, IDC_SESSIONS ),
                LB_SETITEMDATA, index, (LPARAM)session );

    if( selectedSession == session )
      SendMessage( GetDlgItem( window, IDC_SESSIONS ),
                  LB_SETCURSEL, index, 0 );

    session = g_engine->GetNetwork()->GetNextSession();
  }

  if( selectedSession == NULL )
    SendMessage( GetDlgItem( window, IDC_SESSIONS ), LB_SETCURSEL,
                0, 0 );
```

```
        SendMessage( GetDlgItem( window, IDC_SESSIONS ), WM_SETREDRAW,
                     true, 0 );
        InvalidateRect( GetDlgItem( window, IDC_SESSIONS ), NULL,
                        false );
    }
```

You will notice that there are quite a few `SendMessage` function calls. This is the primary function used to communicate with the controls on a dialog. This function allows you to send a message or data to a control. If you ignore all the dialog specific code for a moment, you will see that right at the start we call `EnumerateSessions` on the engine's network object. Remember that this is a synchronous call, so it won't return until it has finished, which may take several seconds. During this time nothing else can be processed so you will notice that the application appears to stop responding until the call returns.

Once the engine has finished enumeration, we can iterate through the list of found sessions by using the `GetNextSession` function on the engine's network object. This gives us access to the `SessionInfo` structure of each found session, one at a time. Using this, we can access extra information such as the name of the session, which can be added to a list box (or any other list display mechanism) as shown in this example. This kind of approach facilitates joining a session as the user can simply select a session from the list box and click the join button on the menu dialog.

Before the user can host or join a session, the three text boxes at the top of the menu dialog need to be filled in. You can see from Figure 11.2 that they each contain default text, which will name the local player "Unknown Player" and load the "Marine.txt" character for the local player. If the player decides to host a game, then the last field is used to determine which map is loaded, which would be "Abandoned City.txt" by default. Obviously, this kind of data needs to be communicated to the other clients (or potential clients) in the session. For example, when joining a session, the other clients will need to know which character you have chosen so that your player object can be loaded correctly across all the clients in the session. Now what if you hosted a session and then other clients tried to join your session? In this case, the other clients would need to know which map you have chosen so that their games can be loaded correctly. This is where the `PlayerData` structure comes into play.

PLAYER DATA

ON THE CD

Since we didn't look at the entire implementation of the `Menu` class, you will have missed something if you didn't go through the implementation on the CD-ROM. In the dialog procedure call-back function (where we handle dialog events, such as the user clicking a button) we use a little structure call the `PlayerData` structure, which is shown here and can also be found in `Main.h`:

```
struct PlayerData
{
  char character[MAX_PATH];
  char map[MAX_PATH];
};
```

The `PlayerData` structure houses two `char` arrays, which are used to store the name of the character and the map you have chosen when you host or join a session. As soon as you click either the Join button or the Host button on the menu dialog, the contents of the text boxes used for specifying your character and desired map are copied into the appropriate `char` array in the `PlayerData` structure.

Once an instance of the `PlayerData` structure has been filled out, it is then passed to either the `Host` or `Join` function (depending on whether the Host or Join button was clicked) on the engine's network object. Both of these functions allow you to pass in user data, which is stored by the network object. This data can then be queried by any other client that joins the session, or is already active in the session. If your client is just another player, then it will only be queried for its character name. Otherwise, if your client is the host, then all the other clients will query it for the map name in addition to your character name. If you're not sure how all this works, refer to Chapter 7, which covers the implementation of the networking system.

THE GAME STATE

Finally, we are ready to look at the game state. This is the primary state that our game will spend the most amount of time in; therefore, you could call it the main workhorse of our game. Just like the menu state, the game state class derives from the State class, as shown here. The `Game` class definition can also be found in `Game.h`.

```
class Game : public State
{
public:
  Game();

  virtual void Load();
  virtual void Close();

  virtual void RequestViewer( ViewerSetup *viewer );
  virtual void Update( float elapsed );
  virtual void Render();
```

```
void HandleNetworkMessage( ReceivedMessage *msg );

private:
  Material *m_crosshair;

  char m_scoreBoardNames[MAX_PATH];
  char m_scoreBoardFrags[MAX_PATH];
  char m_scoreBoardDeaths[MAX_PATH];
  Font *m_scoreBoardFont;
}
```

The class supports all the standard `virtual` functions exposed by the `State` class—no surprises there. It does, however, have an extra function called `HandleNetworkMessage`, which, as the names suggests, is used to handle incoming user-defined (or game-specific) network messages. Remember that the call-back function pointer in the `EngineSetup` structure is called whenever a user-defined network message arrives. This is the function that is eventually called, along with a pointer to a `ReceivedMessage` structure instance that contains the data relating to the network message. Finally, you will notice that the class has some member variables for a crosshair and a scoreboard. `m_crosshair` is a material that we will use to render a crosshair texture in the center of the screen. The scoreboard is built from several `char` arrays, which are then rendered onto the screen using a font. Let's have a look at the implementation of the `Game` class to see how all this works, which can be found in `Game.cpp`.

If you take a look at the `Load` function (shown here), you will see how we prepare the member variables. Notice that we load a material called `Crosshair.dds.txt`, which has a texture of a crosshair, providing this texture is the only purpose served by this material. You can also see that we create a font for rendering our scoreboard and we use the `ShowCursor` function to hide the mouse cursor on the screen as it won't be needed during game play.

```
void Game::Load()
{
  ShowCursor( false );

  m_crosshair = g_engine->GetMaterialManager()->Add(
                  "Crosshair.dds.txt", "./Assets/" );

  m_scoreBoardFont = new Font( "Arial", 14, FW_BOLD );
  m_scoreBoardNames[0] = 0;
  m_scoreBoardFrags[0] = 0;
  m_scoreBoardDeaths[0] = 0;
}
```

The Close function (which is shown below) is pretty straightforward. The first thing we do is show the mouse cursor using the ShowCursor function again. Since this Close function is called when we leave the game state, we know that the user must be going back to the menu state where a mouse cursor is needed. We also need to destroy the scoreboard font and the material used for the crosshair. The final point of interest is how the game is terminated with just two lines of code. The first closes the active network connection using the Terminate function on the engine's network object, and the second destroys the scene using the DestroyScene function on the scene manager.

```
void Game::Close()
{
  ShowCursor( true );

  g_engine->GetNetwork()->Terminate();

  g_engine->GetSceneManager()->DestroyScene();

  SAFE_DELETE( m_scoreBoardFont );

  g_engine->GetMaterialManager()->Remove( &m_crosshair );
}
```

The Update function only serves two purposes at the moment. The first is to populate the scoreboard, and the second is to exit the game state, which switches back to the menu state. If you look at the code for the Update function (which is shown here), you can see that the scoreboard is only populated when the Tab key is held down. The reason for this is that it will only be rendered when it is held down, so there is no need to continually populate it every frame unless it is being rendered. You should also note that there is no player data being added to the scoreboard at the moment simply because we have yet to implement the players into our game. Finally, you can see that the user can exit out of the game state using the Esc key.

```
void Game::Update( float elapsed )
{
  if( g_engine->GetInput()->GetKeyPress( DIK_TAB, true ) == true )
  {
    sprintf( m_scoreBoardNames, "PLAYER\n" );
    sprintf( m_scoreBoardFrags, "FRAGS\n" );
    sprintf( m_scoreBoardDeaths, "DEATHS\n" );
  }
```

```
    if( g_engine->GetInput()->GetKeyPress( DIK_ESCAPE ) )
      g_engine->ChangeState( STATE_MENU );
}
```

The final function is the Render function, which like all the others, is pretty basic at the moment. If you look at the Render function shown here, you can see that the first step is to check if a valid scene is loaded. There is no point in continuing with the rendering process if there is nothing to render. If we do have a valid scene (i.e., a map is loaded into the scene manager), then we can perform any game-specific rendering. Remember that the scene manager handles the rendering of the entire scene, including all the players and objects in it. Therefore, in the game state Render function we only need to worry about rendering things like the scoreboard and the crosshair. You can see that we only render the scoreboard when the Tab key is held down. The crosshair, on the other hand, is rendered every frame using the engine's sprite interface, which allows us to render a texture on the screen in 2D. This means that the crosshair will not be affected by the z-axis and will therefore have no depth in the scene, which prevents anything from being rendered over the top of it.

```
void Game::Render()
{
  if( g_engine->GetSceneManager()->IsLoaded() == false )
    return;

  if( g_engine->GetInput()->GetKeyPress( DIK_TAB, true ) == true )
  {
    m_scoreBoardFont->Render( m_scoreBoardNames, 20, 100,
                              0xFFFF7700 );
    m_scoreBoardFont->Render( m_scoreBoardFrags, 180, 100,
                              0xFFFF7700 );
    m_scoreBoardFont->Render( m_scoreBoardDeaths, 260, 100,
                              0xFFFF7700 );
  }

  g_engine->GetSprite()->Begin( D3DXSPRITE_ALPHABLEND );
  g_engine->GetSprite()->Draw( m_crosshair->GetTexture(), NULL,
                  NULL, &D3DXVECTOR3(
                  g_engine->GetDisplayMode()->Width / 2.0f - 15.0f,
                  g_engine->GetDisplayMode()->Height / 2.0f - 15.0f,
                  0.0f ), 0xFFFFFFFF );
  g_engine->GetSprite()->End();
}
```

The sprite interface is perfect for rendering heads-up display (HUD) elements. For example, you may want to render a health bar in the corner of the screen that displays the player's health. Using the sprite interface allows you to render the health bar in the foreground at all times so that it will never be covered up by any of the geometry in the scene.

This brings us to the end of our Game class implementation, and you are probably thinking that there has to be more to it than this. The reality is that our engine handles so much of the underlying work for us that we only have to put in the minimal effort to produce a working game, which (in case you didn't realize) is a good thing.

You may be wondering what happened to the HandleNetworkMessage function. The reason we didn't cover it is that it essentially does nothing at the moment. We haven't implemented any user-defined network messages yet, so it has nothing to do right now. In the next two chapters, we will add our game specific network messages, which will bring this function to life. This class will be a real hot spot later on, so keep your eyes on it as it will come alive in the coming chapters as we add more functionality to our game.

TESTING THE GAME

If you are excited about testing the game to see what we have so far, bear in mind that we don't have any game play yet. For that matter, we don't even have any players or weapons yet, which leads us to a slight problem. The problem is that without players, we have no virtual camera (since the camera is linked to the local player), and without a camera we cannot see anything—you can probably see where this is leading. It's the old thought exercise that if a tree falls in the woods and nobody is there to hear it, does it make a sound?

When you test the game you will first be presented with the graphics settings dialog per normal. Once you have passed this you will then encounter the game's menu dialog. If you click on Host, you will see that the application's window appears to go blank (actually it will probably be a mess since we are not clearing the target render surface, only the z-buffer) and nothing is rendered. This does not mean that the game is not loaded, quite the contrary. Actually, the game is loaded, but the scene has not been loaded as the players have not been implemented yet. Since there are no players, there is no camera; and since there is no camera, there is no way of viewing the scene, so it is not loaded yet. Although we could have worked around this and forced the scene to load despite not having anything to view it with, it would be futile. Any code we write to achieve this would have to be removed in the next chapter when we do it properly, so it is better to just wait until then—it builds suspense.

SUMMARY

Another chapter down and the end is drawing near. You will probably agree that this chapter has been a rather pleasant relief after some of the previous chapters. Nevertheless, that doesn't make the information in this chapter any less important. We began this chapter with a discussion about the basic design of our game and then went on to implement the foundations for that design. This included the basic data requirements of our game such as the custom game material, as well as the two main states that will control the processing of our game. At this point, the supporting blocks are in place and everything is looking great. In Chapter 12, we will build off of these blocks and implement one of the most important aspects of any computer game: the players.

12 Players

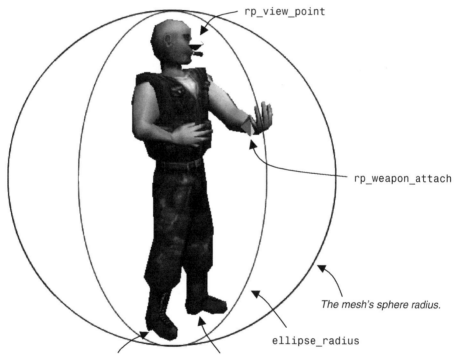

rp_view_point

rp_weapon_attach

The mesh's sphere radius.

ellipse_radius

rp_right_foot and rp_left_foot
are inside the feet at the base.

In This Chapter

- Learn about the concept of players and how they are represented in a FPS.
- Add the player object to our game, which will build off of the base scene object.
- Implement the player manager, which will coordinate player interaction in the game.

In the last chapter, we laid down the foundations of our game, which we built upon the engine we developed in Part I. Now it is time to introduce into our game the important concept of players. You can find the workspace for this chapter in the /Source/Chapter 12/ directory on the CD-ROM.

REPRESENTING THE PLAYER

When you think of the term *players*, the first thought that comes to mind is the idea of people physically sitting down to play a game. There is nothing wrong with this idea, and it is most definitely correct. In our context, a player can be defined as a person who plays a game. However, we need to look beyond the physical player and think more about what the player means to the actual game. In other words, how is the player represented in the game? What does the player look like in the game? How does the player interact with the game? These are just a few of the questions we need to answer before we can endeavor to add players to our game.

Fortunately, we are developing a game from a fairly common genre: a FPS, so you shouldn't have any problems identifying how the players work in this style of game. In order to satisfy this genre we need to fulfill certain requirements, as shown in the following list:

- The players need to be represented by a visible 3D model (or mesh).
- The camera must be linked to the movements of the local player's model.
- The camera must be positioned in such as way that it provides a first person perspective from the local player's model.
- The local player needs to be able to move relative to the camera's view (i.e., moving forward will move the player in the direction the camera faces).

This list outlines the basic requirements of incorporating players into the game. Of course, there are a lot of other aspects such as allowing the players to interact with their environment and collecting weapons, for example. We also need to consider the fact that this is a multiplayer game, so the players need to be able to see one another in order to play the game. By playing the game, we are referring to the fact that the players need to be able to fight one another with the weapons they collect. This immediately infers that our players need to be able to use weapons and, more importantly, need to be able to hurt one another. This leads us to the idea that our players will need health, so to speak. We need some sort of value that tracks how much more damage the player can suffer before he is eliminated and his opponent scores a frag. So, as you can see, there are quite a number of angles to consider when incorporating players into your game.

Our implementation of "players" will use four elements, that (when linked together) will produce a system to incorporate and manage players in our game. Table 12.1 shows the four elements with a brief description of each.

TABLE 12.1 Player System Elements

Player Scripts	We will use a script for each character that can be chosen by the players. This script will identify the mesh used by the character as well as properties used for collision detection and handling weapons.
Player Meshes	Each player script will point to a mesh that represents that character. This will be a 3D articulated mesh with animations for idling, running, dying, etc.
Player Objects	A new type of object will be built off of the scene object, which will be capable of handling the players. It will store all of the data relevant to a single player in the game.
Player Manager	The player manager will collate and manage all of the players in the game. It will assist in facilitating the interactions between the players, their environment, and each other.

The brief descriptions of each element given in Table 12.1 may leave you with questions, but that's okay as we are about to begin the development of our player system. We will look at each element in detail as we progress. By the end of this chapter, you will have a much better understanding of the role each element plays and how they work together. One last thing before we dive into implementation: Figure 12.1 highlights the components of our game that we will be developing in this chapter, which are shaded in gray.

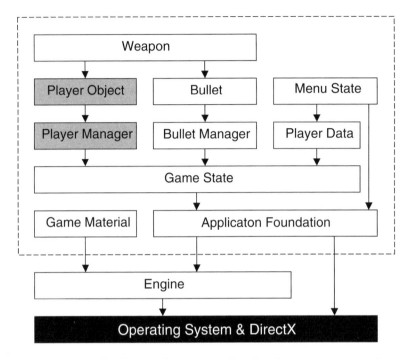

FIGURE 12.1   The design of our game, showing the components to be developed in this chapter.

PLAYER SCRIPTS

The first element of our player system that we will look at is the player scripts, which are really very basic. Take a look at the following script. It is the complete listing for our marine character in the game.

```
#begin

name              string Marine

mesh_name         string Marine.x
mesh_path         string ./Assets/Characters/

ellipse_radius    vector 0.3 0.75 0.3

view_weapon_offset vector 5.0 55.0 0.0

#end
```

As you can see, there really isn't anything to it, and if you are familiar with our scripting system you will have no problem identifying the types of variables in this script. The first question that probably comes to mind is: why do we need these scripts? If you have a good look at the script, the first important point that you should be able to pick up is that it is used to identify the mesh associated with this character. At the moment, our game will only have one character to choose from, but later on you may want to add a second, and a third, and so on. With each new character, you just create another script that gives the character a name and identifies the mesh to use for the character. This allows you to create multiple characters that each use the same mesh but have different properties.

Our game only requires two properties for each character at the moment, but remember you are free to add more when the situation arises as you add new features. The two properties that our game currently uses for each character are `ellipse_radius` and `view_weapon_offset`. The first of the two is used to identify the ellipsoid radius around the character's mesh, and the second is used to position the player's weapon in the first person view in relation to the origin (0.0, 0.0, 0.0) of the character's mesh. This is actually an offset in model space. If we use the example given in the previous script, then the player's weapon will be positioned 5.0 units along the x-axis and 55.0 units along the y-axis in the mesh's model space. By using model space we ensure that the weapon will be in the same position no matter where the mesh is placed or how it is orientated in world space.

You can experiment with both of these values to see the affects they have in the game. Obviously, adjusting the `view_weapon_offset` now will be of little use as the weapons won't be implemented until the next chapter. However, when you finish this chapter you can try adjusting the `ellipse_radius`. By increasing the radius you will give the player a larger bounding volume, which will result in smoother but less accurate collision detection with the environment. Decreasing the radius will give you tighter collision detection with the 3D environment; however, it will increase the chances of the player becoming "stuck" on unusual geometry. Figure 12.2 shows how the different properties relate to the character's mesh. You should note that the two reference points are in fact attached to the mesh's bone hierarchy, which has been removed in Figure 12.2 for clarity.

NOTE

Don't forget that the ellipsoid radius is specified as a percentage of the sphere radius. Therefore, a value of 1.0 on any of the axes indicates that the ellipsoid radius is equal to the radius of the bounding sphere along that axis. Likewise, a value of 2.0 will give an ellipsoid radius of double the sphere radius and a value of 0.5 will result in an ellipsoid radius of half the sphere radius. You should also note that the size of the player's bounding volume does not affect accuracy when shooting at another player. Projectiles fired from weapons will be tested against the player's mesh, not its bounding volume, which gives a far more realistic experience.

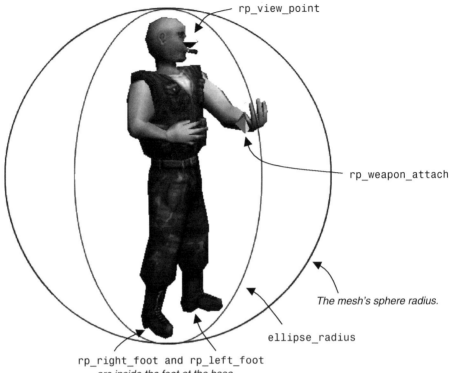

rp_view_point

rp_weapon_attach

The mesh's sphere radius.

ellipse_radius

rp_right_foot and rp_left_foot
are inside the feet at the base.

FIGURE 12.2 The properties of a character mesh.

There is one final point that should be brought to your attention before we move on. There is a small security issue when using scripts so liberally like we are. The problem is that anybody (i.e., the end user) can simply open up any of the scripts and modify the values to change the way the game behaves. This is not always bad, if you want the end user to be able to modify the game and add new features to it through the use of the scripts. However, it does pose a problem when you are trying to play the game across a network with players who have modified their scripts. In this case, the way one client processes the game will be different from how another client processes the same game.

To ensure a fair and proper game, the scripts across every game on the network must be the same. The most common approach to solve the problem is to check each client when they join a session to ensure their scripts match the host's scripts. If you want to eliminate the possibility of the end user modifying the scripts, you can package them up into an encrypted file. We won't bother with anything like this as we are just learning how to make a FPS. Besides, we want to be able to modify the scripts whenever we want, however we want. This really only becomes an issue if you are planning to release your game for public consumption.

PLAYER NETWORK MESSAGES

Before we move on to probably the most important aspect of the player system (the player object), let's take a little detour and run through the user-defined (or game-specific) network messages that will be used by our player system. We won't actually look at how they are handled just yet as we will cover that at the end of the chapter. However, we need to introduce them now as they will be used by the player object and the player manager that we are about to implement. Get acquainted with each of the following network messages and their structures so you won't be alarmed when you see them being used later in the chapter. As previously mentioned, at the end of the chapter we will look at how these messages are actually handled when they are received by our application's network message handler. So don't worry about them for now.

The following shows the identifiers used for the seven player specific network messages, which can be found in Game.h. Notice how we start numbering them at 0x12005. This is because we have reserved the first few for engine specific network messages. You will also notice that messages 0x12009 and 0x12010 appear to be missing. These two are actually weapon specific so we do not need to cover them just yet. We will look at those two in the next chapter.

```
#define MSGID_PLAYER_HEALTH          0x12005
#define MSGID_PLAYER_MOVE_UPDATE     0x12006
#define MSGID_PLAYER_LOOK_UPDATE     0x12007
#define MSGID_PLAYER_SCORE           0x12008
#define MSGID_SPAWN_POINT_REQUEST    0x12011
#define MSGID_SPAWN_POINT            0x12012
#define MSGID_SPAWN_PLAYER           0x12013
```

Now take a look at the following six structures for these network messages, also found in Game.h. You can line up each message with its appropriate structure by just matching the names. The comments have been left in so that you can identify each member of the structures.

```
struct PlayerHealthMsg : public NetworkMessage
{
  float health; // Absolute health of the player.
};
```

```
struct PlayerMoveUpdateMsg : public NetworkMessage
{
  D3DXVECTOR3 translation; // Player's translation.
  float drive; // Player's drive direction.
  float strafe; // Player's strafe direction.
  bool fire; // Indicates if the player is firing their weapon.
};

struct PlayerLookUpdateMsg : public NetworkMessage
{
  float viewTilt; // Player's view tilt (i.e. rotation around the
                     x axis).
  float rotationY; // Player's rotation around the y axis.
};

struct PlayerScoreMsg : public NetworkMessage
{
  unsigned long frags; // Player's frag count.
  unsigned long deaths; // Player's death tally.
};

struct SpawnPointMsg : public NetworkMessage
{
  long spawnPoint; // ID of the spawn point to use.
};

struct SpawnPlayerMsg : public NetworkMessage
{
  D3DXVECTOR3 translation; // Translation to spawn the player at.
};
```

You will notice that MSGID_SPAWN_POINT_REQUEST *does not appear to have its own structure. This is simply because it does not need one. This message is sent to the host when your client requests a new spawn point. The host does not need any special information from this message. The message alone is all the information required; therefore, the standard* NetworkMessage *structure is sufficient for this type of message.*

THE PLAYER OBJECT

Now we are at the business end of things. This is where it all starts to come together, starting with the PlayerObject class. This class represents the most complex, advanced, and exciting object we have implemented so far, and it is the first to make use of the `AnimatedObject` class—since our player will be represented by an animated mesh. The definition of the `PlayerObject` class is shown here, and it can also be found in `PlayerObject.h`:

```
class PlayerObject : public AnimatedObject
{
public:
  PlayerObject( PlayerInfo *player, Script *script,
                unsigned long type = TYPE_PLAYER_OBJECT );
  virtual ~PlayerObject();

  virtual void Update( float elapsed, bool addVelocity = true );
  virtual void Render( D3DXMATRIX *world = NULL );

  virtual void CollisionOccurred( SceneObject *object,
                                  unsigned long collisionStamp );

  void MouseLook( float x, float y, bool reset = false );

  void Hurt( float damage, PlayerObject *attacker );
  void Kill();

  DPNID GetID();
  char *GetName();

  void SetHealth( float health );
  float GetHealth();
  void SetDying( bool dying );
  bool GetDying();

  void SetIsViewing( bool isViewing );

  void SetFrags( unsigned long frags );
  unsigned long GetFrags();
  void SetDeaths( unsigned long deaths );
  unsigned long GetDeaths();

  void SetDrive( float drive );
  float GetDrive();
  void SetStrafe( float strafe );
  float GetStrafe();
  void SetFire( bool fire );
  bool GetFire();
```

```
      void SetViewTilt( float tilt );
      float GetViewTilt();
      D3DXVECTOR3 GetEyePoint();

   private:
      virtual HRESULT CALLBACK HandleCallback( THIS_ UINT Track,
                                               LPVOID pCallbackData );

   private:
      enum{ ANIM_IDLE, ANIM_DEATH, ANIM_FORWARDS, ANIM_BACKWARDS,
            ANIM_LEFT, ANIM_RIGHT };

      DPNID m_dpnid;
      char *m_name;
      float m_health;
      bool m_dying;
      bool m_isViewing;

      unsigned long m_frags;
      unsigned long m_deaths;

      float m_drive;
      float m_strafe;
      bool m_fire;

      D3DXVECTOR3 m_viewPoint;
      float m_viewTilt;

      float m_viewSmoothing;
      float m_viewSensitivity;

      AnimationCallbackData m_callbackData[2];
      RayIntersectionResult m_stepResult;

      AudioPath3D *m_leftStepAudioPath;
      AudioPath3D *m_rightStepAudioPath;
};
```

Now that's a long class! You can recognize the fact that this is an object simply by the virtual functions, which have been overridden from the AnimatedObject class, which in turn are overridden from the SceneObject class—there's a whole lot overriding going on here. However, everything from the MouseLook function, down, is new. Fortunately, a lot of the functions are pretty self-explanatory just by looking at their names. This is an important point of programming; you should always endeavor to give your functions and variables meaningful names. It increases code readability and makes debugging and maintenance a whole lot easier.

Functions such as `SetHealth` and `GetHealth` are fairly obvious as they simply set the value of a member variable and return the value of that same member variable, respectively. If you take a look at the member variables you should be able to find the variables that are affected by these types of functions and match them up to the functions that use them. For example, `m_drive` is obviously affected by `SetDrive` and `GetDrive`.

A lot of the functions in the `PlayerObject` class are quite small and simple, and really not worth covering here. For example, the constructor is mainly used to set all the default values for the member variables. However, there are a few interesting points that we should discuss in more detail, such as the footsteps implementation and the `Update` function. We will look at those now, which in turn will explain a number of the member variables. You are encouraged to take a look at the complete implementation found in `PlayerObject.cpp`.

FOOTSTEPS WITH ANIMATION KEYS

The sound of footsteps as you run around a virtual environment helps to create an immersive experience for the player, not to mention the strategic advantages gained when using 3D sound, which allows you to hear your opponents creeping up behind you or sneaking down an alley on your left. Adding footsteps may appear to be a little complicated at first, but once you wrap your head around the short implementation, you will realize there really isn't a lot to it. Besides, we already have some of the foundations in place, which we implemented in the last chapter. So let's begin by adding a little more to the foundations with the following structure that can be found in `PlayerObject.h`.

```
struct AnimationCallbackData
{
  char foot;
};
```

The `AnimationCallbackData` structure is used by our `HandleCallback` function, which we will implement shortly. Here's an overview of how it all works. We set up two keys in our walking animation that are triggered at certain times (timed for when a foot hits the ground). There is one key for the left foot and one for the right foot, and the `foot` member of the `AnimationCallbackData` structure is used to distinguish between the two. Whenever a key is triggered in the animation, our `HandleCallback` function is called and an instance of the `AnimationCallbackData` structure is passed to it containing the data in the triggered key. The following snippet of code is taken from the `PlayerObject` class constructor. It shows you how the two footstep keys are set up on the player's mesh's movement animations.

```
m_callbackData[0].foot = 0;
m_callbackData[1].foot = 1;

D3DXKEY_CALLBACK keys[2];
keys[0].Time = 0;
keys[0].pCallbackData = &m_callbackData[0];
keys[1].pCallbackData = &m_callbackData[1];

LPD3DXKEYFRAMEDANIMATIONSET oldAS;
LPD3DXCOMPRESSEDANIMATIONSET newAS;
LPD3DXBUFFER buffer;

for( char a = 1; a < 5; a++ )
{
  GetAnimationController()->GetAnimationSet( a,
                          (LPD3DXANIMATIONSET*)&oldAS );

  keys[1].Time = float( oldAS->GetPeriod() / 2.0f *
                          oldAS->GetSourceTicksPerSecond() );

  oldAS->Compress( D3DXCOMPRESS_DEFAULT, 0.4f, NULL, &buffer );

  D3DXCreateCompressedAnimationSet( oldAS->GetName(),
        oldAS->GetSourceTicksPerSecond(), oldAS->GetPlaybackType(),
        buffer, 2, keys, &newAS );
  SAFE_RELEASE( buffer );

  GetAnimationController()->UnregisterAnimationSet( oldAS );
  SAFE_RELEASE( oldAS );

  GetAnimationController()->RegisterAnimationSet( newAS );
  SAFE_RELEASE( newAS );
}
```

There are a few technical bits in there, so don't be too concerned with the details. Instead, let's discuss what the code is actually doing. First, we set the call-back data by using a 0 for the right foot and a 1 for the left foot, and then create the two keys and assign the call-back data to them. You'll notice that we set `Time` to 0 on the first key. If you look further down in the `for` loop, you can see that we set the `Time` on the second key to equal half of the period of the animation. This will result in a key at the beginning of the animation and one halfway through. Since our movement animations (of which there are four: forward, backward, strafe left, and strafe right) are uniform and consistent, we know that the time between each footstep is the same. Each animation contains two footsteps (one for the left foot and one for the right, which is looped to create a cycle), so by timing the keys evenly in the animation we know they will be triggered when each footstep occurs, as shown in Figure 12.3.

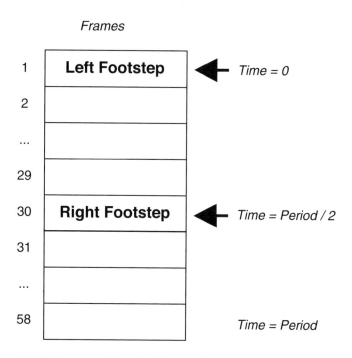

FIGURE 12.3   Timing the footstep keys with the footstep frames in the animations.

Once our keys have been embedded into the animations, we can play the animations and our HandleCallback function will be called by the AdvanceTime function from the animation controller (recall the AnimatedObject class from Chapter 9) every time one of the keys is triggered. All we need to do in the HandleCallback function is check the call-back data to see which key was triggered (i.e., which footstep) and then play the appropriate sound effect for the material that the player is walking on, as we discussed in the last chapter. The implementation of the Handle-Callback function is shown here, and it can also be found in PlayerObject.cpp.

```cpp
HRESULT CALLBACK PlayerObject::HandleCallback( THIS_ UINT Track,
                                               LPVOID pCallbackData )
{
  AnimationCallbackData *data =
                        (AnimationCallbackData*)pCallbackData;

  if( IsTouchingGround() == false )
    return S_OK;

  if( data->foot == 1 )
  {
    m_stepResult.material = NULL;


    if( g_engine->GetSceneManager()->RayIntersectScene(
                &m_stepResult,
                 GetTranslation() + GetMesh()->GetReferencePoint(
                "rp_left_foot" )->GetTranslation(),
                D3DXVECTOR3( 0.0f, -1.0f, 0.0f ) ) == true )
    {
      if( ( (GameMaterial*)m_stepResult.material )
                        ->GetStepSound() != NULL )
        m_leftStepAudioPath->Play(
                            ( (GameMaterial*)m_stepResult.material )
                             ->GetStepSound()->GetSegment() );
    }
  }
  else
  {
    m_stepResult.material = NULL;

    if( g_engine->GetSceneManager()->RayIntersectScene(
                &m_stepResult,
                 GetTranslation() + GetMesh()->GetReferencePoint(
                "rp_right_foot" )->GetTranslation(),
                D3DXVECTOR3( 0.0f, -1.0f, 0.0f ) ) == true )
    {
      if( ( (GameMaterial*)m_stepResult.material )
                        ->GetStepSound() != NULL )
        m_rightStepAudioPath->Play(
                            ( (GameMaterial*)m_stepResult.material )
                             ->GetStepSound()->GetSegment() );
```

```
        }
    }

    return S_OK;
}
```

Now we need to look at how the function determines which sound effect to play. You will remember from the last chapter that we embedded the footstep sound effects into our material scripts so that they could be loaded and attached to the materials. Now we need to determine which one of those materials the player is stepping on. To achieve this we will use the `RayIntersectionResult` structure in conjunction with the `RayIntersectScene` function from the `SceneManager` class. The `RayIntersectionResult` structure can be found in `SceneManager.h` and it is used by the `RayIntersectScene` function to return the results of a ray intersection test with the scene.

A ray intersection test simply means that you shoot an imaginary line (called a ray) through the 3D environment and check if it hits any of the faces in the scene. The best way to think of it is to imagine a bullet flying in a straight line through your scene. All we are doing is checking if that bullet hits anything or just sails right through unobstructed. The D3DX library provides functions that can perform this test for us. All the `RayIntersectScene` function is doing is using those functions to perform the test on our whole scene for us. The `RayIntersectionResult` structure is then used to provide us with user-friendly data that is specific to our game, such as which face was hit by the ray and most importantly, what material is on the face. Have a look at the implementation of the `RayIntersectScene` function we discussed in Chapter 10, if you have forgotten how it works.

To perform the ray intersection test for a foot, we simply cast a ray from the foot straight down, which gives us the details of the first face the ray hits. Casting a ray from the foot is just a matter of finding the translation of the foot in world coordinates, which is done using reference points in the mesh. If you take the left foot for example, you will notice that we cast the ray from:

```
GetTranslation() + GetMesh()->GetReferencePoint( "rp_left_foot" )
                        ->GetTranslation()
```

This means that we take the translation of the `rp_left_foot` reference point and add the player's translation to find the location in world space. We used reference points in Chapter 10 when we created the scene mesh. They were used for positioning player spawn points and spawner objects. These reference points are exactly the same and they can be placed in any kind of mesh. You just need to prefix the reference point with rp_ and the mesh system will know to store that frame as a reference point that you can access in the code as we are doing here.

Once the ray intersection test is complete, we use the returned RayIntersectionResult structure to find the material that was stepped on. If that material has a footstep sound effect attached to it, then we play it through the appropriate foot's audio path.

UPDATING THE PLAYER OBJECT

The only other important function from the PlayerObject class that we should look at is the Update function. There are three primary steps in the Update function: calculating the view matrix, updating the player's movement, and updating the footstep audio paths. Take a look at the implementation of the Update function shown and see if you can pick these three steps. You can also find the implementation of this function in PlayerObject.cpp.

```
void PlayerObject::Update( float elapsed, bool addVelocity )
{
  AnimatedObject::Update( elapsed, addVelocity );

  m_forward.x = (float)sin( GetRotation().y );
  m_forward.y = (float)-tan( m_viewTilt );
  m_forward.z = (float)cos( GetRotation().y );
  D3DXVec3Normalize( &m_forward, &m_forward );

  m_viewPoint = GetMesh()->GetReferencePoint( "rp_view_point" )
                        ->GetTranslation();

  D3DXVec3TransformCoord( &m_viewPoint, &m_viewPoint,
                          GetRotationMatrix() );

  if( m_isViewing == true )
  {
    D3DXMATRIX rotationXMatrix;
    D3DXMatrixRotationX( &rotationXMatrix, m_viewTilt );

    D3DXMATRIX combinedRotation;
    D3DXMatrixMultiply( &combinedRotation, &rotationXMatrix,
                        GetRotationMatrix() );
```

```
        D3DXMATRIX viewPointTranslationMatrix;
        D3DXVECTOR3 finalViewPointTranslation = GetTranslation() +
                                                    m_viewPoint;
        D3DXMatrixTranslation( &viewPointTranslationMatrix,
            finalViewPointTranslation.x, finalViewPointTranslation.y,
            finalViewPointTranslation.z );

        D3DXMatrixMultiply( &m_viewMatrix, &combinedRotation,
                        &viewPointTranslationMatrix );
        D3DXMatrixInverse( &m_viewMatrix, NULL, &m_viewMatrix );
    }

    if( m_dying == true )
      return;

    if( m_drive != 0.0f )
      Drive( m_drive * 8000.0f * elapsed );
    if( m_strafe != 0.0f )
      Strafe( m_strafe * 4000.0f * elapsed );

    m_leftStepAudioPath->SetPosition( GetTranslation() +
                    GetMesh()->GetReferencePoint( "rp_left_foot" )
                        ->GetTranslation() );
    m_leftStepAudioPath->SetVelocity( GetVelocity() );
    m_rightStepAudioPath->SetPosition( GetTranslation() +
                    GetMesh()->GetReferencePoint( "rp_right_foot" )
                        ->GetTranslation() );
    m_rightStepAudioPath->SetVelocity( GetVelocity() );
    }
```

The first step involves recalculating the forward vector of the object since the
SceneObject class does not take into account the fact that the PlayerObject can tilt
its view (when you push the mouse forward or backward). The forward vector
could be extracted from the player's view matrix, but since we have not calculated
the view matrix for this frame yet, we only have the view matrix from the last frame.
In order to create the correct view matrix, we need the correct forward vector for
this frame (as the player has probably moved since the last frame). Once we have
the new forward vector we then need to request the view point matrix from the
player's mesh. The view point matrix is stored in a reference point frame called
rp_view_point within the mesh. This is just another reference point that was embedded in the mesh when it was created, just like the reference points used for the
footsteps. This reference point is positioned at the eyes of the player's mesh so that
the game knows where to put the camera.

If you want to create your own player meshes, you must remember to include a reference point for each foot and one for the view point. You should create these reference points using bones and attach them to the bone hierarchy used to animate the mesh. This way they will move with the mesh and you will be able to request the position and matrix of the reference points even when the mesh is animating. Refer to Figure 12.2 to see where these reference points should be placed in the mesh.

If this player is being used as the viewing object to view the scene, then we go through the process of calculating the view matrix for the player, which takes into account the view point, the new forward vector, the player's rotation, and view tilt, as well as the player's location in 3D space. To achieve the desired results we use a whole lot of matrix manipulation functions provided by the D3DX library. You have seen all of these functions before, so we won't go over them again. However, a quick flip through the DirectX SDK documentation should refresh your memory if you are unclear about any of them.

The next step involves moving the player for the current frame. This is done by simply calling the Drive and Strafe functions on the PlayerObject. You should be aware that although we are calling these functions on a PlayerObject, they are actually exposed by the base SceneObject class. Both of these functions accept a value that indicates how far to move. If m_drive is equal to 0, then the player will not move forward or backward. When the player wants to move forward, m_drive will be set to 1, and when the player wants to move backward, m_drive will be set to -1. This will create a positive or negative thrust that will move the player in the appropriate direction. m_strafe works in exactly the same way, but instead of moving the player forward or backward, the player is strafed left or right depending on the value of m_strafe.

You will notice that we have hard coded in the actual amount by which the player can drive or strafe. Generally, this is not the best practice as it can increase the difficulty of maintaining the code. The best way to approach this is by placing these types of values in an easily accessible medium such as a script or a header file. By removing the hard-coded values, you do not have to recompile the code every time you want to make a small change.

The final step is to update the footstep audio paths. This is just a matter of setting the position and velocity of both audio paths to match that of the player. You will notice, though, that we modify the position of the audio paths by the position of the foot reference points in the player's mesh. This ensures that any sounds played from these audio paths will appear to originate from the player's feet, which is exactly what you want in a 3D environment.

THE PLAYER MANAGER

We now have our `PlayerObject` implemented and ready to be used; the only problem is that we don't have anything to manage our players. We don't need to worry about rendering them as our scene manager handles that, since the players derive from the base `SceneObject`. However, we need something that can handle tasks such as spawning players and the input for the local player. This brings us to the final class for this chapter: the `PlayerManager` class. The definition of this class is shown here and can also be found in `PlayerManager.h`:

```
class PlayerManager
{
public:
  PlayerManager();
  virtual ~PlayerManager();

  void Update( float elapsed );

  void SpawnLocalPlayer( long spawnPoint = -1 );
  void SpawnPlayer( DPNID dpnid, D3DXVECTOR3 translation );

  PlayerObject *AddPlayer( PlayerInfo *player );
  void RemovePlayer( DPNID dpnid );

  PlayerObject *GetLocalPlayer();
  PlayerObject *GetPlayer( DPNID dpnid );
  PlayerObject *GetNextPlayer( bool restart = false );
  PlayerObject *GetViewingPlayer();

private:
  LinkedList< PlayerObject > *m_players;
  PlayerObject *m_viewingPlayer;

  bool m_localMovement;
  float m_localDrive;
  float m_localStrafe;
  bool m_localFire;

  bool m_spawnLocalPlayer;
  bool m_requestedSpawnPoint;
};
```

From looking at the functions in this class you can see that it has the ability to manage and update all of the players in our game. Whenever a new player is created, it will be added to the player manager, which will store the new player object in the m_players linked list. Likewise, when a player leaves the game, it will be removed from the player manager. Every frame the player manager will be updated, which will allow it to collect input for the local player. The player manager is also used in conjunction with the scene manager to perform player spawning. Finally, you can use the player manager to gain access to the player object of any player in the game, including the local player and the currently viewing player (i.e., the player that is being used to view the scene).

We are going to look at the two most important topics covered by the player manager. The first involves handling the local player. The player manager will be used to collect the local player's input and then send any required network messages in order to keep the other players in the game updated. The second important topic involves spawning the players. This includes requesting a spawn point for the local player as well as spawning other players when they do so. Remember that every client in the game will run their own instance of the player manager specifically for their local player. When their local player performs an action such as moving or spawning, it needs to update all of the other clients in the game so that their player managers can stay synchronized. Let's look at how this is achieved through the player manager's Update function.

UPDATING THE PLAYERS

As you already know, the primary task of the player manager's Update function is to facilitate input from the player. In our game, we want the player to be able to perform four direct actions as a result of using an input device (such as the keyboard or the mouse).

- The player needs to be able to move using the w, a, s, d keys, which allows the player to move forward, strafe left, move backward, and strafe right, respectively.
- The player also needs to be able to look around to control the direction of facing by moving the mouse. Pushing the mouse forward should tilt the player's view down, while pulling the mouse back should tilt the players view up. Pushing the mouse either left or right should rotate the player's view in the appropriate direction.
- The player will eventually need to be able to fire its weapon by pressing the left mouse button.

■ The player must be able to switch between multiple weapons (when carrying more than one) by using the scroll wheel on the mouse or the number keys on the keyboard.

This gives you an idea of what we need to achieve in this function, so let's step through it together and look at each of the key areas.

```
void PlayerManager::Update( float elapsed )
{
  if( g_engine->GetSceneManager()->IsLoaded() == false )
    return;

  PlayerObject *localPlayer = m_players->GetFirst();
  if( localPlayer == NULL )
    return;
```

When we first enter the function we need to ensure that the scene is loaded and a local player exists. If there is no scene loaded then the game cannot be running, so there is no need to continue processing. If there is no local player, we stop here since the rest of the code in this function is specific to the local player.

```
  if( localPlayer->GetHealth() <= 0.0f && m_spawnLocalPlayer
      == false )
  {
    if( g_engine->GetInput()->GetButtonPress( 0 ) == true )
      m_spawnLocalPlayer = true;

    return;
  }
```

The first step now is to check if the local player needs to be spawned. There are two occasions when the local player will need to be spawned; when the player first enters the game and after the player has been fragged. When a player has been fragged, its health will be less than or equal to zero. If this is the case, we just wait for the player to press the left mouse button, which will set m_spawnLocalPlayer to true. When this member is set to true it means that the local player is waiting to spawn. In order to spawn the local player, the system needs to send a request to the host for an available spawn point and then send a message back to inform the other players that this player has spawned. This process takes time, during which the Update function may be called several times. To prevent it from trying to spawn the local player every frame while it is waiting for the host to reply, we check the `m_spawnLocalPlayer` member. If it is set to `true`, then we know that the local player is waiting to spawn.

```
if( m_spawnLocalPlayer == true && m_requestedSpawnPoint
    == false )
{
  NetworkMessage rspm;
  rspm.msgid = MSGID_SPAWN_POINT_REQUEST;
  rspm.dpnid = g_engine->GetNetwork()->GetLocalID();
  g_engine->GetNetwork()->Send( &rspm, sizeof( NetworkMessage ),
                     g_engine->GetNetwork()->GetHostID() );

  m_requestedSpawnPoint = true;

  return;
}
else if( m_spawnLocalPlayer == true )
{
  return;
}
```

If the local player is waiting to spawn and `m_requestedSpawnPoint` is set to `false`, we know that the system has not requested a spawn point from the host yet, so we must do that now. This is just a matter of sending a `MSGID_SPAWN_POINT_REQUEST` message to the host and then waiting for a reply. Later in this chapter we will look at the process of handling these network messages. We also need to set `m_requestedSpawnPoint` to `true` to prevent the system from trying to request another spawn point while it is waiting for one. If the local player has requested a spawn point and it is waiting to spawn, then we just drop out. The code that handles these network messages will spawn the local player when the spawn point message arrives. You will see this implemented later in this chapter.

```
static float delayedElapsed = 0.0f;
delayedElapsed = delayedElapsed * 0.99f + elapsed * 0.01f;
```

The next step involves calculating the delayed elapsed time. The delayed elapsed time is an accumulation of all the previous elapsed times. We calculate it by taking 99% of the previous elapsed time and adding 1% of the current elapsed time, which results in a slow change between elapsed times. We do this to minimize elapsed time spiking. Suppose that in one frame you had an elapsed time of 0.03

seconds and then in the next frame you had a spike in processing and the elapsed time was 0.3 seconds. That is an effective drop from 30 fps to 3 fps, which is significant. Without using a delayed elapsed time (or smoothing) your movement in the game would become erratic. This means that when you are looking around with the mouse, the movement would be jumpy and would appear to change speed with the change in frame rate. As the frame rate reduced, the amount of movement the mouse applies would increase and vice versa. To prevent this, we use the delayed elapsed time, which smooths out these spikes. If a frame does spike, then it won't contribute to the overall elapsed time and therefore will maintain a smooth elapsed time.

```
if( localPlayer->GetDying() == true )
  return;

localPlayer->MouseLook(
    (float)g_engine->GetInput()->GetDeltaY() * delayedElapsed,
    (float)g_engine->GetInput()->GetDeltaX() * delayedElapsed );
```

We now need to check if the local player is dying (i.e., just been fragged); if so, we can drop out here. Since the dying process takes a few seconds, we do not want the player to be able to apply any input during this process.

If the player is not dying, we can begin to accept input, the first of which is the ability to look around with the mouse. We simply take the movement of the mouse along both of its axes and pass it to the MouseLook function of the local player. This function applies the movement to the player's rotation and view tilt. We must also remember to modify the mouse's movement by the delayed elapsed time to ensure that the view movement will be smooth, even during frame rate spikes.

```
static unsigned long lookUpdate = timeGetTime();
if( lookUpdate + 100 < timeGetTime() &&
                       localPlayer->GetEnabled() == true )
{
  PlayerLookUpdateMsg plum;
  plum.msgid = MSGID_PLAYER_LOOK_UPDATE;
  plum.dpnid = localPlayer->GetID();
  plum.viewTilt = localPlayer->GetViewTilt();
  plum.rotationY = localPlayer->GetRotation().y;
  g_engine->GetNetwork()->Send( &plum,
        sizeof( PlayerLookUpdateMsg ), DPNID_ALL_PLAYERS_GROUP,
                                DPNSEND_NOLOOPBACK );

  lookUpdate = timeGetTime();
}
```

After we have applied the mouse movement to the local player's view, we need to send a network message to inform the other players that this player has moved. The trick is to keep the other players up-to-date without sending too many network messages. In a typical FPS we move the mouse all the time, which means that we would be sending a message every frame. This is infeasible and would bog down the network. To remedy this, we will send a message every tenth of a second. So a message will be sent 10 times a second, which is every third frame if you are running at 30 fps, which is much better. Although the other players will not be kept perfectly in tune with this player's movements, it is close enough for a game.

To perform the view movement update, we simply send a MSGID_PLAYER_ LOOK_UPDATE message to all of the other players in the game. In the message we need to provide the local player's view tilt as well as the player's rotation around the y-axis. When this message is processed at the other end, these values will be applied directly to the appropriate player. Therefore, the other players will see this local player change rotation. You will see how this network message is handled later in this chapter. For now, take a look at the next snippet of code, which handles the actual movement of the local player.

```
float desiredDrive = 0.0f;
float desiredStrafe = 0.0f;
bool desiredFire = false;

if( g_engine->GetInput()->GetKeyPress( DIK_W, true ) )
  desiredDrive = 1.0;
else if( g_engine->GetInput()->GetKeyPress( DIK_S, true ) )
  desiredDrive = -1.0;

if( g_engine->GetInput()->GetKeyPress( DIK_D, true ) )
  desiredStrafe = 1.0;
else if( g_engine->GetInput()->GetKeyPress( DIK_A, true ) )
  desiredStrafe = -1.0;

desiredFire = g_engine->GetInput()->GetButtonPress( 0, true );

if( m_localDrive != desiredDrive )
{
  m_localDrive = desiredDrive;
  m_localMovement = true;
}
```

```
if( m_localStrafe != desiredStrafe )
{
  m_localStrafe = desiredStrafe;
  m_localMovement = true;
}

if( m_localFire != desiredFire )
{
  m_localFire = desiredFire;
  m_localMovement = true;
}
```

You can see that we check each key to see if it is either pressed or released. We also keep track of the state of each key in the previous frame, which we use to compare the two values. If a key was not pressed in the previous frame but is now pressed in the current frame, we know that the local player has started moving in that direction. This works in the opposite way too. If the key was pressed but is now released, we know that the local player has stopped moving in that direction. Whenever one of the keys changes like this, we set m_localMovement to true to indicate that the local player has changed its movement this frame.

```
if( g_engine->GetInput()->GetButtonPress( 0, true ) == true )
{
  if( m_localFire != true )
  {
    m_localFire = true;
    m_localMovement = true;
  }
}
else
{
  if( m_localFire == true )
  {
    m_localFire = false;
    m_localMovement = true;
  }
}
```

The left mouse button, which acts like the fire button, is treated in exactly the same way. We have a variable (m_localFire) that is used to track the previous state of the button, which is then compared to the current state. This tells us whether or not the local player has started (or stopped) firing its weapon this frame.

```
static unsigned long moveUpdate = timeGetTime();
if( ( m_localMovement == true || moveUpdate + 200 <
        timeGetTime() ) && localPlayer->GetEnabled() == true )
{
  PlayerMoveUpdateMsg pmum;
  pmum.msgid = MSGID_PLAYER_MOVE_UPDATE;
  pmum.dpnid = localPlayer->GetID();
  pmum.translation = localPlayer->GetTranslation();
  pmum.drive = m_localDrive;
  pmum.strafe = m_localStrafe;
  pmum.fire = m_localFire;
  g_engine->GetNetwork()->Send( &pmum,
          sizeof( PlayerMoveUpdateMsg ), DPNID_ALL_PLAYERS_GROUP,
                                         DPNSEND_NOLOOPBACK );

  m_localMovement = false;

  localPlayer->SetDrive( m_localDrive );
  localPlayer->SetStrafe( m_localStrafe );
  localPlayer->SetFire( m_localFire );

  moveUpdate = timeGetTime();
 }
}
```

If m_localMovement is set to true then we know that the local player moved (or stopped moving) in some way this frame. If this is the case then we need to send a network message to inform the other players that this player is moving. If the local player is not moving then we will send a movement message every two hundredths of a second (i.e., five times a second). We will do this to ensure that every player is kept up-to-date, just in case a message is lost or not received correctly. If something does go wrong, it can potentially be corrected five times a second.

The movement update message comes in the form of a MSGID_PLAYER_MOVE_ UPDATE message. When we send one of these messages we need to pass in the movement details for the local player, which consists of the local player's drive, strafe, and fire flags. Remember that the drive and strafe flags can be 1, 0, or -1, while the fire flag is either true or false.

After we have sent the network message, we then update the local player's movement and firing states using the SetDrive, SetStrafe, and SetFire functions. Remember that we will look at how the network messages are handled at the end of this chapter. You will see how the other players update their instance of this local player.

SPAWNING PLAYERS

The second important task handled by the player manager is spawning the players. The player manager needs to be able to spawn the local player upon request, but also spawn its instances of the other players in the game when they indicate that they have spawned.

When the local player requests a spawn point from the host, the host finds an available spawn point that does not have any other players in close proximity. The host sends back the ID of the spawn point for the local player to spawn at. When this network message is received, the network message handler calls the SpawnLocalPlayer player function from the player manager. This function is shown here and can also be found in PlayerManager.cpp:

```
void PlayerManager::SpawnLocalPlayer( long spawnPoint )
{
  if( spawnPoint == -1 )
  {
    m_requestedSpawnPoint = false;

    m_spawnLocalPlayer = true;

    return;
  }

  SpawnPlayerMsg spm;
  spm.msgid = MSGID_SPAWN_PLAYER;
  spm.dpnid = g_engine->GetNetwork()->GetLocalID();
  spm.translation = g_engine->GetSceneManager()
                              ->GetSpawnPointByID( spawnPoint )
                              ->GetTranslation();
  g_engine->GetNetwork()->Send( &spm, sizeof( SpawnPlayerMsg ),
                                DPNID_ALL_PLAYERS_GROUP );
}
```

If spawnPoint is -1 then the host could not find a valid spawn point at the moment. This just means that the player manager will have to request again in the next frame and start the process again. Otherwise, the function sends a MSGID_SPAWN_PLAYER message to all the other players in the game to indicate that this local player is spawning now at the given translation. To find the translation of the spawn point, you simply use the GetSpawnPointByID function on the scene manager (passing in the ID of the spawn point given to you by the host) and then access the translation of the returned spawn point using the GetTranslation function as shown.

When a client receives the MSGID_SPAWN_PLAYER message, it calls the SpawnPlayer function on the player manager. This function takes as input the ID of the player to spawn and the translation to spawn the player at in 3D coordinates. The implementation of this function is shown here and it can also be found in PlayerManager.cpp:

```
void PlayerManager::SpawnPlayer( DPNID dpnid,
                                 D3DXVECTOR3 translation )
{
  m_players->Iterate( true );
  while( m_players->Iterate() )
    if( m_players->GetCurrent()->GetID() == dpnid )
      break;
  if( m_players->GetCurrent() == NULL )
    return;

  m_players->GetCurrent()->SetEnabled( true );
  m_players->GetCurrent()->SetVisible( true );

  m_players->GetCurrent()->SetHealth( 100.0f );
  m_players->GetCurrent()->SetDying( false );

  m_players->GetCurrent()->PlayAnimation( 0, 0.0f );
  m_players->GetCurrent()->PlayAnimation( 0, 0.0f );

  m_players->GetCurrent()->SetTranslation( translation );
  m_players->GetCurrent()->MouseLook( 0.0f, 0.0f, true );

  if( m_players->GetCurrent()->GetID() == g_engine->GetNetwork()
                                          ->GetLocalID() )
  {
    m_players->GetCurrent()->SetIsViewing( true );
    m_viewingPlayer = m_players->GetCurrent();

    m_requestedSpawnPoint = false;

    m_spawnLocalPlayer = false;
  }
  else
    m_players->GetCurrent()->SetIsViewing( false );
}
```

First of all, the function iterates through the players in the game to find the player with the matching ID. Once found, it goes through and sets all the properties of the player in preparation to spawn the player back into the game. This includes enabling the player and setting its health back to full. Finally, the player is set to the translation specified, which effectively spawns the player back into the game. If this player is the local player, we must also remember to set both `m_requestedSpawnPoint` and `m_spawnLocalPlayer` back to `false` to ensure that the local player can begin to receive input again and no longer attempts to respawn.

This completes the implementation of our player manager. Of course (as always), there are a number of functions that we didn't cover, however, they are quite small and easy to understand. The general rule of thumb is that if you can understand what is being presented in the book, then you will breeze through what is not presented. The functions that we don't cover are usually mundane utility functions that merely support the more important tasks that we should focus on. By all means, browse through the actual source code to gain a better understanding. You will also receive the added benefit of seeing the many snippets of code from the book put into context.

HANDLING PLAYER NETWORK MESSAGES

The final topic of discussion for this chapter is the many network messages that are sent and received by the game clients in relation to the players. We will run through each of them, starting with the `MSGID_CREATE_PLAYER` message. You can find the implementation of each of these network messages in the `HandleNetworkMessage` function from the `Game` class. This function can be found in `Game.cpp`.

```
case MSGID_CREATE_PLAYER:
{
  PlayerObject *object = m_playerManager->AddPlayer(
              g_engine->GetNetwork()->GetPlayer( msg->dpnid ) );
  g_engine->GetSceneManager()->AddObject( object );

  if( object->GetID() == g_engine->GetNetwork()->GetHostID() )
  {
    g_engine->GetSceneManager()->LoadScene(
              ( (PlayerData*)g_engine->GetNetwork()->GetPlayer(
                  msg->dpnid )->data )->map, "./Assets/Scenes/" );

    g_engine->GetNetwork()->SetReceiveAllowed( true );
  }

  break;
}
```

The MSGID_CREATE_PLAYER message is received by each client whenever a new player joins the game. When received, a new PlayerObject is created for the new player, which is added to both the player manager and the scene manager. If the new player is the host, then the scene manager is instructed to load the scene specified by the host player. Remember that each player has a PlayerData structure associated with it that indicates the character the player is using and the map the host has chosen.

```
case MSGID_DESTROY_PLAYER:
{
  SceneObject *object = m_playerManager->GetPlayer( msg->dpnid );
  g_engine->GetSceneManager()->RemoveObject( &object );
  m_playerManager->RemovePlayer( msg->dpnid );

  break;
}
```

The MSGID_DESTROY_PLAYER message is basically the opposite of the MSGID_CREATE_PLAYER message. This message is received whenever a player leaves the game; it simply removes the player from the player manager and the scene manager.

```
case MSGID_PLAYER_HEALTH:
{
  PlayerHealthMsg *phm = (PlayerHealthMsg*)msg;

  m_playerManager->GetPlayer( phm->dpnid )->SetHealth(
                                          phm->health );

  if( phm->health <= 0.0f )
    m_playerManager->GetPlayer( phm->dpnid )->Kill();

  break;
}
```

The MSGID_PLAYER_HEALTH message is received every time a player's health changes due to being shot. The health is set to the value specified by the message on the appropriate player. If the health drops below zero, then the player has been fragged and the Kill function is called on the player. This function disables the player so that it can no longer respond and begins playing the death animation.

```
case MSGID_PLAYER_MOVE_UPDATE:
{
  PlayerMoveUpdateMsg *pmum = (PlayerMoveUpdateMsg*)msg;

  PlayerObject *player = m_playerManager->GetPlayer(
                                            pmum->dpnid );

  if( player->GetEnabled() == false )
  {
    player->SetEnabled( true );
    player->SetVisible( true );
  }

  player->SetTranslation( pmum->translation.x,
                          pmum->translation.y,
                          pmum->translation.z );
  player->SetDrive( pmum->drive );
  player->SetStrafe( pmum->strafe );
  player->SetFire( pmum->fire );

  break;
}
```

The MSGID_PLAYER_MOVE_UPDATE message is received whenever a player moves just like you saw in the player manager's Update function. When this message is received, the player (specified by the message) is set to the correct translation and its movement and firing flags are updated as specified by the network message. You should also note that if this message is received about a player that appears to be disabled, then the player is actually enabled; this client just doesn't realize it yet. So we just enable the player and make sure it is visible before we go about updating it.

```
case MSGID_PLAYER_LOOK_UPDATE:
{
  PlayerLookUpdateMsg *plum = (PlayerLookUpdateMsg*)msg;

  m_playerManager->GetPlayer( plum->dpnid )->SetRotation( 0.0f,
                                      plum->rotationY, 0.0f );
  m_playerManager->GetPlayer( plum->dpnid )->SetViewTilt(
                                      plum->viewTilt );

  break;
}
```

The MSGID_PLAYER_LOOK_UPDATE message is received 10 times a second from each player in the game, as you saw in the player manager's Update function. This is the message that updates the rotation and view tilt of the remote players based on their mouse movements. As you can see, it calls the SetRotation and SetViewTilt functions on the appropriate player and sets them to the values specified by the network message.

```
case MSGID_PLAYER_SCORE:
{
  PlayerScoreMsg *psm = (PlayerScoreMsg*)msg;

  m_playerManager->GetPlayer( psm->dpnid )->SetFrags(
                                           psm->frags );
  m_playerManager->GetPlayer( psm->dpnid )->SetDeaths(
                                           psm->deaths );

  break;
}
```

The MSGID_PLAYER_SCORE message is received every time the score changes. In other words, every time a player frags another player, this message is sent to every player in the game to ensure the scores remain synchronized. When the message is received the number of frags and deaths are set on the player specified by the network message.

```
case MSGID_SPAWN_POINT_REQUEST:
{
  SpawnPointMsg spm;
  spm.msgid = MSGID_SPAWN_POINT;
  spm.dpnid = msg->dpnid;
  spm.spawnPoint = g_engine->GetSceneManager()->GetSpawnPointID(
      g_engine->GetSceneManager()->GetRandomPlayerSpawnPoint() );
  g_engine->GetNetwork()->Send( &spm, sizeof( SpawnPointMsg ),
                                msg->dpnid );

  break;
}
```

The MSGID_SPAWN_POINT_REQUEST message is received whenever a client requests a spawn point. Since the host is the only player with the authority to delegate spawn points, this message is only sent to the host. The host requests a random spawn point ID from the scene manager and passes it back to the requesting player in the form of a MSGID_SPAWN_POINT message.

```
case MSGID_SPAWN_POINT:
{
  SpawnPointMsg *spm = (SpawnPointMsg*)msg;

  if( spm->dpnid != g_engine->GetNetwork()->GetLocalID() )
    break;

  m_playerManager->SpawnLocalPlayer( spm->spawnPoint );

  break;
}
```

The MSGID_SPAWN_POINT message is received from the host after requesting a spawn point. When a player receives this message it calls the SpawnLocalPlayer function on the player manager and passes the ID of the spawn point to spawn at. You should note that this message is only processed in regard to the local player, since each player handles its own spawning as delegated by the host.

```
case MSGID_SPAWN_PLAYER:
{
  SpawnPlayerMsg *spm = (SpawnPlayerMsg*)msg;

  m_playerManager->SpawnPlayer( spm->dpnid, spm->translation );

  break;
}
```

The final message is the MSGID_SPAWN_PLAYER message, which is received whenever a player spawns (either into the game or after being fragged). When the message is received it calls the SpawnPlayer function on the player manager and passes in the ID of the player to spawn and the translation to spawn the player at.

This should give you a much clearer understanding of how the network messages work. If you had any difficulties understanding how the PlayerObject and the PlayerManager classes worked, you should have a look at them again now that you have seen the relationships that the network messages form between the players in the game.

TESTING THE GAME

Finally, we have come to the most enjoyable part of every chapter. Before you rush off to see the results of your labor, you should look at Game.cpp to see how the new player manager is put to use. You will notice that it is created by the Game class and updated every frame in the Update function of the Game class.

If you run the game now, you will notice that you can walk around our scene with full collision detection and gravity holding you to the ground. You will also notice that as you walk, the view appears to bob with every footstep. This is because we have linked the camera to the player's mesh at the view point reference point. Since this reference point is in fact a bone that is connected to the rest of the mesh's bone structure, it moves when the mesh is animated. This means that the camera moves with the animation of the mesh and therefore the view moves. So when the player is standing idle the view will move slightly with the idle animation that makes the mesh look like it is breathing. The great part about this is that when you are fragged and the death animation (which throws you onto your back) is played on your player's mesh, the view flies back with your falling body. Unfortunately, you won't be able to see that until Chapter 13 when we implement weapons—a good reason to keep reading.

Another point to take note of is that you can now collect the weapons from the weapon spawners. When you touch a weapon it will disappear only to reappear (i.e., respawn) after a set amount of time as specified by the script for the particular object spawner. You should also hear the weapon collection sound effect played too. At the moment, nothing happens when you collect the weapons, but you will be able to use these weapons once we implement them in Chapter 13.

The final point of interest is that the footstep sound effects now work. When you walk around the scene you should hear a footstep sound effect played with every step. Not only this, but the footsteps will also change based on what you step on. So load it up now and give it a try.

SUMMARY

This has been an exciting chapter, and the second (including Chapter 10) to give us some real rewards. We can actually walk around our scene now with full collision detection, gravity, footstep sound effects, and collectible object spawners. In this chapter, we discussed how our players will work and what we need to handle them. We then went on to implement the PlayerObject and the PlayerManager classes. Finally, we looked at the network messages that relate to our players and discussed their workings.

We are almost at the end now and there is only one last primary area of functionality left to be implemented: the weapons. By the end of Chapter 13 you will be able to use those weapons that are now just lying around the scene. You will be able to frag other players and be fragged yourself. A score will be kept and finally we will have something that we can actually call a game.

13 Weapons

In This Chapter

- Create the base functionality for our weapons, which includes handling projectiles.
- Implement the classes that put the weapons in the hands of the players.
- Cover supporting topics like changing weapons and handling weapons over a network.

We have come a long way and covered quite a bit. By now your head is probably spinning with information overload—the bad news is that you have to wade through one more chapter. However, if you crave information and have enjoyed the book then the effect is probably reversed. It's always a sad feeling to reach the end of a book you've enjoyed.

To ensure that we savor the last chapter, we will focus on the most exciting topic of all: weapons. In the previous chapter, we added players to our scene so we can move around our 3D environment like we are playing a FPS. We even have multiplayer support in place so two or more players can see each other moving around. Now it is time to add the final ingredient that ties everything together for our little FPS. You can find the workspace for this chapter in the /Source/Chapter 13/ directory on the CD-ROM.

ON THE CD

IMPLEMENTING WEAPONS

Obviously, the primary goal of putting weapons into a game (especially a FPS) is to allow the players to fight one another in order to score and hopefully win the game. No doubt, the most common response from a game player when asked why he is carrying a weapon in a game is "so I can blow my opponents away!" or something along those lines. As game creators, this is the experience we aim to create for the player. From a player's perspective this is the only purpose a weapon really serves, but from our perspective weapons must do a whole lot more than this. In our game, weapons must fulfill a number of basic requirements:

- Each weapon needs to be unique, both visually and functionally.
- Weapons must be viewable from an object spawner, from the first person view, and from a third person view.
- Players need to be able to collect weapons, possibly carrying more than one at a time.
- When carrying more than one weapon, players need to be able to switch between these weapons.

■ Most importantly, weapons need to be able to fire a projectile at the player's will.

As you can see, players mainly focus on the last point. This does not mean that they don't recognize the other points; they just place more importance on the last one. We, as developers, definitely need to recognize all of these points and ensure that we have a strategy for covering each of these basic primary points of functionality. Figure 13.1 shows the new (and final) components of our game that we will implement in this chapter, which are shaded in gray.

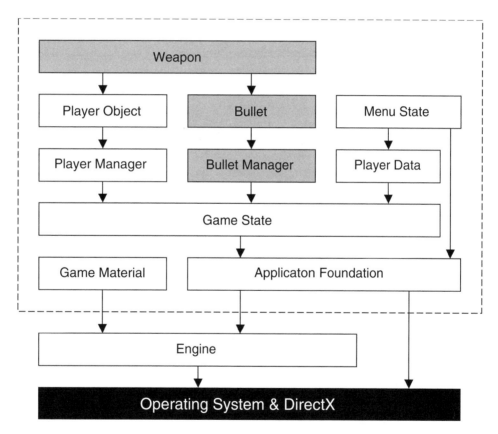

FIGURE 13.1 The design of our game, showing the components to be developed in this chapter.

Rather than discussing each of the components and the previously mentioned points in detail, let's begin implementation and we will discuss them as we go. By the end of the chapter you will see how we have covered all of these bases in the implementation of our weapons. To start with, we will implement the class that handles the projectiles fired from the weapons. Since the weapons need this functionality, it makes sense to implement it before we implement the actual weapons.

THE BULLET CLASS

The first class we will look at it is the Bullet class. As the name suggests, this class is used to manage a single bullet in the game. By saying this we immediately imply an assumption that all of our weapons are only capable of firing bullets, which is true. We are not going to look at other types of projectiles such as explosive projectiles. We will simply assume that all of our weapons fire bullets that are too small and move too fast to be visible. The beauty of this assumption is that we do not have to render anything for our bullets, which means that adding more bullets to our scene only creates extra load for the CPU, not the GPU.

Of course, later on you can modify the Bullet class so that it derives from the SceneObject class, which will allow your projectiles to have a mesh associated with them. Then you can fire whatever you like from your weapons and have a visible mesh to represent the projectile. For now, we'll stick with "invisible" bullets, so take a look at the Bullet class definition shown here, which can also be found in Bullet.h.

```
class Bullet
{
public:
  Bullet( SceneObject *owner, D3DXVECTOR3 translation,
          D3DXVECTOR3 direction, float velocity, float range,
          float damage );
  virtual ~Bullet();

  void Update( float elapsed );

  bool IsExpired();

private:
  SceneObject *m_owner;
  RayIntersectionResult *m_hitResult;
  float m_totalDistance;
  bool m_expired;

  D3DXVECTOR3 m_translation;
  D3DXVECTOR3 m_direction;
  float m_velocity;
  float m_range;
  float m_damage;
};
```

The `Bullet` class constructor is used to create a new bullet based on the parameters passed to it. Every bullet needs to have an owner (i.e., the player that fired the bullet); this way the game knows who shot whom when the bullets start hitting the players. Each bullet also needs to have a starting translation in 3D space, which would be at the end of the barrel of the weapon. To ensure the bullet moves correctly it also needs a direction and a velocity. The direction is obviously going to be the direction the player is pointing the weapon. The velocity is simply how fast the bullet travels and is dependent on the weapon that fired it. The final two parameters indicate the effective range the bullet can travel and the damage it causes when it hits a player. Both of these parameters are also dependent upon the weapon that fired the bullet.

You can see where each parameter is stored by looking at the member variables of the class. As for the `Update` function and the other member variables, we'll look at them now. We will step through the `Update` function of the `Bullet` class. You can also find the implementation of the `Bullet` class in `Bullet.cpp`.

```
void Bullet::Update( float elapsed )
{
  m_hitResult->material = NULL;
  m_hitResult->distance = 0.0f;
  m_hitResult->hitObject = NULL;
```

Every time this `Update` function is called we have to move the bullet through 3D space in its direction of travel, but before we move the bullet we have to check its flight path to ensure it isn't going to hit anything. To achieve this we use a `RayIntersectionResult` structure that we pass to the scene manager by calling `RayIntersectScene`. When we call this function we give it the details necessary to compute a ray from the bullet's current translation to its intended translation at the end of this frame. Then the function checks if this ray hits anything, and passes the details of the collision back to us using the `RayIntersectionResult` structure. First, we have to clear our instance of the structure and then pass it to the `RayIntersectScene` function as shown here:

```
if( g_engine->GetSceneManager()->RayIntersectScene( m_hitResult,
    m_translation, m_direction, true, m_owner, true ) == true )
{
  if( m_hitResult->distance <= m_velocity * elapsed )
  {
    m_totalDistance += m_hitResult->distance;
    if( m_totalDistance > m_range )
    {
      m_hitResult->material = NULL;
```

```
        m_hitResult->distance = 0.0f;
        m_hitResult->hitObject = NULL;

        m_expired = true;

        return;
    }
```

If the ray does hit something we first have to check if the collision occurred within the maximum distance that the bullet can travel this frame. If so we also need to check if the collision occurred within the maximum range that the bullet is allowed to travel in its life. Every frame that we move the bullet, we will keep track of how far it has moved in its life with m_totalDistance. If m_totalDistance ever exceeds m_range then the bullet has moved beyond its maximum effective range and any collisions beyond this range are ignored. This means that the bullet has expired and will no longer be updated. Instead, it will be removed from the system.

```
        m_expired = true;

        if( g_engine->GetNetwork()->IsHost() == false )
            return;

        if( m_hitResult->hitObject == NULL )
            return;
```

If all the range tests passed, then we can flag the bullet as expired as we know it has hit something this frame. By expiring the bullet we ensure that it will not be processed in future frames and it will later be removed from the system. We then need to check if the local player is in fact the host of the game. If not, we drop out here as we only want the host to be able to determine hits on players, which is the next step. To determine this we must first check if the hitObject member of m_hitResult is valid. If it is NULL, we know that the bullet did not hit an object, but hit a wall or some other static face that makes up the scene. If this is the case we can ignore it.

```
        if( m_hitResult->hitObject->GetType()
            == TYPE_PLAYER_OBJECT )
            ( (PlayerObject*)m_hitResult->hitObject )->Hurt( m_damage,
                                        (PlayerObject*)m_owner );

        return;
    }
    else
    {
```

```
        m_hitResult->material = NULL;
        m_hitResult->distance = 0.0f;
        m_hitResult->hitObject = NULL;
    }
}
```

Assuming the bullet hit an object, we need to ensure that the object is actually a player by checking its type. If it is a player then we can hurt it with the bullet by calling Hurt on the player object that the bullet hit. Once we have hurt the player we simply return because we do not want to continue processing this bullet.

If the bullet did not hit anything then we just clear out our RayIntersection-Result structure instance and continue processing the bullet this frame, which means that we are going to move the bullet.

```
m_totalDistance += m_velocity * elapsed;
if( m_totalDistance > m_range )
{
  m_expired = true;

  return;
}

m_translation += m_direction * ( m_velocity * elapsed );
}
```

We first apply the bullet's velocity to the total distance the bullet has traveled, which we use to check if the bullet has moved beyond its maximum range and if so, flag it as expired. Otherwise, we move the bullet by adding the bullet's velocity in the direction of travel to the bullet's current translation as shown.

When performing movement like this you must always remember to multiply all movement by the elapsed time to ensure that the movement is consistent across frames and across multiple players in the game.

NOTE

THE BULLET MANAGER

The bullet manager is used to keep track of all the bullets in the game and is a very basic system. It is really nothing more than a glorified linked list. Take a look at the BulletManager class definition, which can also be found in Bullet.h:

```
class BulletManager
{
```

```
public:
  BulletManager();
  virtual ~BulletManager();

  void Update( float elapsed );

  void AddBullet( SceneObject *owner, D3DXVECTOR3 translation,
                  D3DXVECTOR3 direction, float velocity,
                  Float range, float damage );

private:
  LinkedList< Bullet > *m_bullets;
};
```

You can see that the class has the AddBullet function, which is simply used to add another bullet to the linked list. The Update function does nothing more than iterate through the list of bullets and call their respective Update functions each frame. If you take a look at the implementation of the bullet manager (found in Bullet.cpp) you will realize that there is no point covering it in the book. In fact, if you were to derive your bullets from the SceneObject class and allow it to handle the movement of your bullets, you could eliminate the bullet manager altogether.

The only reason we are using this simple class is for clarity. It allows us to separate the management of our bullets from the rest of the scene. So feel free to change the implementation so that the bullets are handled by the scene manager. In fact, you can consider this to be an exercise. However, you may find the bullet manager comes in handy if you want to incorporate more advanced features that are applied only to the bullets in the game.

WEAPON RESOURCES

Now that we have our bullets implemented we can safely start to discuss the implementation of our weapons, knowing that they have something to fire when the time comes. Like many other objects in our game, a weapon is made up of a number of assets. In fact, a weapon can be considered a complex asset as it is comprised of many primitive assets, as shown in Table 13.1.

NOTE

There are a couple of important points to note about the two meshes. First, the first person mesh must also include the hands and arms of the player's mesh. Second, both meshes must include a reference point called rp_sight at the end of the barrel of the weapon. This is the location (in model space) that is used to spawn new bullets when the weapon fires. It is also the location where the flash is displayed when the weapon fires.

TABLE 13.1 Weapon Assets

Player Scripts	We will use a script for each character that can be chosen by the players. This script will identify the mesh used by the character as well as properties used for collision detection and handling weapons.
First Person Mesh	This is the mesh that is displayed in the first person view, when a player is holding and firing the weapon.
Third Person Mesh	This is the mesh that the players see when the weapon is floating on an object spawner waiting for collection. It is also the mesh that is displayed to other players when you are holding the weapon. In other words, this mesh is attached to your player's mesh so that the other players can see what weapon you are using.
Flash Textures	These are comprised of one or more textures that are displayed (at random) when the weapon fires. A weapon should have at least two or three of these to give some variety to the flash.
Shot Sound	The sound effect that is played whenever this weapon is fired.
Weapon Script	A script that ties together all of the above resources and specifies the individual properties of the weapon. Remember that each weapon has individual traits such as how far it can shoot and how much damage it delivers.

The most important of the four assets is the weapon script, which we will look at in more detail. The following shows the contents of a typical weapon script:

```
#begin

type            number 0
name            string "Gun 1"
ellipse_radius  vector 1.0 1.0 1.0

list_position   number 0
rate_of_fire    float  0.3
muzzle_velocity float  200.0
max_damage      float  25.0
range           float  50.0
```

```
flash0              string Flash1_1.dds.txt
flash1              string Flash1_2.dds.txt
flash_path          string ./Assets/Objects/Gun1/

mesh                string "3rd Person.x"
mesh_hands          string "1st Person.x"
mesh_path           string ./Assets/Objects/Gun1/

sound               string ./Assets/Sounds/shot1.wav

#end
```

You can see that the bottom half of the script is used to define the various resources used by this weapon as well as the path to each of these resources. You can have as many flash textures as you like; just remember to name the variables appropriately. They must be in a numerical sequence starting with zero (i.e., flash0, flash1, flash2, etc.).

The first three properties, type, name, and ellipse_radius, are used to identify the type of spawn object, the name of the weapon, and the ellipsoid radius around the weapon's mesh respectively. Don't forget that the ellipsoid radius is specified as a percentage of the mesh's sphere radius (so 1.0 equals 100% and 0.0 equals 0%). The type of spawn object is used to inform the engine that any object spawner that spawns this object is in fact spawning a weapon (since we have defined 0 as a weapon spawn object in Game.h). Later you can add more objects of different types and then you can apply the appropriate effects based on the type of object the player collects from any object spawner. The next five properties are used to define the individual traits of each weapon. Table 13.2 details each of these properties.

TABLE 13.2 Weapon Properties

list_position	The position in the player's inventory where the weapon will be stored. A player has a maximum of 10 available slots in its inventory, which match up to the numerical keys along the top of your keyboard. The weapon in the first slot is accessed by pressing the 1 key on your keyboard and the weapon in the last (or 10th) slot is accessed by pressing the 0 key on your keyboard. Setting the list_position to 0 will put the weapon in the first slot when it is collected. Setting it to 9 will put the weapon in the last slot when it is collected. Just remember that you can only have one weapon per slot.

→

TABLE 13.2 Weapon Properties

`rate_of_fire`	Specifies how fast the weapon fires in seconds. A value of 1.0 will allow the weapon to fire once per second while a value of 0.1 will allow the weapon to fire 10 times a second.
`muzzle_velocity`	The speed at which the bullet is fired in units/second. The unit of measure depends on the scale you have chosen to work in. Needless to say, the higher the value the faster the bullet travels.
`max_damage`	This is the damage the weapon causes when a bullet (fired by this weapon) hits its target. The value is specified as a percentage of a player's full health. In other words, a player starts with 100% health so a bullet fired from a weapon that inflicts 35% damage will reduce the player's health to 65% when hit by this bullet.
`range`	The effective range of a bullet fired by this weapon—beyond this range the bullet is lost. This is measured in the same units used by `muzzle_velocity` and once again depends on the scale you have chosen to work in. Technically speaking, if a weapon can fire a bullet with a `muzzle_velocity` of 200.0 units/second and a range of 50.0 units, then the bullet should cover its effective range within a quarter of a second.

THE WEAPON CLASS

With our bullet implementation in place and our weapon resources ready, it is time to begin to implement the `Weapon` class. This is the class that is used to house all of the details of a single weapon carried by a player in the game. This means that if two players have both collected the same weapon (i.e., they hold it in their inventory), then two instances of this class will exist for that weapon, one for each player. Before we cover any more details of how the class works, take a look at its definition, which can also be found in `Weapon.h`.

```
class Weapon
{
public:
  Weapon( Script *script, D3DXVECTOR3 viewWeaponOffset );
  virtual ~Weapon();
```

```
    void Update( float elapsed, bool fire, SceneObject *parent,
                float viewPointY );
    void Render( SceneObject *parent );

    void RaiseLowerWeapon( float elapsed, SceneObject *parent,
                            float move );

    void UseViewWeapon( bool use );

    char *GetName();

    void SetValid( bool valid );
    bool GetValid();

private:
    char *m_name;
    bool m_valid;
    D3DXVECTOR3 m_viewWeaponOffset;

    float m_lastViewPointY;
    float m_offsetViewPointY;

    float m_rof;
    float m_velocity;
    float m_damage;
    float m_range;

    float m_fireTimer;
    D3DXVECTOR3 m_muzzlePoint;

    bool m_useViewWeapon;
    SceneObject *m_bodyWeapon;
    SceneObject *m_viewWeapon;

    bool m_displayFlash;
    LinkedList< Material > *m_flashes;

    Sound *m_shotSound;
    AudioPath3D *m_shotAudioPath;
};
```

Don't let its length fool you. A close inspection reveals that much of the class can be matched up to the resources and the script used for each weapon. In fact, if you take a look at some of the member variables you can see exactly which ones are used to store the details from the weapon script.

Since this is the last class we have to look at to complete our game (and the book), there is not much point in discussing each of the functions of this class in great detail here as we are going to spend the rest of this chapter covering the implementation of the Weapon class. This includes topics such as updating and rendering the weapons, as well as collecting and changing weapons. So let's begin by looking at the Update function first.

UPDATING WEAPONS

The Update function serves two primary purposes. First, it is used to keep the weapon's mesh position correct as the player moves, and second, it is used to keep track of when the player is firing the weapon. To maintain the two different meshes used for the weapon, we will use two scene objects. The first scene object will be used to store the third person view mesh (otherwise referred to as the body weapon) and the second scene object will be used to store the first person view mesh (otherwise referred to as the view weapon). By storing them in scene objects we gain the added benefit of the positional data that comes with the SceneObject class. This means that we can easily position the meshes in 3D space so that they appear where we want them whether in the first person or viewing another player (i.e., the third person view). With this background information, let's begin stepping through the Update function to see how it works. You can also find the implementation of this function in Weapon.cpp.

```
void Weapon::Update( float elapsed, bool fire,
                     SceneObject *parent, float viewPointY )
{
  if( m_useViewWeapon == false )
    m_bodyWeapon->Update( elapsed, false );
  else
  {
    D3DXVECTOR3 offset;
    D3DXVec3TransformCoord( &offset, &m_viewWeaponOffset,
                            parent->GetRotationMatrix() );

    if( m_lastViewPointY == 0.0f )
      m_lastViewPointY = viewPointY;

    m_offsetViewPointY += ( viewPointY - m_lastViewPointY )
                          * 0.8f;
    offset.y += m_offsetViewPointY;
    m_lastViewPointY = viewPointY;
```

```
      m_viewWeapon->SetTranslation( parent->GetTranslation()
                                    + offset );
    m_viewWeapon->SetRotation( parent->GetRotation() );
    m_viewWeapon->AddRotation( ( (PlayerObject*)parent )
                               ->GetViewTilt(), 0.0f, 0.0f );
    m_viewWeapon->Update( elapsed, false );
  }
```

First we check which mesh needs to be used. This depends on whether or not the owning player is the local player. If we are processing the local player's weapon, we use the view weapon; otherwise, we use the body weapon for all the other players. If this weapon does belong to the local player, we need to calculate its position so that it is viewed correctly in the first person view. This is a matter of taking into account the view weapon offset (from the player's character script), the translation of the player (in world space), the rotation of the player, and the player's view tilt. With this data we can calculate where (in world space) we need to place the view weapon's mesh so that it appears correctly in the player's first person view.

```
    m_fireTimer += elapsed;

  if( fire == false )
     return;
```

The next step is to increment the timer used to keep track of when the weapon is allowed to fire. This is done by simply adding the elapsed time to the timer. After that, we need to check if the player wants to fire the weapon (which is determined by checking the fire flag passed into the function). If not, we can drop out as the rest of the Update function relates to firing the weapon.

```
    if( m_fireTimer > m_rof )
    {
       m_displayFlash = true;
```

At this point we know that the player wants to fire the weapon, but we have to make sure that the weapon does not fire too fast (remember the rate of fire property). We do this by checking if the timer exceeds the rate of fire set for the weapon. If so, we know it is time to fire off another bullet. In this case, we set m_displayFlash to true, which is used by the Render function so that it knows to display a flash since the weapon is firing.

Now that we know the weapon is definitely firing, we now need to find the location of the weapon's muzzle point in 3D space. The muzzle point location is used for two things. We need it so that we know where to display the flash in world space and so that we can position the audio path that plays the shot sound effect. How we calculate the muzzle point depends on whether we are using the body weapon or the view weapon. This is just a matter of checking the m_useViewWeapon flag (which we used previously). If it is set to true then we are using the view weapon, otherwise we are using the body weapon.

```
if( m_useViewWeapon == true )
{
  m_muzzlePoint = m_viewWeapon->GetMesh()
                      ->GetReferencePoint( "rp_sight" )
                      ->GetTranslation();

  D3DXMATRIX rotationXMatrix;
  D3DXMatrixRotationX( &rotationXMatrix,
                ( (PlayerObject*)parent )->GetViewTilt() );

  D3DXMATRIX combinedRotation;
  D3DXMatrixMultiply( &combinedRotation, &rotationXMatrix,
                    parent->GetRotationMatrix() );

  D3DXVec3TransformCoord( &m_muzzlePoint, &m_muzzlePoint,
                    &combinedRotation );

  m_muzzlePoint += m_viewWeapon->GetTranslation();

  m_shotAudioPath->SetMode( DS3DMODE_HEADRELATIVE );

  m_shotAudioPath->SetPosition( m_viewWeapon->GetMesh()
                          ->GetReferencePoint( "rp_sight" )
                          ->GetTranslation() );
  m_shotAudioPath->SetVelocity( parent->GetVelocity() );
}
```

When using the view weapon, we calculate the muzzle point in much the same way as calculating the position of the view weapon. The only major difference is that we need to offset the position by the rp_sight reference point found on the weapon's mesh. This ensures that the muzzle point is actually located at the end of the weapon's barrel rather than in the center of the weapon.

The final step is to set the position of the audio path that plays the shot sound effect. This is actually quite simple as we just use the DS3DMODE_HEADRELATIVE flag so that we can position the audio path using the position rp_sight reference point in model space. Remember that when using this flag you are actually positioning the audio path in the player's model space, not world space.

```
        else
        {
          m_muzzlePoint = m_bodyWeapon->GetMesh()
                          ->GetReferencePoint( "rp_sight" )
                          ->GetTranslation();

          Frame *attach = ( (PlayerObject*)parent )->GetMesh()
                          ->GetReferencePoint( "rp_weapon_attach" );
          D3DXMATRIX transform;
          D3DXMatrixMultiply( &transform,
                              &attach->finalTransformationMatrix,
                              parent->GetWorldMatrix() );

          D3DXVec3TransformCoord( &m_muzzlePoint, &m_muzzlePoint,
                              &transform );

          m_shotAudioPath->SetMode( DS3DMODE_NORMAL );

          m_shotAudioPath->SetPosition( m_muzzlePoint );
          m_shotAudioPath->SetVelocity( parent->GetVelocity() );
        }
```

If we are using the body weapon, calculating the muzzle point is a little different. First, we need to calculate the position of the weapon's mesh when it is attached to the player's mesh. This is done by finding the position where the weapon attaches to the player's mesh, which is located at the reference point rp_weapon_attach (which is a reference point in the player's mesh). We can then offset from this position using the rp_sight reference point to find the exact muzzle point.

Once we have calculated the muzzle point, we need to set the position of the audio path that is used to play the shot sound effect. This time we will use the DS3DMODE_NORMAL flag as this is not the first person view so we need to be able to position the audio path somewhere in world space. This is done by simply setting the audio path's position to match the muzzle point location.

Don't forget to include the rp_weapon_attach reference point when you create your own player meshes. This reference point should be created as a bone that is attached to the rest of the mesh's bone hierarchy. This ensures that the reference point moves when the mesh animates. The actual weapon mesh will be placed so that its center lines up with the position of the reference point in model space. You should also note that the orientation of the weapon depends on the orientation of the reference point. Take a look at Figure 13.2, which is the same figure from the last chapter. It illustrates where the reference points should be positioned on a character mesh.

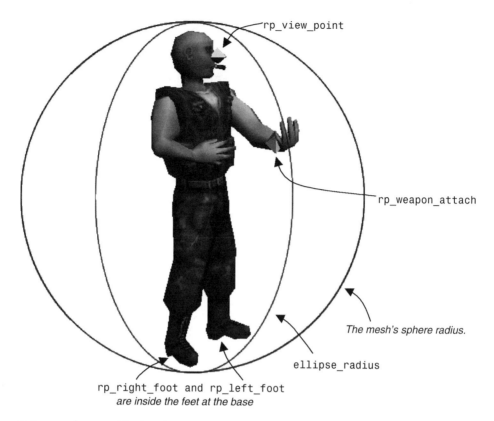

rp_view_point

rp_weapon_attach

The mesh's sphere radius.

ellipse_radius

rp_right_foot and rp_left_foot
are inside the feet at the base

FIGURE 13.2 Positioning the reference points on the character mesh.

We can finally wrap up the Update function as there are only three more steps left after we have calculated the muzzle point.

```
m_shotAudioPath->Play( m_shotSound->GetSegment() );

g_game->GetBulletManager()->AddBullet( parent,
                ( (PlayerObject*)parent )->GetEyePoint(),
                ( (PlayerObject*)parent )->GetForwardVector(),
                  m_velocity, m_range, m_damage );

    m_fireTimer = 0.0f;
  }
}
```

First we need to play the shot sound effect on the audio path, second, we need to add a new bullet to the bullet manager, and third we need to reset the fire timer back to zero so that it begins counting for the next shot.

You will notice that when we add a new bullet, we use the player's eye point and forward vector to determine where the bullet starts and the direction that it travels. The reason for this is that we do not know where the weapon's muzzle point will be and it may very well be completely out of alignment with the crosshairs in the center of the screen. In other words, if we were to start the bullet at the muzzle point and fire it in the direction the weapon is facing, the bullet will most likely be off course from where the player is actually aiming.

Warning: this only works with bullets you cannot see. If you were to use a visible mesh to represent the projectiles that are fired from the weapon, the projectile's mesh would appear to originate from the player's eye point rather than from the muzzle of the weapon. In this situation you would have to change the code so that the bullets are fired from the weapon's muzzle point. You would also need to ensure that the view weapon is aligned with the crosshairs.

RENDERING WEAPONS

Rendering the weapons is really very easy and is done in two parts. First, we need to render the actual weapon itself and then we need to render a flash (at the weapon's muzzle point) if it is firing. When rendering the weapon we need to determine if we are using the body weapon or the view weapon, which is done by simply checking the m_useViewWeapon flag as we did in the Update function. Let's have a look at the Render function shown here, and also found in Weapon.cpp.

```
void Weapon::Render( SceneObject *parent )
{
  if( m_useViewWeapon == true )
    m_viewWeapon->Render();
  else
  {
    Frame *attach = ( (PlayerObject*)parent )->GetMesh()
                    ->GetReferencePoint( "rp_weapon_attach" );
    D3DXMATRIX transform;
    D3DXMatrixMultiply( &transform,
                        &attach->finalTransformationMatrix,
                        parent->GetWorldMatrix() );

    m_bodyWeapon->Render( &transform );
  }
```

If we are using the view weapon, we can just call the Render function on it as we have already positioned it back in the Update function. If we are to render the body weapon, we must first find the correct position to render it in on the player's mesh. This is done by finding the position of the rp_weapon_attach reference point on the player's mesh (in model space). This position is then transformed into world space and used to render the weapon so that it appears to be held by the player's mesh.

```
if( m_displayFlash == true )
{
  Material *material = m_flashes->GetRandom();

  D3DXMATRIX view, world;
  D3DXMatrixIdentity( &world );
  g_engine->GetDevice()->GetTransform( D3DTS_VIEW, &view );
  g_engine->GetSprite()->SetWorldViewLH( &world, &view );
  g_engine->GetSprite()->Begin( D3DXSPRITE_BILLBOARD |
                                D3DXSPRITE_ALPHABLEND );
  g_engine->GetSprite()->Draw( material->GetTexture(), NULL,
                  &D3DXVECTOR3( material->GetWidth() / 2.0f,
                   material->GetHeight() / 2.0f, 0.0f ),
                  &m_muzzlePoint, 0xFFFFFFFF );
  g_engine->GetSprite()->End();

  m_displayFlash = false;
}
}
```

The next step is to render a flash at the muzzle point if the weapon is being fired. We know when the weapon is being fired because the m_displayFlash flag will be set to true (which was set in the Update function). It is then just a matter of taking one of the flash textures at random and displaying it at the muzzle point using the sprite interface. After we have rendered the flash we need to restore the m_displayFlash flag back to false so that it does not try to display another flash in the following frame (assuming the weapon is no longer firing).

COLLECTING WEAPONS

At this point a player can carry and fire a weapon, but there is one problem. How can a player carry a weapon (let alone fire it) if the player cannot pick the weapon up? If you've checked out our sample scene you will notice that there are a few weapon spawners around. At the moment, we can touch them and the weapon will disappear only to reappear again after a short while. This is just the programmed behavior of the weapon spawner and does not indicate that we have actually picked the weapon up. To do that we need to do more work. We need to go back to our `PlayerObject` class and implement the `CollisionOccurred` function. Remember that this is a call-back function, which is called by our collision detection code every time two objects collide with one another. Let's step through the implementation of this function, which you can also find in `PlayerObject.cpp`.

```
void PlayerObject::CollisionOccurred( SceneObject *object,
                                      unsigned long collisionStamp )
{
  if( m_dying == true )
    return;

  SceneObject::CollisionOccurred( object, collisionStamp );

  if( object->GetType() != TYPE_SPAWNER_OBJECT )
    return;
```

As soon as we enter the function we need to check if the player is dying. If so, we can drop out here as we don't want our players doing a dying leap into the weapon spawner, collecting it on their way down. If the player is not dying then the first step is to call the `CollisionOccurred` function on the base `SceneObject`, which allows it to update its internal collision stamp. The next step is to check the type of object that the player has collided with. We only care if the player has bumped into an object spawner so we check for this type. If it is not an object spawner then we can simply drop out here and ignore the collision.

```
  SpawnerObject *spawner = (SpawnerObject*)object;

  if( *spawner->GetObjectScript()->GetNumberData( "type" )
      == WEAPON_SPAWN_OBJECT )
  {
```

At this point we know that we have collided with an object spawner so we now need to check what type of object is actually being spawned. At the moment, we only have one type (`WEAPON_SPAWN_OBJECT`), but later on you may want to add more types and this is where you distinguish between them when they are collected.

```
    char listPosition = (char)*spawner->GetObjectScript()
                              ->GetNumberData( "list_position" );

    if( m_weapons[listPosition] == NULL )
    {
```

```
    m_weapons[listPosition] = new Weapon(
                 spawner->GetObjectScript(), m_viewWeaponOffset );

    if( m_dpnid == g_engine->GetNetwork()->GetLocalID() )
    {
      m_weapons[listPosition]->UseViewWeapon( true );

      ChangeWeapon( 0, listPosition );
    }
    else
    {
      m_weapons[listPosition]->UseViewWeapon( false );
    }
  }
  else if( m_weapons[listPosition]->GetValid() == false )
  {
    m_weapons[listPosition]->SetValid( true );

    ChangeWeapon( 0, listPosition );
  }
 }
}
```

The final step is to actually "collect" the weapon from the object spawner. First, we need to check if the weapon slot (in the player's inventory) is already taken. If so, we know that this weapon has already been collected (since you can only have one weapon per slot). In this case, we just ensure that the weapon is valid and then change to it.

If the weapon is new (i.e., the weapon slot for it is empty) then we need to add it to the player's inventory. Once the weapon has been added we can then change to it. However, before we change to the new weapon we need to check if we are working with the local player. If so, we must set the weapon to use the view weapon; otherwise, we must set it to use the body weapon for the other players.

As you can see, collecting weapons isn't especially difficult. You may have noticed that we are using a new function called ChangeWeapon, which is obviously used to change the player's weapon. If you're wondering how that function works, you're in luck, as the next topic we are about to look at is all about changing weapons.

CHANGING WEAPONS

There are two steps involved with changing weapons. The first step informs the game and the other players that this player (i.e., the local player) has changed weapon, and which weapon the player has changed to. The second step is purely visual and involves the lowering of the old weapon and the raising of the new one into view. This way the old weapon doesn't just disappear and the new one appear in its place in the first person view.

Players can change weapons by simply turning the scroll wheel on the mouse to cycle through the weapons or by pressing the numerical keys along the top of the keyboard to switch to a specific weapon (assuming the player is carrying a weapon in the chosen slot). This input is received by the player manager and the `ChangeWeapon` function is called on the local player when the player attempts to change to a different weapon. The following code snippet is taken from the player manager's `Update` function, which you can find in `PlayerManager.cpp`:

```
char changeWeapon = 0;
if( g_engine->GetInput()->GetDeltaWheel() > 0 )
  changeWeapon = 1;
else if( g_engine->GetInput()->GetDeltaWheel() < 0 )
  changeWeapon = -1;

if( changeWeapon != 0 )
  localPlayer->ChangeWeapon( changeWeapon );

if( g_engine->GetInput()->GetKeyPress( DIK_1 ) == true )
  localPlayer->ChangeWeapon( 0, 0 );
```

The first few lines of code check if the mouse wheel has been moved and then sets the `changeWeapon` variable to either 1 or −1 depending on the direction the mouse wheel was turned. If the mouse wheel was moved we then call the `ChangeWeapon` function on the local player and pass the `changeWeapon` variable to it so that it knows which way to cycle through the weapons.

Alternatively, if the mouse wheel was not moved, we then proceed to check the numerical keys to see if the player is trying to change to a specific weapon. In this snippet we only see the test for the 1 key; however, the real code tests all of the numerical keys are tested in the same fashion. If the player did press the 1 key, we call the `ChangeWeapon` function and pass in 0 as the first parameter to indicate that the mouse wheel was not used. For the second parameter we pass in 0 to indicate that we want to change to the first weapon slot. If the player had pressed the 2 key, then we would pass in 1 for the second parameter, and so on.

Now let's step through the `ChangeWeapon` function to see what actually happens when it is called. The implementation of this function can also be found in `PlayerObject.cpp`.

```
void PlayerObject::ChangeWeapon( char change, char weapon )
{
```

```
if( m_dying == true )
  return;

if( m_changingWeapon > 0.0f )
  return;

m_oldWeapon = m_currentWeapon;
```

First, we check if the player is dying as we do not want dying players to be able to change weapons. The next step is to check the m_changingWeapon timer, which is used to prevent the player from changing weapons while they are already in the middle of a change. Whenever the player changes weapons, this timer is set for two seconds, which is enough time for the visual raise and lower operation to take place. The last step (before we actually begin changing the weapon) is to store the index of the current weapon. The current weapon's index (since the weapons are stored in an array) is stored in m_currentWeapon; we just copy over to m_oldWeapon. Now we are ready to begin the weapon change operation.

```
if( change == 0 )
{
  m_currentWeapon = weapon;
  if( m_weapons[m_currentWeapon] == NULL )
    m_currentWeapon = m_oldWeapon;
  else if( m_weapons[m_currentWeapon]->GetValid() == false )
    m_currentWeapon = m_oldWeapon;
}
```

If the change parameter (which is passed into the ChangeWeapon function) is set to 0, we know that the scroll wheel was not used so a specific weapon slot must have been specified. All we need to do is set the current weapon to the weapon parameter that is passed into the ChangeWeapon function. If there is no weapon in the new slot or the new weapon is not valid, we just change back to the old weapon. Since no visual change has taken place, then technically the weapon change never occurred as far as the player is concerned.

NOTE

The only time a weapon slot will contain a weapon that is not valid is when the player has collected a weapon and then he is fragged. The player loses the weapons that he has collected and then has to recollect them. However, instead of removing the weapon from the player, we just invalidate it. When the player collects it again we simply revalidate the weapon.

```
else
{
  do
  {
    do
    {
      m_currentWeapon += change;

      if( m_currentWeapon < 0 )
        m_currentWeapon = 9;
      else if( m_currentWeapon > 9 )
        m_currentWeapon = 0;
    }
    while( m_weapons[m_currentWeapon] == NULL );
  }
  while( m_weapons[m_currentWeapon]->GetValid() == false );
}
```

If the change parameter is not set to 0 then we know that it must be either 1 or −1, in which case the mouse wheel has been used to change weapons. To change weapons with the scroll wheel we need to use two do...while loops. The first loop is used to ensure that a weapon exists in a given weapon slot and the second is used to check if the weapon is valid.

To cycle to the next weapon we simply add the change parameter to the m_currentWeapon variable. The sign of the change parameter determines the direction that the weapons are cycled. If the m_currentWeapon cycles out of bounds, we simply loop back to the other side. We continue cycling until we find a slot with a weapon in it. If the weapon in that slot is valid then we have found the next weapon.

```
if( m_oldWeapon == m_currentWeapon )
  return;

m_changingWeapon = 2.0f;

NetworkMessage pwcm;
pwcm.msgid = MSGID_PLAYER_WEAPON_CHANGING;
pwcm.dpnid = g_engine->GetNetwork()->GetLocalID();
g_engine->GetNetwork()->Send( &pwcm, sizeof( NetworkMessage ),
              DPNID_ALL_PLAYERS_GROUP, DPNSEND_NOLOOPBACK );
}
```

The final step involves checking the new weapon against the old weapon. If they are the same then we don't want to bother changing weapons as we would be just changing to the same weapon. Assuming we are changing to a new weapon, we set the `m_changingWeapon` timer for two seconds and then send a `MSGID_PLAYER_WEAPON_CHANGING` network message to all of the other players in the game. This informs them that this local player is in the process of changing to a new weapon. Don't worry about how the network messages work for now as we will look at them later. For now let's have a look at the function to raise and lower the weapons when a change weapon operation is invoked.

When the system has determined that a weapon change is to take place (which occurs in the `Update` function of the `PlayerObject` class), the `RaiseLowerWeapon` function is used to lower the old weapon and raise the new one into place. Take a look at the implementation of this function, which is shown here and can also be found in `Weapon.cpp`:

```
void Weapon::RaiseLowerWeapon( float elapsed, SceneObject *parent,
                               float move )
{
  D3DXVECTOR3 offset;
  D3DXVec3TransformCoord( &offset, &m_viewWeaponOffset,
                          parent->GetRotationMatrix() );

  D3DXVECTOR3 up;
  D3DXVec3Cross( &up, &parent->GetForwardVector(),
                 &parent->GetRightVector() );

  offset += up * move;

  m_viewWeapon->SetTranslation( parent->GetTranslation()
                                + offset );
  m_viewWeapon->SetRotation( parent->GetRotation() );
  m_viewWeapon->AddRotation(
          ( (PlayerObject*)parent )->GetViewTilt(), 0.0f, 0.0f );
  m_viewWeapon->Update( elapsed, false );
}
```

The function uses the `move` parameter as an offset from the weapon's original position. The weapon is then moved along the player's up vector (i.e., the vector that points straight up) in the appropriate direction based on the sign of the `move` parameter. If the sign is negative then the weapon is lowered down along the up vector; otherwise, it is raised up. Once the new position of the weapon is found, the view weapon is then positioned correctly and updated.

This process is repeated several times to create a smooth animation of the old weapon lowering and the new one rising into position. The entire operation takes around two seconds to complete and for the first second the offset is gradually increased in the negative direction to lower the weapon. After one second the process is reversed with the offset gradually being increased back in the positive direction. You can look at how this process is handled at the end of the Update function found in the PlayerObject class. You can find this code in PlayerObject.cpp, but the important part is reproduced below. The comments have been left in to help you follow the code.

```
static float move = 0.0f;
if( m_changingWeapon > 0.0f )
{
  m_changingWeapon -= elapsed;

  if( m_changingWeapon > 1.0f )
  {
    // Lower the old weapon.
    move -= 100.0f * elapsed;
    m_weapons[m_oldWeapon]->RaiseLowerWeapon( elapsed, this,
                                              move );
  }
  else if( m_changingWeapon < 0.0f )
  {
    // The new weapon is in place.
    m_changingWeapon = 0.0f;
    move = 0.0f;

    // Send a message to inform the other players the weapon
    // is ready.
    PlayerWeaponChangeMsg pwcm;
    pwcm.msgid = MSGID_PLAYER_WEAPON_CHANGE;
    pwcm.dpnid = g_engine->GetNetwork()->GetLocalID();
    pwcm.weapon = m_currentWeapon;
    g_engine->GetNetwork()->Send( &pwcm,
                  sizeof( PlayerWeaponChangeMsg ),
                  DPNID_ALL_PLAYERS_GROUP, DPNSEND_NOLOOPBACK );
  }
  else
  {
    // Raise the new weapon.
    move += 100.0f * elapsed;
    m_weapons[m_currentWeapon]->RaiseLowerWeapon( elapsed, this,
                                                  move );
  }
}
```

```
else
{
  // Update the player's current weapon, when not changing
  // weapons.
  if( m_weaponChanging == false )
    m_weapons[m_currentWeapon]->Update( elapsed, m_fire, this,
                                        m_viewPoint.y );
}
```

Hopefully, you should have a solid understanding of how weapons are changed. Don't be alarmed about the network messages that are being sent as we are going to look at them next.

WEAPON NETWORK MESSAGES

We have almost completed the implementation of our weapons. All that stands between us and a playable game is two small network messages that we need to look at to round off our discussion. The following shows the identifiers used for these two network messages, which can be found in Game.h:

```
#define MSGID_PLAYER_WEAPON_CHANGE   0x12009
#define MSGID_PLAYER_WEAPON_CHANGING 0x12010
```

The MSGID_PLAYER_WEAPON_CHANGING message can be handled with a generic NetworkMessage structure as it does not require any special parameters. This message exists only to inform the other players that a weapon change is taking place.

The MSGID_PLAYER_WEAPON_CHANGE message, on the other hand, does require a specific structure as it is used to inform the other player which weapon we have changed to when the weapon change operation is complete. The definition of the structure used for this message is shown here and can also be found in Game.h:

```
struct PlayerWeaponChangeMsg : public NetworkMessage
{
  char weapon;
};
```

The following code snippet (taken from the HandleNetworkMessage function in the Game class) shows how we handle a MSGID_PLAYER_WEAPON_CHANGE network message when it arrives. All we need to do with the message is call the WeaponChanged function on the appropriate player and pass in the index of the new weapon. This causes all further processing and rendering to use this new weapon.

```
case MSGID_PLAYER_WEAPON_CHANGE:
{
  PlayerWeaponChangeMsg *pwcm = (PlayerWeaponChangeMsg*)msg;

  m_playerManager->GetPlayer( pwcm->dpnid )
                 ->WeaponChanged( pwcm->weapon );

  break;
}
```

Finally, the MSGID_PLAYER_WEAPON_CHANGING network message is handled in the following manner. This code snippet is also taken from the HandleNetworkMessage function in the Game class and shows how we call the WeaponChanging function on the appropriate player when this network message is received. The WeaponChanging function simply informs the player object that it is changing its weapon so that it doesn't try to process, render, or fire the weapon during the weapon change operation.

```
case MSGID_PLAYER_WEAPON_CHANGING:
{
  PlayerWeaponChangeMsg *pwcm = (PlayerWeaponChangeMsg*)msg;

  m_playerManager->GetPlayer( pwcm->dpnid )->WeaponChanging();

  break;
}
```

This concludes the topic of weapon changing and the entire topic of weapons implementation. You have probably been itching to try out the game with weapons (unless of course you've cheated and already tried it out) and now is your big chance as that is what we're going to do.

TESTING THE GAME

There really isn't much more to say about the game at this point. We have covered every topic necessary to produce a basic FPS, so all that is left is to test it. The main area of interest that you will want to note especially is the new weapons. Load up the game and try everything out. Try firing your weapon, collecting weapons from the object spawners, and changing between them with the scroll wheel and the numerical keys along the top of the keyboard. Figure 13.3 shows a screen shot from our completed game, with weapons and all.

FIGURE 13.3   A screen shot from our completed game.

To really appreciate the introduction of weapons you really need to play with two or more players. If you have access to a second computer (and they are on a LAN), then copy the executable and the assets across to it and load the game on both computers. Host a new game on one of the computers and then enumerate for the session by clicking the Refresh button on the other game client. When you see the session display in the list, simply select it and click the Join button.

After the game has finished loading, both players will exist in the same game. You will be able to move around, collect weapons, and fight against one another. Every time you score a frag on another player your frag count is incremented, and every time you are fragged your death count is incremented. At any time during the game you can hold down the Tab key to view the current score.

EXPANDING THE GAME

After you have played through the game a few times you may be a little bored. This is natural as the novelty wears off and you begin to crave something bigger and better. When this happens you have the perfect opportunity to expand upon the game we have created. There are many more features that you can add to the game to make it more enjoyable. Here is a short list of features that you might add:

■ New scenes, characters, and weapons
■ More materials, sound effects, and music
■ Nicer (graphical) menu system rather than the plain dialog
■ In-game heads-up display (HUD) to display details such as the player's health
■ In-game chat facility so that players can talk to one another with text
■ Ammunition tracking so that weapons can run out of ammo, and players have to collect more ammo and reload
■ New types of objects that can be spawned into the game, such as ammo (if you have implemented ammunition tracking), and medical packs to heal players when they are low on health
■ New types of game play such as team play (meaning that you work together with your teammates to frag the players on the other team)
■ A "capture the flag" style of game to team play (you would have an object spawner that spawns a flag for each team; you score by collecting the other team's flag and bringing it back to your flag)
■ A modified network system so that you can host and join games across the Internet (this way you can play with friends from all over the world)

Don't forget to periodically visit *www.coderedgames.com*. I will have a forum set up there so that you can discuss any problems you might experience. It will also be the place where you will find any source code updates as they become available. Whenever bugs are fixed or new features are added, the updated source code will be posted on the site. Feel free to e-mail me (vyoung@coderedgames.com) if you have any comments.

SUMMARY

Is this really the end? Well yes and no. We may have come to the end of this book, but you have by no means come to the end of your game development journey. In this chapter, we finished off our game by adding the last key ingredient, the weapons. However, weapons should not be the last feature you add to your game. As you saw from the short list of possibilities, there are many additional features to enhance your game.

If you are new to game development, then you have a great resource at your finger tips. You should read through the source code meticulously. Rewrite sections the way you like, change things you don't like, and constantly add new features. The best way to learn is by doing, so tinker with the code, break it, and bend it to your will. That's what it's there for. Of course, if you've been doing this for a while now, you have probably already broken and bent many lines of source code—so here are a few more for you to try your hand at.

You will probably appreciate this as a nice foundation from which to launch your own projects. However, don't let this code restrict you. If you don't like the scene manager, for example, then don't use it. Scrap it and rewrite your own. The fact that you can do that is a testament to your learning and ability to make the code work for you, not the other way around.

Finally, I would personally like to say, congratulations on coming this far and tackling some tough subjects. I hope you have enjoyed reading this book (and playing the game) as much as I enjoyed writing it and I hope this is not the last game development endeavor you undertake, but one of many. So what are you waiting for, make that game into everything you really want it to be. Good luck!

Appendix A

About the CD-ROM

The CD-ROM included with *Programming a Multiplayer FPS in DirectX* is organized into several directories to facilitate easy browsing. The content of each directory, as well as instructions on using the CD-ROM, is detailed below.

Article: In this directory, you will find the "Improved Collision Detection and Response" article written by Kasper Fauerby. You are encouraged to read the article if you are interested in learning more about the collision detection algorithm used in the sample game.

DirectX: This directory contains the DirectX SDK installation package used to develop the code throughout this book. Simply double-click on the setup file and follow the prompts to install the SDK.

Exporter: Here you will find the Panda DirectX Exporter created by Andy Tather. You can use this exporter in conjunction with 3ds max to produce meshes in DirectX's native .x file format.

Paint Shop Pro: In this directory, you will find the setup file for a trial version of Paint Shop Pro. This is a great, fully-featured product that is relatively inexpensive and perfect for creating textures to use as materials for your 3D meshes.

Source: This directory contains all of the source code used throughout the book. It has been further arranged into subdirectories, which contain the source code as presented in each chapter. Please refer to the section entitled *Preparing Visual Studio* in the Introduction for details about compiling the source code.

REQUIRED SOFTWARE

In order to compile the source code provided on this CD-ROM, you will need a C++ compatible compiler. Microsoft Visual Studio 6 was used to create and compile this source code. Although the source code will most likely compile without any problems under another version of Visual Studio (or a different product), it has not been tested. The workspaces provided on the CD-ROM are for Visual Studio 6.

SYSTEM REQUIREMENTS

To run the sample game that you will create throughout the book, it is recommended that you have at least a 1 GHz CPU. It is also recommended that your system has at least 256 MB of RAM. Finally, you will need a 3D accelerated video card with at least 32 MB of onboard memory. Although we will be using DirectX 9, we will not be using any version-specific features that will require you to have a DirectX 9 compliant video card. Therefore, any video card supporting DirectX 8 or above should be fine.

INSTALLATION

The directory containing the source code can be copied to your hard drive where you can modify and compile it. Remember to always ensure your system matches the minimum system requirements before installing any of the third-party products.

PREPARING VISUAL STUDIO

Before you can rush off and begin compiling the source code on the CD-ROM, you need to ensure you have your development environment correctly prepared. The source code in this book was compiled using Microsoft Visual Studio® 6, so we will quickly run through the steps you need to take to prepare Visual Studio 6. If you are using a newer version of Visual Studio (or a different compiler all together), most (if not all) of these steps will still apply; how you go about them will be a little different. In this case, you may need to refer to your compiler's documentation to determine how to carry out a particular step.

Step 1: Ensure that Visual Studio is properly installed on your computer. You should also ensure that your compiler has the latest patches and service packs applied to correct any known issues and bugs.

ON THE CD

Step 2: Install the DirectX 9.0c SDK, which you can find on the CD-ROM in the DirectX directory.

Step 3: The next step is to ensure you have the DirectX Include and Library directories set within your compiler. In Visual Studio 6, open the Options dialog from the Tools menu. From there, select the Directories tab. In the "Show directories for" drop-down list, select Include files. Ensure that your DirectX Include directory is at the top of the Directories list. If not, simply use the Up arrow on the right to push it to the top of the list. This will ensure that it is searched before the other directories. If it is not in the list at all, you will need to add it by using the New button and browsing your hard drive. Once this is done you can go to the Library files in the "Show directories for" drop-down list. You just need to repeat the process for the DirectX Library (Lib) directory, ensuring that it is located at the top of the Directories list.

Step 4: As of the DirectX 9.0c release, Visual Studio 6 is no longer supported. However, Microsoft did release a modified version of one of the core DirectX libraries, which makes it possible to compile DirectX 9.0c applications with Visual Studio 6. If you are using a later version of Visual Studio then you can ignore this step. For everyone else, you will need to copy the Visual Studio 6 compatible d3dx9.lib file from the DirectX directory on the CD-ROM to the Lib directory on your hard drive where you installed the DirectX 9.0c SDK (C:\Program Files\ Microsoft DirectX 9.0 SDK (October 2004)\Lib by default). Simply replace the existing d3dx9.lib file when prompted. If you plan on upgrading to a future version of Visual Studio, you may want to consider making a backup of the existing d3dx9.lib file before you replace it, as it is needed for future versions.

Step 5: There is one more file required to compile DirectX 9.0c applications with Visual Studio 6, called BaseTsd.h. If you have a later version of Visual Studio you may be able to skip this step. The file can only be obtained by updating your Platform SDK from the Microsoft Platform SDK Update Web site at www.microsoft.com/msdownload/platformsdk/sdkupdate/. From here you can navigate to Downloads and select Install, which will allow you to install the updated Platform SDK. Once you have the Platform SDK installed, you need to ensure the paths are set up correctly in Visual Studio. This is done in exactly the same fashion as setting the DirectX SDK paths. You need to ensure that you have both the Include and the Library paths set, which are located at <Platform SDK Installation Path>\Include\ and <Platform SDK Installation Path>\Lib\ respectively.

If you cannot download the Platform SDK for some reason, there is a quick "hack" that you can apply to the code in this book that will allow it to compile and run without the updated Platform SDK. However, it is strongly recommended that you use the Platform SDK instead. To apply this hack, simply place the following line of code at the beginning of one of the main header files, such as `Engine.h`*.*

```
typedef unsigned long DWORD_PTR;
```

That's it. Now you are ready to compile DirectX 9.0c applications (and the book's source code) in Visual Studio 6. Remember, if you are using a different compiler (or a different version of Visual Studio), you may need to double check if all of these step are necessary for you. You may also need to refer to your compiler's documentation about the specific steps involved for adding the DirectX (and Platform SDK) Include and Library directories. If you are using a newer version of Visual Studio, you can open up the workspaces on the CD-ROM and allow the conversion wizard to upgrade them for you. Once it is finished, you should be able to compile the code without any major issues.

A FINAL NOTE

You should keep an eye on my Web site (*www.coderedgames.com*) or visit *www.charlesriver.com* for updates to the book and the code as necessary. I will also have a forum set up on my Web site to allow you to raise any issues you may have with any of the material in the book, or the source code.

Competition

If you have read this book from cover to cover and developed the game, you are probably wondering what to do next. At the end of Chapter 13 there were a number of suggestions given as to how you can continue the development of your game by enhancing the game with new features and richer content. You obviously have a passion for computer game development (otherwise you wouldn't have read this book, right?), so naturally you will go away now and spend countless hours in a labor of love to produce the game of your dreams. So, what if you could take your final creation and show it off to the world? What if you could be rewarded for all those long hours? Well, here is your opportunity.

This is your chance to be a part of a competition to create the best first person shooter your imagination can conceive. The competition will run for approximately 12 months from the release of this book. All submissions must be received by **November 4, 2005** at 11:59 p.m. Eastern Standard Time (U.S.). To win the competition, all you have to do is take the engine and the game you have developed with this book and expand upon it. The bigger, bolder, and brighter, the better. You can add new features to the engine, new game play, better graphics, more sound effects, new maps, weapons, characters . . . the list goes on.

Now you are probably wondering what's in it for you? Well, the good news is there are prizes. At the time of publishing, the final prizes for the competition have not been determined, however, we can confirm that Charles River Media will be offering the entire *Game Programming Gems* series (volumes 1 to 5) as one of the prizes. The fifth volume of this great series is scheduled for publication in March 2005. Bearing in mind that each one of these volumes costs $69.95 (U.S.), that is a prize value of $349.75 (U.S.) just for these books alone. You can read more about the *Game Programming Gems* series at *www.gameprogramminggems.com*. The exact prizes for the competition will be listed and updated on the competition Web site (*www.coderedgames.com*) as more information becomes available.

Entering the competition is very simple. All you need to do is go to *www. coderedgames.com* and read the details about the competition, including the terms and conditions. It is very important that you read the terms and conditions carefully

ON THE CD

as you must agree to them before entering the competition. The next step is to open the competition entry form, which can be found on the accompanying CD-ROM. Simply complete the form and then e-mail it to *competition@coderedgames.com*. The final step then is to go away and build the winning game!

Just remember that you must submit your entry form before you can submit your game, so if you want to be a part of this competition, fill out the entry form and send it in right now. Details as to where and how to submit your actual game will be provided on the competition Web site at the appropriate time. We may also e-mail you with specific details as necessary.

Remember to always keep a close eye on the competition Web site for the most up-to-date details regarding the competition.

Index